Anglistik

International Journal
of English Studies

Volume 23 · Issue 2 · September 2012

Edited by
RÜDIGER AHRENS
HEINZ ANTOR

Focus on
Scottish Studies:
A New Agenda for the Field

Focus editor
CARLA SASSI

Universitätsverlag
WINTER
Heidelberg

THE YEARBOOK OF LANGLAND STUDIES

The Yearbook of Langland Studies is the sole journal
devoted to *Piers Plowman* studies.

1 volume per year - pay-per-view available: http://brepols.metapress.com
ISSN 0890-2917

Since 1987, YLS has significantly shaped the expanding critical attention to the poem and its contexts. Each volume – including essays, debate, reviews, and annual annotated bibliography – offers access to the most significant and up-to-date scholarship on the poem and its literary, historical, codicological, and critical contexts. Articles are written in English.

The editors of YLS are:
Andrew Cole, English Department, Princeton University, USA - **Fiona Somerset**, English Department, Duke University, USA - **Lawrence Warner**, Department of English, University of Sydney, Australia

Table of Contents volume 25 (2011):

Illustrations
Commentary
Jill Mann, *Some Observations on 'Structural Annotation'* – Andrew Galloway, *Non-literary Commentary and its Literary Profits: The Road to Accounting-ville* – Andrew Cole, *Commentaries on Unknown Texts: On Morton Bloomfield and Friedrich Nietzsche* – Traugott Lawler, *Langland Versificator* – Michael Van Dussen, *Parsing the Peacock: Langland's Wills and the Limits of voluntas* – Ellen K. Rentz, *Half-Acre Bylaws: Harvest-Sharing in* Piers Plowman – John Burrow, *An Alliterative Pattern in* Piers Plowman B – Miċeal F. Vaughan, *Where is Wille Buried?* Piers Plowman, *A. 12.* – S. Melissa Winders, *'Bad, harsk spech and lewit barbur tong': Gavin Douglas's Langlandian Prologue* – Stephen Yeager, *Lollardy in* Mum and the Sothsegger: *A Reconsideration* – Gordon Teskey, *Review Essay: Langland's Golden Bough*
Reviews:
Derrick Pitard, *Ethics and Power in Medieval English Reformist Writing* (by Edwin D. Craun) – Stephanie Trigg, *Medieval Alliterative Poetry: Essays in Honour of Thorlac Turville-Petre* (ed. by John A. Burrow and Hoyt N. Duggan) – Simon Horobin, *The Lost History of 'Piers Plowman': The Earliest Transmission of Langland's Work* (by Lawrence Warner) – Sister Mary Clemente Davlin, OP, *Willing to Know God: Dreamers and Visionaries in the Late Middle Ages* (by Jessica Barr)
Annual Bibliography, 2010

Abstracting & Indexing Services:
International Medieval Bibliography • *Iter* • *Medioevo Latino*
MLA International Bibliography • *New Testament Abstracts*

For institutional subscriptions please contact Brepols Publishers:
(The International Piers Plowman Society will administer individual subscriptions)

BREPOLS PUBLISHERS

Begijnhof 67 · B-2300 Turnhout (Belgium)
Tel: +32 14 44 80 35 · Fax: +32 14 42 89 19 · periodicals@brepols.net · www.brepols.net

TABLE OF CONTENTS

FOCUS ON SCOTTISH STUDIES: A NEW AGENDA FOR THE FIELD

CARLA SASSI, Verona:
Introduction — 7

DAFYDD MOORE, Plymouth:
"Kings unborn of Fingal's royal race:" *Ossian*, Scottishness, and the Aesthetics of Collaboration in the Age of Napoleon — 17

PAULINE ANNE MACKAY, Glasgow:
Objects of Desire: Robert Burns the 'Man's Man' and Material Culture — 27

CAROLINE MCCRACKEN-FLESHER, Laramie, WY:
Prediction of Things Past: Scott and the Triumph of the Author's Antiquity — 41

OLIVER S. BUCKTON, Boca Raton, FL:
"It touches one too closely:" Robert Louis Stevenson and Queer Theory — 51

EMMA DYMOCK, Edinburgh:
A Gaelic Antisyzygy? Philosophical Idealism and Materialism in the Poetry of Sorley MacLean — 61

SCOTT HAMES, Stirling:
Diasporic Narcissism: De-sublimating Scotland in Alice Munro and Alistair MacLeod — 73

SUZANNE GILBERT, Stirling:
The Scottish Ballad: Towards Survival in the 21st Century — 83

IAN BROWN, Kingston upon Thames:
"Arts first; politics later:" Scottish Theatre as a Recurrent Crucible of Cultural Change — 95

GLENDA NORQUAY, Liverpool:
Untying the Knots: Gender and Scottish Writing — 107

DONNA HEDDLE, Kirkwall:
"The North Wind Doth Blow:" A New Agenda for Northern Scottish Studies — 119

ALAN RIACH, Glasgow:
What Good is a Canon? The Case of Scottish Literature — 129

ARTICLES

MICHAEL MEYER, Koblenz:
Antonia S. Byatt's Intermedial "Art Work:" The Empire Knits Back — 139

RENATE BROSCH, Stuttgart:
Third Space in Rohinton Mistry's "Swimming Lessons" — 149

ALBERT-REINER GLAAP, Düsseldorf:
Palace of the End by **Judith Thompson** – A Canadian Playwright's View of the Iraq War ... 159

REVIEWS

Peter Erlebach. *Natur und Spiritualität in der englischen Literatur- und Geistesgeschichte*
- by FELIX SPRANG, Hamburg ... 165

Wendy Marie Hoofnagle and Wolfram R. Keller, eds. *Other Nations: The Hybridization of Medieval and Insular Mythology and Identity*
- by NICOLE NYFFENEGGER-STAUB, Bern ... 166

Christian Huck. *Fashioning Society, or, The Mode of Modernity. Observing Fashion in Eighteenth-Century Britain*
- by BIRGIT NEUMANN, Passau ... 171

Dirk Schulz. *Setting the Record Queer: Rethinking Oscar Wilde's* **The Picture of Dorian Gray** *and Virginia Woolf's* **Mrs. Dalloway**
- by SYLVIA MIESZKOWSKI, Berlin ... 174

Bernfried Nugel and Jerome Meckier, eds. *Aldous Huxley Annual. A Journal of Twentieth-Century Thought and Beyond*
- by ANDREA BECK, Greifswald ... 177

Joachim Frenk and Christian Krug, eds. *The Cultures of James Bond*
- by JULIKA GRIEM, Frankfurt am Main ... 179

Jan Rupp. *Genre and Cultural Memory in Black British Literature*
- by DORIS TESKE, Karlsruhe ... 182

Silke Stroh. *Uneasy Subjects. Postcolonialism and Scottish Gaelic Poetry*
- by CARLA SASSI, Verona ... 183

Joanna Rostek. *Seaing through the Past: Postmodern Histories and the Maritime Metaphor in Contemporary Anglophone Fiction*
- by SARAH HEINZ, Mannheim ... 185

Marie-Hélène Gutberlet and Sissy Helff, eds. *Die Kunst der Migration. Aktuelle Positionen zum europäisch-afrikanischen Diskurs. Material – Gestaltung – Kritik*
- by CECILE SANDTEN, Chemnitz ... 187

Ellen Dengel-Janic. *'Home Fiction.' Narrating Gendered Space in Anita Desai's and Shashi Deshpande's Novels*
- by OLIVER LINDNER, Kiel ... 189

Mark Aronoff and Kirsten Fudeman. *What is Morphology?*
- by GIANINA IORDĂCHIOAIA, Stuttgart ... 191

Andrea Cabajsky and Brett Josef Grubisic, eds. *National Plots: Historical Fiction and Changing Ideas of Canada*
- by MARTIN LÖSCHNIGG, Graz — 193

Stefan L. Brandt and Astrid M. Fellner, eds. *Making National Bodies: Cultural Identity and the Politics of the Body in (Post-)Revolutionary America*
- by KARIN HÖPKER, Erlangen — 196

Waldemar Zacharasiewicz, ed. *Riding/Writing Across Borders in North American Travelogues and Fiction*
- by EVA-MARIE KRÖLLER, Vancouver — 197

Stefanie Schäfer. *"Just the two of Us:" Self-Narration and Recognition in the Contemporary American Novel*
- by ANNA FLÜGGE, München — 199

Greta Olson, ed. *Current Trends in Narratology*
- by SANDRA HEINEN, Wuppertal — 201

Christoph Bode. *The Novel: An Introduction*
- by HEIDE ZIEGLER, Stuttgart — 203

Isabell Ludewig. *Lebenskunst in der Literatur. Zeitgenössische fiktionale Autobiographien und Dimensionen moderner Ethiken des guten Lebens*
- by JAN RUPP, Heidelberg — 205

Stephanie Waldow, ed. *Ethik im Gespräch. Autorinnen und Autoren über das Verhältnis von Literatur und Ethik heute*
- by STEFANIE SCHÄFER, Jena — 207

Stefan Horlacher. *"Wann ist die Frau eine Frau?" "Wann ist der Mann ein Mann?" Konstruktionen von Geschlechtlichkeit von der Antike bis ins 21. Jahrhundert*
- by DIRK SCHULZ, Köln — 209

Friedrich Balke and Marc Rölli, eds. *Philosophie und Nicht-Philosophie: Gilles Deleuze – Aktuelle Diskussionen*
- by ULF SCHULENBERG, Eichstätt — 211

Maria Eisenmann, Nancy Grimm, and Laurenz Volkmann, eds. *Teaching the New English Cultures and Literatures*
- by JANA NITTEL, Bremen — 213

Peter Fenn. *A Student's Advanced Grammar of English*
- by ILSE WISCHER, Potsdam — 215

Jörg-U. Keßler and Anja Plesser. *Teaching Grammar*
- by CLAUS GNUTZMANN, Braunschweig — 218

Holger Schmitt. *Phonetic Transcription: From First Steps to Ear Transcription*
- by JÜRG STRÄSSLER, Zürich — 220

Anne Schröder. *On the Productivity of Verbal Prefixation in English. Synchronic and Diachronic Perspectives*
- by ALEXANDER TOKAR, Düsseldorf   222

Tanja Rütten. *How to Do Things with Texts. Patterns of Instruction in Religious Discourse 1350-1700*
- by LEENA ENQVIST, Helsinki   224

Marco Schilk. *Structural Nativization in Indian English Lexicogrammar*
- by GEORG MAIER, Hamburg   227

Björn Rothstein. *Wissenschaftliches Arbeiten für Linguisten*
- by MATTHIAS MEYER, Kiel   229

Isabel Karremann and Anja Müller, eds. *Mediating Identities in Eighteenth-Century England. Public Negotiations, Literary Discourses, Topography*
- by FELIX SPRANG, Hamburg   232

LIST OF CONTRIBUTORS   235
STYLE SHEET   238
CALL FOR DONATIONS   240

FOCUS ON SCOTTISH STUDIES: A NEW AGENDA FOR THE FIELD

CARLA SASSI, Verona

Introduction

There is no such thing as an academic discipline that represents a stable field of knowledge – on the contrary, academic disciplines always are, and arguably have to be, contested domains. To argue on similar lines, there is no such thing as an academic discipline (or indeed, an epistemological practice) that can exist in even relative isolation from the global horizon of cultural production and knowledge formation. Scottish Studies, a relatively young discipline, whose field directly intersects and partly overlaps, among others, with English, Celtic and Nordic Studies (and, through its involvement in the British Empire, with postcolonial scholarship) is no exception. And yet, it is important to acknowledge here, at the very beginning of this special issue, the specific history of this discipline, both as a contested territory, and in its changing relationship with other established or emergent disciplines – it is in fact only through an awareness of its shifting borders, and of its many fissures and tensions, and also with a memory of its past that we can gauge our present concerns and look forward. It is indeed this double intent – to engage with a critical analysis of the discipline's history and to evaluate new paths and approaches – that underlies the present collection of articles.

The interdisciplinary field of Scottish Studies – first introduced as a markedly ethnographic and folkloric field of investigation by the School of Scottish Studies of the University of Edinburgh, founded in 1951 with the aim to record the culture, customs, folklore, songs and stories of Scotland – established itself in its present interdisciplinary set-up between the 1980s and the 1990s. The European Society for the study of English, founded in 1990, and endowed with a Constitution in 1995, included Scottish Studies among the list of its area subjects, while the 3rd ESSE conference, held in Glasgow in 1995, further reinforced its institutional status by devoting a substantial section of its academic and cultural programme to Scottish writing. Since the 1980s, several Scottish Studies centres have been established in Scotland and around the world (it is worthwhile to remember here that the Scottish Studies centres respectively of the Université Stendhal, Grenoble, founded by Henri Gibault and Pierre Morère in 1979, and of the Johannes Gutenberg-Universität, Mainz, founded by Horst Drescher in 1981, were the first of their kind in 'continental Europe').[1] Since 1999, Scottish Literature has also been listed as a Modern Language Association of America discussion group (founded by Cairns Craig, Ian Duncan and Charles Snodgrass).[2] The

---

[1] The Mainz Centre maintains a website, listing events and useful links, and publishing a *Newsletter* at http://www.fb06.uni-mainz.de/englisch/183.php. Also, the The French Society for Scottish Studies maintains a website at http://sfee.univ-tours.fr/Scotland/conferences.htm.
[2] See Brown, Clancy, Manning and Pittock (2007) for further analysis and details on "Scottish Literature: Criticism and the Canon."

number of scholars who today engage with this field – either directly as area specialists, or indirectly, intersecting with their research its many subfields and topics – is possibly larger than ever before, including researchers from different disciplinary and methodological backgrounds, as well as from outside Scotland and Britain.[3] The first World Congress of Scottish Literatures will be held in 2014 at the University of Glasgow, with the involvement of the Association for Scottish Literary Studies.[4] This will no doubt represent an important step forward towards a further internationalisation of the field and a wider articulation of the critical debate.

However, as is the case with most nationally specific academic subjects, even the young discipline of Scottish Studies traces its roots back to the 19th century, a time when the national focus became the grid through which humanistic studies were re-organised at a global level in a shift towards what has been aptly labelled as "methodological nationalism," and which marked the consolidation of historical knowledge and "the dominance of national categories [which] reinforced a way of reading social development essentially as the result of internal dynamics" (Conrad 2010, 400) leading, *in primis*, to the institutionalisation of history as national history in countries across the globe (Germany, France, the USA and Japan, among others). Within the wider context of the national re-compartmentalisation of knowledge, however, Scotland's case presents at least one central specificity, as it involved, since the Union of Parliaments in 1707, a simultaneous engagement on a double front. Politically, it performed simultaneously a centripetal movement, by conforming to the rules and language of the new centre of institutional power (London), and a centrifugal one, by firmly protecting its national interests and networks within and outside Britain (most conspicuously within what has been aptly termed "Scotland's Empire," see Devine 2003). An equivalent double pull towards the same two distinct (but, at least in the 18th and 19th century, not incompatible) poles of Scottish life ('home' and London), also characterised Scotland's re-organisation of institutionalised knowledge. On the one hand, in fact, Scottish institutions became responsible for the "invention of English literature" as a university discipline, first with the establishment of the first official university course on 'rhetoric and belles-lettres,' focused on modern writers in English as well as in the Classical languages, taught by Adam Smith (Professor of Logic and Rhetoric and then of Moral Philosophy) in 1751 at the University of Glasgow, and then with the establishment in 1762 of what is today regarded as the first Chair of English literature in the world, held by Hugh Blair, Regius Professor of Rhetoric and Belles-Lettres at the University of Edinburgh (see Crawford 2008). And yet, in the same period, Scotland also committed itself to the preservation of the memory of its own past, at a time when its minoritarian status within the Union posed a tangible threat to its survival as a distinct national entity. Antiquarianism – an important aspect of Scotland's cultural life between the 18th and the 19th century – was indeed "a sort of shadow-history [...] created through antiquarian collections of arte-

---

3 The website of the Association for Scottish Literary Studies offers an up-to-date list of call for papers, recent publications and upcoming conferences held worldwide at http://www.arts.gla.ac.uk/ScotLit/ASLS/index.html. Also the e-zine of the ASLS, *The Bottle Imp*, whose aim is to promote and support the teaching and study of Scottish literature and language, beside articles and reviews, provides information on new developments in Scottish literature and literary criticism: http://www.arts.gla.ac.uk/ScotLit/ASLS/SWE/TBI.html.
4 For further information, see http://www.gla.ac.uk/colleges/arts/research/scottishstudiesglobal/worldcongressofscottishliteratures/.

facts, tales, songs, myths and legends of the nation, which brought a more diverse past into the popular present to celebrate the continuities of national identity" (Manning 2007, 48). Given that in the antiquarian practice "conventions of evidence and authenticity were flexible," and that they "existed within a continuum of antiquarian recovery and literary impersonation," evident, for example, in James Macpherson's *The Poems of Ossian* (1760-1765) or in Walter Scott's *Minstrelsy of the Scottish Border* (1802) (Manning 2007, 48), it is indeed possible to identify in it a first nucleus of that academic construction of Scottish literature as national mythology that will establish itself (via Walter Scott) between the end of the 19th century and the early decades of the 20th century.

The first chair in the field of Scottish literary and linguistic studies was that of Celtic, founded in 1882 at Edinburgh: its establishment, however, also marked the artificial separation between Gaelic and English/Scots literature as academically distinct subjects, perpetuated to the present day in the departmental structure of Scottish universities, where 'Scottish literature' still stands for writing in English and/or Scots. Very much in line with "the consolidation of the internalist paradigm of historical knowledge" (Conrad 2010, 400), which characterises the 19th century worldwide, but also as a response to the specific political-cultural set-up described above, the first Chair of Scottish History was founded in Edinburgh in 1901, to be followed by that in Glasgow in 1903. And it was again in Glasgow that in 1913 the first chair of Scottish History and Literature was established, with the proceeds of the Scottish Exhibition held at Kelvingrove in 1911 – a child of the Empire as much as of a nationalist *and* unionist middle class. This does not seem so distant (either in time or space) from England's institutionalisation of its own national literature – the first Chair of English Literature being established in 1828 at University College, London, followed by Oxford only in 1904. Yet, the institutional knot binding Scotland's literature to its national history (which lingered at least until the creation of two separate departments for Scottish history and Scottish literature in Glasgow in 1971 – the first Chair of Scottish literature here was established only in 1995) is meaningful, and it signals the two very different (and yet related) ideological lines along which the academic constructions of, respectively, Scottish and English literature developed in the course of the 20th century: the former explicitly and firmly inscribed with (local) historical and social meaning, the latter shaping itself as a 'great tradition,' in theory detached from local or national concerns, in practice generating a subtle conflation between a notion of English literature as a 'local' expression, conveying nationally-specific values and perspectives, and a 'cosmopolitan' one, embracing selectively (and by criteria that remain largely undefined to the present day) authors and texts from the English-speaking regions and nations of the British-Irish archipelago, as well as from the (ex-)British Empire. While it is a common practice among scholars to investigate the strategies and ends underlying each of such constructions separately – each seen as largely independent from the other – it is only fair to claim that the births of both English and Scottish literature as academic subjects are deeply intertwined – developing in the same cultural and ideological climate (i. e. under the shadow of the British Empire, to whose construction both countries, in different ways, contributed) and in a close and complex dialectic relationship with each other, made up of antagonism as much as of collusion. This complex dialogue is possibly best represented through the inter- and intra-textual dialogue between Samuel Johnson's *Journey to the Western*

Islands of Scotland (1775) and James Boswell's *Journal of a Tour to the Hebrides* (1785), both accounting the same event – the tour of the Hebrides and Western Islands of Scotland which the two had undertaken in 1773 – and engaging with or referring to a number of contemporary issues and events which both divided and united the two authors and the two nations they represented: the transformation of the Highlands in the years after the second Jacobite rising, the legacy of Jacobitism, the might and prospects of the British Empire, the impact of the Scottish Enlightenment, among others. That the focal place (both physically and discursively) of this dialogue should be the western islands of Scotland – 'primitive' and 'picturesque' Scotland, marginal and yet seductively at the centre of Romantic imagination, remote and yet attracting a new brand of middlebrow, "antiquarian tourists," searching "for the unsophisticated culture of declining rural localities" at a time when the traditional practice of the aristocratic grand tour was declining (Pittock 1999, 39) – is in itself meaningful of the complex relationship that binds the new centre to the new periphery. And while the periphery resists its peripherality by asserting (like Boswell) its own relevance in the new British order, the centre is not always so self-confident about its own centrality, as several waves of virulent anti-Scottish feeling in this historical period (as that staged by the popular London newspaper the *North Briton,* see Crawford 2000, 63-64) witness.

Within the dynamics of the Union, Scotland is indeed "always at least two places at the same time: both Scotland and Britain, an ancient or imaginary space and a modern political force, synecdochal for northerness in general and a singular position generating its own national character" (Fielding 2008, 38-39). Such 'duplicity' can, however, be seen as having two conflicting outcomes: empowerment and subordination, as effectively illustrated by Britain's first 'political novel,' John Galt's *The Member: an Autobiography* (1832), a first-person account of the adventures of a Scottish nabob, newly returned to Britain from India – Archibald Jobbry – who decides to become an MP at Westminster by unscrupulously availing himself of the iniquitous rules and practices that the political system, in this historical period, codes as legal. His mixed strategies and role playing, involving both assimilation and resistance (in)to the British parliamentary system, first secure his success, then seal his failure and definitive marginalisation (see Sassi 1999).

While, arguably, representations of Scotland and England's relationship in the course of the 18th and 19th century oscillate from a discourse of sameness and identification with the British and imperial super-identity to a discourse of difference, within which each nation becomes each other's Other – and there is no doubt that literary representations as well as constructions of national literary traditions held a central role in this complex dialectical process – it would be certainly naive to see this as a game played fairly and on equal terms, and with the same impact on both nations. The unbalanced relation of political power between the two nations is clearly mirrored in the different fate of English and Scottish Literature as academic subjects, which unfolded in the course of the 20th century, after the 1921 Anglo-Irish War of Independence ended with the establishment of the Irish Free State and with the 'devolution' of Irish culture and literature, thus reinforcing "'little Englandism' [...] [and making] it easier to think of 'Britain' as England writ large" (Kerrigan 2008, 245). A pivotal role in the definition of the role and status of both fields was no doubt played by T. S. Eliot's re-definition of 'tradition' and of the role of the literary critic. As postcolonial scholarship has highlighted, T. S. Eliot's theorisation of tradition, and his famous request that a writer should write with an historical sense, involving "a perception, not only of the pastness of the past, but of its presence [...] not merely with his own generation in his bones, but with a feeling that the whole of the literature of Europe from Homer and within it the whole of the literature of his own country has a simultaneous existence" (Eliot 1952, 14), put the European tradition firmly at the centre of academic knowledge, and within this, it inevitably privileged those countries which could boast a continuous and consistent narrative of their own past. Eliot thus embraces the national taxonomy of literatures, and identifies a national tradition worthy of this name as endowed with universal value. It is 'universality' then – articulated largely in Eurocentric terms and ambiguously defined – that represents the measure of literary greatness. An exhaustive reading of Eliot's essay, which should certainly be evaluated in its complexity, is beyond the scope of the present article, yet it is worthwhile to point out that "Tradition and the Individual Talent" (1919) – Eliot's possibly most canonical critical text – was instrumental in re-defining English literature as both a national and a 'cosmopolitan' construct, thus authorising the conflation between the two terms. In the same year of the publication of "Tradition and the Individual Talent," Eliot also published an article virtually unknown beyond the 'borders' of Scottish Studies: in "Was There a Scottish Literature?" (*Athenaeum*, August 1919) he responds to G. Gregory Smith's *Scottish Literature: Character and Influence* (1919) by firmly denying Scottish literature the status of tradition. Interestingly, his effort here is not so much aimed at evaluating Scottish writing along 'universal' aesthetical criteria, but rather at assessing the consistency and quality of Scotland's nationness: by drawing on 19th-century defining criteria (among which language unity, 8) he argues that Scotland as a nation does not satisfy the pre-requisites necessary for the building of a proper literary tradition. Its writers, therefore, are either identified as Scottish, and therefore as "provincial," or assimilated into the English tradition, and therefore metropolitan and universal. The language of literariness, especially in the conclusive part, is entirely subsumed by the utterly pragmatic language of the imperial vision, which informs the article:

> A literature does not maintain itself simply by a continual production of great writers. The historian of literature must count with as shifting and as massive forces as the historian of politics. In the modern world the struggle of capitals of civilization is apparent on a large scale. A powerful literature with a powerful capital, tends to attract and absorb all the drifting shreds of force about it. (Eliot 2004, 10)

This "power of attraction" is also seen as a powerful shield against "the danger of disintegration of English literature and language" posed by the English-speaking (ex)colonies – "people too remote (for geographical or other reasons) to be able to pool their differences in a common metropolis" (Eliot 2004, 10). The close nexus between Empire, Union and the construction of English literature is here fully revealed, even though not for the first time – Eliot, after all, had followed into Matthew Arnold's footsteps in this and other matters – providing an extraordinarily sharp illustration of its pervasive and yet elusive power in this historical period.

Much of the history of the intertwined constructions of English literature and Scottish literature in the 20th century can be seen as a development of, or a response to such imperial instrumental views of literature. And so can the 'hostility' which has often permeated their dialogue. Both constructions, in fact, have attracted deserved criticism, especially starting from the 1980s, after the cultural turn, for different and yet connected reasons: 'EngLit' has been attacked by postcolonial and archipelagic scholars as promoting imperialist and Anglocentric values; 'ScotLit' has been accused of constructing itself narrowly along stifling nationalist lines – of subordinating literariness to nation-ness, crystallising the role of literature to the preservation of cultural memory and to the staging of political resistance. As Bell has aptly observed:

> There has been a tendency in Scottish Studies to equate history with literature, so that literature tends to be regarded as the *effect* of cultural processes, rather than as an intervention in those processes, or indeed as a relatively autonomous act of aesthetic, ethical or political engagement. Subsequently, there is a certain factor of reducibility at work, where texts produced by Scottish authors must in the first instance be explained in terms of their Scottishness. (Bell 2004, 2)

Both fields, since the 1980s, have gone a long way to reshape their respective methodological and disciplinary set-ups.[5] No doubt the gradual devolution of Scottish literature and the consolidation of the more articulated and self-confident field of Scottish Studies have contributed indirectly also to the re-articulation of English Studies (in an archipelagic direction, for example) and to a further questioning of its literary canon, but they are also having an impact on other theoretical/comparative fields. Research on Caribbean-Scottish postcolonial relations, for example, opened new methodological perspectives and investigative paths in both fields, either by

> mapping a transnational Circum-Atlantic in which widely complex conflicts, connections, and interferences are accounted for – a map showing colonial inscriptions, social contrasts, cultural interconnections, and lived relations between the Caribbean and Scotland (Covi 2007, 13)

or by performing a "displacement of Scottishness" through a focus on the West Indies as "a powerfully destabilising *lieu de mémoire*" (Sassi 2007, 135), while Silke Stroh and Stephanie Lehner's challenging studies have undertaken for the first time a sustained gauging of postcolonial theories against, respectively, Scotland's and Scotland and Ireland's complex relation with the centre of empire, also investigated through a comparative approach in Michael Gardiner, Graeme Macdonald and Niall O'Gallagher's volume of collected essays.

The post-devolution decade, in particular, has released energies that were for a long time repressed by a defensive (and yet necessary and, for a long time, even radical) nationalist stance. This 'post-nationalist turn' has been heralded and welcome by many scholars in the past ten years: Christopher Whyte, one of the first voices in Scotland to denounce the restrictions of a nation-oriented criticism, in his *Modern Scottish Poetry* sets out "to reclaim a degree of autonomy for the creative [...] Reclaiming such autonomy means that both history and politics must renounce any privileged status as tools for the interpretation of Scottish literature" (Whyte 2004, 7, 8); along similar lines, Gavin Miller and Eleanor Bell's volume of collected essays purports to draw "attention to new types of criticism which are able to challenge the cultural-nationalist paradigm, and which also reflect the sociological and intellectual

---

5   For an exhaustive investigation of the history and recent developments of "The Study of Scottish Literature," see Craig (2007).

changes now taking place" (Miller and Bell 2004, 11). As Berthold Schoene has aptly put it, "undeniably [...] devolution has changed and will continue to change Scotland's structure(s) of feeling, and the nation's present preoccupations and priorities are bound to differ markedly from late 20th-century political concerns" (Schoene 2007b, 4).

And yet, it is foreseeable that the national question will remain *one* of the strands of Scottish Studies, even though freed from the intra-British hegemonic discourse of sub/national traditions and re-visioned through the lens of contemporary theorisations that reconcile the nation with cosmopolitan practices by maintaining, for example, that global democracy is best achieved through the strengthening of local and nationally based democratic citizenship (Thompson), or by identifying in patriotic sentiment the basis for global concern (Nussbaum). A sense of (partial) continuity with the past, for example, has been recently implied by Caroline McCracken-Flesher in her prediction that Scottish Studies' "disciplinary boundaries [will] bend and shift; history and culture will fold together but oppositions multiply; presents and pasts will connect to futures" (McCracken-Flesher 2011b, 18), while a more explicit re-evaluation of "the matter of the *nation* [...] and the value of national identity" is articulated by Alan Riach, who reframes nationalism postmodernly "as a curious unanswered question, the unfinished business of home" and points out how "in a world of globalised interest, self-determined nationality may be the only viable opposition to imperial power" (Riach 2005, 240).

The present collection is of course not the first to attempt to provide an agenda for Scottish Studies for the 21st century (see, among others, Schoene 2007a and McCracken-Flesher 2011a); furthermore, a sense of innovation and renovation has indeed inspired most critical works published in the past decade or so – the three-volume *Edinburgh History of Scottish Literature* and the series of the Edinburgh Companions to Scottish Literature (which, starting from 2013, will be continued by ASLS, under its newly launched academic imprint, Scottish Literature International) provide ample illustration of this. And it is equally obvious that eleven articles may only represent the tip of the iceberg: the exclusions, motivated only by reasons of space limitations, outnumber here the inclusions, both in terms of fields of investigation represented (Linguistics and Medieval Studies being among the most notable ones) and of theoretical approaches. Yet, some sort of inclusivity is achieved in the micro- and macro-mapping of focuses and trends offered, and *inclusivity* is indeed a keyword here, as the collection purposes to chart the diversity of scholarly interests and approaches and to inscribe them on the same standing in the new agenda for the field, beyond the somewhat simplified anti/nationalist diatribe that has too often stifled or sidelined other important investigative paths.

The collection opens aptly with Dafydd Moore's investigation of 18th-century Scotland's most internationally renowned writer – James Macpherson – aimed at reassessing his work in a wider, European context, and also at raising methodological issues which are relevant not only to the study of the writer under consideration, but to the understanding of British Romanticism at large. Pauline Anne Mackay undertakes an original investigation of the uses of Robert Burns (a writer firmly and controversially at the centre of the Scottish literary canon) as a cultural icon, unveiling a continuum linking the Bard's poems as 'objects' of cult to the material culture of male and patriotic social circles. Caroline McCracken-Flesher delves into an equally original revisitation of Walter Scott as an aging man/writer by strategically reconsidering old age "as the site of unpredictable power," and thus disclosing a new autobiographical and meta-literary facet of one of Scotland's most polyhedric and complex writers. Oliver S. Buckton articulates a challenging re-reading of R. L. Stevenson's work from a queer theory perspective by focusing on recurrent same-sex erotic figurations, and by revealing how Stevenson often subverts the hierarchy of gender roles (based on the binary of masculine/feminine) coded by 19th-century law and social conventions. Emma Dymock provides a new historical and theoretical framework for the critical appreciation of one of Scotland's greatest 20th-century poets: Sorley MacLean's work is here revisited in its complex affiliations with the Scottish Renaissance as well as with transnational political and philosophical currents. Scott Hames's probing assessment of Alice Munro and Alistair MacLeod's representations of diasporic Scottishness engages with issues of (diasporic) memory and rememorisation as well as with displaced identities, thus unsettling Scotland's established narratives of national identity. Suzanne Gilbert engages with the notion of tradition by charting and analysing the recent developments of one of Scotland's quintessentially traditional genres, the ballad, highlighting its intrinsically polymorphic and adaptable quality: "the ballad's paradoxical conjunction of stability and variation" becomes therefore a key to revise the very notion of tradition as a fixed and ritual practice. Ian Brown's retrieval of the lost sense of importance of drama in Scottish society provides evidence of the significant 'archaeological' work awaiting scholars in the re/writing of whole chapters of Scottish cultural and literary history; furthermore, by focusing on the notion of theatre "as crucible of change," it foregrounds an idea of tradition that is – as above – dynamic and fluid. Glenda Norquay in her article provides an up-to-date state of the art of the controversial relation between Gender and Scottish Studies: her critical reconstruction of the different stages and voices in the process of "gendering the nation" opens new, exciting investigative paths to the understanding of Scottish literature, and suggests the possibility of a radical re-mapping of the canon. Donna Heddle articulates both a regionalist and a transnational approach by reporting on the development of the new field of Northern Scottish Studies at UHI: the 'militant' attention to native communities here combines with a conventional activity of empirical and theoretical research and reminds us of the often radical role of the 'local' within Scottish Studies. Finally, Alan Riach's important article aptly closes the collection by alerting us to what is indeed a central issue in contemporary Scotland's cultural debate: the lack of institutionalisation of Scottish literature in Scottish schools and the consequent difficulty at defining a shared core literary canon. Riach also reminds us of how the role of a canon – even when defined, as it should be, in a flexible and pluralistic way – remains an important tool in cultural transmission, as well as a form of cultural empowerment.

By way of conclusion, I would like to identify a core proposition for this new agenda for the field in the 'making of connections' – in the engaging of Scottish Studies in a fruitful dialogue with other disciplinary fields and theoretical perspectives. I am borrowing the image from James Robertson's latest novel, *And the Land lay Still* (2010), an 'epic' novel whose subject is Scotland itself, from 1950 to the present day. Here, Robertson sounds the depths of his country's complex recent history through the disconnected lives and voices of several characters. At the end of the novel, the main character takes on the task of connecting them – connecting lives and stories is not the same as creating a homogeneous unity, as the act of connecting is respectful of individual features and local specificities:

> He thinks, where do you begin? How do you tell a man that he has a granddaughter he never knew existed? How do you introduce someone who never knew her father to her grandfather? How do you make the connections between Don and Marjory and Ellen and Kirsty that must be made, that will be made? He doesn't yet know. But the connections, more of them even than he can know or imagine at this moment [...] the connections will be made, and he understands that it has fallen to him to make them. (Robertson 2010, 671)

The time has indeed come to make the connections, it has fallen on us to make them.

Works Cited

Bell, Eleanor. *Questioning Scotland: Literature, Nationalism, Postmodernism*. Basingstoke: Palgrave Macmillan, 2004.
Brown, Ian, Thomas Owen Clancy, Susan Manning, and Murray Pittock. "Scottish Literature: Criticism and the Canon." *The Edinburgh History of Scottish Literature: Vol. 1*. Eds. Ian Brown, Thomas O. Clancy, Murray Pittock, and Susan Manning. Edinburgh: Edinburgh University Press, 2007. 3-15.
Conrad, Sebastian. *Globalisation and the Nation in Imperial Germany*. Cambridge: Cambridge University Press, 2010.
Covi, Giovanna. "Footprints in the Sand: Attornies, Redlegs, and Red-Haired Women in African-Caribbean Stories." *Caribbean-Scottish Relations: Colonial and Contemporary Inscriptions in History, Language and Literature*. Eds. Giovanna Covi, Joan Anim-Addo, Velma Pollard, and Carla Sassi. London: Mango Publishing, 2007. 12-45.
Craig, Cairns. "The Study of Scottish Literature." *The Edinburgh History of Scottish Literature: Vol. 1*. Eds. Ian Brown, Thomas O. Clancy, Murray Pittock, and Susan Manning. Edinburgh: Edinburgh University Press, 2007. 16-31.
Crawford, Robert. *Devolving English Literature*. Edinburgh: Edinburgh University Press, 2000.
—. *The Scottish Invention of English Literature*. Cambridge: Cambridge University Press, 2008.
Devine, Thomas M. *Scotland's Empire: 1600-1815*. London: Allen Lane, 2003.
Eliot, T. S. "Tradition and the Individual Talent." 1919. *Selected Essays*. London: Faber and Faber, 1952. 13-22.
—. "Was There a Scottish Literature?" 1919. *Modernism and Nationalism: Literature and Society in Scotland, 1918-1939. Source Documents for the Scottish Renaissance*. Ed. Margery P. McCulloch. Glasgow: Association for Scottish Literary Studies, 2004. 7-10.
Fielding, Penny. *Scotland and the Fictions of Geography: North Britain, 1760-1830*. Cambridge: Cambridge University Press, 2008.
Gardiner, Michael, Graeme Macdonald, and Niall O'Gallagher, eds. *Scottish Literature and Postcolonial Literature: Comparative Texts and Critical Perspectives*. Edinburgh: Edinburgh University Press, 2011.
Kerrigan, John. *Archipelagic English: Literature, History, and Politics, 1603-1707*. Oxford: Oxford University Press, 2008.

Lehner, Stefanie. *Subaltern Ethics in Contemporary Scottish and Irish Literature: Tracing Counter-Histories*. Basingstoke: Palgrave Macmillan, 2011.

Manning, Susan. "Post-Union Scotland and the Scottish Idiom of Britishness." *The Edinburgh History of Scottish Literature: Vol. 2*. Eds. Susan Manning, Ian Brown, Thomas O. Clancy, and Murray Pittock. Edinburgh: Edinburgh University Press, 2007. 45-56.

McCracken-Flesher, Caroline, ed. *Culture, Nation, and the New Scottish Parliament*. Lewisburg: Bucknell University Press, 2007a.

—. "Introduction." *Culture, Nation, and the New Scottish Parliament*. Ed. Caroline McCracken-Flesher. Lewisburg: Bucknell University Press, 2007b. 9-18.

McCulloch, Margery P., ed. *Modernism and Nationalism: Literature and Society in Scotland, 1918-1939. Source Documents for the Scottish Renaissance*. Glasgow: Association for Scottish Literary Studies, 2004.

Miller, Gavin and Eleanor Bell. "Introduction." *Scotland in Theory: Reflections on Culture and Literature*. Eds. Eleanor Bell and Gavin Miller. Amsterdam: Rodopi, 2004. 11-15.

Nussbaum, Martha C. "Toward a Globally Sensitive Patriotism." *Daedalus* 137.3 (2008): 78-93.

Pittock, Murray G. H. *Celtic Identity and the British Image*. Manchester: Manchester University Press, 1999.

Riach, Alan. *Representing Scotland in Literature, Popular Culture and Iconography: The Masks of the Modern Nation*. Basingstoke: Palgrave Macmillan, 2005.

Robertson, James. *And the Land Lay Still*. London: Hamish Hamilton, 2010.

Sassi, Carla. "Acts of (Un)willed Amnesia: Dis/appearing Figurations of the Caribbean in Post-Union Scottish Literature." *Caribbean-Scottish Relations: Colonial and Contemporary Inscriptions in History, Language and Literature*. Eds. Giovanna Covi, Joan Anim-Addo, Velma Pollard, and Carla Sassi. London: Mango Publishing, 2007. 131-207.

—. "Subverting Britannia's (Precarious) Balance: a Re-reading of John Galt's *The Member: An Autobiography*." *RSV – Rivista di Studi Vittoriani* 8 (1999): 25-45.

Schoene, Berthold, ed. *The Edinburgh Companion to Contemporary Scottish Literature*. Edinburgh: Edinburgh University Press, 2007a.

—. "Introduction. Post-Devolution Scottish Writing." *The Edinburgh Companion to Contemporary Scottish Literature*. Ed. Berthold Schoene. Edinburgh: Edinburgh University Press, 2007b. 1-4.

Stroh, Silke. *Uneasy Subjects. Postcolonialism and Scottish Gaelic Poetry*. Amsterdam: Rodopi, 2011.

Thompson, Dennis. "Democratic Theory and Global Society." *Journal of Political Philosophy* 7.2 (1999): 111-125.

Whyte, Christopher. *Modern Scottish Poetry*. Edinburgh: Edinburgh University Press, 2004.

DAFYDD MOORE, Plymouth

"Kings unborn of Fingal's royal race:" *Ossian*, Scottishness, and the Aesthetics of Collaboration in the Age of Napoleon

In recent years James Macpherson's *Poems of Ossian* (1759-1763) have enjoyed a return to critical prominence in Anglo-American literary critical discourse not seen since the mid-19th century. So much so, that in his important exploration of archipelagic criticism John Kerrigan felt able to suggest that "anyone seriously interested in English Romanticism reads *Ossian*," a claim that in its matter-of-fact tone would have provoked surprise amongst the *Poems*' most ardent advocates twenty years earlier (Kerrigan 2008, 3). This renewed attention has broadly focussed on two dimensions to the work. On the one hand, significant attention has been paid to the *Poems*' cultural politics, be that in relation to their Highland-Gaelic inspiration, their Scottish Enlightenment genesis, their engagement with questions of wider British identity, or in the debates that surrounded the provenance of and Macpherson's claims for the *Poems*.[1] On the other hand, there has been further work on the reception of and response to *Ossian*, almost exclusively beyond the British Isles.

Any consideration of the latter, perhaps in the shape of Howard Gaskill's *Reception of Ossian in Europe*, will almost certainly lead one to ponder the paucity of such work in connection with writing from the British Isles.[2] This volume is part of a series of reception studies that on the whole takes that rather English view of what 'Europe' might mean (that is to say, non-Anglophone and continental), but in fact, Gaskill persuaded his editors that, given *Ossian's* nigh-on unique hybrid national identity, Ireland, Gaelic Scotland, Wales and Lowland Scotland and England counted as Europe even for a British readership, and thus were the subject of chapters. This rhetorical triumph only highlighted the vacuum its essays on these subjects went some way to being able to fill. Despite Jerome MacGann's claim that *Ossian*'s influence on the literature of the late 18th century "eclipsed all others" (MacGann 1996, 33), Dunn's unpublished PhD thesis from 1965 remains the only comprehensive attempt to come to terms with Macpherson's relation to British Romanticism, even if the last thirty years of revisionism have produced the occasional individual essay.[3] There are nearly as many articles devoted to Thomas Jefferson's enthusiasm for *Ossian* as there are on *Ossian* and British Romantic writers put together. This can be accounted for in a number of ways, from the mundanely coincidental (scholars interested in *Ossian* have not had the interest in or perhaps felt themselves ill-equipped to tackle this project), through to the more culturally significant and interesting.

---

1   The body of Macpherson scholarship is now substantial. As a *very* selective introductory sample, see Stafford (1988), Gaskill (1991), Stafford and Gaskill (1998), Moore (2003; 2004), Weinbrot (1993) and Trumpener (1997).
2   Stepping outside the Anglophone world momentarily, we could also add Schmidt (2003). In terms of the comparison noted here, the comparison with the non-Anglophone world (in terms of reception and scholarship) is even more stark if one takes into account the number of French, German and Italian works devoted to the influence of *Ossian* within their respective national literatures.
3   See Dunn (1965). There has been one article on Coleridge, a couple on Wordsworth, an article and some passing commentary on Blake and a few other publications cited below. It is notable that Nigel Leask has recently made this self-same observation in relation to Robert Burns (2011, 128).

The questions of Macpherson's moral character, and the reliability of his claims about Ossian, are, in fact, much more troubling features in the Anglo-American critical tradition than the European one. This led to complex and contradictory responses at the time of the *Poems*' publication and still leads to reluctance to engage now. It is still possible for Thomas Curley's *Samuel Johnson, the Ossian Fraud and the Celtic Revival in Great Britain and Ireland* (2009) to not only focus exclusively on the question of *Ossian's* authenticity (genuinely new insights on this self-evidently important topic are always welcome), but also to conflate the final word on the *Ossian* controversy with the final word on *Ossian*, and thus categorically deny that there is anything else to say about Macpherson.

That said, Macpherson does not owe his critical rehabilitation to Johnsonites, but to revisionists seeking to correct the Anglo-centric nature of English literary studies. Thus, a more important factor is the suspicion with which four nations or the archipelagic approaches have tended to view reception or influence-oriented criticism. As a range of important books on the nature of Scottish and Irish Romanticism have emphasised over the last ten years:

> in reaching for a more neutral understanding of British Romanticisms, one where the plural is more than a facile gesture towards inclusion, we need to understand the structures of earlier literary history, or we may risk abandoning them only to rebuild with some of the same materials. (Pittock 2008, 8)[4]

In other words, archipelagic criticism is more engaged in interrogating the fundamental tenets of British Romanticism than it is in exploring the unexamined influence of previously neglected writers on established figures. More importantly, it is suspicious of the tendency such readings can have of re-inscribing a literary history in which a writer's (perhaps only) value resides in the impact on or similarity to an English writer already established as worth reading.[5]

Caution in the face of the siren call of "facile gesture[s] towards inclusion" (Pittock 2008, 8) is entirely right, but it is possible to appreciate the new subtleness and insight brought to the understanding of the literary culture of the British Isles at the turn of the 19th century by this scholarship (and hopefully go some way towards emulating it) and still feel that there is a place for a more thorough examination of Macpherson's place within British Romanticisms through the responses provoked by the *Poems*. Furthermore, such an examination should be limber enough to stay methodologically true to the overall aim of devolutionary critical studies to broaden and reconfigure, rather than unwittingly reinforce, accepted narratives of Anglo-centric literary historiography. One of the ways it might do this is through renewed attention to the desperate and more fugitive ways in which *Ossian* drew responses and was part of the British cultural bloodstream in the fifty years following its publication.

With this in mind, this article offers a modest case study in the form of a consideration of a minor theatrical work, pulled together for a very specific purpose. *The Druid, or The Vision of Fingal, A Choral Masque* was performed as part of a benefit

---

4 See also Carruthers and Rawes (2003; 2010), Davis, Duncan, and Sorenson (2004), Duff and Jones (2008) and Pittock (2011).
5 This is of course a generalisation, and like all such ultimately flawed. But it is the case that when Macpherson's influence is considered, it is more likely to be in terms that deny the Anglo-axis than confirm it, such as Ó Gallchoir (2008).

evening for the Caledonian Asylum at the King's Theatre Haymarket on the evening of Thursday 25 May, 1815. Copies of the text were printed by MacMillian, "printer to his Royal Highness the Prince Regent" (Moore 2004, vol. 4), and available for sale for one shilling. It is but one of the myriad adaptations of Macpherson's *Poems* for stage and music in Britain and across Europe, and indeed *Ossian* provided source material for opera as late as the 1920s. They did not share the commercial success or critical attention of their inspiration, and some share the undignified fate of remaining unperformed to this day. Unsurprisingly, they have received very little scholarly attention and little consideration of what they might offer to our understanding of the story of *Ossian*'s reception.[6] However, texts such as *The Druid,* demonstrate some of the things that the Ossianic milieu meant, and the purposes to which it could be put, in the opening decades of the 19th century. Consideration of *The Druid* also draws together the two strands of current *Ossian* criticism, since it can only be fully understood within the context of a cultural politics existing within a European frame of reference for *Ossian's* reception.

Before discussing the masque, it is worth establishing the context of the performance. The Caledonian Asylum was founded in 1815 under the patronage of the Prince Regent (and boasting an extensive set of royal princes and princesses as vice patrons and patronesses). Its purpose, according to the announcement of the benefit evening in *The Times*, was "educating and supporting such children of soldiers, sailors, and marines, natives of Scotland, as cannot be admitted into the Royal Institutes of Chelsea and Greenwich, and of indigent Scotch parents resident in London, not entitled to Parochial Relief" (Anon. 1815, 2). The evening wore its Scottishness on its plaid sleeve. The tone was set in *The Times*, where all the vice-patrons were styled with their English and Scottish titles, as in "His Royal Highness the Duke of Clarence and St Andrews K. T." (the initials standing for Knight of the Order of the Thistle). The main attraction of the evening came before the masque in the shape of a performance of John Home's *Douglas* (1756), in which Kemble took the role of Old Norval. *Douglas*, a historical tragedy set in the Scottish medieval past (and itself an influence on *Ossian*), had in its time been the subject of wild acclaim (and nationalist boasting) in Edinburgh, and anti-Scottish audience riots when Garrick had been unwise enough to attempt a transfer to London. Whichever way one looks at it, the evening was one of high octane Scottishness, and it is tempting to view the association of the Royal Household (four Princes, ten Princesses, the Prince Regent and the Queen) with such a Scottish charity and, by extension, the benefit evening, as part of the growing royal interest in Scotland that would find its most striking expression seven years later, in George IV's tartan-clad visit to the country in 1822.[7]

As is perhaps the case with many charity gigs, *The Druid* appears to have been a rather *ad hoc* affair, as the printed text is at some pains to point out. A postscript to the argument notes that it was originally intended "for a ballet only" before attempts were made to fashion a full play, only for the work to ultimately be "a mere vehicle for Music and Action" (Moore 2004, vol. 4, 259). The notes also suggest that because many of the singers have other engagements that night "it is impossible to fix the period of their performance" (260), while the text bears witness to its being formed in

---

6 See Malek (1975) and Moore (2004), which contains a number of reprints (vol. 4) and some critical discussion of their potential value (vol. 1: xcvii-cvii).
7 I am grateful to Frank O'Gorman for reminding me of what no doubt felt like the obvious here.

large measure around the availability of particular performers, notably the celebrated *prima donna* Miss Mortimer, for whom a grand scena was introduced. Evidence that this rather provisional state of affairs was not merely a pre-emptive fiction on the part of the author to avoid criticism might be provided by the fact that *The Times* advertised the identity of the performer taking the role of Ossian, yet the published text contains no such part. The suspicion of a rather hurriedly assembled melange is further heightened by the intelligence that the choruses were borrowed and adapted to an Ossianic purpose from Kinnaird's translation of Winter's grand cantata *The Liberation of Germany* of the same year (Peter Winter himself had written an Ossian-inspired piece nine years earlier, in 1806).[8] Overall, the musical extravaganza and pot-pourri that is *The Druid* does not evince a confident organic structure or firm artistic purpose. But it is nonetheless valuable as a document of the ways in which *Ossian* was read and understood as emblematic of Scottishness on the eve of Waterloo.

The masque owes relatively little to Macpherson's *Ossian*, though significantly more than merely names and an all-purpose Scottishness. It recounts the efforts of Fingal's wife and attendant Druid to cheer the King up, and in this narrative trigger at least something of Macpherson survives. Fingal has defeated the Romans, but fears that they will soon be back for more:

> [...] our victorious ranks beheld
> The foe defeated, but not quell'd
> The snake you scotch'd, and think is slain,
> Will close, and be itself again:
> The eagle that today had fled
> Again will fill the vales with dread. (Moore 2004, vol. 4, 260)

Besides, Fingal has more profound fears within what he calls his "boding breast:"

> Fingal's race, the race of song,
> Shall sink amidst that current strong,
> And silence brood where bards in Selma sing,
> And fluttering ivy climb where hangs the tuneful string. (Moore 2004, vol. 4, 261)

These "twilight thoughts of shadowy dread" (as Roscrana rather nicely characterises them) are very much at one with the mood of Macpherson, where triumph is only ever temporary and where all achievement comes haunted by the knowledge of more profound defeat and decay, as in "Carthon" from *Fingal and Other Poems* (1761):

> Raise the song of mourning, O bards, over the land of strangers. They have but fallen before us: for one day, we must fall.– Why dost thou build the hall, son of the winged days? Thou lookest from thy towers today; yet a few years, and the blast of the desert comes; it howls in thy empty court, and whistles round thy half-worn shield. (Moore 2004, vol.2, 132)

What happens next is not, however, at one with Macphersonian entropy. Roscrana calls forth a Druid who relates the history of Scotland and "the kings unborn of Fingal's royal race." The history the Druid relates is one of wars and martial kings, of "Highland arm and Highland steel," of the "sons of the mountains to battle advanc-

---

8 *The Times* advertises other borrowings: the "celebrated Movement by Salvator Rosa [...] and for the first time in this country, the Triumphal Polonaise, composed by her Imperial Majesty the Empress Catharine II" (Anon. 1815, 2).

ing" (Moore 2004, vol. 4, 264, 265). Fingal himself notes the emphasis on "battle, blood and death" and asks of the "genial hours of leisure" (265) brought by peace. The Druid's reply invokes a vision of war and peace as alternate states through which nations move as night follows day. The Druid's vision is rather obscure, and the reader is aided by a couple of footnotes: one notes that a passage referring to a time of "wild and wasteful conflict" is "allusive to the Feudal Wars and domestic contentions," and another clarifies that the five-line description of regicide and slaughter refers to the French Revolution. Fingal, lacking the benefit of the footnotes, is ultimately moved to exclaim "O! That these eyes could pierce the veil / That shuts such glory from the sight" (266), a request that moves the prophecy of national destiny and glory for Fingal's royal line to its climax:

> A prophetic vision, commemorative of the battle of the Nile and the rescue of Egypt, concluding with an Allegory expressive of the public visit of the Allied Sovereigns to the Prince Regent. (Moore 2004, vol. 4, 259)

It is possible to see how the decisive engagements of the Egypt campaign could have been staged.[9] However, it is tempting to say that it would be worth good money (especially for charity) to have witnessed exactly how the state visit of Tsar Alexander of Russia, King Frederick William III of Prussia and Prince Metternich, the Austrian Chancellor, (along with other dignitaries including Field Marshall Blucher) between 6 and 26 June 1814 was represented on stage, however allegorically. Their itinerary included a trip to Ascot Races, a visit to Oxford, tours of Woolwich Arsenal and Portsmouth naval dockyard, inspections of the fleet (including some sort of live firing exercise in the Solent), as well as sundry honorary dinners, investitures, opera trips, levees and other ceremonial events. Doubtless the point about British military-technological-fiscal might was not lost on the foreign dignitaries as they subsequently made their way to the Congress of Vienna, but nevertheless the visit itself was not obviously the stuff of national allegory, even by the standards of an age obsessed with pageantry and which readily dealt in this currency.[10]

The Druid's prophecy lays out a history of Scottish martial endeavour with its roots in the resistance to Roman invasion (a notion that stretches back to the 1st century AD and Tacitus' *Agricola*), but treads a careful, unspoken and possibly ambiguous line on the question of Anglo-Scottish relations. The "feudal wars and domestic contentions" referred to in the note are significantly non-specific, and certainly non-dynastic. The point is consistent opposition to foreign aggression, even if the particular foreignness is left usefully obscure. As the prophecy progresses, so we move to an explicit reference to the French Revolution, and a resolution in the vision in terms of the British struggle against Napoleonic France. The focus of the vision of "Fingal's royal race" moves from a Scottish to a wider British history, from the Celtic warrior king to the Hanoverian British Regent.

The construction of Scottish history, and of the contribution of Scotland to the project of Britain, in military terms, is a familiar notion. Whether in the form of the Jacobite rebel charge or the thin red line – defeat on Culloden Moor or victory on the

---

9 If we are to take the distinction of events noted in the argument literally, presumably this would be a reference to Nelson's victory at the Nile on 1 August 1798 and the subsequent eviction of the French following the second Battle of Aboukir (22 March 1801).

10 For the period's interest in pageantry, see Hilton (2006, 33-34).

Plains of Abraham – more than one commentator has observed the almost exclusively martial character of the way that Scottishness functioned (and indeed in many ways still functions) in the British imaginary.[11] And the timing of the event is surely significant. The masque was performed less than two months after Britain had, along with her allies, pledged to field 150,000 men to rid Europe of Napoleon once and for all, and, as it turned out, less than three weeks before the decisive battle of Napoleon's one hundred days at Waterloo on 18 June, a battle that would in turn enter the pantheon of Scottish military honours. It may have been that the horrors and glory of Waterloo were still to come, but the sacrifice that had led to the founding of the Caledonian Asylum for the orphans of Scottish veterans was recent history, and so the charitable context of the performance reinforces the point of the vision of "Highland steel."

If a vision of Scottish martial heritage in the service of Britain is not unexpected, the location of a Hanoverian Regent at the culminating point of the vision of national greatness originating with Fingal might raise some eyebrows. It is widely accepted that in *Ossian* Macpherson plays on the established associations between Gaelic myth, Celtic heroism and Jacobite iconography to lend the *Poems* at least part of their resonance. In Murray Pittock's words, *Ossian* represents, through its "context, imagery and authorial connection" a "reconfiguration of Jacobite experience post Culloden," even if any one definition of the politics of Macpherson the man is likely to be "too categorical" for such a janus-faced figure (Pittock 1998, 41). The critical consensus holds that the Jacobitism offered by *Ossian* is fundamentally sentimental, a coming to terms with defeat, a valedictory and nostalgic patriotism that seeks to repackage contemporary political matters as aesthetic, the stuff of epic, "of far off unhappy things and battles long ago," as Wordsworth would put it in his own imaginative engagement with what Gaelic song might mean in "The Solitary Reaper" (1807). There are dissenting voices to this sentimental Jacobite position, but no-one has yet suggested that this cultural sell out (if sell out it be), extends to typing Fingal as the progenitor of a Hanoverian Regent.

In fact, the accommodation between heroic Celticism, crypto-Jacobitism, and the Hanoverian dynasty is only one of the accommodations in this short text. There are others, all operating at different levels. The Druid himself represents a significant one. It is surprising to discover that there are no druids in Macpherson's *Ossian,* given the association of druids with the Celto-mania the *Poems* did so much to promote, but it is the case nonetheless. According to the pre-Fingalian history outlined by Macpherson in the "Dissertation concerning the Antiquity, Etc, of the Poems of Ossian the Son of Fingal" that accompanied the *Fingal* volume, the druidic order was crushed by Fingal's immediate forefathers on account of its opposition to the establishment of a hereditary monarchy: as Macpherson notes, "it is a matter of little wonder then, that Fingal and his son Ossian make so little, if any, mention of the druids, who were the declared enemies of their succession to the supreme majesty" (Moore 2004, vol. 2, v). In effect, 1688 is re-run, only this time the exclusionist whigs are banished forever, leaving the way clear for the eventual reign of Fingal himself, while the more respectable and politically neutral bards live on as guardians of history and social ethics into Ossian's time. Of course this did not stop imitators of (and indeed some commentators on) *Ossian* pretending that they were present, so the Druid's appearance in the masque

---

11 See, for example, Pittock (1991), Womack (1989) and Clyde (1995).

is not in itself worthy of comment. More significant is the reference to the previous unpleasantries between the druidic order and Fingal's family. He is introduced by Roscrana in good Ossianic fashion as "the last of all the Druid train" (Moore 2004, vol. 4, 262), and the argument had made clear that he "is supposed to be the last of that order of Priesthood, their worship and institutions being abolished by the time of Fingal" (259). This glance in the direction of Macpherson's pre-history of *Ossian* is doubtless in the interests of the creation of an Ossianic sole survivor, but it also affords a tiny drama of accommodation and reconciliation. Fingal is cheered up, and the greatness of his nation and line outlined to him by the last representative of an outlawed order; an order outlawed, furthermore, because it questioned the right of Fingal's recent forebears to establish the political conditions of benevolent dictatorship Fingal enjoys during his reign.

The future the Druid foresees is also marked by examples of accommodation, of setting aside differences in the interest of a common purpose. In the move from Scottish to British history there is the (here) unspoken Union of England and Scotland, while its culmination provides another example: the visit of the Allied Sovereigns to celebrate the defeat of Napoleon in 1814, an alliance being newly tested by the time of *The Druid's* performance by Napoleon's reappearance on the continent. Thus, when the Fingal of *The Druid* laments the constant state of war and asks after the "genial hours of leisure" brought by peace (Moore 2004, vol. 4, 265), one of the things he is in effect doing (or could be understood to be doing), is advocating exactly the sort of art of public diplomacy embodied by such choreographed state visits. Alliances in war are always important and often fragile, but few can have been more important or fragile than the Sixth Coalition that finally came into being between 1812 and 1814 to defeat Napoleon. The formation and maintenance of this fraught but crucial alliance was a masterly exhibition of the accommodation and co-ordination of disparate, even antagonistic elements and interests. It involved, for example, overlooking the fact that, with the exception of the British, virtually all the other members had at one time or the other in the previous ten years sided with France against the others; while the British, to paraphrase Canning paraphrasing Caligula, had contented themselves with seeking to cure European hatred of them with fear (cit. in Hilton 2006, 211).

Perhaps even in its formal construction *The Druid* contains a version of accommodation in its integration of elements drawn from across Europe, as the supercharged Scottishness of the evening and the masque, with its "original Highland airs of great antiquity," is set off by the incorporation of, most notably, adapted elements from the *Liberation of Germany*. One might push it a little further and wonder whether the self-conscious nature of the published text, in drawing attention to the contingency of the performance (which goes so far as to indicate alternative versions of what was planned for the event), does not emphasise the air of coalition, of collaborative effort. In practical terms this was doubtless the result of a fund-raising desire to produce a commemorative text for purchase on the evening, before the details of performance could be nailed down, but the apologies and defensiveness do provide their own little drama of fraught collaboration. In the context of other examples of accommodation and co-ordination, displayed or implied, this is a pleasing, if coincidental, parallel.

There is, however, a further dimension to the association of the Ossianic hero Fingal with the Prince Regent in the context of the struggle against Napoleon. Bluntly put, Macpherson's *Poems* were big in France, where *Ossian*'s "patriotism, violence and secularism struck emotional chords in French readers during the Revolutionary and Napoleonic periods" (Dawson and Morère 2004, 19). Indeed they were not above expressing this enthusiasm through an effort to co-opt *Ossian* as part of French heroic myth. One of the most famous of all *Ossian*-inspired works of visual art – Anne-Louis Girodet's painting *Ossian Receiving the Generals of the Republic* (1802) – envisages Ossian as a tutelary deity not for Highland warriors but heroes of the French Revolution. The line of Fingal, the painting suggests, runs not through kings of Britain but through the fallen heroes of the French Republic.

No-one was more enthusiastic about *Ossian*, or so the story goes, than the French Emperor himself, who supposedly carried a copy of the *Poems* with him everywhere, including exile. Some of the myths surrounding Napoleon's enthusiasm for *Ossian* have been debunked in recent years. For example, it has been established that Jean-François Le Sueur's opera *Ossian ou Les Bardes* (1804) was started in 1795, much earlier than previously thought, and therefore not commissioned by the Emperor as previously assumed (Smith 1998, 153-163). That said, Napoleon does seem to have been involved in the eventual staging of the work at the Paris Opera (then enjoying a new title as the Académie Impériale de Musique), publically congratulated Le Sueur for the work and granted him membership of the Légion d'honneur. Other products of the French enthusiasm for *Ossian* are no less closely implicated with the Emperor. Girodet's painting was commissioned for a Napoleonic residence (though never hung), while Jean-Augustine-Dominique Ingres' *The Dream of Ossian* (1812) was commissioned for one of Napoleon's rooms in the Quirinal Palace in Rome. Overall there is, as Smith notes, something other than merely "a certain pose of modish sensibility" about Napoleon's interest in Macpherson and his Celtic heroes (Smith 1998, 154).

In the light of this appropriation of *Ossian*, the Caledonian Asylum's choice of Ossianic subject matter for its fundraiser, and its attempts to associate the Prince Regent with a tradition of heroism stretching back to Fingal, takes on a further significance. *The Druid* makes clear the patriotic Britishness, and the underpinning of British monarchical identity, represented by Fingal and his race of Celtic warriors. Furthermore, the legitimacy that this prophetic vision bestows on the Regent is significant in a domestic political argument about British policy towards Napoleon. If, as Stuart Semmel has argued, British attempts to prop up an unpopular Bourbon king against the claims of a ruler apparently enjoying the support of the people of France could be seen, in the context of the British constitutional settlement that had installed William III on the throne, as "hypocritical to the core," then visions of British history that located the Regent within a line of kings stretching back to Fingal was highly convenient (Semmel 2004, 183). *The Druid* performs then a double function: it reasserts the Britishness of Fingal against French appropriation of his legacy, and offers a version of legitimacy based on blood for a Hanoverian monarchy otherwise uncomfortably caught in the paradox of defending the inalienable right of royal lines to rule, while being themselves the beneficiaries of an alternative model of royal prerogative. This was not, of course, the beginning of a sustained campaign. Despite what Macpherson had hoped, the Irish folk hero Fionn does not fit comfortably into Anglo-British myth-making, unlike King Arthur, who would provide a more stable "Celtic keystone in the architecture of British monarchical identity" (Pittock 1999, 19). But if the accommodation was not long-standing, it was at this moment at least available and apparent.

Attention to texts such as *The Druid*, then, offers a way into the history of *Ossian*'s reception and casts a reciprocal light onto literary and popular culture in the early 19th century that does not rely on simplistic claims to influence upon established writers. In particular, interest in these more ephemeral treatments provides a richer picture of the ways in which Macpherson's *Poems* played a role in the cultural life blood of the period. In particular, it shows us the close association by this time (or at least the availability of such an association) between *Ossian* and a form of Scottish identity based upon martial endeavour and sacrifice made in the British cause. In terms of *Ossian* itself, texts such as *The Druid* remind us that the *Poems*' role within music and song is amongst their most significant bequests, while also speaking of the longevity of interest in *Ossian*. 1815 was 55 years after the first appearance of the *Poems* and, perhaps more significantly, ten years after the appearance of the two great debunking texts of 1805, Malcolm Laing's edition of the *Poems*, which traces every example of their (modern) derivation, and Henry Mackenzie's *Report of the Committee of the Highland Society of Scotland [...] into the Poems of Ossian*. It is not so much that people did not care about authenticity, they just cared differently, and about other things too, and for long enough for it to be the case that when a charity with Royal patronage wanted to sell box tickets to a benefit night for £1.1s, it did so in part on the strength of a choral work derived from *Ossian*.

The Druid has one further value. Emphasising the competition over the idea of Ossian in the Napoleonic era offers a way of uniting the two recent strands of Macpherson criticism of cultural politics and international reception. It is an anxiety that archipelagic criticism sometimes has about itself that it merely swaps a set of London or Anglo-centric blinkers for a set of Scottish/Irish/Welsh/English blinkers; that however nuanced and neutral our notions of Britishness are, they may nonetheless fall into the trap of a larger parochialism when considered on a global scale. Understanding *Ossian*'s reception in Britain in the context of, or as part of, a wider reception within Europe (and indeed beyond), is one way of offering some reassurance on that count.

Works Cited

Anon. "Advertisement for *The Druid*." *The Times* (20 May 1815): 2, column B.
Carruthers, Gerard and Alan Rawes, eds. *English Romanticism and the Celtic World*. Cambridge: Cambridge University Press, 2003 [reprinted 2010].
Clyde, Robert. *From Rebel to Hero: The Image of the Highlander 1745-1830*. Edinburgh: Tuckwell Press, 1995.
Curley, Thomas. *Samuel Johnson, the Ossian Fraud and the Celtic Revival in Great Britain and Ireland*. Cambridge: Cambridge University Press, 2009.
Davis, Leith, Ian Duncan, and Janet Sorenson, eds. *Scotland and the Borders of Romanticism*. Cambridge: Cambridge University Press, 2004.
Dawson Deidre and Pierre Morère, eds. *Scotland and France in the Enlightenment*. Cranbury, NJ: Associated University Presses, 2004.
Duff, David and Catherine Jones, eds. *Scotland, Ireland and the Romantic Aesthetic*. Lewisburg: Bucknell University Press, 2008.
Dunn, John. *The Role of Macpherson's Ossian in the Development of British Romanticism*. University of Michigan: Unpublished doctoral thesis, 1965.
Gaskill Howard, ed. *Ossian Revisited*. Edinburgh: Edinburgh University Press, 1991.
—, ed. *The Reception of Ossian in Europe*. London: Continuum, 2004.

Hilton, Boyd. *A Mad, Bad, and Dangerous People? England 1783-1846.* Oxford: Oxford University Press, 2006.

Kerrigan, John. *Archipelagic English: Literature, History, and Politics 1603-1707.* Oxford: Oxford University Press, 2008.

Leask, Nigel. "Robert Burns and Romanticism in Britain and Ireland." *The Edinburgh Companion to Scottish Romanticism.* Ed. Murray Pittock. Edinburgh: Edinburgh University Press, 2011. 127-138.

MacGann, Jerome. *The Poetics of Sensibility: A Revolution in Literary Style.* Oxford: Oxford University Press, 1996.

Malek, James. "Eighteenth-Century Dramatic Adaptations of Macpherson's Ossian." *Restoration and Eighteenth-Century Theatre Research* 14 (1975): 36-41.

Moore, Dafydd. *Enlightenment and Romance in the Poems of Ossian.* Aldershot: Ashgate, 2003.

—, ed. *Ossian and Ossianism.* 4 vols. London: Routledge, 2004.

Ó Gallchoir, Clíona. "Celtic Ireland and Celtic Scotland: Ossianism and *The Wild Irish Girl.*" *Scotland, Ireland and the Romantic Aesthetic.* Eds. David Duff and Catherine Jones. Lewisburg: Bucknell University Press, 2008. 114-130.

Pittock, Murray. *The Invention of Scotland: The Stuart Myth and Scottish Identity 1638 to the Present.* London: Taylor Francis, 1991.

—. "James Macpherson and Jacobite Code." *From Gaelic to Romantic: Ossianic Translations.* Eds. Fiona Stafford and Howard Gaskill. Amsterdam: Rodopi, 1998. 41-50.

—. *Celtic Identity and the British Image.* Manchester: Manchester University Press, 1999.

—. *Scottish and Irish Romanticism.* Oxford: Oxford University Press, 2008.

—, ed. *The Edinburgh Companion to Scottish Romanticism.* Edinburgh: Edinburgh University Press, 2011.

Schmidt, Wolfgang, ed. *"Homer des Nordens" und "Mutter der Romantik:" James Macphersons Ossian und seine Rezeption in der deutschsprachigen Literatur.* 4 vols. Berlin: Walter de Gruyter, 2003.

Semmel, Stuart. *Napoleon and the British.* New Haven: Yale University Press, 2004.

Smith, Christopher. "*Ossian, ou Les Bardes*: An Opera by Jean-François Le Sueur." *From Gaelic to Romantic: Ossianic Translations.* Eds. Fiona Stafford and Howard Gaskill. Amsterdam: Rodopi, 1998. 153-163.

Stafford, Fiona. *The Sublime Savage: James Macpherson and the Poems of Ossian.* Edinburgh: Edinburgh University Press, 1988.

— and Howard Gaskill, eds. *From Gaelic to Romantic: Ossianic Translations.* Amsterdam: Rodopi, 1998.

Trumpener, Katie. *Bardic Nationalism: The Romantic Novel and the British Empire.* Princeton: Princeton University Press, 1997.

Weinbrot, Howard. *Britannia's Issue: The Rise of British Literature from Dryden to Ossian.* Cambridge: Cambridge University Press, 1993.

Womack, Peter. *Improvement and Romance: Constructing the Myth of the Highlands.* Basingstoke: Macmillan, 1989.

PAULINE ANNE MACKAY, Glasgow

Objects of Desire: Robert Burns the 'Man's Man' and Material Culture

The reputation of Robert Burns as a 'man's man,' indeed an impulsive, energetic lover, is propelled by poems such as the iconic "Tam o' Shanter" (1790), by the poet's correspondence, by documentary records of his affairs with the opposite sex and by the bawdy literature circulated by Burns for the enjoyment of his male cronies and reproduced in *The Merry Muses of Caledonia* (1799). But what does the object record tell us? On 19th-century "Tam o' Shanter" pen and ink snuff boxes, drinking ephemera and various other objects sold with male recipients in mind, we frequently encounter images of cronies drinking, or scantily clad witches dancing, watched by the enthusiastic voyeur Tam. These objects stress the priapic conviviality apparent in the poem, and celebrate Burns's overt, at times infamous, libido to a degree which is untypical of the early biographical record of the Bard's life and unusual for 19th-century society.

The article that follows will examine the commemoration of Robert Burns's life and literary output via objects (or what we might also call the material cultural record), with particular reference to sexuality and masculinity. It will consider the way in which certain excerpts from Burns's "Tam o' Shanter" were appropriated for objects aimed at an exclusively male market, and examine the ways in which the material cultural depiction of Burns and his most iconic text converges with and/or diverges from the biographical commemoration of Scotland's 'National Bard.' Drawing upon the research findings of the AHRC-funded *Beyond Text* project, "Robert Burns: Inventing Tradition and Securing Memory, 1796-1909,"[1] this article is the culmination of two emerging strands of Burns scholarship that have, until recently, been largely neglected: the study of Robert Burns's bawdy sensibility (here taken to extend to "Tam o' Shanter" itself),[2] and the examination of the commemoration of the poet and his texts via material culture.

"Tam o' Shanter" is Burns's most iconic and most commemorated poem. Written for the antiquary Captain Francis Grose (1731-1791), one of Burns's male cronies, it was published in *Antiquities of Scotland* (1791) and immediately met with emphatic

---

1 The AHRC-funded *Beyond Text* project, "Robert Burns: Inventing Tradition and Securing Memory, 1796-1909" has opened up a new and exciting avenue of interdisciplinary scholarly investigation, incorporating literature, history and history of art (among other disciplines) in the study of the effects of material culture, and the cultural environment, on memory. Directed by Murray Pittock and based at the University of Glasgow, the project team's research sought to demonstrate the role played by material culture in preserving and creating the reputation and cultural memory of a poet via two new web resources: a detailed online catalogue of Burns statues and major public memorials erected prior to 1909, and a taxonomy of private and domestic Burns-related objects produced during the same period. These resources document the memorialisation of Robert Burns (1759-1796) through objects and public monuments, enabling an extensive range of images and items used in the transmission of Burns's reputation into the sphere of cultural memory to be openly available for consultation in one place for the first time. Images reproduced in this essay can be viewed on the project website, with commentaries by Murray Pittock: http://www.gla.ac.uk/robertburnsbeyondtext.
2 The author's PhD thesis represents the first extensive critical study of Robert Burns's bawdy song and verse (Mackay 2011).

critical acclaim. In a letter to Burns dated 12 March 1791, the Edinburgh Advocate Alexander Fraser Tytler (1747-1813) declared that:

> I have seldom in my life tasted of higher enjoyment from any work of genius than I have received from this composition; and I am much mistaken if this poem alone, had you never written another syllable, would not have been sufficient to have transmitted your name down to posterity with high reputation. In the introductory part, where you paint the character of your hero and exhibit him at the ale-house *ingle*, with his tippling cronies, you have delineated nature with a humour and *naiveté* that would do honour to Matthew Prior; but when you describe the infernal orgies of the witches' sabbath and the hellish scenery in which they are exhibited, you display a power of imagination that Shakespeare himself could not have exceeded. (Chambers 1896, vol. 3, 256)

Significantly, the particular excerpts from "Tam o' Shanter" that Tytler deems most praiseworthy – the convivial drinking scene "painted" in the opening lines of the poem, and Burns's detailed description of "the witches' sabbath" – are scenes that would be reproduced in statuary and upon all manner of private and domestic objects (from whisky jugs to souvenir woodware, pottery and handcrafted snuff boxes) for centuries to come. Consequently, the material cultural celebration of male cronyism, conviviality and masculine sexual appetite, all of which "Tam o' Shanter" is deemed to represent, can scarcely be underestimated as regards its impact upon the cultural appropriation of Burns as a 'man's man:' an appropriation that is also supported with reference to Burns's activities as a Freemason,[3] and as a member of gentlemen's clubs such as The Crochallan Fencibles.[4] As Murray Pittock and Christopher Whatley have pointed out, by the time of the first Ayr Burns Festival in 1844, "markers of Burns's identity as a Scot were already strongly linked to love, male conviviality and alcohol, popular signs of Burns's universality as a human being" (Pittock and Whatley 2012). Certainly, throughout the 19th century, the popular celebration and commemoration of the Scottish National Bard increasingly paid tribute to Burns's 'humorous,' 'naïve' and therefore accepting treatment of human 'nature,' using "Tam o' Shanter" as a cultural vehicle.

"Tam o' Shanter" is a highly skilful and multi-faceted work which, when we scratch below the surface of the poem's colourful and energetic survey of antiquarianism, folklore and the supernatural, yields a complex and interesting consideration of human nature, gender and sexuality. While simplistic readings of "Tam o' Shanter" advocate the poem's inscription and reinforcement of stereotypical gender roles, re-

---

3   Robert Burns was initiated to St David's Masonic Lodge, No 174, Tarbolton in 1781. He then became a Master of St James's Lodge, Tarbolton on 27 July 1784, and was made a member of Canongate Kilwinning Lodge, No 2, during his time in Edinburgh in 1786. Robert Crawford describes the Tarbolton Freemasons as, "a band of initiated 'brothers' who drank together, paid for glasses they smashed, processed on occasion to the parish kirk to hear Brother Woodrow preach, and enjoyed manly fellowship" (Crawford 2003, 94). Significantly, the Freemasons played an important part in the commemoration of the National Bard by helping to secure the tradition of the Burns supper (at which "Tam o' Shanter" is ceremoniously performed), and by commissioning and/or contributing to numerous statues and memorials erected in the poet's honour.

4   It is believed that Burns became a member of The Crochallan Fencibles whilst he resided in Edinburgh in 1787. Although little is known about the Fencibles, it is believed that a great deal of Burns's bawdy poetry and song was composed for recitation at this particular social club. The title of the first ever publication of *The Merry Muses of Caledonia; a Collection of Scots Songs, Ancient and Modern; Selected for the use of the Crochallan Fencibles* in 1799, is a clear signal of the club's association with Burns's bawdy literature.

cent criticism has increasingly identified and addressed such complexities. Gerard Carruthers and Sarah Dunnigan posit that "Burns does not *deal* in [gender] stereotypes, but utilises and deconstructs them. Burns is sceptical about received roles" (Dunnigan and Carruthers 2000, 38). Elsewhere, Carruthers suggests that "the poem essays, in fact, male irresponsibility and 'fear' of the female, rather than fear of any more mysterious unknown" (Carruthers 2006, 87), and so it is apparent that the poem, to quote Sarah Dunnigan, "opens up a Pandora's box of gendered readings" (Dunnigan 2009, 33). Similarly, while the representation of convivial scenes from "Tam o' Shanter" on 19th-century objects emphasises the masculine and fraternal aspects of the poem, it can also be argued that detailed depictions of the witches' dance and "Cutty Sark's" (or rather the young witch Nannie's) pursuit of the poem's principal character, encompass the problematisation of gender to which Carruthers and Dunnigan refer.

The opening lines of "Tam o' Shanter" place the tale's main protagonist, "bousing at the nappy" (l. 5) with his male cronies, ("*Tam* loe'd him like a vera brither;/ They had been fou for weeks thegither," ll. 44-45) and cavorting with the landlady ("The landlady and *Tam* grew gracious;/ Wi favours secret, sweet and precious," ll. 47-48) (Kinsley 1968, vol. 2, 557-564). Fraternal camaraderie (with other characters and with an imagined, seemingly male, reader) is enforced by the deployment of the words, "we," "us," "our:"

> We think na on the lang Scots miles,
> The mosses, waters, slaps and styles,
> That lie between us and our hame,
> Whare sits our sulky sullen dame,
> Gathering her brows like gathering storm,
> Nursing her wrath to keep it warm. (ll. 7-12)

These famous lines convey comedic notions of stereotypical gender roles: the sociable, fraternal male with his wandering eye, suppressed by conjugal responsibility; his wife no longer attractive and sexually arousing, but "sulky" and "sullen" with her increasing displeasure inscribed upon her "gathering brows." And so, wives are not sexual beings, but sources of unwanted advice ("O Tam! Hadst thou but been sae wise,/ As ta'en thy ain wife *Kate*'s advice!," ll. 17-18) and reprimand ("She tauld thee weel thou was a skellum,/ A blethering, blustering, drunken blellum," ll. 19-20). It should be noted here that, just as Kate's physical body is notably absent from "Tam o' Shanter" (in which the conjugal relationship is invariably presented as a-sexual), images of Tam's wife rarely, if ever, appear on commemorative objects.

Instead, a wealth of objects depicting the opening lines of the poem are emblazoned with seemingly more desirable images of "Tam" drinking with "Souter Johnny," laughing, glass in hand, and cavorting with a hospitable landlady. A large whisky jug in the shape of Souter Johnny's head by Caledonian Pottery (c. 1840-1850) invites its owner to enter into the convivial and fraternal celebration of the poem, by drinking with Tam's very companion. Another typical illustration may be observed on a whisky jug manufactured by Bells Pottery in Glasgow, c. 1840 – 1911 (Fig. 1). Here, a jovial Tam and Souter Johnny are depicted sitting with the landlord, Tam's glass raised to a buxom landlady (perhaps in a toast, or perhaps with the expectation of more liquor). The scene is littered with tankards and whisky jugs placed atop tables or hanging on the wall, while joints of meat are suspended above a fire place. These features make explicit the function of this room as a convivial space, but also as a place where appetites may be quenched.

Extremely similar depictions appear on ceramic figurines manufactured by Dunmore Pottery, Scotland (c. 1866-1902), whisky jugs and plates by Clyde Pottery Co., Greenock (1900-1905), and wall plaques produced by Osborne of Kent in the late 19th to early 20th century (to name but a few).[5] Despite occasional differences (varying degrees of drunkenness and sexual suggestion, or alternative representations of the interior of the inn), it should be noted that the images reproduced on these objects are all very clearly based upon the first statuary renderings of "Tam o' Shanter" by the Ayrshire stonemason, James Thom (Fig. 2).[6] And so, although an in-depth study of related statuary is out with the scope of this essay, we might recognise that the commemoration of the convivial aspect of "Tam o' Shanter" (and therefore Burns's association with masculine fraternity and drinking culture), was reinforced by objects produced for both the public and private spheres.

Figure 1: Whisky Jug by Bells Pottery. Image © Hunterian, University of Glasgow, 2012.

As research undertaken as part of the Robert Burns *Beyond Text* project has demonstrated, this emphatic celebration of Burns's association with drinking culture is a striking example of the way in which the popular celebration of Burns in the 19th century diverged from early biographies of the poet's life. Burns's biographers often expressed disapproval of the poet's male appetites and conviviality. On the basis of little or no evidence, Dr James Currie (who produced the first posthumous edition of Burns's life and works) referred to Burns as "[p]erpetually stimulated by alkohol in one or other of its various forms" and suffering from "the pollution of inebriation" (Currie 1803, vol. 1, 220-221). Similarly, Rev. George Gilfillan purported that:

---

5   For images of objects mentioned here, see http://www.robertburnstaxonomy.arts.gla.ac.uk/.
6   James Thom (1802 – 1850) produced two groups of statues commemorating "Tam o' Shanter." The four figures pictured in Fig. 2 were unveiled at Kirkoswald (the former residence of "Souter Johnny," Burns's acquaintance John Davidson) on 1 July 1829. Beginning in 1828, a further set of statues depicting "Tam" and "Souter Johnny" were exhibited in Ayr, Edinburgh, Glasgow and London before being inaugurated at Alloway, the poet's birthplace, in 1830. That Thom's statues attracted widespread attention both north and south of the Scottish border, and that the commemoration of the poem had quickly extended to associational figures and locations, is testament to the fact that, by the early 19th century, "Tam o' Shanter" was the most widely celebrated of the poet's works. For further images of Burns-related statuary, see http://www.robertburnsmemorials.arts.gla.ac.uk/.

[The] blood of John Barleycorn furnished him with a false and hollow semblance of the true inspiration he had met in the solitary field [...] through the misty light of the presiding punch-bowl, he saw the most ordinary specimens of female nature transformed into angels; and fancied that, like divinities, they should be adored.[7] (Gilfillan 1856, vol. 1, xii)

Figure 2: Tam o' Shanter by James Thom, Kirkoswald. Unveiled 1829. Image © Robert Burns *Beyond Text*.

Ironically, while Currie and Gilfillan regretted Burns's human frailty, the object record demonstrates that the poet's ability to essay the shortcomings of man in poems such as "Tam o' Shanter," without imposing harsh judgements, only increased his popularity and enhanced his status as a universal figure. Robert Burns the 'man's man' was celebrated for his sociability and for his perceived common humanity.

As "Tam o' Shanter" progresses and the poem's drunken hero journeys home, he is drawn to Alloway Kirk where he discovers "Warlocks and witches in a dance" (l. 115). The witches' "dance" defies presbyterian religious orthodoxy insofar as dancing was considered to be a sinful activity;[8] defiance made even more vehement by Burns's introduction of Satan, ("There sat auld Nick, in shape o' beast," l. 120) who literally propels this 'sinful' behaviour ("He screw'd the pipes and gart them skirl,/ Till roof and rafters a' did dirl," ll. 123-124). And so Burns introduces a scene of bestiality and carnal festivity, promptly embellished by a list of bodily grotesquery and mutilation, where we encounter dead bodies and various weapons, or rather blades, coated in bodily fluids ("Five tomahawks, wi' blude red-rusted;/ Five scimitars wi' murder crusted," ll. 135-136). Notions of danger and horror are conveyed by reference to human bodies and to the weapons that destroy them.

Burns's imagery here has been carefully retained in material culture. Frequently on early 19th-century pen and ink snuff boxes, both bodies and weapons are assiduously

---

7   Burns's association with drinking culture is also celebrated by objects commemorating the poet's famous drinking song, "Willie Brew'd a Peck o' Maut."
8   Burns himself makes reference to this in his famous autobiographical letter to Dr. John Moore, where the poet recalls his defiance in attending dance classes against the wishes of his strict presbyterian father: "In my 17th year, to give my manners a brush, I went to a country dancing school. – My father had an unaccountable antipathy against these meetings; and my going was, what to this hour I repent, in absolute defiance of his commands" (Roy and DeLancey Ferguson 1985, vol. 1, 139).

incorporated. Here we might examine a snuff box held at the Robert Burns Birthplace Museum in Alloway (Fig. 3). Open coffins and skeletons surround the witches' festivities, while Satan, thoroughly bestial with horns and a coat of dark hair, is watchfully perched above the action as he plays the pipes. The enthusiastic voyeur, Tam, is pictured to the right of the scene, straddling his mare and gazing through a hole in the wall as lightning strikes above his head: an ominous forewarning of the consequences of his leering curiosity. Significantly, the scantily clad witches are in the throes of a Scottish sword dance: a reference to Burns's status as the national bard which is reinforced by the presence of an elaborate Scottish thistle design on the sides and base of the box. However, the swords might also be interpreted as a phallic symbol, and as a clever incorporation of the cutting imagery that the poet employs in his verse. In the bottom right-hand corner of the snuff box is another blade, an axe. Such details suggest that the maker of this snuff box has adhered very carefully to Burns's poetic vision. Furthermore, by making prominent the young, attractive and barely dressed "Nannie," and by incorporating the three lines from the poem which culminate in Tam's famous exclamation, "Weel done, Cutty-sark!" (l. 89), the box maker has successfully incorporated the sexual suggestion of the poem and emphasised Tam's overt masculinity for the male consumer.

Figure 3: Early 19th Century Pen & Ink Snuff Box. Image © Robert Burns *Beyond Text*.

Figure 4: The Celebrated Tam O' Shanter Razor Hone. Image © Robert Burns *Beyond Text*, Courtesy of Glasgow Museums.

That the subject matter of "Tam o' Shanter" was readily and easily appropriated for a thriving market of male tobacco consumers is apparent from the fact that, by the 1820s, Burns-related illustrations, and particularly depictions of "Tam o' Shanter," were "the most commonly reproduced on snuff boxes" (Trachtenberg and Keith 2002, 25-26). Certainly, in the 19th century, snuff-taking was a distinctly masculine activity. Here we might refer to Woodruff D. Smith who states that:

> Ladies (that is to say, respectable women whose behaviour patterns were framed by the context of domestic femininity) were not supposed to smoke or, in most countries, to employ tobacco in any form. In part, this prohibition arose from notions about the peculiar physical susceptibility of women to the harshness of tobacco smoke, and partly it derived from tobacco's particular identification with rational masculinity. (Smith 2002, 169)

Pen and ink snuff boxes, then, were produced with male consumers in mind, but not just any consumer. The timely process of intricately hand-crafting a pen and ink snuff box necessarily rendered these objects more expensive than mass-produced, point-of-purchase items. As such, it is likely that these objects would have been privately commissioned by gentlemen, or presented to acquaintances as gifts much in the same way that Burns's bawdy writing was motivated by homo-social culture, presented by the poet to close acquaintances, and eventually privately printed and circulated for the convivial enjoyment of men, and men alone.[9]

Larger-scale manufacturers of Burns memorabilia were particularly resourceful in their appropriation of "Tam o' Shanter" for products aimed solely at a male market. Established in 1810, W & A Smith of Mauchline were inspired by 19th-century tourists' flourishing interest in the 'Land of Burns' to corner the market in souvenir woodware. Initially stonemasons and manufacturers of hone stones (used to sharpen blades), the Smiths' seized the opportunity to appropriate the cutting imagery and masculine appeal of "Tam o' Shanter" to produce an object which combined the family's industrial interests. And so, by the 1830s W & A Smith were successfully marketing "The Celebrated Tam o' Shanter Razor Hone" (Fig. 4). It should be noted that this object is not decorated with images of blades or bodies, but with images of Alloway Kirk (a key location in the poem) and Burns Cottage (the poet's birthplace and, as such, the heart of the 'Land of Burns'). Superficially, the razor hone functions as both a souvenir and an advertisement at a time when the Victorian penchant for literary tourism was at its peak (see Watson 2006). The significance of its more meaningful association with "Tam o' Shanter" depends upon a more nuanced understanding of the poem's main preoccupations as regards male (and female) sexuality. As the present author and Murray Pittock have pointed out, the cutting imagery of the poem "emblematizes masculinity and some of its deepest anxieties, evoked but in the end avoided by the drinking, lecherous hero: the 'razor hone' is in this context an outstanding product, created 'beyond text' to re-inscribe the textuality of "Tam o' Shanter," and some of its deeper meanings, in the minds of its purchasers" (Mackay and Pittock 2011, 158). Indeed, overtly masculine in its function, and yet

---

9   The likelihood that such objects were commissioned may be supported with reference to the base of the snuff box pictured in Fig. 3, where the name "T McFadzane" appears. McFadzane does not appear on any extant records of box makers, and so we might consider that this is the name of the owner as opposed to the manufacturer. For a list of known box makers, see Trachtenberg and Keith (2002, 92).

symbolic of male anxiety, "The Celebrated Tam o' Shanter Razor Hone" might be considered a remarkable material cultural demonstration of the complexities of Burns's most iconic poem.

Notions of masculine anxiety are reinforced in Burns's "Tam o' Shanter" as representations of the physical body increasingly drive the narrative, and Burns begins to play upon the notion of gender as a marker of supernatural threat. Indeed, an acute fear of the typically female 'witch' remained very present in 18th-century folk and religious culture. Informed and reinforced by patriarchal constructions of gender and an irrational fear of the feminine, the feminisation of witchcraft can be traced as far back as the 15th century to the *Malleus Malleficarum* ("The Witch Hammer") – a monumental religious tract against witchcraft, commissioned by Pope Innocent VIII and composed by the Dominicans Heinrich Kramer and Jakob Sprenger c. 1486. Exuding from this text is an acute fear of the feminine, firmly rooted in original sin. Women are very much portrayed as 'other;' even the term 'witch' is distinguished from the typically more masculine, 'wizard.' Women are described as "sinful," "bitter," "wheedling," a "secret enemy" and "a snare" of devils. Their powers to tempt men render them powerful agents of evil. As such, women represent potential disorder, a physical and ideological threat to the order of patriarchal society, a threat that is realised when a woman becomes "infected with the heresy of witchcraft," and manifested in a witches' supposed supernatural powers. The *Malleus Malleficarum* also provides an interesting example of the sexualisation of woman and witch as carnal, sensual beings by positing the notion that woman is driven to witchcraft, or rather to "consort with devils," when her insatiable bodily appetite cannot be satisfied by man (Kramer and Sprenger 1971, 47) Her sexual appetite is not therefore natural, but supernatural. The notion of woman as insatiable was still very much present in 18th century folk culture, and can be readily identified in humorous bawdy songs such as Burns's "Nine Inch Will Please a Lady" (1789). However, Burns, rather than subscribing to superstition or fear of the supernatural, seems attracted to the sexual and subversive qualities attributed to witchcraft, and can be seen to harness these ideas more creatively, wittily, positively even, in "Tam o' Shanter."

As Tam continues his voyeuristic examination of the witches' celebration, the focus shifts from grotesque depictions of the dead human body to the portrayal of bodies animated in dance, and the imagery becomes increasingly carnal:

> They reel'd they set, they cross'd, they cleekit,
> Till ilka carlin swat and reekit,
> And coost her duddies to the wark,
> And linket at it in her sark! (ll. 147-150)

Notions of carnal frenzy are developed with reference to bodily exertion and the expulsion of bodily fluid, the "carlins'" physical bodies gradually exposed as they cast off their clothes. The bodies of these "wither'd beldams, auld and droll" and "Rigwoodie hags" (ll. 159-60), although they are not sexually arousing, nevertheless possess the potential to provoke physical reaction and a bodily expulsion of sorts: "I wonder didna turn thy stomach" (l. 160). Here we might examine another early 19th-century pen and ink snuff box, produced by J. Cooper and held in the private collection of Alex Wilson (Fig. 5). Blades are present in the form of four axes which lie across a table and function as a barrier to separate Tam (who is pointing through the window) from the festivities. Once again the blades symbolise the danger courted by the main protagonist of the poem and, we might consider, Tam's vulnerability when confronted with insubordinate female sexuality. The dancing witches (with one exception) are adorned with wings and pointed hats, rendering them both bestial and alien, and reinforcing their subversive, supernatural qualities. However, Nannie, the central subject of Tam's gaze, is depicted as both young and attractive, her legs and breasts exposed as she dances around a pole: an obviously phallic symbol which simultaneously connotes pagan ritual.

A. D. Harvey tells us that, "During the 18th century, and for some hundreds of years previously, it had not been customary for lovers or even married couples to see each other naked" (Harvey 2001, 21). Both men and women in the 18th century slept in undergarments, which were lifted during sexual intercourse, but even then they were not typically removed. Bare legs, then, were a sexual stimulus that could be accounted for by 18th- and 19th-century sexual mores, and this might go some way towards explaining Burns's recurring references to women's legs as an index of sexual attractiveness in poems such as "The Fornicator" ("Those limbs so clean where I between/ Commenc'd a Fornicator," ll. 15-16) and "The Vision" ("And such a *leg*! my bonie Jean/ Could only peer it," ll. 63-4) (Kinsley 1968, vol. 1, 103-113). Also in keeping with the sexual mores of the time, exposed breasts do not appear anywhere in Burns's literary canon. The highly detailed illustration of Nannie's breasts pictured in Fig. 5 is, therefore, sexually explicit to a degree unusual for the 19th century, and so it would appear that J. Cooper has playfully emphasised Burns's notion of the sexually subversive witch for the male consumer. Indeed, it seems likely that objects produced privately for male consumers were significantly more explicit and less abashed in their celebration of human sexuality than mass-produced material culture.[10]

Figure 5: Early 19th Century Pen & Ink Snuff Box. Image © Robert Burns *Beyond Text*, Courtesy of the Alex Wilson Collection

---

10 Unsurprisingly, my research here has been hampered by the scarcity of any extant sales records. However, early indications would suggest that the representation of sexuality on objects privately produced by and for men can be aligned with the underground publication of bawdy song and verse in the study of male consumers' acquisition and circulation of 'unofficial' products in the 18th and 19th centuries.

Notions of physical stimulation are developed and become increasingly sexualised when Tam's male gaze falls upon Nannie, "ae winsome wench and wawlie" (l. 164), in her "cutty sark" (l. 171):

> But here my Muse her wing maun cour;
> Sic flights are far beyond her pow'r;
> To sing how Nannie lap and flang,
> (a souple jade she was, and strang),
> And how *Tam* stood, like ane bewitch'd,
> And though his very een enrich'd;
> Even Satan glowr'd, and fidg'd fu' fein,
> And hotch'd and blew wi' might and main:
> Till first ae caper, syne anither,
> *Tam* tint his reason a' thegither,
> And roars out, 'Weel done, Cutty-sark!'
> And in an instant all was dark: (ll. 179-190)

Nannie's body is not "wither'd" but young, healthy and, significantly, "strang." As such she commands both Tam's male gaze and Satan's, whose bodily sexual arousal is indicated and demonstrated by the alliterative, onomatopoetic description of the lines, "Even Satan glowr'd, and fidg'd fu' fein,/ And hotch'd and blew wi' might and main." Certainly, the depiction of frenzied physical movement serves also as an allusion to the sexual act, this accumulation of explicitly sexual energy climaxing in Tam's famous exclamation (or rather, ejaculation): "Weel done, Cutty-sark!" Significantly, this forthright expression of male sexual desire is one of the quotations most frequently inscribed upon material culture commemorating "Tam o' Shanter." The implications of Tam's inability to contain his sexual excitement and his verbal objectification of Nannie's female form are immediate, and he is plunged into darkness, only to be pursued by the "hellish legion" of "skreeching" witches:

> For Nannie, far before the rest,
> Hard upon noble Maggie prest,
> And flew at Tam wi' furious ettle;
> But little wist she Maggie's mettle –
> Ae spring brought off her master hale,
> But left behind her ain grey tail:
> The carlin claught her by the rump,
> And left poor Maggie scarce a stump. (ll. 211-18)

Tam is no longer the drunk, swaggering male of the beginning of the poem, but fearful and pursued by Nannie, a "strang" female, clearly representative of male fear of the feminine, who seeks revenge for her sexual objectification by the main protagonist of the poem.

Tam's fear is made apparent in an illustration of the witches' chase which appears on the reverse of the aforementioned whisky jug by Bells Pottery of Glasgow. Tam attempts to shield himself as lightning strikes directly towards him, whilst Nannie straddles and determinedly tugs upon his mare's tail: an act of obvious sexual and phallic significance which alludes to the notion of the insatiable female/witch and reinforces notions of masculine anxiety (Fig. 6). The phallic symbolism of this excerpt from Burns's poem is similarly emphasised on a whisky jug produced by Macinn & Potts of Staffordshire in 1834. Tam's grotesque and terrified face emerges from the lip of the jug whilst the handle is comprised of Maggie's tail, once again firmly grasped by Nannie's sinister hand (Fig. 7). On the vessel of the jug we observe Tam in the throes of a convivial gathering at the inn, and so this extremely effective object encompasses the moral of Burns's tale: the dangers of drink and sex.

Figure 6: Whisky Jug by Bells Pottery. Image © Hunterian, University of Glasgow, 2012.

Figure 7: Macinn & Potts Whisky Jug. Image © Robert Burns *Beyond Text*, Courtesy of Mitchell Library.

If the moral of the poem is that Tam is punished for his male conviviality, and for his leering and sexually forthright masculinity, ("I wad hae gi'en them off my hurdies,/ For ae blink o' the bonie burdies!" ll. 157-8), it is interesting that the poem ends with the violent removal of Tam's female horse's tail. This is commonly interpreted as pointing to Tam's emasculation (a metaphorical castration) and material cultural interpretations of the poem do much to reinforce this (Fig. 8). On one particularly striking carved wooden snuff box, a jubilant Nannie grasps Maggie's completely severed tail in her left hand, and what appears to be a Scottish thistle in her right (again, re-inscribing Burns's status as the Scottish National Bard, the poem's status as his most iconic work and, perhaps, the cultural importance of Scottish folklore). However, we might consider that the device of the severed tale further problematises notions of gender insofar as the true victim of Tam's convivial and sexual dalliances is Maggie (a passive, female character). Although Nannie is, in one sense, empowered by her subversive female sexuality, her physical strength and her "furious mettle," and Tam's role changes from pursuer of the female sex (in the sexual sense) to the pursued, Tam himself evades any real consequences, and so masculinity reigns supreme. We might therefore consider that, on a very basic level, it was this perceived triumph of masculinity that informed the material cultural appropriation of "Tam o' Shanter" for men.

Figure 8: Carved Snuff Box. Image © Robert Burns *Beyond Text*, Courtesy of the Alex Wilson Collection.

Certainly, it can be argued that "Tam o' Shanter" acknowledges the fluidity and complexity of received gender roles and male-female sexual relationships. Similarly, it may be argued that the artists and manufacturers of "Tam o' Shanter" memorabilia have re-inscribed the problematic subject matter of the poem upon material culture by consistently replicating images of Tam's fearful (yet thrilled) facial expression, blades symbolic of masculine anxiety, sexualised witches, Nannie's determined flight and, ultimately, poor Maggie's violently severed tail. However, the appropriation of particular excerpts from "Tam o' Shanter" for drinking vessels, smoking paraphernalia and cutting accessories, reinforced the gendering of Burns's most iconic work towards the celebration of male conviviality and appetites, ultimately helping to cement Robert Burns's reputation as a 'man's man.'[11] As research undertaken as part of "Robert Burns: Inventing Tradition and Securing Memory, 1796-1909" has demonstrated, and as this essay has sought to elaborate, much is to be gained from an understanding of the way in which both texts and objects contribute to the cultural memory of the Scottish National Bard and his works.[12]

Works Cited:

Burns, Robert. "Tam o' Shanter." *Antiquities of Scotland*. Ed. Francis Grose, 1790.
Carruthers, Gerard. *Robert Burns*. Tavistock: Northcote, 2006.
Chambers, Robert, ed. *The Life and Works of Robert Burns*, Revd. William Wallace. 4 vols. Edinburgh: Waverley, 1896.
Crawford, Robert. *The Bard: Robert Burns, A Biography*. London: Jonathan Cape, 2009.

---

11 This can also be said of objects commemorating "Willie Brew'd a Peck of Maut." See Mackay and Pittock (2011, 154-155).
12 This essay is complemented by an online exhibition, "Robert Burns: Objects of Desire," which can be viewed on the "Robert Burns: Inventing Tradition and Securing Memory, 1796-1909" website: http://www.gla.ac.uk/robertburnsbeyondtext.

Currie, James, ed. *The Works of Robert Burns; with an account of his life, and a criticism on his writings. To which are prefixed some observations on the character and condition of the Scottish peasantry.* 4 vols. London: Cadell & Davis, 1803.

Dunnigan, Sarah. "Burns and Women," *The Edinburgh Companion to Robert Burns.* Ed. Gerard Carruthers. Edinburgh: Edinburgh University Press, 2009. 20-33.

— and Gerard Carruthers. "Two Tales of 'Tam o' Shanter.'" *Southfields* 6 (2000): 36-43.

Gilfillan, George, ed. *Poetical Works of Robert Burns with Memoir, Dissertation and Explanatory Notes.* Edinburgh: J. Nichol, 1856.

Harvey, A. D. *Sex in Georgian England: Attitudes and Prejudices from the 1720s to the 1820s.* London: Phoenix Press, 2001.

Kinsley, James, ed. *The Poems and Songs of Robert Burns.* 3 vols. Oxford: Clarendon Press, 1968.

Kramer, H. and J. Sprenger. *The Malleus Maleficarum: Translated with an Introduction, Bibliography and Notes by the Reverend Montague Summers.* New York: Dover Publications, 1971.

Mackay, Pauline Anne. *Bawdry and the Body in the Works of Robert Burns: The Poet's Unofficial Self.* Glasgow: University of Glasgow, 2011.

— and Murray Pittock. "Beyond Text: Burns, Byron and their Material Cultural Afterlife." *The Byron Journal* 39.2 (2011): 149-162.

Pittock, Murray and Pauline Mackay. "Highland Mary: Objects and Memories." *Romanticism.* Forthcoming 2012.

Pittock, Murray and Christopher Whatley. "Poems and Festivals: Text and Beyond Text in the Popular Memory of Robert Burns." *Scottish Historical Review.* [Forthcoming] 2012.

Pittock, Murray et al. "Robert Burns: Inventing Tradition and Securing Memory, 1796-1909." 2011. *University of Glasgow.* 27 January 2012. <http://www.gla.ac.uk/robertburnsbeyondtext>.

Roy, G. Ross and J. DeLancey Ferguson, eds. *The Letters of Robert Burns.* 2nd ed. 2 vols. Oxford: Oxford University Press, 1985.

Smith, Woodruff D. *Consumption and the Making of Respectability, 1600-1800.* London: Routledge, 2002.

Trachtenburg, David and Thomas Keith. *Mauchline Ware.* Woodbridge: Antique Collector's Club, 2002.

Watson, Nicola. *The Literary Tourist.* Basingstoke: Macmillan, 2006.

Anglistik

Universitätsverlag
WINTER
Heidelberg

PREUSS, STEFANIE

A Scottish National Canon?

Processes of Literary Canon Formation in Scotland

2012. 381 Seiten,
10 Abbildungen. (Anglistische Forschungen, Band 427)
Gebunden € 66,–
ISBN 978-3-8253-6013-9

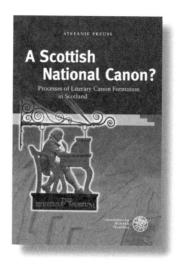

The „Best Scottish Book of All Time" is Lewis Grassic Gibbon's novel Sunset Song. This, at least, was the result of a public vote organised in 2005. But what is a Scottish book? And who decides which books are considered canonical? Until the 1960s, the apprehension of Scottish literature as merely a lesser sub-branch of English literature was a common notion. Since then, however, Scottish literature, as well as academic scholarship on Scottish writing, has been systematically promoted by means of grants, bursaries or literary awards. This revival was the result of a concerted policy of canonisation by literary institutions, which had its beginning in the eighteenth century. Such strategies of Scottish canon formation since the Union of Parliaments are the concern of the present study. For the first time, it identifies the different agents involved in Scottish canon formation and analyses how canon formation in Scotland is related to nationalist identity politics.

D-69051 Heidelberg · Postfach 10 61 40 · Tel. (49) 62 21 / 77 02 60 · Fax (49) 62 21 / 77 02 69
Internet http://www.winter-verlag.de · E-mail: info@winter-verlag.de

CAROLINE MCCRACKEN-FLESHER, Laramie, WY

Prediction of Things Past:
Scott and the Triumph of the Author's Antiquity

In an "Agenda for the 21st Century" it may seem odd to invoke a "Prediction of Things Past," especially for Walter Scott. Scott has long been considered the author of nostalgia – he writes, we are told, of a romanticized past, and pushes Scotland "Out of History" (in Cairns Craig's compelling 20th-century terms). However, Scott meets 21st-century concerns through his prescient interest in old age – in his characters, in the "Author of Waverley," and in himself. Foregrounding apparently superannuated players, Scott accomplishes a meditation on age and antiquity, not so much as lack and loss, but as duration, persistence, excess, mystery, and creativity.

Specifically, Scott embraces the translation of self into thing through the aging body. Paradoxically, his elderly and problematic characters, from the significantly named Jonathan Oldbuck (in *The Antiquary*) to the "Eidolon," or "Author of Waverley" (see *The Fortunes of Nigel*), and the aging author himself, thereby resonate with an unknowable and excessive vitality. For a 21st century that in the western world seems compelled to rise to the challenge of an aging population, Scott offers a strategic reconsideration of old age, at the furthest edge of life and even as a "thing past," as the site of unpredictable power.

Everything Old is New Again

In 1825, Walter Scott began a new literary venture: his journal. Trying to construct the present moment as a memorable past for family and other readers, Scott emulated the deceased Lord Byron, whose memoranda he had recently viewed (*Journal*, 3). But the author's timing seems unfortunate. At the outset, he acknowledges that already he has forgotten much – and more serious losses accumulated from the moment he started to write. The journal begins on 20 November; on the 30th Scott laments:

> I am come to the time when those who look out at the windows shall be darkend.[1] I must now wear spectacles constantly [...]. I feel my lameness becomes sometimes painful and often inconvenient. [...] Seams will slit and elbows will out quoth the tailor – and as I was fifty four on 15 August last my mortal vestments are none of the newest. (*Journal*, 26)

Scott's finances, unbeknownst to him, were in a worse state of repair. On 14 January 1826, he caught the first hint of the news that would eventually threaten to sweep away not just money and reputation, but even his home at Abbotsford (70).

Thus the *Journal*, at first glance, seems a record of decline, rather than a triumph of biographical recuperation for an authorial self. Moreover, the Byron memoranda Scott admired pointed only to the impossibility of self-expression: two days after

---

[1] Ecclesiastes 12:13: "In the day when the keepers of the house shall tremble, and the strong men shall bow themselves, and the grinders cease because they are few, and those that look out of the windows be darkened" (King James Version).

Scott took them as his model, he recorded the Byron family's rapacious pursuit and destruction of his fellow poet's memoirs (9).[2] And if Scott's own journal did not require purgation by fire for the sake of the family reputation, as did Byron's, it suffered an arguably worse fate. Although Scott had imagined a "Life" would raise the value of the new edition of his works, J. G. Lockhart, his son-in-law and literary editor, and Robert Cadell, his publisher, did not produce the author's meditations on his closing years (448). Presuming that Scott's declining health mapped a dwindling of powers, and that further writing on the author's part would undermine the value of the Magnum, they instead programmatically sought to shut down his later work, intrusively critiquing his plots, rewriting his sentences, and ultimately substituting for his memoirs Lockhart's *Life of Sir Walter Scott, Bart* (1837-1838). In this context, Scott's journal signifies not the life but the slow demise and the deliberate killing off of Sir Walter. This is the "Death of the Author" with a vengeance.

What did Scott's journal do that required its usurpation by Lockhart's strange mix of hagiography and unwitting character assassination?[3] The journal, standing for a life accumulating toward its ending, in Scott's son-in-law and the author's literary relations provoked anxieties about age and death. But with their focus on Scott's failing powers, Lockhart and Cadell missed something remarkable. Duration, Heidegger tells us, escapes us all. We are beings only in time. Yet, in the journal, Scott achieves persistence through the assertively told story of his decline. It is a persistence that can bother today's readers as much as it bothered his heirs, awaiting his death, and their assumption of his publishable properties.

Scott's journal, in fact, constitutes a foregrounding and even a celebration of the downward spiral toward death. Day to day, Scott recognizes a public discourse that shifts him, as he ages, from subject to object, and day to day he seizes upon it, aggressively turning himself into a thing. Such a move flies in the face of our most commonly held and deeply feared assumption – all that lives must die. For as Scott objectifies himself, he gains duration and intensifies the possibility of signifying when the bodily self is no more.

Such a claim needs philosophical context. Let me begin with Kathleen Woodward, who in her book *Aging and Its Discontents* critiques the Freudian notion that aging castrates all subjects. To Freud, the ego is "a mental projection of the surface of the body" (Freud 1962, 16 n. 1).[4] Consequently, Woodward observes, "the aging body [is] [...] a narcissistic wound to the ego" (Woodward 1991, 10). Freud's later self-analysis, performed in age and illness, suggests to Woodward that we defend ourselves by a process of encrustation, becoming "progressively *inorganic*" (48). Indeed, for Freud, she says, "aging [was] more threatening than death itself. The emphasis on death [...] as an *event*, conceals a denial of aging" (39). Woodward, by contrast, seeks an understanding of aging that privileges "new forms of creativity in late life" (10). Still, she stumbles up against "[the] facticity of the mortal vulnerability of the body in

---

2   Scott had just reencountered Thomas Moore (28 May 1779 – 25 February 1852), the Irish poet, singer, and songwriter now best remembered for the lyrics of *The Minstrel Boy* and *The Last Rose of Summer*. He was responsible, with John Murray, for burning Byron's memoirs after his death.
3   Thomas Carlyle lamented that Lockhart had "recorded much that ought to have lain suppressed," and yet that his Scott was "altogether lovely" (Carlyle 1838, 299, 301).
4   The footnote appeared in the 1827 English translation, and was marked as authorized by Freud: "The ego is first and foremost a bodily ego; it is not merely a surface entity, but is itself the projection of a surface" (Freud 1962, 16).

old age" (19). Heidegger, while emphasizing that being is possible only within time, nonetheless argues for an intensification of meaning in the context of impending demise: "being in the world" means having our horizons limited by daily needs and interactions – our awareness is forfeit to the world; however being in the context of the Nothingness that is death invites awareness and allows "authenticity" in those who can be in existence but not subject to the social world (Heidegger 2010, 241, 244, 250-253). Yet, once again, we come up against our mortality. As Jean-Luc Nancy points out, we exist in the body alone (Nancy 2006, 15). The flash of authenticity may only highlight the non-duration of being.

Here is where Scott's practice and Thing Theory helpfully align. For the intractable problem of psychological being that is posed by the declining body and by the fact of death, the author who embraces his objectification as an aged body, and through the artifacts that constitute the residue of a life once lived, suggests a further possibility. Merleau-Ponty wrestles with the oddity that in unexpected contexts "[a] thing presents itself to the person who perceives it as a thing in itself," not as something that exists merely in relation to ourselves. Things in such contexts "disclose the non-human element which lies hidden in them" (Merleau-Ponty 2004, 139-140). Bill Brown extrapolates: "[suddenly ...] things seem to assert their presence and power" (Brown 2004, 4). The thing, Merleau-Ponty suggests, then stands forth as "hostile and alien, no longer an interlocutor, but a resolutely silent Other, a Self which evades us no less than does intimacy with an outside consciousness" (Merleau-Ponty 2004, 140). The body itself, Brown quotes Merleau-Ponty, emerges as "a thing among things" (Brown 2004, 4). Inanimate objects, that is, refuse recognition and disturb identity in others; they seem to enjoy meaning beyond Heideggerian being. Further, insofar as death marks the end of the human context that confines meanings within the social world, it is, Michael Taussig implies, "the harbinger and index of the thing-world" (Brown 2004, 381). At the end of being, our "death awakens life in things" (381). Perhaps, this paper will suggest, being erupts even as we are recast as things by death.

This brings us back to the objectification, the de-humanizing of the aging body – and why Walter Scott embraces his own failing body and advertises the damage inherent to his texts as the product of that body. The issue is not that Scott rises above the fact or discourse of decline. He wishes for "Bodily Health" as much as the next man, recognizing it as "the mainspring of the microcosm;" he fears for himself and his texts "that whoreson touch of the Apoplexy;" he laments "a wavering in my composition sadly visible. I am not the man that I was" (*Journal,* 68, 695). Moreover, he anticipates Freud's dread of aging, concerned that "I should linger on 'an idiot and a show'" (692). And his aging is a reality. Indeed, he fits Freud's theories and practices distressingly well. Abbotsford, with its accumulated artifacts, might figure at large that encrustation against the anxieties of decline, that transformation into the uncaring inorganic older self, which is recognized by Woodward in Freud's life as well as in his theory.

Moreover, Scott was fully subject to the discourse of aging. When he got confused about money, Cadell described him in bestial terms as "howling" about it (Cadell copy letter to Major Scott, 30 April 1832, NLS MS 21003, f 43).[5] This was some months before the author actually did follow his father, degenerating beyond speech in his last days.[6] This "howling" author stood in no position of authority to his own texts, especially since he persisted in adding to their number. Cadell pondered to himself:

> Sir Walter [cannot] get on with the Castle Dangerous [...] of the Tales of a Grandfather [...] there is about two volumes done – and as to Count Robert he has not touched it since I condemned the third volume – so that here are three unfinished works – Mr Laidlaw and I are quite agreed that it would be a most fortunate circumstance if he were not to write any more. (Cadell's Notebook, 9 August 1830, NLS MS21043 f 110)

When Scott wrote frenetically to beat the clock, yet failed to catch up with proto-Victorian sensibilities, Lockhart and Cadell registered his productivity as a process of encrustation that would only devalue the property of the Magnum. These active and relatively young men (in their own view) colluded to hustle the now objectified Sir Walter off the stage (Cadell to Scott, 15 December 1830, NLS MS 3915, f 172-75). Cadell stresses: "it might be as well to fix on either the Count or his successor being the closing work of Fiction," together with "a *farewell announcement*" (Cadell to Scott, 28 December 1830, NLS MS 3915, f 216-7). At the same time, the two encroached more and more upon Scott's texts in their role as editors (Cadell to Scott, nd, MS 21003, f 31-32). To the author's late requests, Cadell declared, "*I pay no attention*" (Cadell to Major Scott, 30 April 1832, NLS MS 21003, f 43). From the evidence of his body, Scott was delimited by youth according to the discourse of age. Of course, those whose being is "in the world," in Heidegger's terms, can recognize no other authenticity.

But strangely, in his work and in himself, Scott embraced this discourse of aging in a way that ultimately would trump it, and convert Lockhart and Cadell's momentary triumph of (apparent) youth into an anxiety of persistent and inescapable influence emanating from the space that once was the Author of Waverley. Scott was not naive about the problems of aging and the subjection of the aged through fact and discourse. He knew that he himself had acted against others on the grounds of age. Early in the journal, this prematurely old fifty-four-year-old laments the financial need to "[turn] old age and infirmity adrift" as he retrenches his household expenses (*Journal,* 95). And Crystal Croftangry, the character who in *The Chronicles of the Canongate* (1827) both coincides with and fictionally reenacts Scott's financial crash, through his age proves trivial to his new acquaintances and unrecognizable to his onetime friends. Age betokens the loss of presence and persistence both. When the sexton in *Castle Dangerous* (1831) feeds his fire with the funerary relics of long ago, Scott provokes us to wonder if even the supplemental signs of death can last.

So how can this author make decline resonate? How can the subject achieve persistence in the space of non-being – on the other side of death? Notably, Scott does not simply touch on his diminishing health and impending demise now and again in his journal. Rather, he insists on his decline into an object. Throughout this text,

---

5 NLS references manuscripts held by the National Library of Scotland. Permission granted by the Trustees.
6 In 1830 Cadell recorded Scott's fear that he would become "like my father – a man done before my days are done" (Cadell's Notebook, 19 December 1830, NLS MS21043 f 80).

which he advertises as for family and strangers alike, he discusses his illnesses and his treatments in ways that foreground his suffering and decaying body. Early on, a stumble compels him to give up walking: the body becomes a falling object that must be transported by the complex prosthetic that is a coach and horses (*Journal,* 17). Scott is remorselessly blistered and cupped (638, 708, 729). At the insistence of family, he suffers the installment of a "seton" to cut off an anal fistula.[7] That is, unmentionable parts of the body and unspeakable illnesses usurp the conventional subject of autobiography, the unified mind coherently embodied. And as an assemblage of damaged body parts, the author repeatedly points out, he is detached from and an embarrassment to the world – mortified to be seen sprawling atop a pony, sorry to be tedious to his friends (*Journal* 705, 563). He even begins a count down to death, knowing that "[the] step of time is noiseless as it passes over an old man," and expecting to "be in the Secret next week" (631, 729). Scott, with a creativity perhaps not even Kathleen Woodward could have imagined, deliberately turns his body into a cynosure for the public eye. In so doing he recasts the self into a thing that can persist and insist well beyond the usual realms of identity. It is by his assertive unhealthiness that the author gains presence. Thus for putative literary heir Thomas Carlyle, Sir Walter becomes even in death that obtrusively "healthiest of men."[8]

Significantly, Scott's late strategy was no innovation in his work. Rather, the journal, with its focus on the aging body, epitomizes a long-standing practice. Woodward observes that age is the ultimate difference; it is what cannot be recognized and accepted (Woodward 1991, 16). From early in his career, however, Scott had expressed age and its resistance to containment. Generations of critics have wrestled to understand Scott's ingénue heroes. Yet, who even remembers the hero of *The Lay* in the context of the "Last Minstrel" or, even more so, Michael Scott (it is Baron Henry Cranstoun)? Baron Bradwardine provides the most memorable moments of *Waverley*, not the eponymous hero; Lovel fades into insignificance in the presence of the antiquary.

It is worth noting that all these supporting, yet usurping, players figure disease and decline. The minstrel is fading into the landscape at the beginning of *The Lay* ("Introduction"); the Baron with the boot-jack constitutes a weak-minded comic butt for the young men of the Chevalier's court in *Waverley*; *The Antiquary*'s Monkbarns, with his misrecognized relics, enacts the encrustation of age that insulates it from the experience – good and bad – that is real life. All three are turned toward the past; all three seem static and should be even less heroic than a wandering *Waverley* protagonist. Yet all three display an astonishing intensity of life, a vibrancy that cannot be diminished by the smirks of a Fergus McIvor or the embarrassed condescension of an Edward Waverley. Conventional heroes may strive to fence these elders within the confines of the family plot or the discourse of age as opposed to youth, but such heroes are forfeited, in Heidegger's terms, to the world. Their being is only in the world, and a shallow being it is. They are easily trumped by those whose near relation to death has recast them not as persons, but as authenticities on the declining side of life. As

---

7 Anal abscesses, penetrating to the surface, create a track or 'fistula.' Pain and potentially lethal infection can ensue. The fistula can be treated by threading through it a 'cutting seton,' and gradually pulling the seton tight. The seton cuts through the flesh and allows for healing (Cirocco and Rusin 1991).

8 "An eminently well-conditioned man, healthy in body, healthy in soul; we will call him one of the *healthiest* of men" (Carlyle 1838, 305).

Waverley and his cohort discover, it is difficult to patronize an intractable object. Worse, the more annoying, ridiculous, or encrusted one of these anti-heroes becomes – the more the minstrel corrects his audience, the more Bradwardine insists on ritual, the more trash the antiquary accumulates – the more they move to the center of Scott's texts. The efforts of Scott's young men to evade them and of his readers to ignore them, only install them more obtrusively in the place of the increasingly inadequate hero.

Is this agency? Not really – for any protagonist, or at least any non-Scott hero, should be able to anchor his own book. Usurping a Lovel or a Nigel (see Sir Mungo Malagrowther in *The Fortunes of Nigel*, 1822) may seem no great achievement. But it implies a being – or at least a disturbing – from beyond the ending. What these elder characters figure is a kind of assertive objectness – the trait that a wavering hero is only learning as he is passed around from pillar to post. And this is a trait that makes Scott, through his illnesses, his decline from agency into suffering object and objectified character, the hero of his own journal.

Woodward explains when she recognizes in Freud's fear of aging not just a dislike of but also an obsession with the body: "we turn our attention away from the world and concern ourselves with our own bodies" (Woodward 1991, 48). The aging body, she argues, from this perspective can be seen as a tomb for the living well in advance of death (56). During the course of Scott's journal, a succession of strokes brought this reality progressively upon him (*Journal,* 661, 728-729). However, Scott had long ago demonstrated that we should not consider either the body entombed or the entombing body as the end, or as the limit point of effectiveness. In *The Lay of the Last Minstrel* (1805), Michael Scott epitomizes the connection between premature objectness and a deeply disturbing being beyond the ending. Interred – but never specified as dead – Michael is exhumed. Now light streams from the tomb; the wizard lies, years after his burial, as irreducible as an object (*Lay*, Canto 2 verses 18 and 19). When the mystic book is removed from his hand, the dead man seems to frown (verse 21). Are these light effects only? They matter nonetheless, for in the presence of the preternaturally persistent corpse of Michael Scott, the monk who assists in the book's theft is dead before the deed breaks on daylight (verse 23). Soon, the wizard, or random bits of him, intrude upon the wedding banquet (canto 6 verse 26). Death stalks the feast in the inaccessible object that is Michael Scott.

Lockhart, in *Peter's Letters to his Kinfolk* (1819), registered this unusual vitality in a character who has passed into the tomb and thus beyond subjectivity. And he knew which way it tended. He drew upon the *Lay* to describe the younger Walter Scott's imagination as "one majestic sepulchre, where the wizard lamp burns in never-dying splendour, and the charmed blood glows for ever in the cheeks of the embalmed, and every long-sheathed sword is ready to leap from its scabbard" (Lockhart 1977, 136). Perhaps it was this awareness that made the older Lockhart strangely anxious about his declining father-in-law. The tomb, Lockhart understood – at least as built by Walter Scott – does not so much contain the body as facilitate its expression. The detritus of a life, whether body or book, dangerously intrudes from the other side of death. It enacts the unmanageable otherness of the self when translated into a 'mere' thing.

Scott's practice further suggests that the aging, objectified, and perhaps even dead author can enjoy a potency that is enhanced through the supposedly disempowering gaze of others. For Woodward, the constrictions of old age arise in part through a perversion of the mirror stage. The first mirror stage unifies internal and external selves, but, drawing on Christopher Lasch's suggestion that "our dread of old age has its origins not in a cult of youth but in a cult of the self," she infers that the mirror stage of old age divorces the two (Woodward 1991, 69). The outward image is further inflected by the unsympathetic and objectifying audience against which the aging subject must construct itself, for the mirror stage of old age "is inherently triangular, involving the gaze of others as well as two images of oneself" (69). Scott, again, recasts a weakness as a strength: he multiplies these points of triangulation and instances of objectification. He thus makes impossible the limiting positioning performed by those who seek to find their being, set against that of their community's elders, in a narrowly social world.

Scott well understood the inverted equation that fragmented and yet multiplied the self as object. Michael Scott persists not just in the body but in the book, and in the hand or the arm as much as in the whole. However, this division of selves allows for an intensification of effect; so dispersed, his powers cannot easily be directed by the Lady of Branksome Tower. In fact, they work against her and install the wizard as ever more potent. Not surprisingly, then, just as the antiquary encrusted himself with objects, the author encrusts himself with selves. Notoriously, as Ian Duncan has hinted, Scott went from being lawyer to poet to Author of Waverley and back to Walter Scott (Duncan 2007, 281). He vogued as President of the Royal Society of Edinburgh and companion to kings. Furthermore, the Author was *Eidolon*, or representation, and fittingly – given Woodward's observation that age alone trumps the hierarchies of gender – looms as either or neither man or woman in *The Fortunes of Nigel* (Woodward 1991, 16; *Nigel*, 5). Then too, s/he is a "postman," shifting according to various points of perspective as his/her works are delivered to one reader or another (*Nigel*, 9). Readers also multiply. In *Nigel* and in the journal, the reader alternately does and does not matter to the reception of Scott's novels: the author is "their humble jackall, too busy in providing food for them, to have time for considering whether they swallow or reject it" (9). "The publick favour is my only lottery," Scott insists, locating himself as an object/subject to the play of a randomized audience (*Journal*, 73). This variable reader in turn encounters books presented not as ideas, or even as stories, but as objects. *Waverley* is ostentatiously denied any generic category in Scott's introduction, and recast in his postscript as the equivalent of fishing tackle (*Waverley*, 3-4; "General Preface," xvii). Volumes are so many pages, wont to be used for scouring pots by over-enthusiastic cook maids (*Nigel*, 11-12). Abbotsford, in this context, is no expensive stately home, but an *Antiquary*-like hodge-podge of objects in lieu of a self. And the assemblage that tumbles together as "Walter Scott" allows no reductive triangulation of authorial identity.

So what did it mean when Scott eventually took his works upon himself? Was this a closing down into limited selfhood and toward the conventional death of the author – placed in time and according to literary and geriatric criticism? In February1826, after the financial crash that required his writings to be declared as property and assessed according to monetary value, Scott was outed as the Author of Waverley. At the Theatrical Fund dinner, he accepted the role in terms that seem oddly absolute: "He meant, when he said that he was the author, that he was the total and undivided author: [...] there was not a single word that was not derived from himself" (Vedder 1997, 38). To his journal he declared: "I am firmly and resolutely determined that I will tilt under my own cognizance" (*Journal*, 244). Yet, by this time there were so many Scotts in circulation, as a thing and in things such as books and houses, that belated insistence on the body of the author only foregrounds an objectification that had long escaped any individual or temporally located definition of the self. If we exist in the body, and cannot exist outside the body, thus only "ex-isting" and only at the time we cease to be, according to Jean-Luc Nancy, Scott ostentatiously was and was not in numerous bodies, partial and whole, among which the Scott at the Theatrical Fund dinner was simply one more (Nancy 2008, 15). Ian Duncan suggests in *Scott's Shadow* that Scott's fiction so haunted his literary successors because it stood as "inexhaustible surplus, cultural production as the sublime, redemptive double of an industrial political economy" (Duncan 2007, 284). But the stories were only part of the surplus that betokened Walter Scott. Woodward ponders whether "the 'essence' of a memory of someone would [...] have to be that which we could *not* remember, never having known it" (Woodward 1991, 119). A being thus dispersed into many simultaneously different yet overlapping things cannot be avoided, but cannot be remembered in place or contained in time.

Can such being yet come to an end? Scott himself deploys a discourse of ending. In his journal, increasingly he wishes for death: "when the awakenings came a strong feeling how well I could dispence with it for once and for ever" (*sic*, *Journal*, 78). But this discourse, too, was of long standing. If Freud looked to death as an event to conceal the fact of aging, Scott had drawn lastness out over so many years, the discourse itself had aged. To give just a few examples: in Scott's first long poem the minstrel is already "the last of all the bards" (*Lay*, "Introduction," line 7); Scott ended as a poet even as he began as a novelist; *The Antiquary* supposedly "[completed] a series of fictitious narratives" (*Antiquary*, "Advertisement" [3]). During Scott's latter years this discourse accumulates: *Castle Dangerous* went under the imprint "Tales of My Landlord, Fourth and Last Series;" its postscript insists the novel is "the latest tale which it will probably be the lot of the present author to submit to the consideration of the gentle reader;" the belated introductory address purveys it as the last manuscript of Peter Pattieson; and the author steps from behind his personae to cap Jedediah Cleishbotham's account of Cervantes's last days with a statement about his last voyage and his own impending death (*Castle Dangerous*, 193, 189, 195, 207-208). The novel vies for last place with *Count Robert of Paris*, *The Siege of Malta*, and *Bizarro*, each of which Scott determines as his last (*Count Robert*, 361; and as an example: Cadell to Scott 15 December 1830, NLS MS3915 f 172-75). Scott insisted upon lastness so much, in fact, that this discourse trumped criticism in the novel's reviews: *The Border Magazine* runs on: "In all human probability, these Tales of my Landlord are not only the last of the series, but the finale of the whole" (Anon. 1831a, 90-91); the *Edinburgh Literary Journal* began by declaring Scott's ending: "THE LAST! The last echo of the last Bard's harp – the farewell prophecy of the silenced oracle" (Anon. 1831b, 317).

Did Scott know what he was doing? His epilogue to *Count Robert* characterizes the novel "as being very probably the last work of fiction in which [I] may be tempted to engage," but he jokes that "[this] assertion has been, for different reasons, so often solemnly made – and reiterated – and again departed from [... I have] very little credence to expect from the mildest of critics" (*Count Robert*, 361). Against the discourse of decline, Scott had instantiated a discourse of authenticity at the point of death – a finishing that escapes an ending. Thus even *The Centenary Memorial of Sir Walter Scott, Bart*, which we might imagine able to use its long view to force into perspective one Sir Walter, still resounds with this language of many lastnesses: contributors to Charles Stewart Montgomerie Lockhart's volume obsessively remember Scott's last days, his last words, his last works. That is, Scott's being emanates from the moment in which he insisted on himself as no longer a person but, transmuted by death, about to be a thing. From early in his writing, and long after his decease, Scott was always and already damaged, dispersed, belated, fractured, irreducible – and thus ever being past the ending.

Bruno Latour ponders how matters of fact require, in order to exist, to figure as matters of concern (Brown 2004, 172). Scott, by embracing his objectification, fragmenting it and multiplying it, produced himself, in Latour's terms, as "a bewildering variety of matters of concern" for those working to maintain their own being in the world. Thus, even as Scott died, Lockhart and Cadell struggled to stop his persistence as story and his disruption of their own more romanticized and commercial tale. When James Hogg and William Laidlaw verged to publication with their biographies, which would further multiply and fragment Sir Walter, Scott's heirs degraded the one and feared that the other would "do us [the *Life*] an unwitting injury" (see Mack's introduction to *Anecdotes*, and Major Walter Scott to Cadell, 29 July 1833, NLS MS21003 f 164-165). But lives swarmed upon them. The objectification embraced by the author only increased, and Sir Walter persisted as a disturbing thing, such that even Lockhart's seven volume *Life* and Carlyle's devastating critique of it stand only as symptoms of a containment, a closing down of Scott into the life before death, that they cannot achieve.

Woodward suggests that one of the most unsettling phenomena of aging is that bodies lose their coherence; but at the same time in psychic space they can lose their boundaries (Woodward 1991, 100). "[As] we move toward the limits of old age – and that limit is death – "she says, "we move toward the limits of representation" (194). Scott demonstrated that the limit of representation as a self, the decline into the thing that is produced at the moment of death, also constitutes the horizon of opportunity for being hereafter. Scott, despite Heidegger, operates as authenticity *beyond* death.

One final story tells the tale for Scott and for that other preeminent author, already outdistanced by time and the tomb, William Shakespeare. At the moment when Scott shockingly falls, instantancously transmogrified into that degraded object, the failed Author of Waverley, he is simultaneously transmuted into a transcendent matter of concern: "Funny thing at the theatre," he writes:

> Among the discourse in *High Life below Stairs* one of the Ladies' ladies asks who wrote Shakespeare. One says "Ben Johnson" [*sic*] another "Finis." "No" said [another player], "it is Sir Walter Scott; he confessd it at a publick meeting the other day." (*Journal*, 322)

Rumors of Scott's death, it seems, have always been "greatly exaggerated."[9]

Works Cited

Anon. "Rev. of *Tales of My Landlord. Fourth and Last Series.*" *The Border Magazine* 1 (December 1831a): 90-93.

—. "Rev. of *Tales of My Landlord. Fourth and Last Series.*" *Edinburgh Literary Journal* (3 December 1831b): 317-321.

—. "Mark Twain Amused." *New York Journal* (2 June 1897): n. p.

---

9   Mark Twain responded to his premature obituary, "The report of my death was an exaggeration" (Anon. 1897) – popularly misquoted as in the text.

Brown, Bill. *Things*. Chicago: University of Chicago Press, 2004.

Carlyle, Thomas. "Review of *Memoirs of the Life of Sir Walter Scott, Baronet* Vols. I–VI." *London and Westminster Review* 6.23 (1838): 293-345.

Cirocco, William C. and Lawrence C. Rusin. "Simplified Seton Management for Complex Anal Fistulas: A Novel Use for the Rubber Band Ligator." *Diseases of the Colon & Rectum* 34.12 (1991): 1135-1137.

Craig, Cairns. *Out of History: Narrative Paradigms in Scottish and English Culture* Edinburgh: Polygon, 1996.

Duncan, Ian. *Scott's Shadow: The Novel in Romantic Edinburgh*. Princeton: Princeton University Press, 2007.

Freud, Sigmund. *The Ego and the Id*. 1923. Trans. Joan Riviere. Rev. James Strachey. New York: Norton, 1962.

Heidegger, Martin. *Being and Time*. 1953. Trans. Joan Stambaugh. Rev. and Ed. Dennis J. Schmidt. Albany, NY: State University of New York Press, 2010.

Hogg, James. *Anecdotes of Sir W. Scott*. Ed. Douglas S. Mack. Edinburgh: Scottish Academic Press, 1983.

Lockhart, Charles Stewart Montgomerie. *The Centenary Memorial of Sir Walter Scott, Bart*. London: Virtue & Co. 1871.

Lockhart, J. G. *The Life of Sir Walter Scott, Bart*. 7 vols. Edinburgh: Cadell, 1837-1838.

—. *Peter's Letters to his Kinsfolk*. 1819. Ed. William Ruddick. Edinburgh: Scottish Academic Press, 1977.

Merleau-Ponty, Maurice. *Basic Writings*. Ed. Thomas Baldwin. London: Routledge, 2004.

Nancy, Jean-Luc. *Corpus*. 2006. Trans. Richard A. Rand. New York: Fordham University Press, 2008.

Scott, Walter. *Castle Dangerous*. 1831. Ed. J. H. Alexander. Edinburgh: Edinburgh University Press, 2006. [= *Castle Dangerous*]

—. *Count Robert of Paris*. 1831. Ed. J. H. Alexander. Edinburgh: Edinburgh University Press, 2006. [= *Count Robert*]

—. *The Antiquary*. 1816. Ed. David Hewitt. Edinburgh: Edinburgh University Press, 1995. [= *Antiquary*]

—. *The Lay of the Last Minstrel*. 1805. Eleventh Edition. London: Longman, Hurst, Rees, and Orme, 1810. [= *Lay*]

—. "General Preface." *Waverley*. 1814. New Edition of the Waverley Novels. Vol. 1. Edinburgh: Cadell, 1829. v-cvi.

—. *The Journal of Sir Walter Scott*. 1890. Ed. W. E. K. Anderson. Edinburgh: Canongate Classics, 1998. [= *Journal*]

—. *The Chronicles of the Canongate*. 1827. Ed. Claire Lamont. Edinburgh: Edinburgh University Press, 2000.

—. *The Fortunes of Nigel*. 1822. Ed. Frank Jordan. Edinburgh: Edinburgh University Press, 2004. [= *Nigel*]

—. *Waverley*. 1814. Ed. P. D. Garside. Edinburgh: Edinburgh University Press, 2007. [= *Waverley*]

Vedder, David. "Memoir of Sir Walter Scott, Bart." *Scott. Lives of the Great Romantics* II. Vol. 3. Ed. Fiona Robertson. London: Pickering and Chatto, 1997. 23-43.

Woodward, Kathleen. *Aging and Its Discontents: Freud and Other Fictions*. Bloomington: Indiana University Press, 1991.

OLIVER S. BUCKTON, Boca Raton, FL

"It touches one too closely:"
Robert Louis Stevenson and Queer Theory

In 1886, shortly after the publication of Robert Louis Stevenson's *Strange Case of Dr Jekyll and Mr Hyde*, his friend John Addington Symonds – the art historian and poet – wrote him a letter responding to the horrific tale of duality:

> At last I have read Dr Jekyll. It makes me wonder whether a man has the right so to scrutinize "the abysmal deeps of personality" […]. The fact is that, viewed as an allegory, it touches one too closely. Most of us at some epoch of our lives have been on the verge of developing a Mr Hyde. (Symonds 1969, 120-121).

Symonds was living a double life, being married with four daughters, while secretly engaging in homosexual relationships with a variety of working-class men, including British soldiers, a Venetian gondolier, and a Swiss peasant. Symonds – who had come to know Stevenson while both men were convalescing in Davos in the Swiss Alps – evidently picked up on the parallels between Jekyll's situation and his own. As Jeffrey Weeks observes, Symonds – along with Havelock Ellis and Edward Carpenter – "set the tone for most of the discussion concerning homosexuality in liberal and left-wing circles, and through their work […] was transmitted much of the most progressive of European thought on sexual matters" (Weeks 1990, 48).

In this letter to Stevenson, however, Symonds discloses a more personal response to the possibility of sexual revelation. Indeed, Symonds's letter is the first in a series of interpretations of Stevenson's story that have focused on its representation of concealed and fractured queer desires. Recently biographers have suggested that Stevenson himself was involved in relationships with other men that we would today term queer: Clare Harman wonders whether

> perhaps this mesmeric, magus power over other men arose from a desire in Stevenson himself, not necessarily a conscious one. Stevenson could have been in much deeper denial than someone like Symonds, with his forthright image of "the wolf leaping out" when he saw a homosexual graffito, or Gosse, who spoke of his true self being "buried alive," while "this corpse […] is obliged to bustle around and make an appearance." (Harman 2005, 214).

Harman asserts that Jekyll and Hyde "dramatizes both men's dilemmas very accurately" (214) – but the issue of which "both men" she refers to is unresolved.

Literary critics have also argued that *Jekyll and Hyde* functioned as a homosexual code: Elaine Showalter, for example, claims that "Some men, like Symonds and Wilde, may have read the book as a signing to the male community" (Showalter 1990, 115) that expressed the painful self-division of homosexual men. Given this critical history of the story, it is perhaps inevitable that a discussion of Stevenson's work in the light of queer theory should begin here, with narrative that has dominated the readings focusing on same-sex eroticism.

The place of *Jekyll and Hyde* as a queer text has been established by readings of the late-Victorian gothic of which it is a prime example. Eve Sedgwick's *Between Men* (1985) provided a critical framework for discussing features of gothic narrative that indicate a paranoid queer desire, projecting disavowed desires onto 'doubles' that take on a sinister and violent aspect. While Sedgwick did not discuss *Jekyll and Hyde* in detail, her work traces "emergent patterns of male entitlement, friendship, and rivalry" (Sedgwick 1985, 1) that clearly apply to the novella. Sedgwick's discussion of the male paranoid gothic created the conditions for later readings and points to a vocabulary of the Gothic genre that serves a double-function as a language of queer desire:

> One of the most distinctive of Gothic tropes, the 'unspeakable,' had a symptomatic role in this series of shifts. Sexuality between men had, throughout the Judaeo-Christian tradition, been famous among those who knew about it at all precisely for having no name [...] Of course, its very namelessness, its secrecy, was a form of social control. (Sedgwick 1985, 94)

This "defining pervasiveness in Gothic novels of language about the unspeakable" (94) can be found in *Jekyll and Hyde*, in the vows of silence made between the male characters, for example when Gabriel Utterson reproaches himself for speaking of Mr Hyde: "Here is another lesson to say nothing [...] I am ashamed of my long tongue. Let us make a bargain never to refer to this again" (Stevenson 2003, 12). Utterson, we are told in the story, "was embarrassed in discourse; backwards in sentiment" (7) and it is this secretiveness that leads Showalter to designate him as a "Jekyll manqué," whose "demeanor is muted and sober" (Showalter 1990, 109).

The all-male cast of central characters leads Sedgwick to include the story in her discussion of the later-Victorian "bachelor literature" in *Epistemology of the Closet* (1990) – a form in which the "paranoid gothic" finds a new incarnation as "male homosexual panic was acted out as a sometimes agonized sexual anesthesia that was damaging to both its male subjects and its female non-objects" (Sedgwick 1990, 188). However, the difference that provokes transgressive desire in Jekyll is less that of gender than that of class.

This connection between queerness and class transgression has been observed in perhaps the most influential interpretation focusing on queer desire in Stevenson: Elaine Showalter's chapter, "Dr Jekyll's Closet," in *Sexual Anarchy*. Showalter notes, "Jekyll's apparent infatuation with Hyde reflects the late-19th-century upper-middle-class eroticization of working-class men as the ideal homosexual objects" (Showalter 1990, 111). Hence Hyde's status as what Showalter terms "a loutish younger man, who comes and goes as he pleases" (111), is precisely what might make him attractive to an upper-class gentleman such as Jekyll.

Similarly to Sedgwick, Showalter takes note of a gothic language of the unspeakable in Stevenson's novella, linking it to both sexual and class transgression: the potent combination that would be the cause of Oscar Wilde's downfall in 1895. As Showalter notes:

> The reaction of the male characters to Hyde is uniformly that of "disgust, loathing, and fear," suggestive of the almost hysterical homophobia of the late 19th century. In the most famous code word of Victorian homosexuality, they find something *unspeakable* about Hyde "that gave a man a turn," something "surprising and revolting." (Showalter 1990, 112; original emphasis).

As an example of the paranoid gothic, Stevenson's story nonetheless eludes Sedgwick's triangular structure in which "it is the use of women as exchangeable, perhaps symbolic, property for the primary purpose of cementing the bonds of men with men"

(Sedgwick 1985, 25-26). For *Jekyll and Hyde*, as is well known, contains almost no women. Commenting on the various adaptations of the story, Showalter writes "not one tells the story as Stevenson wrote it – that is, as a story about men. All of the versions add women to the story and either eliminate the homoerotic elements or suggest them indirectly" (Showalter 1990, 115-116).

Focusing on the exclusively male context of the story, Showalter examines in cultural terms "the shadow of homosexuality that surrounded clubland and the nearly hysterical terror of revealing forbidden emotions between men" (Showalter 1990, 107). Showalter's emphasis on male sexual secrecy proves compelling in its attention to key textual details, as she notes "Jekyll cannot open his heart or his breast even to his dearest male friends. Thus they must spy on him to enter his mind, to get to the bottom of his secrets" (110). Showalter established a pattern in which same-sex desire finds uneasy representation in imagery of doors, penetration, darkness and secrecy. Thus, those features of landscape and climate in the text that contribute to the gothic atmosphere, are read by Showalter as signs "suggestive of anality and anal intercourse. Hyde travels in the 'chocolate-brown fog' that beats about the 'back-end of the evening'" (113). As these quotations indicate, Showalter's reading of queer references in *Jekyll and Hyde* is sometimes lacking in subtlety, and also depends at times on stereotypes of male homosexuality, such as the narcissism associated with the mirror which she terms "an obsessive symbol in homosexual literature" (111). No less problematic is her conflation of male homosexuality and other fin-de-siècle public concerns such as disease, syphilis in particular.

Showalter's argument is not biographical in focus. Nonetheless, the male clubland of Jekyll's environment does mirror Stevenson's circle in some intriguing ways. Like Jekyll, Stevenson had a circle of close male friends, finding himself at the center of currents of male desire. His friend and fellow-author Andrew Lang observed that Stevenson "possessed more than any man I ever met, the power of making other men fall in love with him" (cited in Harman 2005, 213). Jekyll exudes a similar magnetism, as when he "gave one of his pleasant dinners to some five or six old cronies, all intelligent, reputable men and all judges of good wine; and Mr Utterson so contrived that he remained behind after the others had departed" (Stevenson 2003, 19). One detects here a reminder of the possessiveness and jealousy over Jekyll's friendship that Lang refers to concerning Stevenson.

Such biographical parallels raise the possibility that *Jekyll and Hyde*, rather than being an exception or aberration in Stevenson's work in its portrayal of tortured sexual duality, actually forms part of a larger pattern of representations of queer desire. For example, the bitter struggle between the Durie brothers, James and Henry, in *The Master of Ballantrae*, replays the dual personality in the context of a sibling rivalry. James Durie also resembles Hyde in the threat he poses to the conspiracy of silence that maintains the homosocial order: "I have still one strong position – that you people fear a scandal, and I enjoy it" (Stevenson 1996b, 140). The sibling rivalry flares up no less significantly in a memorable duel by torchlight in which Henry apparently fatally wounds his older brother. The miraculous or supernatural reanimation of James, suggests that Henry Durie – like his earlier namesake Jekyll – has tried to destroy desires that cannot be eliminated but recur as an uncanny "return of the repressed:" as he later tells the family servant Mackellar about his brother,

"He's not of this world [...] I have struck my sword throughout his vitals [...] I have felt the hilt dirl on his breastbone, and the hot blood spirt in my very face, time and time again [...]. But he was never dead for all that" (Stevenson 1996b, 209).[1]

The violent penetration and quasi-orgasmic violence of the duel is suggestive of a diverted sexual desire. Sedgwick argues that the Gothic novel typically features "one or more males who not only is persecuted by, but considers himself transparent to and often under the compulsion of, another male" (Sedgwick 1985, 91). Stevenson's gothic male doubles – such as Jekyll and Hyde, and the Durie brothers – strongly illustrate this theme, with Henry's refusal to believe in James's death serving as a manifestation of his paranoia, "the psychosis that makes graphic the mechanisms of homophobia" (91).

The Master may be included in the Scottish Gothic tradition discussed by Sedgwick in her chapter on James Hogg's *Confessions of a Justified Sinner*. Even after moving to Samoa in the South Seas, however, Stevenson maintained his interest in the dynamics of male attraction and conflict in these exotic contexts. Such is the case with the ambivalent relationship between John Wilshire – a British trader – and his rival Case, in "The Beach of Falesa" (1892). Initially friendly, the two traders become bitter enemies and the climax of the story occurs in the High Woods where Wiltshire discovers Case's secret lair – from which he has been manipulating the superstitions of the native islanders to secure a monopoly on trade. Wilshire's final, triumphant dispatch of Case using a knife involves a violent penetration that recalls Henry's duel with James Durie, and connects it with the queer gothic tradition of Jekyll and Hyde:

> I drew my knife and got it in the place. "Now," said I, "I've got you; and you're gone up, and a good job too! Do you feel the point of that?" [...] With that I gave him the cold steel for all I was worth. His body kicked under me like a spring sofa; he gave a dreadful kind of a long moan, and lay still [...]. I tried to draw the knife out to give it him again. The blood came over my hands, I remember, hot as tea. (Stevenson 1996a, 67-68)

The ejaculatory gushing of blood echoes Henry Durie's recollection of spilling James's blood in *The Master*, emphasized here by the word "came," suggesting an orgasm of violence. As Ralph Parfet argues, in Stevenson's work "Narratives of violence become in a sense a substitute for narratives of sexuality [...]. Thus attention is steered quite explicitly away from sex to violence [...]; the knowledge of violence is eroticized" (Parfet 2006, 196). Yet one of the purposes of queer theory is to reverse this process, steering attention back to the displaced representation of transgressive sexual desires. An apt illustration of Parfet's claim that Stevenson's South Seas writing "involves the recognition that violent transactions may be informed by powerful libidinal desires" (197), the scene is disturbing in its blending of intimacy and murder.

The queer intimacy of white men in the South Seas recurs in *The Ebb-Tide*, the third and last collaboration between Stevenson and his stepson Lloyd Osbourne. In this narrative, the drifter Robert Herrick is recognized by Attwater, the colonizer of the Pearl Island, as being of equal class and education, despite his evident decline. The growing intimacy between the two men – Attwater says to Herrick "you are at-

---

[1] In his essay "The Uncanny," Freud forges a link between repressed desire and the uncanny, arguing that "every affect belonging to an emotional impulse, whatever its kind, is transformed, if it is repressed, into anxiety," such that "the frightening element can be shown to be something repressed which recurs. This class of frightening things would then constitute the uncanny" (Freud 2010, 833).

tractive, very attractive" (Stevenson 1996a, 205) – is marked by Herrick's imagining a scene of Attwater's death that is strangely eroticized: "the thought of him lying dead was so unwelcome that it pursued him, like a vision, with every circumstance of colour and sound. Incessantly, he had before him the image of that great mass of man stricken down in varying attitudes and with varying wounds" (208).[2] The gaze between men does appear to be "lustful" (Parfet 2006,191), as when Herrick admires Attwater's manly appearance: "they were able at last to see what manner of man they had to do with. He was a huge fellow, six feet four in height, and of a build proportionately strong." Herrick notes his "eye of an unusual mingled brilliancy and softness, somber as coal and with lights that outshone the topaz; an eye of unimpaired health and virility" (Stevenson 1996a, 191). These scenes powerfully figure the role that violence plays in representing conflicted or repressed desire between men in Stevenson's South Seas fiction.

Following the pioneering work of Sedgwick and Showalter, critical attention to the gothic violence and uncanny scenes of male doubling has certainly been at the forefront of queer readings of Stevenson. More recently, however, a radically different approach to queer theory has emerged, helping us to recognize the emergence of same-sex desire in contexts of tenderness and intimacy, rather than rivalry and violence. A good example is Holly Furneaux's *Queer Dickens* (2009) which challenges what the author terms the "anti-social" school of theorists, claiming "a queer theory that rejects domestic and familial possibilities impoverishes the field of enquiry" (Furneaux 2009, 12).

Furneaux's interpretations emphasize the tender, domestic, and positive queer energies of Victorian fiction, rather than violence, aggression, and despair, which have often been viewed as the chief symptoms of a suppressed queer desire. As Furneaux argues, there has been "a long-held critical bias towards moments of violence in queer readings [...]. Under this thinking of the homosexual as the antisocial, that which must be aggressively repudiated in order for homosociality to be maintained, critical attention has focused on instances where same-sex desires energetically break out as acts of destruction and violence" (Furneaux 2009, 207). One can learn from Furneaux's example in order to attend to the more tender and positive connections between men in Stevenson, signs that the tragic outcome of Jekyll and Hyde is not the only available narrative for characters involved in same-sex passion.

In *Kidnapped* – published the same year as *Jekyll* – there is an extended example of an affectionate male relationship, in the companionship of David Balfour and Alan Breck. Despite deep differences of political affiliation and temperament – Alan is the hotheaded Jacobite, David the cautious Loyalist – a bond of intimacy is forged between the two men in their "flight through the heather." Linked by being joint suspects in the Appin murder and forced to take flight together, their bond is confirmed by the wanted posters: "It seemed it was noised on all sides that Alan Breck had fired the shot; and there was a bill issued for both him and me, with one hundred pounds reward" (Stevenson 2001, 187).

Crucially, at the point at which the relationship threatens to turn into violent antagonism – when David rashly challenges Alan to a duel – the crisis is avoided by

---

2   See chapter 8 of Buckton (2007) for a fuller discussion of the relationships between Herrick, Attwater, and Davis.

Alan's deep affection: "drawing my sword, I fell on guard as Alan himself had taught me. 'David!' he cried. 'Are ye daft? I cannae draw upon ye, David. It's fair murder" (Stevenson 2001, 221). Avoiding the gothic crises of *The Master, Kidnapped* emphasizes the passionate attachment between men that is not driven by paranoia: as Alan tells David, "For just precisely what I thought I liked about ye, was that ye never quarreled; – and now I like ye better!" (223). Alan's tenderness towards David is further illustrated by his care for him when the younger man is unwell, which nicely illustrates Furneaux's point that that "male nursing, as well as wider forms of restorative male tactility […] have tended to get under a critical radar more attuned to acts of masculine aggression" (Furneax 2009, 177). Perhaps most tellingly, David's reaction to being separated from Alan discloses a passion that the narrative has not fully confronted at this point, is all the more emphatic for occurring at the end of the novel:

> Neither one of us looked the other in the face, nor so long as he was in my view did I take one back glance at the friend I was leaving. But as I went on my way to the city, I felt so lost and lonesome that I could have found it in my heart to sit down by the dyke, and cry and weep like any baby (Stevenson 2001, 276).

It may be significant that Alan, at his parting from David, "held out his left hand" (276) – associated with queer desire in the late Victorian period – suggesting what Showalter terms "the Victorian homosexual trope of the left hand of illicit sexuality" (Showalter 1990, 115). The shame at such "illicit sexuality" – the novel being written just after the Labouchere Amendment criminalizing "gross indecency with another male person" (Weeks 1990, 14) – is reflected in the refusal of each man to meet the other's eye, and is also connected to David's subsequent "cold gnawing in my inside like a remorse for something wrong" (Stevenson 2001, 277).

Stevenson's comic writing represents another significant context in which queer desire circulates in Victorian literature in ways that have sometimes evaded critical scrutiny. As critics such as Christopher Craft have demonstrated, Oscar Wilde's verbal wit embeds allusions to sexual inversion and sodomy, and similar displacements of sodomitic desire also occur in Stevenson's comic masterpiece, *The Wrong Box* (1889), co-authored with his stepson Lloyd Osbourne (Craft 1994, 119).[3] Stevenson's morbidly humorous fantasy revolves around the concealment of a corpse – that of Joseph Finsbury – in order to prevent the loss of a valuable tontine fund. In the course of the narrative, the corpse is concealed in a water butt and a grand piano, among other containers, and becomes a disruptive figure for masculine desire. In a key scene, Michael decides to bury the corpse in the back garden of William Dent Pitman, one of the corpse's reluctant recipients. Michael's words suggest an unspeakable sodomitic desire, as he notes "I tell you we should look devilish romantic shovelling out the sod by the moon's pale ray" (Stevenson 1995, 65). "The sod" doubles as a term for earth and an abbreviated word for "sodomite" – installing the corpse as a queer secret in the text, which Pitman suggests "you might put […] in the closet there – if you could bear to touch it" (65).

In a similar fashion to Wilde's pun on "Bunbury," Stevenson's text invokes an absurd context for the emergence of a criminal sexual impulse. The hostile critical re-

---

3   Craft does acknowledge a darker side to such sodomitic representations, noting an "allusion to the thanatopolitics of homophobia, whose severest directives against disclosure only too axiomatically ensure that what finally gets disclosed will be, as in *Dorian Gray*, a corpse, homicide or suicide" (Craft 1994, 118).

ception that *The Wrong Box* provoked, was ostensibly focused on Stevenson's promiscuous collaboration with Osbourne: as the reviewer in the *The Scotsman* anxiously remarked, "It bears the name of a collaborator, Mr Lloyd Osbourne. What Mr Osbourne's share in the story may be it is hard to determine" (Maixner 1981, 337). Yet the charge made by the *Pall Mall Gazette* that Stevenson "ought to be ashamed of himself" for having chosen "so repellant a subject" (Maixner 1981, 336) indicates more serious misgivings about the transgressive sexual meanings of the text. The claim that the novel presents "a kind of ghastly game at hide and seek with a dead man's body" (337) reveals a critical distaste for the extended sodomitic pun about burying an object in the back garden. One reviewer's remark that the plot "is run through with sufficient rapidity to prevent the olfactory nerve discovering the whereabouts of the concealed carcase" (337) further indicates sensory disapproval at the unsavory subject.[4]

The critical discussion of the comic possibilities and manifestations of queer desire in Stevenson is sparse – particular in comparison to the rich interpretive discourse on Wilde. Yet it offers a potentially vital field for investigation, and reminds us that queer representation in Stevenson does not always take on a gothic, tragic form. Such comic forms also draw our attention to the fact that queer energies surface in Stevenson's texts across genres and modes, and are not restricted to the kind of paranoid gothic narratives addressed by Sedgwick and Showalter. In addition to causing "gender trouble" through their challenges to dominant Victorian definitions of masculinity and femininity, Stevenson's texts also promote "genre trouble," by confounding cherished distinctions between literary forms and styles. A neglected yet nonetheless significant example of how gender and genre are both contested and disrupted by Stevenson, is the novel *Prince Otto* (1885).

Occupying an unstable ground between historical fantasy, romantic adventure, and political critique, *Otto* was the object of intensive labor by Stevenson, yet he had doubts as to its likely popular appeal, writing to his friend and mentor, W. E. Henley: "'Otto' is, as you say, not a thing to extend my public on. It is queer and a little, little bit free; and some of the parties are immoral; and the whole thing is not a romance, nor yet a comedy; not yet a romantic comedy; but a kind of preparation of some of the elements of all three in a glass jar" (Maixner 1981, 176).

The protagonist Otto is an ineffectual and passive head of the imaginary State of Grunewald – as unlike the Machiavellian Prince as one could conceive – who is also dominated by his wife, and the novel also inverts the traditional Victorian gender roles by fashioning the Princess Seraphina as the active political force in the relationship. In a clear subversion of the Victorian hierarchy of husband and wife, Otto subserviently praises Seraphina as "in all things my superior" and refers to his "love, slavish and unerect" (Stevenson 1907, 219). Indeed the novel is punctuated by numerous references to Otto's impotence, emasculating him both politically and sexually. As Otto himself states, "I did not believe this girl could care for me; I must not intrude; I must preserve the foppery of my indifference. What an impotent picture!" (58–59). Otto's self-lacerating verdict of "impotence" finds an echo in the observations of Sir John Crabtree, the English traveler who records his opinions in a manuscript in which Otto is described as having "the mark of some congenital deficiency,

---

[4] See chapter 1 of Buckton (2007) for a more detailed discussion of the comic representation of queer desire in narratives including *The Wrong Box* and *New Arabian Nights*.

physical or moral" with his "mouth a little womanish" (65). In this language Stevenson suggests the "type" of the homosexual, anticipating – in Foucault's terms – "a certain way of inverting the masculine and the feminine in oneself" (Foucault 1980, 43). It is this "kind of interior androgyny, a hermaphrodism of the soul" (43) that Stevenson incorporates in his portrait of Prince Otto, thus creating what we have come to recognize, following Judith Butler, as "gender trouble" in the novel.

In *Jekyll and Hyde*, as we have seen, Stevenson draws attention to a late-Victorian crisis in masculinity, disclosing with the dissolution of Jekyll's persona the lack at the center of the Victorian gentleman. *Otto* – published the year before *Jekyll* – achieves a similar effect but in a very different mode. Otto's failure to live up to the expectations of the Victorian male subjects him to the contempt of his subjects: as the narrator comments in the opening chapter, the Grunewald people "looked with an unfeigned contempt on the soft character and manners of the sovereign race" (Stevenson 1907, 12). As Harman argues, "*Prince Otto* is most interesting now for the gender anarchy it portrays" (Harman 2005, 250). Indeed, the novel's inversion of gender roles is an apt illustration of Butler's argument that "gender is a kind of persistent impersonation that passes as the real" (Butler 1999, xxviii) as Otto's transgression "destabilizes the very distinctions between the natural and the artificial, depth and surface, inner and outer through which discourse about genders almost always operates" (xxviii).

Otto's violation of the hierarchy of gender roles – based on the binary of masculine/feminine – consists of subversive bodily acts that attract hostility from critics both within and outside the text. As in the case of *The Wrong Box*, reviewers attacked *Otto* for its undermining of Victorian conventions of sexual propriety, but with the added slight on the hero's masculine identity. The *Saturday Review* noted of Otto: "He tries by fits and starts [...] to pluck up a little manhood" but "[t]he Prince of Grunewald is a fool and a wittol who leaves affairs of State to his wife and her alleged paramour, Baron Gondremark" (Maixner 1981, 184). In contrast to the hypermasculine bravado of characters such as Alan Breck, James Durie and Attwater, Otto demonstrates a far more ambivalent view of gender roles and records the circulation of queer desires. The hostility and neglect that has been suffered by *Otto* is an indication that its dissident sexual meanings were not embraced by the critical establishment, and that it therefore failed to secure a place in the literary canon.

This discussion so far has remained focused on Stevenson's fiction, reflecting the strong preference for the treatment of fictional genres in queer theory's approach to literary texts. Yet Stevenson, as we have noted, also wrote and published extensively in non-fictional genres, in particular travel writing. Indeed, Stevenson's literary career began in earnest with two volumes of travel writing – *An Inland Voyage* (1878) and *Travels with a Donkey in the Cevennes* (1879) – before Stevenson dedicated his energies to writing a successful novel, which resulted in *Treasure Island*. By way of concluding this discussion of queer theory and Stevenson, I want to suggest that certain elements of queer desire and the contesting of conventional gender roles are already apparent in Stevenson's early travel writing, using the example of *Travels with a Donkey*.

This work has sometimes been read within the context of Stevenson's troubled romance with his future wife, Fanny Vandergrift Osbourne. Richard Holmes, in an influential reading of *Travels*, notes Stevenson's reference to the donkey Modestine, reminding him of "a lady of my acquaintance who had formerly loaded me with kindness, and this actually increased my horror of my cruelty" (Stevenson 1992, 141). Holmes points out that Stevenson's journey in the Cevennes began in the month that Fanny returned to California, apparently terminating her fledgling romance with the author. Indeed, for Holmes the journey "brought out his intense sexual loneliness and longing for Fanny Osbourne" (Holmes 1996, 56). Holmes also argues that Stevenson censored his own journal for publication, "deleted or generalized the amorous reflections that were originally written with Fanny in mind" (64).

Yet Stevenson's role in the narrative is not that of heterosexual lover, but of the controller of Modestine's sexuality, as we witness when she meets another donkey: "I had to separate the pair and beat down their young romance with a renewed and feverish bastinado" (Stevenson 1992, 141). The phallic symbol of the "bastinado" suggests that Stevenson – like Modestine's previous owner, from whom he tries to distance himself – "had a name […] for brutally misusing the ass" (136). The sodomitic implications of "misusing the ass" are hard to ignore, and Stevenson's guilt is palpable in the term "horror" and his prayer that "God forbid […] that I should brutalise this innocent creature" (139). Despite the sexually proper associations of her name, Modestine has the power to invoke forbidden desires in Stevenson, and his repeated punishment of her is at once a displacement and acting out of those impulses. Stevenson's focus of his violence on Modestine's "rear" (138) or "stern-works" (139) indicate the sodomitic aspects of this desire, and he notes his "secret shame" (138) at his conduct.

Later in the narrative, Stevenson introduces and curiously identifies with the notorious "Beast of Gévaudan" – a legendary wolf in the Cevennes that preys on women and children. In some ways reflecting Stevenson's own flight from conventional heterosexual domesticity, the Beast becomes an object of admiration for the young author: "What a career was his! He lied ten months at free quarters in Gévaudan and Vivarais: he ate women and children" (Stevenson 1992, 150). Stevenson, himself at the beginning of what he hopes will be a great "career," admires the beast's "free quarters" to roam the landscape, trampling or destroying the weaker beings that stand in its path. As Mr Hyde embodies the suppressed queer desires of Victorian patriarchy – the unspeakable impulses that bind the clubbable men together in shared secrecy – so the Beast reminds us of Stevenson's outlaw status, and his sense (anticipating Jekyll's) that his bond with the Beast – which proves to be "a common wolf" (150) – may be permanent.

Such uncanny associations between Stevenson and bestial impulses return us to the anxious appeal of Symonds to Stevenson in his letter about Jekyll, with which we began this essay. Symonds's letter expresses the concern of a secret homosexual about the protection of his own identity, but also a fear that Stevenson may have entered dangerous territory in exploring "the abysmal deeps of personality." As Harman notes, "Symonds was clearly also shocked by how self-revealing Stevenson had been in his 'strange case'-history" (Harman 2005, 214). This solicitous concern of one man for another – "Jekyll seems to me capable of loosening the last threads of self-control in one who should read it" (Symonds 1969, 121) – may be less significant as a fear of recognition and exposure, than as an eloquent expression of a desired intimacy between men that evades compulsory heterosexuality. Throughout his career – in his writings, his travels, and his friendships – Stevenson discovered forms and techniques with which to articulate a dissident view of Victorian gender roles and sexual desires, while also forging a profound challenge to the conventional forms and moral assumptions of Victorian narrative. In this respect, the "queerness" of Stevenson is ultimately textual no less than sexual.

Works Cited

Buckton, Oliver S. *Cruising with Robert Louis Stevenson: Travel, Narrative, and the Colonial Body*. Athens: Ohio University Press, 2007.
Butler, Judith. *Gender Trouble. Feminism and the Subversion of Identity*. New York: Routledge, 1999.
Craft, Christopher. *Another Kind of Love: Male Homosexual Desire in English Discourse, 1850-1920*. Berkeley: University of California Press, 1994.
Foucault, Michel. *The History of Sexuality. An Introduction. Volume 1*. Trans. Robert Hurley. New York: Vintage, 1980.
Freud, Sigmund. "The Uncanny." *The Norton Anthology of Theory and Criticism*. 2nd ed. Ed. Vincent B. Leitch. New York: Norton, 2010. 824-841.
Furneaux, Holly. *Queer Dickens: Erotics, Families, Masculinities*. Oxford: Oxford University Press, 2009.
Harman, Claire. *Robert Louis Stevenson: A Biography*. London: HarperCollins, 2005.
Holmes, Richard. *Footsteps: Adventures of a Romantic Biographer*. New York: Vintage, 1996.
Maixner, Paul. *Robert Louis Stevenson: The Critical Heritage*. London: Routledge and Kegan Paul, 1981.
Parfet, Ralph. "Violence in the South Seas: Stevenson, the Eye, and Desire." *Robert Louis Stevenson: Writer of Boundaries*. Eds. Richard Ambrosini and Richard Dury. Madison: University of Wisconsin Press, 2006. 190-198.
Sedgwick, Eve Kosofsky. *Between Men: English Literature and Male Homosocial Desire*. New York: Columbia University Press, 1985.
—. *Epistemology of the Closet*. Berkeley: University of California Press, 1990.
Showalter, Elaine. *Sexual Anarchy: Gender and Culture at the Fin de Siècle*. New York: Penguin, 1990.
Stevenson, Robert Louis. *Prince Otto and The Wrong Box*. 1889. The Works of Robert Louis Stevenson. Pentland ed. Vol. 7. London: Cassell, 1907.
—. *Travels with a Donkey in the Cevennes and Selected Travel Writings*. 1879. Ed. Emma Letley. New York: Oxford University Press, 1992.
—. *South Sea Tales*. 1893. Ed. Roslyn Jolly. New York: Oxford University Press, 1996a.
—. *The Master of Ballantrae*. 1889. London: Penguin, 1996b.
—. *Kidnapped, or the Lad with the Silver Button*. 1886. Ed. Barry Menikoff. New York: Modern Library, 2001.
—. *Strange Case of Dr Jekyll and Mr Hyde*. 1886. Ed. Katherine Linehan. New York: Norton, 2003.
— and Lloyd Osbourne. *The Wrong Box*. 1892. Oxford: Oxford University Press, 1995.
Symonds, John Addington. *The Letters of John Addington Symonds*. Vol. 3. 1885-1893. Eds. Herbert M. Shueller and Robert L. Peters. Detroit: Wayne State University Press, 1969.
Weeks, Jeffrey. *Coming Out: Homosexual Politics in Britain from the Nineteenth Century to the Present*. Rev ed. London: Quartet, 1990.

EMMA DYMOCK, Edinburgh

A Gaelic Antisyzygy? Philosophical Idealism and Materialism in the Poetry of Sorley MacLean

In the introduction to "An Cuilithionn," in *O Choille gu Bearradh/From Wood to Ridge: Collected Poems*, Sorley MacLean makes the following statement:

> The first two parts of the poem ["An Cuilithionn"] were made by June 1939, when I was closest to Communism, although I never accepted the whole of Marxist philosophy, as I could never resolve the idealist-materialist argument. I regarded philosophical materialists as generally more idealistic morally than philosophical idealists. (MacLean 1989, 63)

Although this statement refers specifically to "An Cuilithionn," which explores the history and culture of (Gaelic) Scotland and the broader European spectrum against the backdrop of communist-inspired political radicalism, it could apply not only to much of MacLean's work from the late 1930s, but also to later poems from the 1970s and beyond. There is certainly a convincing argument for the idealist-materialist quandary underpinning many of MacLean's poetic themes and motivations. In this one statement there lies the essence of MacLean's poetry, with its oppositional forces and strong sense of soul-searching. This acknowledgement of his difficulty with the idealist-materialist debate could be viewed as a significant statement of an integral part of the development of his belief system.

This article seeks to show that the idealist-materialist issue is a major aspect of MacLean's work and that it can be connected to the philosophical perspectives of other modern Scottish writers, such as Hugh MacDiarmid and Lewis Grassic Gibbon, and to the wider field of literature and politics within the context of the inter-war period and beyond. An outline will be provided regarding what MacLean meant generally by the idealist-materialist argument and some of the ways in which this argument manifests itself in the poet's work will be highlighted. It will be suggested that the struggle to resolve these opposing philosophies is inherently personal for MacLean and may even lead to a new interpretation of his own unique poetic-philosophical system.

1. Materialism and Idealism in Scottish/Gaelic Contexts

Philosophical materialism and philosophical idealism are the two opposing beliefs upon which much of philosophy is based. The Marxist strain of philosophical materialism, encompassing both historical and dialectical materialism, would undoubtedly have been the most familiar to MacLean and other writers of his generation. Hugh MacDiarmid gave dialectics a distinctly Scottish flavour when he introduced the "Gaelic Idea" and the "Caledonian Antisyzygy" into his poetry. The "Caledonian Antisyzygy" was originally discussed by G. Gregory Smith in *Scottish Literature: Character and Influence* (1919), in which he describes the duelling polarities existing within one entity as being typical of the Scottish psyche, with all of its geographical, religious and literary contradictions. MacDiarmid continued this theme and added to it with his "Gaelic Idea," which was envisioned as a dynamic myth like Dostoevsky's "Russian Idea." The "Gaelic Idea" was a cultural and creative ideal in which free reign would be given to a "national genius which is capable of countless manifestations at absolute variance with each other, yet confined within the limited infinity of the adjective 'Scottish'" (MacDiarmid 1931, 152).[1] Unashamedly idealist in terms of his poetic philosophy, MacDiarmid had been influenced by the ideas circulated in *The New Age* periodical (1907-1922). Its editor, A. R. Orage, believed in the potential of human consciousness, which could be expanded through acts of the imagination. He conceived the human mind to be "a rotating and revolving sphere" and human thought as subject "to the tyranny of opposites" and "the inherent duality of the human mind" (McCulloch and Matthews 2011, 55-56). MacDiarmid explored his Gaelic Idea in conjunction with the symbol of the serpent, Cencrastus, in *To Circumjack Cencrastus* (1930), in which he builds up a cultural and creative ideal, offering a "duality between transcendent escape from worldly hindrance and the infinite multiplicity of life" (McCulloch and Matthews 2011, 64).

If "An Cuilithionn" is read in this context, it becomes clear that MacLean has a firm grasp of MacDiarmid's particularly Caledonian strain of dialectics. In Part VI of "An Cuilithionn" there is a case for the imagery of the wheel of fortune (also an image often associated with the Gaelic panegyric code[2]) being a symbol of dialectics, sensing that cyclical movement will result in change – "Thèid a' chuibhle mun cuairt/ is tionnda'idh gu buaidh an càs."[3] However, perhaps even more convincing is the direct reference to MacDiarmid's Cencrastus, a symbolic serpent embodying the tension between reality and transcendence outside worldly experience, in Part VII:

> Thogadh às a' mhuir an uilebheist
> 's chuireadh i air àird a' Chuilithinn;
> bha i cearclach an àm ruagaidh
> a-mach à doimhne nan cuantan,
> ach a-nise tha i dìreach […].[4]

In a typescript of the poem this sea monster was footnoted with a reference to MacDiarmid's Cencrastus (MacLean, MS 29559 f.98), although this was left out of the poem when it was finally published. If, as McCulloch and Matthews have recently suggested, the point of MacDiarmid's serpent was to leave behind the contrasts and dialectical oppositions of *A Drunk Man Looks at the Thistle* (1926) in favour of transcendence, on a plane of pure beauty and pure music (64), there is every possibility that MacLean's use of this symbol, and its transformation from curled to straight, hints at his own attempt to transcend this dialectical struggle in his poetry.

---

[1] The Idealist-Materialist quandary can be viewed in conjunction with the 'Caledonian Antisyzygy' because of the way that the contradiction inherent in it cannot be separated. This particularly Scottish/Gaelic strain of the idealist-materialist quandary clearly manifests itself in the work of writers such as MacDiarmid and MacLean.

[2] The Panegyric Code is the system of rhetoric in traditional Gaelic verse, which contained common themes and motifs that would have been familiar to poets, patrons and a wider Gaelic audience. The repetition of specific motifs allowed for the poetry to contain a storehouse of meaning which could be easily accessed by those with knowledge of the tradition. For a detailed discussion of the Gaelic Panegyric Code, see MacInnes (2006, 265-319).

[3] "The wheel will go round/ and distress will turn to victory." (MacLean 2011, 400-401)

[4] "The monster has been lifted out of the sea,/ and put on the summit of the Cuillin;/ it was coiled when it was routed/ out of the depths of the oceans,/ but now it is straight." (Maclean 2011, 406-407)

This same struggle and the struggle of opposites can also be viewed as a much wider issue for Scottish writers on the lead up to World War II and beyond, and should not be viewed as only relating to the work of MacDiarmid and MacLean. The influence of cultural nationalism, the growth of fascism and communism, and the rise in the awareness of economic and social struggle from within Scotland, with the unfulfilled promise of a 'land fit for heroes' following World War I, meant that Scottish writers could not fail to engage with a myriad of concerns and issues. It is perhaps unsurprising that there emerged a jostling of contraries – on a political level there was the manifestation of this in the permitting of membership to more than one political party at a time. Thus, MacDiarmid, among others, could be a member of both the Communist Party and the Scottish National Party (this continued until 1948, when the SNP changed their rules of membership). In literature, this dialectical quandary appears in Willa Muir's *Imagined Corners* (1931), in which the theme of divided or multiple selves is explored in the characters of Elise Mütze and Elizabeth Shand, while Lewis Grassic Gibbon's Chris Guthrie in *Sunset Song* (1932) speaks of the "two Chrisses there were that fought for her heart and tormented her" (32), and indeed, the whole of *A Scots Quair* (1946) can be viewed through the lens of the polarity of idealism and materialism, with the opposing ideologies of Christianity and Marxism, and the differing rural and urban mindsets coming into play. Likewise, Neil Gunn (incidentally, another writer committed to finding a balance between the ideals of nationalism and socialism) in *The Silver Darlings* (1941) successfully tackles what would seemingly appear to be opposing themes, such as the idealist notion of the 'eternal hero,' with the more materialist social concerns of the clearances and the herring fishing industry. MacLean's work is often praised for its oppositional force and energy, symbolised through his sense of love and duty in many of the poems in *Dàin do Eimhir* (1943). However, I want to propose that the oppositional forces of love and duty are actually symptomatic of a much larger dilemma in his work, which is shaped by the idealist-materialist debate and his concept of his role as a poet in relation to this. Some of MacLean's poems are easier to decipher in this context than others. The likes of "Calbharaigh" and "Ban-Ghàidheal" are inherently materialist in their outlook of the injustices of the world and the oppressive influences which stunt the poor and disenfranchised. In "Ban-Ghàidheal" MacLean levels accusations at the Church and questions the economic circumstances that have put a Highland woman in a state of poverty (MacLean 2011, 16-17), and in "Calbharaigh" he makes it clear that he is not looking towards Calvary but on the places in his own country in which there is suffering:

> Chan eil mo shùil air Calbharaigh
> no air Betlehem an àigh
> ach air cùil ghrod an Glaschu
> far bheil an lobhadh fàis,
> agus air seòmar an Dùn Èideann,
> seòmar bochdainn 's cràidh,
> far a bheil an naoidhean creuchdach
> ri aonagraich gu bhàs.[5]

---

[5] "My eye is not on Calvary/ nor on Bethlehem the Blessed,/ but on a foul smelling backland in Glasgow,/ where life rots as it grows;/ and on a room in Edinburgh,/ a room of poverty and pain,/ where the diseased infant/ writhes and wallows till death." (MacLean 2011, 20-21)

One of the underlying messages in this poem is that those who begin life in poverty often do not have the chances to bring themselves out of this situation. MacLean was undoubtedly influenced not only by his reading of 19th century Highland history as a narrative of oppression, but also by the more present influence of economic crisis, as viewed during and after his student days in the urban context of Edinburgh. "Calbharaigh" can also be interpreted as anti-religious: it is a direct dismissal of Christ in favour of highlighting the suffering of the masses and, on another level, it is also a rejection of 'spiritual' suffering and heroism, countered with a portrayal of suffering more akin to social realism. In the case of MacLean's "Calbharaigh," the materialist wins against the idealist. This is also the case in many of his war poems such as "Curaidhean," in which the 'hero' is the antithesis of the Gaelic heroes of old in panegyric poetry. The everyday horrors of war are revealed and the 'hero' is viewed as a pawn in the game of war, an ordinary soldier whose death means very little in the grand scheme of things:

> Cha do chuireadh crois no meadal
> ri uchd no ainm no g' a chàirdean:
> cha robh a bheag dhe fhòirne maireann,
> 's nan robh cha bhiodh am facal làidir;[6]

Likewise, in "Glac a' Bhàis" it is the circumstances surrounding the soldier's death which take on the real significance – MacLean takes a materialist stance when he reveals that circumstances (in this case, the ambitions of Fascist and Nazi leaders) have put this soldier where he is, and not some spiritual motive of self-sacrifice for a higher cause (MacLean 2011, 206-207).

However, it should be noted that MacLean does not always so readily reject self-sacrificial heroes. The individual heroes in "An Cuilithionn" often take centre stage and the roll call of heroes by Clio, the Muse of history, in Part VI of "An Cuilithionn," succeeds in lending these figures (some of whom are from the very recent past) a mythological license, sanctioning the idealist belief that an individual is somehow imbued with the power of heroism, which exists down through the ages, irrespective of material circumstances. His translation into Gaelic of Hugh MacDiarmid's "If there are bounds to any man" in Part V of "An Cuilithionn" (MacLean 2011, 386-387) also seems to hint at an acceptance of intellectual elitism, that some men will rise higher than others in their quest for heroism and self-fulfilment:

> 'S ma tha mhòr-chuid gu fangte teann,
> a' leantainn slighe crìon,
> 's e 'n leisg fhann fhèin as coireach air,
> an lùths cha dhearbh iad fìor.[7]

This belief in some sort of eternal heroism, in direct opposition with his belief in a more socialist, realistic heroism based on actual circumstance, is something which MacLean shares with MacDiarmid, who also attempted to align the materialist and idealist heroic struggle. Scott Lyall has drawn attention to MacDiarmid's stance, cit-

---

6 "No cross or medal was put to his/ chest or to his name or to his family;/ there were not many of his troop alive,/ and if there were their word would not be strong." (MacLean 2011, 204-205)

7 "And if most men are close curtailed/ and keep a petty grove/ 'tis their own sloth that is to blame,/ their powers they will not prove." (MacLean 2011, 386-387)

ing a letter to Iain Crichton Smith in 1967, in which MacDiarmid defends his communist position:

> I am not really concerned that many people do not think me "a Communist in any ordinary sense of the word"! They are hopelessly mistaken. So are all those who think Communism is concerned with "ordinary humanity" [...] least of all with humanitarianism. They forget that our objective is "to change human nature." (Lyall 2011, 80)

MacDiarmid was not alone in his hope in a communist-spiritual utopia, a union of opposites encompassing the materialist and the mystic. Much of the communist imagery coming out of the Soviet Union after the Revolution did not correspond with philosophical materialism as much as the Soviet leaders would perhaps have liked – artists and poets known as the "god-builders" often portrayed Lenin as a god-like figure, willing to sacrifice himself for the good of the masses. After an assassination attempt on Lenin, the Soviet propagandists were particularly susceptible to idealist themes of the eternal hero and, on the sixth anniversary of the Revolution, Lenin was described as "[n]ot only the name of a beloved leader; [...] Lenin is the suffering for an idea; it is the bleeding of the proletariat; it is the struggle under the most intolerable conditions [...]" (Tumarkin 1997, 83).

Closer to home, before the 1916 Easter Rising in Ireland, the socialist James Connolly, who was certainly the least poetically-driven of the leaders of the Rising, had a moment of idealistic fervour when he said:

> Without the slightest trace of irreverence, but in all due humility and awe, we recognise that of all of us as of mankind before Calvary, it may truly be said – "without the Shedding of Blood there is no redemption." (Howell 1986, 143)

Of course, it should be remembered that James Connolly may have been an ardent socialist, but he was also a catholic operating within a climate of strong nationalism. It may have been virtually impossible for him not to be affected by a heady mix of religion and idealism. Can the same thing be said for MacLean, who was, after all, a poet and not a political leader? It may be that the influence of Free Presbyterianism in his upbringing and his subsequent, ardent rejection of this secederism made him even more suspicious of any tendency to make a 'religion' out of secular, political figures. However, when he writes that "I regarded philosophical materialists as generally more idealistic morally than philosophical idealists" (MacLean 1989, 63), he may be criticizing himself as well as others - there can be no doubt that there are possible dangers in mixing idealism with politics in poetry. But perhaps the most shocking manifestation of MacLean's single-minded hope for the advancement of a political ideal is reserved for his non-poetic writing. In a letter to Douglas Young on 22 February 1941 he struggles to come to terms with the concept of suffering:

> I myself can only work it out by thinking that the sum of all human suffering is not greater than the suffering of one individual, that hence human suffering in wars does not matter more than the inevitable suffering even of a comparative few and that therefore the evolutionary urge must work itself out even with the deaths of thousands of kulaks or of western European people of high or low place. (MacLean, Acc 6419)

This "evolutionary urge" is pure Marxist rhetoric, with connotations of historical and dialectical materialism. MacLean's politics cannot be easily explained away as a product of 1940s revulsion at the fascist/Nazi threat – as late as the early 1970s, MacLean composed a poem entitled "Stàilin," until recently unpublished, which appears to expound the same sort of belief in the moral value of sacrifice and suffering for the greater good:

> Ach their càch
> gu robh do thuigse
> thar tuigse gach aoin eile,
> [...]
> gun do mhurt thu an-dràsta
> air sgàth màireach 's an earar.[8]

The poem also lists Stalin's crimes, and the line "Ach their càch" ("but others say") attempts to provide some distance and objectivity, but the underlying implications of the poem are nevertheless inescapable. In a letter to MacLean on 10 June 1943, Young suggests that the reason for MacLean's extreme views in relation to Stalinism is actually due to his exposure to Secederism in his younger days:

> [...] you say "Socialism was important in casting out just what there was of Secederism." I am far from maintaining that you were ever a converted Seceder. All I note is that you were early exposed intensely to a Dualist view of the world. Now the ancient Greeks didn't go in for Dualism, it is more an Old Testament analysis. The bearing of this on politics is that a Dualist-conditioned mind will see a fundamental antithesis Capitalism-Socialism, Proletariat-Bourgeois etc where a mind less strongly so conditioned may see far more than two conflicting forces. (Young, MS 29540 f. 77)

Young's analysis raises the intriguing question of whether this dualistic worldview makes it theoretically impossible for MacLean's opposing beliefs to reach any form of synthesis or transcendence. It is perhaps astute of Young to go back to MacLean's upbringing, a time when his personal views were being shaped, in order to track MacLean's philosophical and psychological development. Unfortunately, MacLean's subsequent letters to Young never directly address these theories, but it is tempting to read MacLean's personal philosophic system in the light of the influence of a Free Presbyterian-Old Testament structure proposed by Young. The danger with dualism is that it becomes too restrictive and it is only when these alternatives are looked at together, rather than separately, that dialectical synthesis can take place. A tendency to lean towards a dualistic view may have been why MacLean found it so hard to align materialism and idealism in a way that would have satisfied him. It could be argued that the only way for MacLean to 'transcend' his dualism, or to attempt to 'square his circle,' was to come to terms with the different parts of his self on a metaphysical level.

2. Fragmenting the Self: The Role of the Poet

In *Dàin do Eimhir* XXIX, MacLean's poetry takes on a life of its own, separate from the physical person who composes it, and his unwritten poems are envisioned as wolves chasing inspiration in the form of Eimhir across an eternal landscape (MacLean 2011, 132-133). One reason for MacLean finding it possible to turn his poetry

---

8 "But others say/ your understanding/ surpassed all other men's, /.../ that you murdered now/ in the interests of tomorrow and the day after tomorrow." (MacLean 2011, 442-443)

into something with a spirit of its own is that MacLean may have felt that *Dàin do Eimhir* came to him so easily, almost as an unconscious process (he claimed that several of these poems came to him fully formed from dreams, see Acc 6419). Christopher Whyte has described it in similar terms: "one is left with the impression that his conscious, politically engaged self was busy with "An Cuilithionn," the kind of poetry he felt he ought to be writing, while the Eimhir sequence [...] emerged almost of its own accord" (67). Therefore, it can be no coincidence that within *Dàin do Eimhir* the idealist-materialist quandary arises. He exhibits discomfort at his idealism in *Dàin do Eimhir* XXXII, when he appears to yearn for a composition more fitting of socialist realism or, at the very least, the kind of poetry "he felt he ought to be writing" (Whyte 2004, 67):

> Sgatham le faobhar-rinn gach àilleachd
> a chuir do bhòidhche 'nam bhàrdachd,
> 's dèanam dàin cho lom aognaidh
> ri bàs Liebknecht no daorsa.⁹

However, Eimhir's face continues to haunt him, much like the idealism that he goes to such lengths to eschew. Thus, in what could be seen as another aspect of his view of the role of the poet, MacLean also believes that he can give Eimhir immortality through his poems in a reciprocal exchange in which she also gives him inspiration. This immortalisation of Eimhir obviously cannot be a physical preservation of the woman. Instead, he praises specific aspects of the real woman – her face, her hair and, most interestingly, her spirit, which can be accessed through her face in much the same way that the idealist philosophers such as Fichte speculated that the spirit 'speaks' through the physical body.

MacLean's poetic role is not limited to immortalising his muse – he also attempts to immortalise and celebrate his own tradition. As a poet composing in Gaelic, MacLean is aware of the rich heritage which is accessible to him. While his admiration for Màiri Mhór nan Orain could no doubt be viewed as having a socialist agenda (many of Màiri Mhór's songs were, after all, based on material problems and injustices of the day), MacLean seems to be more aware of his place in connection with poets from the past rather than the actual content and concerns of these poets. In "An Cuilithionn" he writes that he was

> Sgitheanach ri taobh Màiri Mòire.
> Ach chan inns mi dha spiorad làidir
> Nach tàinig tilleadh air an tràigh ud;¹⁰

MacLean is clearly following the attitude to the literature of the past which T. S. Eliot discusses in his seminal article "Tradition and the Individual Talent" (13-22), but his respect of tradition goes beyond this to something which can only be described as a spiritual affinity to his tradition and landscape. In "Hallaig," his connection with his own people, his ancestors, is tangible. He writes that the MacLeans and MacLeods are still in Hallaig and that "chunnacas na mairbh beò"("the dead have

---

9   "Let me lop off with sharp blade every grace/that your beauty put in verse,/and make poems as bare and chill/ as Liebknecht's death or slavery." (MacLean 2011, 134-135)
10 "a Skyeman by the side of the great Mary./ But I will not tell her strong spirit/ that no turning has come on that ebb-tide." (MacLean 2011, 372-373)

been seen alive") (MacLean 2011, 232-233). This conviction that traces of human life, of spirit, can still inhabit a landscape in some shape or form is idealistic because it exhibits a belief that the spirit needs no body, that it can survive as an entity without the confines of the physical. Even more tellingly, "Hallaig" ends with MacLean's conviction that the miracle of this continuation of life, symbolised by the deer, is dependent on his own consciousness: "chan fhaighear lorg air fhuil rim bheò" ("his blood will not be traced while I live") (MacLean 2011, 234-235).[11]

MacLean appears to be acting as a spokesperson for the masses or, at the very least, as a voice of his imagined community in one breath and then, in the next instance, he moves towards a more exclusive artistic vision. Within his poetry it seems impossible to trace any kind of coherent psychological timeline at all – often in the same poem, or at least in the same period of composition, he can appear to favour both idealism and materialism. The dislocation of aspects of the self is not restricted to Eimhir with the repetitive haunting of her face, hair and spirit. MacLean also provides many examples in his poetry of the separation between different aspects of his own self. In *Dàin do Eimhir* XXII he writes:

> Choisich mi cuide ri mo thuigse
> a-muigh ri taobh a' chuain;
> bha sinn còmhla ach bha ise
> a' fuireach tiotan bhuam.[12]

This sense of being in motion but of being a little separated from one part of his self is remarkably similar to the last section of "An Cuilithionn," in which MacLean views "am falbhan" ("the journeying one") on the mountain:

> Cò seo, cò seo oidhche chinne?
> Chan eil ach samhla an spioraid,
> anam leis fhèin a' falbh air slèibhtean,
> ag iargain a' Chuilithinn 's e 'g èirigh.[13]

This is an extremely personal and intimate way to end a poem which focuses on the plight of the masses. The repetition of the question "cò seo?" ("who is this?") suggests a questioning of identity. In both these poems, the independent movement of separate parts of MacLean's self brings to mind Julia Kristeva's theory of the self in process. Kristeva has claimed that a person is not simply a unity but is constantly called into question – there is no such thing as a 'fixed' identity. Instead, identity is unstable, being constantly in process, and both suffering and creativity are what comprises these moments of instability. A person is therefore constantly trying to achieve a sense of stability, which may be found by identifying with certain roles (Kristeva 1989, 129). Philosophical materialism and idealism become extremely personal in MacLean's poetry. This philosophical quandary is not just theoretical for MacLean, but actually has serious effects on the type of poetry he produced and, indeed, on the type of poet he viewed himself to be. Kristeva has said that it is possible "that in aesthetic creation we occupy several positions" and role-identity theorists have also put

---

11 I am indebted to Christopher Whyte for his reading of this aspect of "Hallaig" (Whyte 2004, 74).
12 "I walked with my reason/ out beside the sea./ We were together but it was/ keeping a little distance from me." (MacLean 2011, 124-125)
13 "Who is this, who is this in the night of mankind?/ It is only the ghost of the spirit,/ a soul alone going on mountains,/ longing for the Cuillin that is rising." (MacLean 2011, 414-415)

forward the idea that a person can have different identities at any given time, depending on to whom they are relating (132). In his role as poet, MacLean accessed both the philosophical materialist and the philosophical idealist within himself, but this was not an easy opposition to attempt to align, especially during the specific point in his personal history when MacLean was standing between political commitment to communism and the commitment to his role as modernist poet within a Gaelic context.

In many ways, MacLean was always a poet who was destined to balance extremes and to exist on borders. By choosing to compose often distinctly 'unGaelic' poems in Gaelic, and by making the choice to be open to a myriad of influences from his own Gaelic tradition and the wider European literary field, MacLean made it clear from the outset that he was going to defy categorisation, regardless of how literary history now views him in retrospect. The point in history in which MacLean's poetry first came to fruition may have been a time of extremes, in which the political situation called for a 'black or white'/'all or nothing' approach, but this was also the period in which MacLean and his friends and acquaintances (MacDiarmid included) felt it was entirely possible to be simultaneously a member of the Communist Party and the Scottish National Party. MacLean inhabited more than one world in many senses – while he did not give himself the luxury of a pseudonym in the style of Hugh MacDiarmid and Lewis Grassic Gibbon (which must have opened up the potential for even more freedom for multiple voices), he was nevertheless prepared to admit, in poetic terms, that more than one aspect of his self existed and had to be given voice. The psychoanalyst D. W. Hamlyn has written the following, which may shed some light on fragmentary poetic voices and standpoints:

> A person is not a static thing. If there are some constant things about us [...] we are [...] changing entities with both a history and a future. For this reason alone there can be no complete story about what has to be known for adequate self knowledge. (Hamlyn 1977, 196)

The one thing that both philosophical idealism and materialism share within the history of their theory is dialectics – the movement of oppositions which change and transform. MacLean never remained static in his poetry, perhaps because, rather in spite of, not being able to resolve the idealist-materialist debate. Ivana Markova has drawn attention to the theorist K. Kosik's idea of humans as journeyers who wander in the world and who, through their own active transformation of the world, eventually recognise themselves (Markova 1987, 68). Connections can be drawn between this idea and MacLean's image of "am falbhan" ("the journeying one") in "An Cuilithionn" – by exploring both realist and more mystical figures, often within the same poem, MacLean recognised both sides of himself in these figures, as well as the kind of poetry he wanted to write. He could not create a synthesis between Lenin and Christ in "An Cuilithionn" (372-373) any more than he could find transcendence for both sides of his own personality, but at some point, perhaps as late as the composition of the introduction to the 1989 "An Cuilithionn," he must have recognised and accepted that his poetry and his own character needed both these figures, both the brain and the heart, intellect and love. While he did not resolve the idealist-materialist argument in philosophical terms, he did resolve it for himself in poetic terms. The proof of this can be found in his essay "Realism in Gaelic Poetry:"

> The dynamic of poetry is never intellectual contemplation alone, and intellectuality or merely sense impression must be suffused with emotion […]. As a result this fusion of intellectuality and emotion in varying degrees, a feeling of totality, which is simply emotional and intellectual satisfaction, is imparted by great poetry to a degree that philosophy or science cannot impart […]. (MacLean 1985, 15-16)

MacLean was a poet of commitment, but his main commitment was neither to a specific materialist political vision, nor to the love of a woman or an ideal. It was a commitment to emotion, in all its forms, which ensured that MacLean's idealist-materialist quandary was constantly being questioned and resolved in what could be described as the cause and effect of a personal-poetic dialectic of creativity.

Works Cited

Eliot, T. S. *Selected Essays by T. S. Eliot*. London: Faber and Faber, 1951.
Gibbon, Lewis Grassic. *Sunset Song*. London: Jarrolds Publishers, 1932.
—. *A Scots Quair: A Trilogy of Novels*. London: Jarrolds Publishers, 1946.
Gunn, Neil. *The Silver Darlings*. London: Faber, 1941.
Hamlyn, D.W. *The Theory of Knowledge*. London: MacMillan, 1977.
Howell, David. *A Lost Left: Three Studies in Socialism and Nationalism*. Chicago: University of Chicago Press, 1986.
Kristeva, Julia. "A Question of Subjectivity – An Interview." *Modern Literary Theory: A Reader*. Eds. Philip Rice and Patricia Waugh. London: E. Arnold, 1989. 128-134.
Lyall, Scott. "MacDiarmid, Communism and the Poetry of Commitment." *The Edinburgh Companion to Hugh MacDiarmid*. Eds. Scott Lyall and Margery Palmer McCulloch. Edinburgh: Edinburgh University Press, 2011. 67-81.
MacDiarmid, Hugh. "The Caledonian Antisyzygy and the Gaelic Idea." *The Modern Scot* 2.2 (1931): 141-154.
MacInnes, John. "The Panegyric Code in Gaelic Poetry and its Historical Background." *Dùthchas nan Gàidheal: Selected Essays of John MacInnes*. Ed. Micheal Newton. Edinburgh: Birlinn, 2006. 265-319.
MacLean, Sorley. *Letters from Sorley MacLean to Douglas Young*, 1940-1972. Acc 6419 Box 38b. Edinburgh: National Library of Scotland.
—. *Manuscripts and Typescripts of MacLean's Translation of "An Cuilithionn,"* 1939. MS 29559. National Library of Scotland, Edinburgh.
—. "Realism in Gaelic Poetry." *Ris a'Bhruthaich: The Criticism and Prose Writings of Sorley MacLean*. Ed. William Gillies. Stornoway: Acair, 1985. 15-47.
—. *O Choille gu Bearradh/From Wood to Ridge: Collected Poems*. Edinburgh: Carcanet/Birlinn, 1989.
—. *Dàin do Eimhir*. Ed. Christopher Whyte. Glasgow: Association for Scottish Literary Studies, 2002.
—. *Caoir Gheal Leumraich/ White Leaping Flame: Collected Poems*. Eds. Christopher Whyte and Emma Dymock. Edinburgh: Polygon, 2011.
Markova, Ivana. "Knowledge of the Self Through Interaction." *Self and Identity: Psychological Perspectives*. Eds. Krysia Yardley and Terry Honess. Chichester: John Wiley and Sons, 1987. 65-80.
McCulloch, Margery Palmer and Kirsten Matthews. "Transcending the Thistle in *A Drunk Man* and *Cencrastus*." *The Edinburgh Companion to Hugh MacDiarmid*.

Eds. Scott Lyall and Margery Palmer McCulloch. Edinburgh: Edinburgh University Press, 2011. 48-67.

Muir, Willa. *Imagined Corners*. London: M. Secker, 1931.

Smith, Gregory G. *Scottish Literature: Character and Influence*. London: MacMillan, 1919.

Tumarkin, Nina. *Lenin Lives: The Lenin Cult in Soviet Russia*. London: Harvard University Press, 1997.

Whyte, Christopher. *Modern Scottish Poetry*. Edinburgh: Edinburgh University Press, 2004.

Young, Douglas. *Letters from Douglas Young to Sorley MacLean*, 1940-1972. MS 29540. National Library of Scotland, Edinburgh.

Jetzt auch in englischer Sprache!

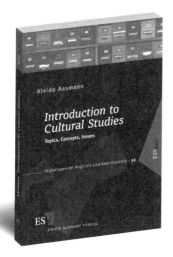

This volume is not only an introduction, but also an important study tool encouraging reader's own endeavours concerning the relationship between reading and major key questions of culture.

»This book by Aleida Assmann consistently surpasses a narrow definition of 'English Studies' and opens up new, fresh perspectives that enable fascinating views on current questions. The theme-centred, coherent and well written Introduction to Cultural Studies can be considered outstanding in every respect: it will take a permanent place among the introductions to English Literature and Cultural Studies.«

Till Kinzel

Introduction to Cultural Studies

Topics, Concepts, Issues

By Aleida Assmann

2012, 248 S., € (D) 17,80
ISBN 978-3-503-13716-9

Grundlagen der Anglistik und Amerikanistik, Band 36

Weitere Informationen:
www.ESV.info/978-3-503-13716-9

Einführung in die Kulturwissenschaft

Grundbegriffe, Themen, Fragestellungen

Von Aleida Assmann

3., neu bearb. Aufl. 2011, 264 S., € (D) 17,80
ISBN 978-3-503-12270-7

Grundlagen der Anglistik und Amerikanistik, Band 27

www.ESV.info/978-3-503-12270-7

ERICH SCHMIDT VERLAG
Auf Wissen vertrauen

Erich Schmidt Verlag GmbH & Co. KG · Genthiner Str. 30 G · 10785 Berlin
Tel. (030) 25 00 85-265 · Fax (030) 25 00 85-275 · ESV@ESVmedien.de · www.ESV.info

SCOTT HAMES, Stirling
Diasporic Narcissism: De-sublimating Scotland in Alice Munro and Alistair MacLeod

In the only sustained exploration of Scottish-Canadian literary relations, Elizabeth Waterston writes:

> The situation in each nation and in its literature seems to clarify that of the other. Here are two northern nations, ironic and sentimental, each quietly resentful of the stronger, more affluent neighbour lying south of the national border, indifferent to or unaware of the impact of its culture on others. Here are two sets of writers whose literary strategies and structures have been sharpened and maybe warped by northernness, the doubleness, the angular spareness of their heritage, and the pressure of alien alternatives. (Waterston 2001, 8-9)

Freud observed that nations with uncertain claims to separateness are liable to the "narcissism of small differences" (Freud 2002, 50-51). Here, Waterston hints that Scotland and Canada's small differences are largely the same, and gradually reconstitutes them as traces of filial provenance passed from parent to child. There is a continual slippage in *Rapt in Plaid* between historically contingent literary tastes and forms (c.g. John Buchan's discovery of an "already strong attachment to his kind of writing" in Canada, Waterston 2001, 9) and totalised national mentalities ("ironic and sentimental") which betoken a linear relation of heritage transfer, rather than a common positionality vis-à-vis "alien alternatives." The shared cultural condition begins as an exogenous parallel – tensions with the encroaching southern neighbour – but is briskly smuggled under the mail-order kilt, endogenised and essentialised. "When Scots immigrants came to Canada in the early 19th century, they brought Robert Burns's values with them, packed into their psyches, just as the volume of his poems was packed into their brass-bound sea trunks" (9). Affinities of circumstance have quickly become organic folkways, legible as family resemblances. The north-south "small differences" of these two countries are re-coded and narrativised within the east-west dynamic of diasporic transmission, estrangement and yearning.

Tracing the problem of Canadian identity "elsewhere," along settler folkways which bypass the influence of the United States, has been a recurring feature of efforts to construct a national imaginary. Accounting for the emotional power of Alistair MacLeod's fiction, his fellow Canadian novelist Jane Urquhart declares:

> We Canadians are, after all, a nation composed of people longing for a variety of abandoned homelands and the tribes that inhabited them, whether these be the distant homelands of our recent immigrants, the abducted homelands of our native peoples, the rural homelands vacated by the post-war migrations to the cities, or the various European or Asian homelands left behind by our earliest settlers. All of us have been touched in some way or another by this loss of landscape and of kin, and all of us are moved by the sometimes unidentifiable sorrow that accompanies such a loss. (Urquhart 2001, 37-38)

The very cosiness of this "we Canadians" universalism, and its glib erasure of the violence of invasion and nation-building, occasions a deep moral unease. A similar kinship-of-the-kinless motif plays a peripheral role in MacLeod's celebrated novel *No Great Mischief*. The central drama is preceded by a roadside tableaux in which Ontario fruit-pickers – "many of them are from the Caribbean and some of them are Mennonites from Mexico and some are French Canadians from New Brunswick and Quebec" – share in the archetypally Canadian tragedy of the Cape Breton MacDonalds: "This land is not their own" (MacLeod 1999, 1). The apparent inclusivity of this trope actually re-inscribes the centrality of white-settler dislocation to Canadian identity, while claiming for those same settlers an additional *frisson* of colonial injury, and compensatory claim to authenticity. We return to the itinerant fruit-pickers in the final pages of the novel, though now they recall not the transplanted Gaels of Nova Scotia but their coastal predecessors, "the native peoples who move across the land, harvesting" (253) – as well, incongruously, as "the tall and arrogant Masai" of Kenya, prospective victims of confinement "to certain 'homelands' which are really not their homes at all" (254). In a bravura twist, the "clannic remnant" (Nairn 2004, 54) at the centre of the novel turn out not to be settlers at all; their Highland heritage entitles them to perennial status as refugees and ethnic underdogs. This fudging nativism sweeps aside the historical complexity of *No Great Mischief*'s core identity-paradox, in which Canada is "won" from the French by ex-Jacobite Highland soldiers distrusted and exploited by their redcoat commanders. At the novel's close Calum MacDonald is in prison for the murder of a French-Canadian rival rendered allegorical by the novel's careful marshalling of such ironies. But in the final jarring pages they are elbowed out the window:

> In Kingston Penitentiary, Calum said, a disproportionate number of the prisoners were from the native population. In many cases they did not fully understand the language of those to whom they were entrusted and condemned. They would hang their woven dreamcatchers in the windows of their cells, he said. (254)

Cell-mates in a Canadian cultural space of universal displacement – one compounded but also clarified by the erasure of Quebecois identity – this is the emblematic scene by which MacLeod's fiction, abetted by responses such as Urquhart and Waterston's, re-routes anxieties of white Canadian identity via the emotional vocabulary of diasporic Scottishness. Cementing the pathos and longing of the Celtic diaspora as the fundamental and even "native" condition of Canadianness, this rhetoric dissolves the historical violence of colonisation and nation-building and presents it as a continuation of internal "British" conflict, already de-realised and assimilated to the realm of ballad and romance. The dreamcatcher in the cell window extends this logic to a pre-appropriated, "New Age" indigeneity, a symptom of the white containment it would seem to protest. And so, despite their trumpeted pre-eminence in Canadian nation-building (McGoogan 2010), the descendants of Scots settlers are restored as heirs to a gloriously suppressed traditional culture.

By now it will be clear that, far from mutually clarifying, I see such Scots-Canadian "recognitions" as a narcissistic attachment: an elective affinity with a national peer constructed, in the same gesture, as the orphan's lost parent, only part of whose inheritance the child is keen to reclaim. In the work of Alice Munro, residues of Scotland are coequal with the archival knowledge by which they are retrieved and reproduced; Scottishness may only be realised as narrative or verbal performance, and even then as one characterised by the deferral of presence.[1] By contrast, MacLeod's diasporic Scottishness is concrete and substantial, directly embodying a heritage of loss, betrayal and communion. In both writers' work we find a de-sublimation and release of – or release *from* – a legendary or ethnic Scottishness held to underpin but also upstage the insipid register of "civic," multicultural Canadianness.[2]

Munro, Scepticism and Textual Diaspora

Famously wry, we would not expect Alice Munro to find any straightforward nostalgic fulfilment in visiting the family homeland. But her disappointment is clear as she visits the Scottish Borders to research her semi-fictional family memoir *The View from Castle Rock*. Underwhelmed by the banality of the ancestral landscape (its brownness evokes "the hills around Calgary," Munro 2006, 5), and feeling "conspicuous, out of place," she writes:

> I was struck with a feeling familiar, I suppose, to many people whose history goes back to a country far away from the place where they grew up. I was a naïve North American, in spite of my stored knowledge. Past and present lumped together here made a reality that was commonplace and yet disturbing beyond anything I had imagined. (Munro 2006, 7)

A recurring pattern in Munro's "Scottish" writing is the Canadian storyteller's disappointment with the revealed drabness and unromance of "real" Scotland. The Ettrick landscape Munro is delighted to associate with "a story of Merlin – *Merlin* – being hunted down and murdered" is reduced in scale to the "twice-a-week Shoppers' Bus" by which she travels there from Selkirk (Munro 2006, 5). Invocations of the legendary are consistently deflated by first-hand tourist experience, itself marked by an ambivalent desire to soberly verify or disprove the informal archive of family tales and letters. The old country is a matter of belief and unbelief, recovered only via correspondence with the "stored knowledge" of texts.

It is impossible to ignore the resonance of the "real" authorial scenario which frames *The View From Castle Rock* with an earlier Munro story. "Hold Me Fast, Don't Let Me Pass" centres on the frustrated researches of Hazel, a Canadian widow visiting the Scottish Borders in search of the people and places of her dead husband's wartime reminiscences. We first encounter Hazel in a hotel lobby, making notes on the day's touristic researches. These notes are instantly subject to revision and correction, but not in the light of any felt experience with which they fail to tally; they are erroneous on the internal terms of history as a closed order of confirmed truths. Hazel mistakenly dates the Covenanters' victory at the Battle of Philiphaugh as 1945 instead of 1645, directly linking the tragic aura of this place to the era of her husband's wartime visit. The cancellation of this easy transposition of historical frames, trading one battle for another, is a recurring feature of the story. Even before we glimpse the character, we catch her editing her descriptive sketch of the area, policing her own embellishments,

---

1 For reasons of space Munro's story "Friend of My Youth" (1990) is not considered here, though it would repay a similar critical treatment.
2 Perhaps ironically, "the conceptual foundation of the Canadian idea of civility" is the deracinated category of Britishness of which the "Scots, historically, were the primary inventors and promoters" (Coleman 2006, 6). Daniel Coleman has noted the prominence of "the enterprising Scottish orphan" in settler fiction constructing "English Canadian" identity (81-127).

quelling a sense of unreality. Our most rounded image of Hazel finds her curiously at home in this posture of writerly groundlessness, both fraught and self-possessed: "she was a person you would not be surprised to find sitting by herself in a corner of the world where she didn't belong, writing things in a notebook to prevent the rise of panic" (Munro 1990, 75).

Hazel is disquieted by the refusal of this place to yield up the expected, faded signs of her husband's visit. "The problem was just the opposite of what she had expected. It was not that people had moved away and the buildings were gone and had left no trace. Just the opposite" (78). Locals from her husband's stories, including a well-preserved lover, are still "in place, right where they used to be" (80). Indeed the sameness and *presence* of this world is excessive; the Borderers do not live up to their reputation for "British" reserve, and are far from withholding (83). For her part, Hazel struggles to maintain her identity as Canadian: "So have you come over here looking for your roots?" asks Dudley, a fixture of the hotel bar. "He gave the word its most exaggerated American pronunciation. 'I am Canadian,' Hazel said quite pleasantly. 'We don't say "roots" that way'" (79). This small difference seems no more than a matter of accent, but verbal performance turns out to be central to authenticating a cultural identity rooted beyond the empirical domain of the notebook.

The teenage lover of Jack's stories, Antoinette, still works in the hotel but insists she does not remember Hazel's husband. As a consolation she takes her to the home of Jack's ancient relative and former landlady. Miss Dobie lives not in the storied idyllic farmhouse but a modern bungalow, "stuccoed, with stones set here and there in a whimsical suburban style" (91). A surprisingly intense emotionalism is contained by this unassuming exterior, which it becomes Hazel's task to uncover and bring to light. Miss Dobie proves unable to recollect Jack, but offers a recitation of the Borders ballad "Tam Lin." This tale of lost maidenhead and fairy bewitchment seems to unite the fabular and contemporary worlds, offering a cold commentary on the dormant love triangle Hazel has stumbled upon and perhaps reactivated. Antoinette shares the affections of Dudley with a young, gloriously red-haired woman who is Miss Dobie's live-in carer. Mother to Dudley's illegitimate child, and herself an orphan, Judy is a blaze of flamboyance among the crockery and patterned upholstery, but one kept in check by Antoinette's barrage of coded feminine reproaches throughout the visit. Boiling with fury at Antoinette's insults, and the personal judgement implied by Miss Dobie's choice of recital ("*gin ye lose your maidenhead / Ye'll ne"er get that agen!*," 99), Judy gives off an atavistic odour "that washing and deodorizing had made uncommon. It poured out hotly from between the girl's flushed breasts" (95). Here we seem to make direct, pungent contact with the suppressed passions of romantic Scotland, the folkway to the more personal recognition Hazel yearns for. Yet the essential Judy we encounter here is one generated by the ballad narrative, and the oblique cruelties of its performance.

On the journey back from Miss Dobie's, Antoinette points out the supposed scene of Tam Lin's escape from the Queen of the Fairies, but "the field was brown and soggy and surrounded by what looked like council housing" (98). This anti-Gothic puncturing of mystique figures both as loss and a form of relief. Just as Tam is released from supernatural bondage by the steadfastness of Jennet, his human lover, the balladic landscape is restored to a space of ordinary modern settlement – an exorcism itself cancelled when we learn, later, that Antoinette has pointed out the wrong brown field owing to a confusion of names. What "being there" expels from this place was never "there" to begin with, even on the doubtful terms of the folktale. What Hazel finds in Scotland is not the object or ground of her desire, but *tradition* as the ritual enactment of longing, deferral and recognition.

Later recognising the ballad from Hazel's description, Dudley seems to accept "Tam Lin" as master-text to his own romantic predicament: "he threw himself back in his chair, looking released, and lifted his head and started reciting" (100). Here, seemingly, is the fulfilment of Hazel's longed-for correspondence: Dudley incarnates Tam Lin, released from the fairy kingdom of the hotel by Jennet/Judy, but also embodies Jack, lover of Antoinette and suddenly attractive to her successor Hazel. These fragile recognitions, however, are sustained only by the memory and voice of the balladeer, whose verbal realisation of "stored knowledge" is a kind of magic. As in Miss Dobie's earlier performance, the Scottishness of Dudley's speech "thickens" and "broadens" as he conjures "Tam Lin"

> with style, in a warm, sad splendid male voice […]. Of course Dudley's style was old-fashioned, of course he mocked himself, a little. But that was only on the surface. This reciting was like singing. You could parade your longing without fear of making a fool of yourself. (101)

The narrative strangeness of the ballad and the potential ironies of its delivery are expelled from this hidden "depth," a flow of emotion that flushes away the question of sincerity itself. The coded displacements and correspondences of "Tam Lin" are de-sublimated in a pure release of romantic orality, a medium of personal expression and ethno-cultural communion beyond ridicule or historical judgment.

In *The View from Castle Rock* Munro is both cagey and fussy about the textual basis of her family saga, but insists that key elements are drawn directly from family letters, official documents and the writings of her ancestor James Hogg. Prominent in this work are tropes which internalise to Scotland the transatlantic fantasy which lingers in Hazel's peripheral vision. The vista of the book's title is a mysterious drunken prank or mistake, in which a male ancestor (Hogg's first cousin, James Laidlaw) claims that the view from Edinburgh Castle encompasses America rather than Fife:

> "Well the sea does not look so wide as I thought," said the man who had stopped staggering. "It does not look as if it would take you weeks to cross it."
> "It is the effect of the height we're on," said the man who stood beside Andrew's father. "The height we're on is making the width of it the less." […] "So there you are my lad and you have looked over at America," [James] said. "God grant you one day you will see it closer up and for yourself." (Munro 2006, 30)

Munro matches this domestication of the emigrant's unknowable destination with a comic acceleration of disillusionment and homesickness. Almost the moment James has led his family onto an emigrant ship bound for Quebec, after years of evangelising about America, the presence of "Black Highlanders" among his fellow passengers moves him to lament "Oh, that ever we left our native land!" (32). Andrew replies "We have not left yet […] We are still looking at Leith" (32). This condensation of the diasporic imaginary – its replacement of the real origin with a false memory – heralds the dramatic explosion of small differences throughout the collection.

Once we have followed Andrew and the rest of Munro's (real-life) ancestors from Leith to Ontario, their anxieties of displacement become refocused along a north-south axis. Prior to his family's emigration to Canada, Munro's great-great-grandfather William Laidlaw (brother to Andrew and son to James) had already estranged himself from the family by moving from the Borders to the Highlands. (Thus the family is fractured and dispersed before the leave-taking at Leith.) Several years later, and upon news of his father's death in the New World, William decides that the time has come to follow his family across the Atlantic; although not precisely:

> His father and his brothers had spoken of going to America, but when they said that, it was really Canada they meant. William spoke accurately. He had discarded the Ettrick Valley for the Highlands without the least regret, and now he was ready to get out from under the British flag altogether – he was bound for Illinois. (Munro 2006, 88)

The "Illinois" story concerns the secondary migration of William's wife and children following his death from cholera. Andrew, now settled in Upper Canada, comes to retrieve the family and move them north. The eldest son Jamie feels an overwhelming attachment to the place of his father's grave, and resists the move to Canada; the youngest child has arrived on the day of William's death, an orphan on her birthday. This becomes a key motif in what follows, as Jamie uses his new-born sister to engineer what he regards as the necessary and fateful return to Illinois, by a misfiring ruse in which she figures as several kinds of decoy orphan in addition to her actual fatherlessness. When the travelling party stop to rest at a "crossroads inn" (95), still on the American side of the border, Jamie conceals the child in a nearby shack. When the alarm is raised, he hints that Becky Johnson, a native girl from back home, "might have been following along trying for a chance to sneak away the baby who she loved unreasonably" (104). The aim is to force a return to the place of the lost parent, to confront the false parent of Jamie's invention. But before the sister can be retrieved from the shack and somehow smuggled back to Illinois, she is discovered by local girls who over-write Jamie's deception, transferring the hungry baby to the sleeping-place of a stable boy they mean to ridicule. They leave a note labelling the foundling – both real and pretend – "*A PRESENT from one of your SWEETHEARTS*" (108), before Andrew eventually hears the baby's cries and cancels both fictions.

Jamie's strategem is, he supposes, guided by the wishes of his dead father, who "is not under that stone" back in Illinois "but in the air or walking along the road invisibly and making his views known as well as if they had been talking together – *his father* was against their going" (103). This presence compels Jamie to thwart the displacement led by Andrew, the Upper Canadian "newcomer who looked and even sounded like his father but was entirely a sham" (103). By contrast, the only concern of the father-inventing local girls, upon finding the child, is "how can we best make a joke, or fool somebody?" (103). This is the precise moment *The View from Castle Rock* shifts into Munro's familiar terrain of small-town secrets and unkindness, and leaves the extravagant longings of its refugees behind. But if the collection begins to put down "Canadian" roots at this juncture, they are shaped by American rather than transatlantic pressures. During the stop at the tavern, Munro has Andrew overtly thematise his brother's fateful "choice of nationality:"

> He had seen enough of the Yankee people by now to know what had tempted Will to live among them. The push and noise and rawness of them, the need to get on the bandwagon. Though some were decent enough and some, and maybe some of the worst, were Scots. Will had something in him drawing him to such a life.

> It had proved a mistake.
> Andrew knew, of course, that a man was as likely to die of cholera in Upper Canada as in the state of Illinois, and that it was foolish to blame Will's death on his choice of nationality. He did not do so. And yet. And yet – there was something about all this rushing away, loosing oneself entirely from family and past, there was something rash and self-trusting about it that might not help a man, that might put him more in the way of such an accident, such a fate. (110)

The alignment of Americanness with "loosing oneself entirely from family and past" positions Canadian rootedness as a kind of emotional loyalism, allied to a watchful scepticism toward self and others. The reckless way in which the orphan herself is loosed from her true place and made a token in serious and silly games played by others embodies a too-cavalier attitude toward the ties of family, past and truth, and the perilous hijacking of the real, vulnerable child by fictions intended to recover – but also to parody – true parentage. The Canadian figure operating as the reality-principle in this story, it should be noted, is the son who doubted the father's vision from Castle Rock ("if he did not understand that his father was drunk [...] he did certainly understand that something was not as it should be" (30)) and who will now play surrogate father to his brother's orphans. Scepticism and substitution are the "real" narrative strands of Munro's Scottish lineage.

MacLeod, Orality and Ethnic Re-inscription

The fetishism of "roots" in contemporary North American culture has nominated a particular vision of Scotland as a preferred site of ancestry (see Hague 2002). The resulting idiom of white indigeneity is re-exported to the mother country and consumed as a kind of exogenous affirmation of the (frequently challenged) "reality" of traditional Scottish culture, based on the salience of its residues abroad. Gerard Carruthers links its remarkable success on both sides of the Atlantic to the fact that *No Great Mischief*

> does not place undue emphasis upon the supposedly catastrophic failure of a past Scotland. This is the kind of vision that is more easily sent back to a modern Scotland which is perhaps beginning to move away from a version of its cultural past that is all loss and (diseased) post-1707 gain. (Carruthers 2009, 173)

We can best illustrate this dynamic of restoration by turning to an iconic passage in the novel. The sister of the Ontarian narrator accompanies her husband on a business trip to Aberdeen, and takes the opportunity to visit the ancestral homeland in Moidart. Here, she encounters an older woman collecting winkles at low tide:

> And then, she said, she met the woman face to face, and they looked into each other's eyes.
> "You are from here," said the woman.
> "No," said my sister, "I'm from Canada."
> "That may be," said the woman. "But you are really from here. You have just been away for a while." (MacLeod 1999, 147)

The sister accompanies the old woman to her home, where she is introduced as a returning native. A rheumy old man marvels at the concept of houses made from wood, before abruptly claiming his ancestors helped to shelter Bonnie Prince Charlie.

This occasions some clunking exposition about "the auld alliance" and a vaguely postcolonial vindication of the Jacobite cause: "It was worth fighting for, our own land and our own people, and our own way of being" (149). To complete the picture, he hints that "some of us [...] may be descendants of the prince" (149).

We seem here to glimpse the roots-tourist's forbidden scene of enjoyment: immediate and warm recognition by timeless ancestor-natives of your self-evident claim to belong, an authentication mirrored by the elevation to ancient royalty. The recovery of lost origins is sealed by the romantic imaginary of vocal co-presence. The sister begins, miraculously, to converse with the womenfolk in fluent Gaelic, a language she has not used since childhood, when she (and the narrator) were raised by their Gaelic-speaking grandparents following the death of their own parents. (The moment of their orphaning on the ice is perhaps the best-known scene of the novel.) The ecstatic linguistic "homecoming" which follows therefore unites cultural and personal recoveries of the true self, in a register of high communal passion:

> I nodded back and it was a few seconds before I realised that she had spoken in Gaelic and that I had understood her. It seemed I had been away from the language for such a long, long time. [...]
> She said everything in Gaelic, and then I began to speak to her and to them in Gaelic as well. I don't even remember what I said, the actual words or the phrases. It was just like it poured out of me, like some subterranean river that had been running deep within me and suddenly burst forth. And then they all began to speak at once, leaning towards me as if they were trying to pick up a distant but familiar radio signal even as they spoke. We spoke without stopping for about five minutes, although it might have been for a longer or shorter time. [...] And then all of us began to cry. All of us sobbing, either standing or sitting on our chairs in Moidart.
> "It is as if you had never left," said the old man. "Yes," said the others all at once, "as if you had never left."
> Suddenly we were all shy again. Wiping our eyes self-consciously. It was like the period following passion. As if we had had this furious onslaught and now we might suddenly and involuntarily drop into a collective nap. (MacLeod 1999, 150-151)

The erotic dimension of this de-sublimation requires no commentary. Boldly refusing the displacements of narrative re-telling, we are brought directly into the presence of the sister's memory and emotionality. Such passages in MacLeod's writing operate by the condensation and discharge of the yearnings "Tam Lin" defers and recirculates in Munro's story. In *No Great Mischief* homilies such as "blood is thicker than water" take on an emblematic function which transcends "story" and the contingency of its quasi-oral style of transmission (here, from sister to brother to reader). In another scene, a Canadian fragment of the ancient clan is recognised from a moving car in a strange city by the redness of his hair alone. Only the direct superposition of one redhead over another, one origin over another ("I'm from Canada" / "You are really from here"), one historical conflict over another (Culloden / The Plains of Abraham / the MacDonalds' battle with Fern Picard) can sustain the unity of this organism. In place of Munro's palimpsestic model of tradition and re-narrativisation, in which the earlier doubtful layer is visible through the present one, but where 1945 can never simply reincarnate 1645, and where Hazel can never truly inhabit Jack's memories, this is a model of irresistible experiential proofs which admits of no misrecognition. There is a sensuous and substantial match between the selves of "home" and "exile," which only awaits the correct circumstance in which to be manifested and released.

The key detail in this scene is "either standing or sitting on our chairs in Moidart," a descriptive superfluity which anchors this dreamlike scene in a realistically prosaic dimension, reversing the pattern of Munro's bathetic deflations. But ultimately *No Great Mischief* is not interested in the ragged particularity of the past. Toward the end of the novel, the sister recalls their own grandfather's taste for history – that of the orphans' adoptive father:

> "He felt that if you read everything and put the pieces all together the real truth would emerge. It would be, somehow, like carpentry. Everything would fit together just so, and you would see in the end something like 'a perfect building called the past.' Perhaps he felt that if he couldn't understand his immediate past, he would try to understand his distant past."
> "Not so easy," I said.
> "I know not so easy," she answered. "And he knew it too. But he tried, and he was interested, and he tried to pass it on to us." (MacLeod 1999, 215-216)

Here the evasion of experience and displacement of "our" past by "theirs" takes on the authority and legitimacy of tradition, as a pattern sanctified by custom and perhaps even the blood (the narrator suggests the habit of idealising absent parents and origins is "genetic," adding, "and I'm not mocking," 216). The notion of a "natural" inclination to indulge such sentimental escapes brings what is emotionally at stake in MacLeod's diasporic writing directly into focus. Not, as in Munro, the articulation of one story to another (or within another) – which contains the possibility of unbelief, exposure and making a fool of yourself – but the *re-inscription* of an essentialised ancestral self into a diasporic subject clamouring to escape the prison of sham kinship and civic nationality.

Diasporic Narcissism and the Recuperation of Essentialism

For Alice Munro, the quest to uncover and release the past is always shadowed by the anticipated moment in which "what has been so compelling is drawn now into a pattern of things we know about" (Munro 2006, 336). She closes the first part of *The View from Castle Rock* – that part centred on family history and a degree of factual reality – with an image counterpointing the sister's orgasmic re-Gaelicisation in *No Great Mischief*. This passage follows a lengthy quotation from her own father's ("real") memoirs, in which he recalls hearing his grandfather speaking Scots to a visiting cousin.

> That is where I feel it best to leave them – my father a little boy, not venturing too close, and the old men sitting through a summer afternoon on wooden chairs [...]. There they spoke the dialect of their childhood – discarded as they became men – which none of their descendants could understand. (Munro 2006, 170)

Accepting the desire to hear this conversation as well as the impossibility of its fulfilment – accepting the need "to leave them" at all – strikes me as a preferable model for imagining Scottish-Canadian cultural relatedness. Here is a longing grounded in the historical condition of a settler society, rather than projected onto emigrant-ancestors in the plenitude of their imagined self-presence. Textual displacement is the fragile "truth" of Scots-Canadian literary heritage, not an ecstatic vocal communion which dissolves the real ground of national memory and contestation.

To be sure, the unsatisfactions of "English Canadian" literary identity have often been traced to the yearnings explored in these texts. In 1912 Professor Pelham Edgar of the University of Toronto lamented that

> all the countries of Europe have passed through the ballad and epic stage of unselfconscious literary production, and we are only vicariously the heirs of all this antecedent activity. They have a mythical as well as a historical past to inspire them, and they possess vast tracts of legends still unexplored which yield [...] stores of poetic material. (cited in Coleman 2006, 17)

The insecurity of English Canada's vicarious heirs seems especially clear in the writing of Alastair MacLeod, rapturous critical acclaim of whose work seems to me inseparable from the jealous heritage-poverty of Canadian whiteness. Almost a century later, MacLeod seems to fully embrace Pelham's logic of dis-inheritance and European antecedence, and to offer an artful recovery of unselfconscious quasi-ethnic belonging. What seem, viewed from within the Scottish literary tradition, exhausted or discredited forms of national imagining (romantic Highlandism, pan-Gaelic blood bonds, balladic enchantment) gain a new life via Canadian fictions which project anxieties internal to the national literary self-image onto a static and archivally "given" Scotland, where they attain the dignity and stability of tradition. The recovery of this Scots-Canadian ur-self, with its readymade folkloric glamour, supplies a watertight historical alibi of cultural distinctiveness, marginality and suppression, reinforcing the fundamental, contrastive identification with the United States. But the resurrected parent also stands to gain. The warm Scottish critical reception of Canadian fictions manufacturing this inheritance, "returning" it to the parent apparently laundered of its essentialist baggage, both completes and authenticates the circuit of diasporic narcissism.

Works Cited

Carruthers, Gerard. *Scottish Literature*. Edinburgh: Edinburgh University Press, 2009.
Coleman, Daniel. *White Civility: The Literary Project of English Canada*. London: University of Toronto Press, 2006.
Freud, Sigmund. *Civilization and Its Discontents*. 1930. Trans. David McLintock. London: Penguin, 2002.
Hague, Euan. "National Tartan Day: Rewriting History in the United States." *Scottish Affairs* 38 (2002): 94-124.
MacLeod, Alistair. *No Great Mischief*. London: Vintage, 1999.
McGoogan, Ken. *How the Scots Invented Canada*. Toronto: Harper Collins, 2010.
Munro, Alice. *Friend of My Youth*. London: Chatto & Windus, 1990.
—. *The View from Castle Rock*. London: Vintage, 2006.
Nairn, Tom. "Death in Canada: Alistair MacLeod and the Misfortunes of Ethnicity." *Edinburgh Review* 113 (2004): 42-61.
Urquhart, Jane. "The Vision of Alastair MacLeod." *Alastair MacLeod: Essays on His Works*. Ed. Irene Guilford. Toronto: Guernica, 2001. 36-42.
Waterston, Elizabeth. *Rapt in Plaid: Canadian Literature and Scottish Tradition*. London: University of Toronto Press, 2001.

SUZANNE GILBERT, Stirling

The Scottish Ballad: Towards Survival in the 21st Century

Figuring prominently in Scottish culture over centuries, ballads have reflected national concerns at significant times of upheaval. Strife over disputed boundaries between Scotland and England in the 16th century leading up to the 1603 Union of Crowns manifested itself in the so-called "debateable lands" and sparked the high-spirited outlawry of the Border ballads. Loss of parliamentary sovereignty in 1707, described as "the end of an auld sang," propelled the self-reflection so central to the explosion of Scottish vernacular expression in the 18th century, when ballads gained new cultural and poetic importance. And questions of political identity underlay the mid-20th-century "Folk Revival," which introduced some of Scotland's most renowned ballad-singers. Indeed, as Sarah Dunnigan argues, ballads are themselves "debateable lands" that open up hermeneutic possibilities (Dunnigan 2005, 1); their very nature renders them appropriate for examination early in the 21st century, when devolution and the constitutional future of Scotland are at the forefront. Ballads fulfil different functions now than in earlier times, but they are nonetheless deeply embedded in Scotland's consciousness. Given the ballad's legacy in Scotland's cultural production, this essay will trace dominant constructions over time in order to assess the genre's manifestations and significance in the 21st century.

As a genre the ballad has remained highly recognizable: "tales of marvel, love and butchery, told in a style strikingly distinct from that of most poetry" (Buchan 1972, 1). This simple description captures the primary subjects of Scottish ballads, including supernatural encounters as in "Tam Lin," tragic romance as in "Love Gregor," and violent revenge as in "The Burning of Auchindoon." The description also points to ballads' most recognizable trait; they tell a story in a peculiar way, in stanzas that pace the dramatic action, employing devices such as incremental repetition, heavily coded "formulaic" language, and images juxtaposed in "a series of rapid flashes" (Hodgart 1950, 28). They are narrative songs, characterised by the interdependence of text and tune: "[T]he music that carries the words and keeps them alive in tradition is an integral and ultimately inescapable half of the subject" (Bronson 1962, vol. 1, xviii-xix). Fundamental, too, is their emotional core. As Thomas A. McKean observes, "within balladry there is complex human emotional interaction, combined with striking imagery polished by use and memory" (McKean 2003, 10).

But ballads are "awkward things," as David Buchan acknowledges: "Few literary genres give so much pleasure to so many kinds of people and yet pose such refractory problems for the scholar and critic" (Buchan 1972, 1). The "ballad enigma" (Hustvedt 1930, 4) has inspired repeated attempts at definition as well as divergent critical lines of enquiry; and from the beginning, literary and cultural agendas have shaped the genre. Disciplinary approaches to ballads do not speak the same language, nor value the same features, and influential formulations have shifted the sense of what a ballad is and how it functions in culture. Literary studies of Scottish ballads, emerging from 18th-century antiquarians' fascination, have been marked by emphasis on diachronic, retrospective assessments of the genre and its position in the canon, particularly its place within a national poetry, over centuries. This approach has also been influenced by the drive to collect and classify variants of ballads, begun by the Danish scholar Svend Grundtvig and applied to British balladry in Francis J. Child's monumental *The English and Scottish Popular Ballads* (1882-1898); it is here, as James Moreira argues, that "the program to not only describe but rigidly define *the* ballad begins" (Moreira 1999, 98). Influenced by classification, but from an entirely different direction, ethnographic studies have featured synchronic treatments of ballad types, regional distribution, and cultural function, with an insistence on song, "tradition-bearing" and, more recently, performance.

Theresa Catarella has identified four paradigms of past ballad studies, which may still be found in current research. She aligns configuration of the ballad as a "relic" with the antiquarian endeavours leading up to the Enlightenment, where a second paradigm emerges in Romantic notions of the ballad as the voice of a "people" or a "nation." A third paradigm traces the ballad as an "inferior adaptation and assimilation of 'higher' culture." Catarella's fourth paradigm marks a point of difference between the first three frameworks and more recent folkloristic or ethnographic understanding of the genre: "the ballad exists through change and is defined by its variability" (Catarella 1994, 469-472). Though overlapping in some cases, these paradigms nonetheless serve as reference points for understanding how Scottish ballads are received. Also to be considered is the changing emphasis on the forms of expression through which ballads are appreciated and delivered (as poetry or song). This essay will examine the Scottish tradition in its preoccupation over time with ballads as poetic texts and as songs, and it will posit a way forward for ballads in terms of adaptability in the 21st century.

A Scottish Tradition

In 1954, Stanley Hyman cited a string of ballads – among them "The Twa Sisters," "Sir Patrick Spens," "Johnie Cock," "Mary Hamilton," "The Bonny Earl of Murray," "Lamkin," "The Cruel Mother," "The Twa Corbies" and "The Demon Lover" – and called the Scottish ballads "a folk literature unsurpassed by any in the world," part of "as rich a poetic heritage as any we know […]. If we seek language that is simple, sensuous, and passionate, a corpus of more than a dozen tragic Scottish ballad texts constitutes almost a classic tradition" (quoted in Henderson 2004a, 26). Parallel to ballad scholarship, a succession of Scottish writers – among them Robert Burns, James Hogg, Robert Louis Stevenson, Hugh MacDiarmid, Nan Shepherd, Willa Muir, Muriel Spark and Liz Lochhead – have engaged in various ways with ballad narratives, motifs, structures and language in their own work. Muir dedicated a book, *Living with Ballads* (1965), to the subject; and Muriel Spark read ballads obsessively as a child and reported in her autobiography: "The steel and bite of the ballads, so remorseless and yet so lyrical, entered my literary bloodstream, never to depart" (Spark 1992, 98). That ballads have formed a strand of Scotland's poetic achievement is clear. They comprised a substantial amount of material chosen by the English collector Thomas Percy for his influential *Reliques of Ancient English Poetry* (1765). Distinguishing 'northern' ballads from 'southern' ones, Percy found a mixture of qualities in ballads written in the Middle Scots used in the Scottish-English Borders: "The old Minstrel-ballads are in the northern dialect, abound with antique words and phrases, are extremely incorrect, and run into the utmost licence of metre; they have also a romantic wildness, and are in the true spirit of chivalry" (Percy 1794, 1: liv). Despite the homogenising effect of centuries of ballad criticism that has subsumed Scottish ballads into a 'British' cultural tradition, they have benefited from depiction as a "distinct and very important species of poetry" (Child 1908, vol. 1, 464).

Reflecting on regional diversity in ballads, David Atkinson finds that "[t]o a significant extent [...] the respective ballad traditions in regions like English or Scotland or Newfoundland remain simply empirically different from one another" (Atkinson 2002, 245); and David Buchan argues that the narrative song tradition "gives expression to the cultural preoccupations of – and sometimes the identity of – a given group" (Buchan 1994, 377). Certain features may be observed regarding predominantly Scottish ballads, among them "a widely shared Scottish idea that the ballads, resonant of earlier times, offered a kind of evocative history" (Brown 2011, 192). Scottish historical ballads may be closely linked to the areas of the country in which the events are thought to have occurred; for example, the reiving ballads such as "Jamie Telfer of the Fair Dodhead" and "Kinmont Willie" are closely associated with the Scottish-English Borders. In another type of ballad, the supernatural element is especially strong. Comparing English and Scottish variants of "The Daemon Lover," Emily Lyle observes that while the supernatural appears in both, "the 'spirit' of the English version is replaced by the much more powerful figure of the devil himself in the Scottish form" (Lyle 1994, 14). Scotland has more ballads revolving around fairies, such as "Tam Lin" and "Thomas Rymer," while the English tradition has produced a greater number of ballads making reference to Christianity (Atkinson 2002, 242). Bothy ballads flourished in north-east Scotland, capturing farming life and practices at a particular time and place. Ballads turning on laconic or macabre humour, such as variants of "Twa Corbies," often bear the stamp of Scottish origins; and ironic juxtapositions that challenge Scottish feudal hierarchies recur in classic ballads such as "Sir Patrick Spens." The Scots language has proved particularly apt for depicting the narratives and dialogue of ballads. Overall, as Lyle suggests, "over a period of several centuries Scotland seems to have initiated ballads and to have provided an especially hospitable environment for those that came from elsewhere" (Lyle 1994, 13).

Ballads captured in print in the 18th century became the subjects of a trend that dominated late in the 19th century and carried well into the 20th: to gather, classify and present specimens of folk expression, mostly from manuscript and print sources. The effect of Francis J. Child's work to obtain what he deemed to be every variant of all the "popular" ballads, resulting in publication of the monumental *The English and Scottish Popular Ballads*, was to downplay the features that reflected regional origin or historical situation, and to foreground their universality. Paradoxically, Child's drive to provide all information known about a ballad also provides clues to the regions where it has been found and even at times the specific informant, to the discerning reader interested in such details. The variant of "Lord Randal," for example, is headed as follows: "From a small manuscript volume lent me by Mr William Macmath, of Edinburgh, containing four pieces written in or about 1710, and this ballad in a later hand. Charles Mackie, August, 1808, is scratched upon the binding." Variant B is headed, "Kinloch's Ancient Scottish Ballads, p. 110. From Mrs Comie, Aberdeen" (Child 1965, 157, 158). Despite the obscuring effect of paratextual framing, the Scottish ballad has retained its own identity and reputation. The Scottish

Cultural Resources Access Network (SCRAN) project at the University of Glasgow identifies 216 of the 205 Child ballads as Scottish "on the basis of theme or informant" (Cowan 2000, 15). In arguing for a distinct corpus of ballads originating in England, Atkinson makes a case for regional, or national, coherence among the ballads originating in particular locations, arguing further that "[i]n principle, no song text exists at any time or place in isolation from its socio-historical context, and it ought therefore to be possible to attempt some relation of specific folk song texts to identifiable social and cultural contexts" (Atkinson 2002, 242). The corpus of Scottish ballads has shown its distinctiveness.

Ballads and Books: Some Shapers of Tradition

Before Percy, Scottish poet Allan Ramsay had gathered what he considered the gems of Scottish tradition in *The Tea-Table Miscellany* (1723-1740), a task taken up later in the century by anthologists such as David Herd in *The Ancient and Modern Scots Songs* (1769; 1776) and by Robert Burns, who collected traditional songs for James Johnson's *Scots Musical Museum* (1787-1803). The cause of ballads was treated more specifically in 19th-century collections such as Walter Scott's *Minstrelsy of the Scottish Border* (1802-1803) and William Motherwell's *Minstrelsy, Ancient and Modern* (1827). For Scots such as Herd, Burns, Scott, Robert Jamieson and James Hogg, the impetus was culturally-nationalist: a post-Union attempt to preserve what were considered remnants of Scotland's cultural identity, quickly, or they would be lost. Significant figures in the history of Scottish balladry contributed to its preservation, but also shaped the genre and its subsequent reception. Among them were Walter Scott, William Motherwell, and the American scholar Francis J. Child, whose antiquarian and literary approaches to the ballad reflect divergent perspectives that have impacted ballad studies then and now.

Scott's *Minstrelsy of the Scottish Border* (1802-1803) represents a reclaiming of material that Percy had heralded as a "native *British*" poetry (under the rubric "English" poetry). For Scott, the attraction of ballads had little to do with affection for folk culture and everything to do with preserving bits of history that could be reconstructed into narratives of an idealized past, one that was no longer tenable in Scotland's move into modernity. Under the rubric of "Border minstrelsy," however, he appropriated ballads from other parts of Scotland as well, resulting in distortion that collectors from the even ballad-richer region of the north-east later felt compelled to correct. An admirer of Percy's *Reliques,* Scott subscribed to his predecessor's belief that ballads are unrefined and require improvement: they were relics but also "inferior" versions of what had been ancient, courtly minstrelsy. Writing to Washington Irving in 1817, Scott declared, "A real old Scottish song is a cairn gorm […] a precious relic of old times, that bears the national character stamped on it, – like a cameo, that shows what the national visage was in former days, before the breed was crossed" (qtd. in Zug 1978, 229). At the heart of Scott's construction of ballads is loss:

> [U]ndergoing from age to age a gradual process of alteration and recomposition, our popular and oral minstrelsy has lost, in a great measure, its original appearance; and the strong touches by which it had been formerly characterised, have been generally smoothed down and destroyed by a process similar to that by which a coin, passing from hand to hand, loses in circulation all the finer marks of the impress" (Scott 1932, vol. 1, 12).

Recalling Joseph Ritson's language in the 1874 *Scottish Songs*, Scott describes tradition as "a species of alchemy which converts gold to lead." The "original" ballad, according to Scott, suffered irrevocably from "passing through the mouths of many reciters," which produced the "impertinent interpolations from the conceit of one rehearser, unintelligible blunders from the stupidity of another, and omissions equally to be regretted, from the want of memory in a third" (Scott 1932, vol. 1, 10). When Scott collected "Auld Maitland" from Margaret Laidlaw Hogg, she chastised him for printing ballads because they were "made for singin' and no for readin'" (Hogg 1999, 38), but the text was all-important in Scott's formulation of the ballad.

While in *Minstrelsy Ancient and Modern* (1827) Motherwell included some tunes, he did not emphasise them. He attempted, however, to maintain the link between informant and ballad. Motherwell recognised the importance of the tradition-bearer – the "old singing women" from whom he transcribed the ballads – in direct opposition to Scott's representation of oral sources. His manuscript records many details regarding his sources, including name, profession or "familial connection," age, when and where he had collected the ballad, and often how it was learned (Brown 2011, 87). Significantly, he embraced the idea that ballads exist in variation. Motherwell was before his time: his recognition of informants paved the way for emphasis on performers and music in the 20th-century Folk Revival, and his articulation of ballad variation inspired subsequent collectors, most notably Child.

The accumulation of ballads in the many collections produced throughout the 19th century was a treasure chest for Child, whose ballad-collecting was achieved largely through correspondence. The prevalence of Scottish ballads in Child's *English and Scottish Popular Ballads* was enhanced by the enthusiasm of his contributors, the most energetic and influential of them being William Macmath, a legal clerk in Edinburgh. Mary Ellen Brown details how "the indefatigable Scot," on whom Child depended to be his eyes and ears in Scotland, played a determining role in what was to become the major canon of ballads (Brown 2011, 142): "The predominance of Scottish materials is due in large measure to his pursuit of manuscripts and even to his collecting. Many other Scots were involved [...], but Macmath's role as a finder, copier, and mediator completely and totally committed to Child's project cannot be overestimated" (Brown 2011, 190-191). There was a nationalist element to Macmath's efforts: "On some level, Macmath felt it was important to keep track of all the Scottish materials, to make copies, so that there would be a Scottish record" (191). Towards the end of his massive project, Child was still dealing with "new discoveries, as usual coming from Scotland and facilitated by Macmath," but by 1882, Child concluded that "the day of ballads in Scotland was over." As Brown observes, Child was "dead wrong, and Macmath was right:" he knew "because he was there" (Brown 2011, 197). There were, indeed, more songs to be found.

"Muckle Sangs" and Singers

Ballads have led parallel lives, current in oral song culture and printed in collections, taking different shapes according to context. Even when distorted by limiting critical assumptions in one corner of society – treated as relics of antiquity, or characterised as the voice of a so-called 'primitive' people – ballads have been sung and transmitted orally in other corners. Literary scholarship has only shown awareness of this occasionally and in restrictive ways, but even this attention has proved important to the ballad's survival. The stories of earlier and highly influential ballad-singers are filtered through literary accounts, with occasional glimpses provided from the records of family members or friends. Anna Gordon (1747-1810), commonly known as "Mrs Brown of Falkland," has been hailed by ballad scholars as "the greatest informant encountered by any collector of traditional ballads," and as "the most important single contributor to the canon of English and Scottish popular ballads" (Fowler 1968, 294; Friedman 1961, 57; see also Rieuwerts 2011). Child included all thirty-three of her ballads in the *English and Scottish Popular Ballads*, twenty of them privileged as "A" texts, noting, "No Scottish ballads are superior in kind to those recited in the last century by Mrs Brown of Falkland" (Child 1882, vol. 1, vii). Another informant found in the drive to preserve tradition was Margaret Laidlaw Hogg (1730-1813), mother of writer James Hogg. Gifted with a strong memory and active imagination, she soaked up the traditional songs and tales of the borders, as J. E. H. Thomson observed: "As she had a vivid imagination and a retentive memory, she eagerly heard, and scrupulously retained, the legendary ballads that were floating about the Border district" (Thomson 1909, 13-14). Among Motherwell's sources was Agnes Lyle of Kilbarchan, a weaver's daughter with a wide range of traditional material who contributed twenty-two songs, some with accompanying tunes.

Fieldwork done at the beginning of the 20th century in the northeast of Scotland reflects a new emphasis on the importance of ballad music. This preoccupation had borne fruit through the folk-song collecting of S. Baring-Gould, Cecil Sharp, the Broadwoods, and others in rural parts of England. Duly inspired by these collectors, in Scotland the school headmaster Gavin Greig and the Reverend James B. Duncan discovered over three thousand song versions, texts and tunes, in Aberdeenshire and surrounding areas; this material was described by Hamish Henderson as one of "the largest collections of traditional song material in the world" (Henderson 2004b, 132). The songs remained little known to the wider world until 1981, when the first volume was published of an eventual eight-volume edition, *The Greig-Duncan Folk Song Collection* (Munro 1996, 2). This collection provides a fascinating, and little-explored, window into Scottish ballads, as this vast amount of material was not available to Child.

Despite recurring prophecies of doom for the oral tradition, in some circles the ballad has proved far more mobile, adaptable, and resilient than Enlightenment thinkers had predicted. A further challenge to ballad scholars' certainty that ballads were no longer part of oral tradition came in the middle of the 20th century. At the close of World War II, fieldworkers in Britain and other areas of Europe were found to have continued, uninterrupted, the practice of ballad-singing and transmission. Making use of new recording technology, Hamish Henderson and others sought to document the ballads of Scottish Travellers for the archives of Edinburgh's newly established School of Scottish Studies. In the process, they were able to preserve the songs of great tradition-bearers such as Jeannie Robertson, Willie Scott, Belle Stewart and Betsy Whyte. Henderson tapped into a rich stream of tradition and reported that the quantity and quality of ancient ballads still being sung – including the so-called "muckle sangs" or big ballads – was overwhelming: recording them "was like holding a bucket under Niagara Falls" (quoted in Stewart 2006, 67).

As in the case of post-Union ballad-collections, there was a strong political impetus for song recovery. Ailie Munro describes how changes in public opinion following World War II opened a space for such cultural exploration: "The 1945 election saw a massive Labour victory [...] the heroic struggle of the Soviet Union gave the left a tremendous credibility among working people. In this moment, songs [...] which celebrated ordinary people in all aspects of their lives spoke to the hopes and fears of a generation" (Munro 1996, 2). American folklorist Alan Lomax left stifling Cold-War America for Scotland, commissioned by Columbia Records to edit the "folk and primitive music of the world" (Henderson 2004c, 16), and was present to record the historic first People's Festival in 1951, organised by the Edinburgh Labour Festival Committee. Left-wing dramatist and songwriter Ewan MacColl was instrumental in introducing Lomax to the People's Festival events, and went on to play an active role in the Folk Revival. The venues for hearing ballads shifted, moving from campfires and private homes to folk clubs, which flourished in the smaller towns throughout Scotland. Folk pubs (such as the famous Sandy Bells in Edinburgh) became central. Festivals began to increase in number; forty years after the Revival Munro reported around sixty festivals in Scotland. And, always, there was the "gatherings of friends in each other's houses, where you will find something nearer the original ceilidh situation" – in Gaelic, literally "a visiting" (Munro 1996, 4).

The Folk Revival brought a new emphasis on music and individual performance, and many of the singing Travellers became known in folk clubs throughout Britain and beyond. Arguably the central figure of the revival, Jeannie Robertson (1908-1975) learned ballads from her mother and grew up travelling six months of the year with families for whom songs and stories were the chief entertainment. In 1953 she was 'discovered' by Henderson, who first recorded her songs. In early life around the campfire, and as an adult living in Aberdeen, Robertson was acknowledged within her family circle as an outstanding singer. But as a mature woman immersed in the Folk Revival she became internationally renowned as a performer of traditional song. Singers such as Robertson were members of a traditional community whose practices helped to preserve tradition, but also became ambassadors for that culture. This emergence of the ballad as song prompted study of "the singer's total conception of a song, comprising both the contextual dimension of the song in its performance situation and more particularly the complex of experiential and subjective meanings the singer brings to the song" (Atkinson 2002, 7); James Porter and Herschel Gower's study, *Jeannie Robertson: Emergent Singer, Transformative Voice* (1995), is based on these criteria.

A distinction that emerged during the Folk Revival had implications for survival of the ballad beyond the 20th century. Whereas singers had tended to be categorised as either 'source' singers, who learned their songs from oral tradition or in childhood, or 'revival' singers, who had learned songs from recorded or printed sources or from other revival singers, this distinction was breaking down: "[T]he categories are not clear-cut. Not a few revival singers have source elements in their backgrounds, while many source singers make use of the written word – both in giving copies to other singers, and in obtaining copies of words to add to their own repertoires" (Munro 1994, 52). One singer, Maddy Taylor, clearly articulates the change: "'*I don't think about it at all.* These categories divide us, don't you think? Can't we just be 'singers' and enjoy the music?'" (quoted in Munro 1994, 52).

Prospects for Survival

Paradigms within ballad studies have both foregrounded and obscured features of ballads, crystallising definitions that, on their face, seem contradictory or at least incomplete. And with paradigm shifts, previously neglected features have become defining attributes of the genre. Clearly, the 18th-century idea of a ballad as a relic crumbles in the wake of the mid-20th-century singing of ballad texts that have been transmitted orally over centuries. The hazy notion of the ballad as representing the "voice of a people," the creation of a "communally poeticising folk" (Catarella 1994, 470), is challenged by the significance of strong individual tradition-bearers in shaping the canon. The idea that "change is equivalent to loss" (471), counters what ballad scholars recognise: that variation is a crucial part of the ballad's identity. At one level of society, throughout the 19th century and well into the 20th in Scotland, little attention was paid to folk music at one level of society, while that art form was preserved at another level: folksong flourished among traditional communities. The Folk Revival brought down some barriers while insisting on others (judging who could sing what songs, and the political significance of song and singing). The "artless peasantry" of the 18th-century was replaced by the politically-left working classes of the 20th. Today, the class and political elements, significant for labouring-class solidarity across Britain in the middle of the 20th century, have receded as crucial for understanding or engaging with the ballad tradition.

These changes are paradigm-shattering and create a space for the ballad's continued relevance within Scottish culture and the global ballad community. With devolution in 1999 returning parliamentary power to Scotland, the emphasis within the country is once again on national identity and the need to retain and nurture those arts deemed important to Scottish culture. Catarella's fourth paradigm accounts for the ways in which the ballad has survived: "That the variant previously viewed as deterioration, could also be admitted as positive transformation was an important step toward the understanding of oral poetry" (472). There can be recognition of the ballad's inherent variability, a combination of dependence on the ballad form and social mechanisms that allow and encourage survival. The ballad is part of the national poetry, but also still functioning at the level of folk song. Ballads have found a new stage as one of the arts showcased at folk festivals. The largest – and most eclectic – festival is Celtic Connections, held annually in Glasgow, which regularly features sessions on ballads. While there are still established folk clubs, much of the training and exchange goes on in informal sessions, still held in pubs across the country. A sign of the health of traditional music is the involvement of both veteran Folk Revival performers and young singers and players, such as singer-songwriter Karine Polwart, who sings ballads "because of their ability to connect human experiences across the details of time and place, and to take on new resonances for new circumstances" (quoted in Harding 2008).

But will today's ballad become so much of a hybrid, so adapted to new circumstances, that it varies itself out of existence? The recurrent worry is that the mechanisms that have stabilised the ballad over centuries have slipped, or are slipping away. Henderson asserted that a proactive approach is needed: "no national tradition can ever afford to 'mark time' – to regard itself as unassailable: there are always possibilities of decline, or even extinction;" but, he insists, "Happily, in Scotland, we have usually been lucky in having champions never sweir to enter the lists in defence of something they valued – in this case, a central part of the country's culture" (Munro 1996, xi). The strong tradition-bearer plays an important role in anchoring traditional practices, but John Miles Foley signals the importance of an "implied audience" of informed listeners in the survival of oral poetry (Foley 1991, 45). Prominent among recent trends in ballad scholarship is acknowledgement of reception and audience interaction in ballad-making. Ideas are being developed regarding audience interaction to "fill the gaps" and the audience's "collaborative" role (McKean 2003, 6), suggesting some possible ways forward for preserving ballads within a wider community. The key may lie in a new – varied, if you will – concept of community, one that can encompass the range of people interested in living tradition. The assertion of a past paradigm that limited the ballad to an "artless multitude," for example, has always been inaccurate. As singer and folklorist Sheila Douglas observes, "[i]n Scotland, folk song has never been confined to any one social class since we have ballads and songs composed by all kinds of people, from kings to ploughmen" (Douglas 2003, 175). Survival through oral tradition alone has been a persuasive myth: singers have always learned songs from every kind of source, and those in the age of mechanical reproduction are no different. The shapers of tradition – from ballad collectors to singers to communities to enthusiasts – have always influenced not only the reception of ballads but the very form itself.

The ballad's paradoxical conjunction of stability and variation has allowed it to survive and even to flourish in many different contexts. Hence, it is a crucial time during which to observe how the functions of this chameleon form are adapting. Whereas historically constructions of ballad survival were based on paradigms that more or less excluded some aspects of narrative song, the way forward demands recognition that such separations do not accurately reflect the state of the art. Scottish ballads' continued relevance may still be found in their intense engagement with human drama, in the ways in which they tell human stories: "ballads offer us intimate access to culture and individual worldview, enabling a richer understanding of ourselves" (McKean 2003, 3). In the 21st century, the Scottish ballad appears on the library shelf, but not there alone; it is also at large in the wider world.

Works Cited

Atkinson, David. *The English Traditional Ballad: Theory, Method, and Practice*. Burlington, Vermont: Ashgate, 2002.
Bronson, Bertrand H. *Traditional Tunes of the Child Ballads*. 4 vols. Princeton, NJ: Princeton University Press, 1962.
Brown, Mary Ellen. *William Motherwell's Cultural Politics, 1797-1835*. Lexington: The University Press of Kentucky, 2001.
—. *Child's Unfinished Masterpiece: The English and Scottish Popular Ballads*. Urbana: University of Illinois Press, 2011.
Buchan, David. *The Ballad and the Folk*. London and Boston: Routledge, 1972.
—. "The Historical Balladry of the North East." *Aberdeen University Review* 192 (Autumn 1994): 377-387.
Catarella, Teresa. "The Study of the Orally Transmitted Ballad: Past Paradigms and a New Poetics." *Oral Tradition* 9.2 (1994): 468-478.
Child, Francis J. "Ballad Poetry." 1874. *Universal Cyclopaedia and Atlas*. Ed. Rossiter Johnson. Rev. Charles K. Adams. 12 vols. New York: Appleton, 1908. 464-68.

—, ed. *The English and Scottish Popular Ballads*. 1882-1898. 5 vols. Boston and New York: Dover Pulbications, 1965.
Cowan, Edward J. "Introduction: The Hunting of the Ballad." *The Ballad in Scottish History*. Ed. Edward J. Cowan. East Linton: Tuckwell Press, 2000. 1-18.
Douglas, Sheila. "The Life and Times of Rosie Anderson." *The Flowering Thorn: International Ballad Studies*. Ed. Thomas A. McKean. Kommission für Volksdichtung and the Elphinstone Institute, University of Aberdeen. Logan, UT: Utah State University, 2003. 175-181.
Dunnigan, Sarah. *Scottish Ballads*. Glasgow: Association for Scottish Literary Studies, 2005.
Foley, John Miles. *Immanent Art: From Structure to Meaning in Traditional Oral Epic*. Bloomington and Indianapolis: Indiana University Press, 1991.
Fowler, David C. *A Literary History of the Popular Ballad*. Durham, NC: Duke University Press, 1968.
Friedman, Albert B. *The Ballad Revival: Studies in the Influence of Popular on Sophisticated Poetry*. Chicago: The University of Chicago Press, 1961.
Greig, Gavin and James Bruce Duncan. *The Greig-Duncan Folk Song Collection*. Eds. Patrick Shuldham-Shaw and Emily Lyle. 8 vols. Aberdeen: Aberdeen University Press, 1981-2002.
Harding, Mike. "Karine Polwart on the Traditional Ballad and Seth Lakeman." 2008. *BBC Radio 2*. 6 August 2011. <http://www.bbc.co.uk/blogs/folk/2008/07/karine-polwart-on-the-traditio.html>.
Henderson, Hamish. "The Ballads." *Alias MacAlias: Writings on Songs, Folk and Literature*. Ed. Alec Finlay. Edinburgh: Polygon, 2004a. 23-27.
—. "Folk-song Heritage of the North-East." *Alias MacAlias: Writings on Songs, Folk and Literature*. Ed. Alec Finlay. Edinburgh: Polygon, 2004b. 132-134.
—. "Scottish Folk-song and the Labour Movement." *Alias MacAlias: Writings on Songs, Folk and Literature*. Ed. Alec Finlay. Edinburgh: Polygon, 2004c. 16-18.
Hodgart, M. J. C. *The Ballads*. London: Hutchinson's University Library, 1950.
Hogg, James. *Anecdotes of Scott*. Ed. Jill Rubenstein. Edinburgh: Edinburgh University Press, 1999.
Hustvedt, Sigurd Bernhard. *Ballad Books and Ballad Men: Raids and Rescues in Britain, America, and the Scandinavian North since 1800*. Cambridge, MA: Harvard University Press, 1930.
Lyle, E. B., ed. *Scottish Ballads*. Edinburgh: Canongate, 1994.
McKean, Thomas A., ed. *The Flowering Thorn: International Ballad Studies*. Kommission für Volksdichtung and the Elphinstone Institute, University of Aberdeen. Logan, UT: Utah State University, 2003.
Moreira, James. "Genre and Balladry." *Ballads into Books: The Legacies of Francis J. Child*. Eds. Tom Cheesman and Sigrid Rieuwerts. Berne: Peter Lang, 1997. 95-109.
Motherwell, William. *Minstrelsy, Ancient and Modern*. 2 vols. Glasgow: John Wylie, 1827.
Muir, Willa. *Living with Ballads*. London: The Hogarth Press, 1965.
Munro, Ailie. *The Democratic Muse: Folk Revival in Scotland. Including Folk Revival in Gaelic Song*. Aberdeen: Scottish Cultural Press, 1996.
Percy, Thomas. *Reliques of Ancient English Poetry*. London: John Nichols, 1794.

Porter, James and Herschel Gower. *Jeannie Robertson: Emergent Singer, Transformative Voice*. East Linton: Tuckwell Press, 1995.

Rieuwerts, Sigrid, ed. *The Ballad Repertoire of Anna Gordon, Mrs Brown of Falkland*. Edinburgh: Scottish Text Society Fifth Series, 2011.

Scott, Walter. *Minstrelsy of the Scottish Border*. 3 vols. Edinburgh, 1803. Rev. and ed. T. F. Henderson. Edinburgh: Oliver, 1932.

Spark, Muriel. *Curriculum Vitae: A Volume of Autobiography*. London: Penguin, 1992.

Stewart, Sheila. *Queen Amang the Heather: The Life of Belle Stewart*. Edinburgh: Birlinn, 2006.

Thomson, J. E. H. "Memoir of the Ettrick Shepherd." *Domestic Manners*. Ed. James Hogg. Stirling: Eneas Mackay, 1909. 9-50.

Zug, Charles III. "The Ballad Editor as Antiquary." *Journal of the Folklore Institute* 12.1 (1976): 57-73.

—. "The Ballad and History: The Case for Scott." *Folklore* 89 (1978): 229-242.

Anglistik

Universitätsverlag
WINTER
Heidelberg

LUCHT, BENTE

Writing Empire

Latin Quotations in Texts on the British Empire

2012. IV, 239 Seiten,
4 Abbildungen. (Anglistische Forschungen, Band 425)
Gebunden € 44,–
ISBN 978-3-8253-5969-0

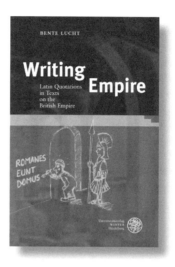

This study explores instances of Latin citation in late nineteenth- and twentieth-century colonial writing (Kipling, Conrad and Orwell), and then also in the postmodern/postcolonial work of Friel and Stoppard. The thesis makes two interlocking cases: first there is the intertextual case for how the investigation of Latin quotation in English texts on the British Empire makes possible a reconsideration of those same colonial or postcolonial texts, and of the value or interpretation they place upon the colonial experience. Second there is the methodological case for how the Latin quotations act as 'loopholes' within the text which can be used to generate meanings against the grain.

The thesis makes important contributions to subfields within colonial discourse analysis and postcolonial critique, expanding our understanding of classical references within British imperial discourse and imperial learning, of post/colonial irony, and of the intertextual values and uses of citation.

IAN BROWN, Kingston upon Thames
"Arts first; politics later:" Scottish Theatre as a Recurrent Crucible of Cultural Change

It is becoming a cliché to observe that there has been a renaissance in Scottish theatre since the 1970s (Brown 2007, 283). It is certainly true that many of the crosscurrents in contemporary Scottish culture have found expression in a revitalised drama sector. This has explored a variety of lively issues, not least the use of Scots language, the revitalisation and reshaping of Gaelic-language drama, radical political themes in the 1970s, the foregrounding, particularly since 1980, when Marcella Evaristi's *Mouthpieces* and *Hard to Get* and Sue Glover's *The Seal Wife* were premièred, of the writing of women and, since the 1990s, radical formal experiments. All these creative impulses can be seen to underlie the launch of Scotland's first National Theatre in 2006. Arguably, this vitality is linked to major recent changes in the culture and indeed the political settlement in Scotland. The quotation in the title – "Arts first; politics later" – is from the Scottish Parliament's second Presiding Officer, the SNP politician George Reid,[1] who thus asserts that the momentum towards the re-establishment of the Scottish Parliament, and all that this has led to politically and culturally, was powerfully led by the arts sector. This view is also that of the unionist Sam Galbraith, first Minister for the Arts for Scotland, whom the present author witnessed saying so in 1999 at the Edinburgh Festival Arts Seminar. This essay, however, also suggests that the importance of the arts – and for present purposes particularly theatre – is not new; there have been significant earlier periods when theatre was just as important to the ways in which Scotland understood its changing cultures. A key argument of this essay is that it is not only in recent years that theatre has provided a forum, a crucible, in which ideas can be contested, celebrated and remoulded. It has regularly explored the potential (and even the need) for change both in religion and church and in social and class structures. Recognition of the earlier importance of theatre as a crucible of cultural change has arisen partly from the development of studies in Scottish drama and theatre following the foundation of the first Chair of Drama in Scotland at Glasgow University in 1965. Following this, in recent years, proper attention has been paid to performative aspects of theatre in Scottish society. This has clarified drama and theatre's importance, somewhat neglected when, in a tradition of text-based literary criticism, study of drama was confused with literary study of dramatic texts.

The significance of earlier phases of Scottish theatre has often been further obscured by a misunderstanding – even among theatre students and practitioners of the highest distinction – that somehow it was, largely as a result of the protestant Reformation, suppressed for long periods. In 2008, even Scotland's Makar, Liz Lochhead, a major theatre practitioner and an artist of the highest calibre, said, "Certainly, our Reformation, early and thorough, stamped out all drama and dramatic writing for centuries" (Lochhead 2008, 7). Yet the historical evidence contradicts this widespread canard:

---

1   Reid said this in an interview with Dolina McLennan in *Dolina*, broadcast by BBC Alba, 1 January 2012.

Drama, the doing of theatre, was never stamped out [...]. Theatre, the watching of drama, certainly occasionally suffered suppression, in the 17th century until 1660, for example, in the absence of a royal court in Edinburgh and for about three decades after William III's Dutch invasion when Whigs took over. In the 1720s, though, Anthony Aston and Allan Ramsay began a theatrical fightback. (Brown 2011a, 1)

Recent research by, *inter alia*, John McGavin (2007), Sarah Carpenter (2011) and Margo Todd (2002) shows that before, during and after the 1560 Reformation, Scots were used to seeing theatre and theatricality as a means of challenging establishment views and exploring social, political and religious change. These impulses might have been to an extent appropriated by the reformed Church of Scotland, the Kirk, when it attacked their earlier manifestations, often perceived as heretical, but drama was never quite successfully suppressed. Theatricality and drama in general had been important before the Reformation and became key means of the Kirk's seeking to stamp its authority post-Reformation on the larger culture of the community.

John McGavin offers an earlier example of how theatricality might be used subversively in pre-Reformation Scotland against the church's hierarchical power even after the savage 1527 example of the burning of Patrick Hamilton for heresy (McGavin 2007, 20-22). As McGavin says:

> The problem for those who would employ theatrical modes to stage their own power in public is that, like any drama, the communal nature of such a performance makes it sensitive to the local circumstances obtaining at the time. (McGavin 2007, 20)

He cites the case of Sandie Furrour who, on returning from imprisonment in England, "discovered that a local cleric, John Dingwall, had been sleeping with his wife and using up his money and possessions." His public complaints led to his being accused of heresy and brought to trial. Then, "He lapp up mearely upoun the scaffold, and casting a gawmound [capering], said 'Whair ar the rest of the playaris?'," so making explicit "the theatrical nature of the event." Furrour proceeded to subvert his examination by "repeatedly referr[ing] to the immediate environment of the stage [...] rather than being drawn into theological discussion" and diverting replies into comments on the immoral behaviour of local clerics, naming the "menis wyffis with whome thei had medled," causing public laughter. Thus he avoided the danger of being burned and shamed the clerics into giving him money to replace his loss and depart (McGavin 2007, 21). As McGavin observes:

> Furrour, though no literary playwright, was a master of social dramaturgy and particularly of the spectatorship upon which it depended. He understood where theatre and reality intersected [...] and he knew which [theatrical] identity would work in this extreme context. (McGavin 2007, 22)

What McGavin sensitises the scholar to is that it is anachronistic to think of theatre or drama in the medieval and early modern period as defined simply by performance on stage, whether at court or in publicly performed religious drama. Bill Findlay notes:

> The earliest recorded example of a rudimentary court masque in Britain took place in 1285 as part of the marriage banquet of King Alexander III in Jedburgh Abbey. Dancers and musicians fell hushed as the figure of Death [...] interrupted the celebrations as a potent reminder of human mortality. (Findlay 1998, 32)

Nonetheless, as Findlay points out, there was by then a wide range of folk and religious drama, while the earliest Scottish performer/actor whose name we know is "Peter the Fool," Robert the Bruce's jester (Maloney 2006, 142).

A recurrent feature of Scottish theatre is the centrality of performers as opposed to playwrights. Such a focus on performativity allows, indeed, encourages, the modern continuity prevailing between legitimate and popular performance domains, marked in the prominent careers since the mid-20th century of actor-entertainers like Duncan Macrae, Russell Hunter, Una Maclean or Elaine C. Smith, all celebrated on both classical and variety or pantomime stages. In other words, when the National Theatre of Scotland held as part of its *Staging the Nation* series a session on "Panto, Variety and the Scottish People" (26 November 2011, King's Theatre, Glasgow) led by Alan Cumming, much contemporary drama, owing dramaturgical debts to popular theatre, was presented. Then on stage were such figures as Johnnie Beattie, Maureen Beattie and Greg Hemphill, representing a performance tradition spanning popular and classical that, arguably, traces its roots back to the Bruce's jester. Cumming, addressing what he sees as specifically Scottish theatrical performance conventions, has observed:

> Being away from Scotland makes you question what it is that makes you Scottish, and when it comes to acting I realise that my performance style is very different to my colleagues' elsewhere in the world. Our whole way of breaking through the fourth wall, indeed never even countenancing its existence, is all derived from our culture that is steeped in variety and music hall and panto. (Anon. 2011)

In fact, the continuity of performativity and performer traditions across theatrical genres – as opposed to the largely text-based focus often seen in English literature's drama studies, embodied in most Shakespeare criticism, with its tight focus on playtext – is a specific feature of Scottish dramatic traditions. This continuity may mark historically an actual benefit of James VI's move to London in 1603 and the removal of royal patronage thereby. Certainly, James was a keen supporter of theatre and when in London he and Anna, his queen, adopted the two leading companies and supported dramatic developments, including the masque, far more dynamically than had his predecessor, Elizabeth. The long-term impact of this has arguably supported the court- and London-centred evolution of forms of and attitudes to theatre that still prevail in England, while Scottish theatre escaped this particular destiny.

Scottish theatre traditions avoided the centralising focus on controlled text that came to characterise the English theatre tradition generally, maintaining a more diffuse drama such as deeply-rooted folk drama in Gaelic, much neglected until recently, as Michael Newton has reminded us (Newton, 2011, 41-46). There was, by 1662, a post-Restoration theatre in the grounds of Holyrood House, the Tennis Court Theatre, which seems to have served nobility, gentry and richer merchant classes for around thirty years. Within that period, during the Duke of York's 1679-82 residence, there was certainly royal court theatre in Edinburgh, but Scotland largely avoided England's experience of royally patronised theatre. In fact, the expense of attending professional theatre at Holyrood, not to mention its general identification with an Episcopalian or Catholic party, seen then as anti-populist, helped make that form of theatre exclusive and unpopular, more reason for theatre to be opposed when drama was not. The range of drama, then, included, but was not coterminous with, Scottish theatre, let alone

Scottish theatricality. This is not, of course, to neglect the occasional importance of playtexts, but rather to place that importance in a wider context.

Carpenter has identified in the late medieval and early modern period at least four major spheres of political and cultural life in which drama and plays served an important function: religion, the town, the court and politics (Carpenter, 2011, 6-21). Certainly the landmark production of David Lindsay's *Ane Satyre of the Thrie Estaitis* (in 1540 as an interlude at court and in 1552/1554 as public performance) draws on a wide range of popular forms and tropes in satirising the corruption of the pre-Reformation church. While its 1540 Linlithgow performance was under James V's protection, its later public performances on the playfields of Cupar and Edinburgh took place after his death and during the regency of Mary of Guise. The potential of drama to address controversial public issues robustly was recognised and apparently accepted even in a Scotland engaged in pre-Reformation spiritual, intellectual and political turmoil. Lindsay's play's production history and themes illustrate clearly Carpenter's four major spheres: religion, town, court and politics. Here, in an almost contemporary way, theatre was a crucible for cultural change and so it continued. While part of the puritan opposition to theatre north and south of the Border was because it involved "telling lies," in Scotland opposition was surely also based on recognition of the power of theatre over ideas.

For drama to serve such a radical function implies that it was embedded in popular consciousness. The very presence of playfields like Cupar's and Edinburgh's in many other towns highlights drama's existence as a regular feature of Scottish civic life. Further, the example already given of Sandie Furrour's performance, not to mention the other cases discussed by McGavin, suggests a society in which expression of potentially subversive (and sometimes conservative) attitudes and ideas through theatricality was well-established. A necessary counterpoint to this is that it might also be retained conservatively in a time of rapidly changing ideas. Where Kirk Sessions record insistence that drama, whether folk, rural, or in the texts of pre-reformation religious plays, be suppressed, McGavin points out that the recurrence of these admonitions, which by implication of their reiteration were not being entirely seriously observed, is telling evidence for the continuance of theatrical manifestations in post-Reformation Scotland. In the summer of 1583, for example, "Iohnne wod & Iohne broun schulmaistiris at ye kirkis of Mwthill & strogayth [Muthill and Strageath, now in Perth and Kinross]" were arraigned before the Stirling Presbytery, accused of "playing of clark playis on ye sabboth day yairby."[2] Both repented, but the issue was not simply the playing, but the fact it was on the sabbath and that it was a 'clark' play. The Presbytery minutes make it clear the ministers wanted to examine the script employed, presumably to check if it was in their eyes heretical. Given the time of year, McGavin suggests it may even have been a May performance.[3] In other words, the Kirk was concerned to control drama.

McGavin, however, has observed that the early 17th-century presbytery in Haddington failed to suppress annual local plays in the nearby villages of Samuelston and Salton. Repeated attempts are made to suppress plays that, if such attempts were successful, would be redundant. Instead, he observes a pattern of movement

---

2 Stirling Presbytery Minutes 1581-89/90 NAS CH2/722/1 Microfilm, Unfol. 21 May 1583.
3 Email: 10 February 2012.

from urban to rural drama [...] [and] from unthinking pleasures to pleasures pointedly enjoyed in opposition to the kirk. [...] [The Presbytery's] flurries of activity against rural drama, our only evidence that such drama took place, were all it could manage in the circumstances. By contrast, instances of adultery and fornication were frequently recorded. (McGavin 1997, 156-157)

The vibrancy of this theatrical tradition as opposed to the relative unpopularity of professional playhouse theatre – for reasons already identified, but also for linguistic and political reasons we shall come to – has been remarked on by Edwin Morgan. Even in Reformation, Restoration and Enlightenment Scotland 'drama' manifested itself in a wide range. Morgan identifies part of that range:

> [P]opular kinds of dramatic or semi-dramatic entertainment, shows and spectacles, communal celebrations don't die out, even if they have to watch their step or go underground in oppressive or authoritarian or anti-hedonistic times, and they are always ready to be thawed out again, like cryogenic Lords of Misrule, whenever society gives them a chance. [...] Lyndsay's *Satyre of the Thrie Estaits* did not come out of a vacuum. If it seems unique, this is because other plays and playwrights that we know about from the medieval period have left no trace except their names or titles. [...] And everywhere there were folk-plays and folk-revels on May Day, at Midsummer and New Year. Guisers with their faces blacked up would dance through the churchyard, men dressed as women and women as men. [...] So it won't do to say that the Scots are by nature undramatic or untheatrical. (Morgan E. 1999)

In fact, Todd provides extensive evidence of the Kirk's difficulty in managing, let alone suppressing, such activities, especially as they related to older rituals surrounding marriage, death or seasonal celebrations at May, midsummer or Christmas (Todd 2002, 213-221). As she says, "The elders were no fools; they chose their battles carefully, and with the priorities of the larger church and community in mind" (Todd, 2002, 185-186). From such subtler, less constantly oppressive approaches than conventional scholarship tended to suggest until recently, she observes:

> The evidence suggests instead that protestantism may have succeeded in part *because* the sessions enforced their legislation against festivity lightly, flexibly and sporadically. Where a heavy hand might have strengthened the opposition to Reformed doctrine as well as discipline, the elders' sense of the inutility of quashing the useful and harmless allowed for a more gradual but secure cultural reconstruction. [...] session minutes reveal them gradually subsuming old traditions into a new kind of festivity, with new ways of demonstrating individual and corporate status and communal cohesion in the face of both the linear and cyclical passage of time. (Todd 2002, 221-222)

Janet Sorensen reinforces the case for the importance of popular theatricalised forms in questioning the status quo and encouraging communal awareness:

> [E]xamining the wide range of public performance, broadly conceived to include not only theatre but also ballad singing, street performance and even sermons, also reveals an expansive diversity of articulations of Scottishness, often in conflict. Oral performance of ballads, for instance, could invigorate subterranean Jacobite sympathies, instil a sense of connection to a larger Scots past or define an emerging, enlightened literate Scotland in contrast to a residual oral culture. Theatre might draw polite spectators into imagined networks of national feeling or arouse depraved drives, creating a community of sinners. (Sorensen 2007, 133)

To such essentially dramatic performances as ballad-singing, which would come to include the overtly political singing and enacting of Jacobite ballads in the streets (Sorensen 2007, 135), one might add the long, quasi-theatrical Scottish tradition of story-telling.

Within the framework of theatricality as a crucible of change, the Kirk itself employed theatre as a means of propagandising its worldview on appropriate personal relationships and responsibilities. Todd talks, for example, of the Kirk's highly theatrical enactments of repentance, social responsibility and forgiveness where, the minister's role included those of "drama coach and director" (Todd 2002, 127):

> Penance was staged and choreographed, with penitents assuming carefully prescribed positions and moving from one place to another in procession within the church, and through particular doors when entering and exiting the building. It was scripted, with allowances for both prescribed, formulaic utterance and *ex tempore* speech, the whole inserted into the larger script of sermon-centred worship. (Todd 2002, 129)

Todd describes such techniques, including specific penitents' costumes, as helping "as in any dramatic performance [...] to communicate the themes of the play [...] on the penitential stage" (Todd 2002, 149).

Meantime dramas were written, often with explicit religio-political intent. Perhaps most famous of these is Archibald Pitcairne's (1652-1713) *The Assembly* (1692). Circulating in manuscript and unpublished until 1722, the play attacks the General Assembly's pedantry and the obscurantism of both Williamite and Jacobite political sectarianism. It mocks presbyterian hypocrisy in a subplot remarkable in its frankness about perceived ministerial lechery: Solomon Cherrytrees, an Assembly member, in a parodic hidden reference to *Song of Solomon*, counsels Laura:

> [T]hese two fair Breasts of yours evidently prove Parity in the Church-Members [...]. Thus and thus they have in brotherly Love and Concord together. Do not imagine that the natural Body there is thus orderly, and that the Wise should suffer such a Blemish in the Mystical (Handling her breasts). (Pitcairne 1722, 50)

Laura responds, "Good Mr Parson ye must fetch your *Similies* elsewhere, I'll assure you I'll be neither Parable nor Metaphor to your Kirk-Government." Solomon is shameless, rather waxing indignant at the use of the "Antichristian name of Parson" as "prelatic" (50). Pitcairne's main plot plods, while his satirical subplot of Presbyterian hypocrisy and love triumphant flows, but both embody anti-Kirk polemic.

As I have noted elsewhere (Brown 2011b, 22-40), an important additional element in late 17th- and 18th-century Scottish drama provision was drama in schools. Throughout more or less the length and breadth of Scotland not only were ministers supporting drama, but required it as part of the curriculum. Even Lundie, a small village in the Carse of Gowrie, produced its play, though in 1688 the Dunkeld Presbytery suspended the master, William Bouok, for "acting a comoedie wherein he made a mock of religious duties and ordinances" (McKenzie 1955, 106), a more pointed offence to the Kirk than that of the Muthill schoolmasters mentioned earlier. It was not the provision of drama that was a problem for the Kirk; it was its possible ideological purpose. As J. McKenzie observes, after the Reformation,

> Kirk Sessions and Presbyteries exercised a stricter control, banning Sunday performances, censoring plays, and restricting the choice of subject. School plays were [how-

ever] [...] used [...] for imparting religious instruction or for revealing the errors of the Roman Catholic faith. (McKenzie 1955, 103)

There was certainly for some a prudish desire to contain the impact of drama; H. G. Graham notes the purpose was to further learning, and "not to pander to any sinful love of playing; and indeed, the pieces selected were admirably gifted to extinguish utterly all fondness for the stage in juvenile breasts throughout their natural life" (Graham 1937, 439).

But the role in the development of 18th-century professional theatre in Scotland, of lawyers, teachers and ministers, those professions that would most have depended on the skills developed through drama in schools, is suggestive. It appears as if in fact school drama actually succeeded in "pander[ing] to the sinful love of playing" and did not "extinguish utterly all fondness for the stage in juvenile breasts throughout their natural life." Let us take only two examples: John Home, author of *Douglas* (1756), was the socially well-connected minister at Athelstaneford and, when the conservative Evangelicals in the Kirk tried to discipline him for writing a play, he simply left his charge and went to write for the London stage, while, according to Adrienne Scullion, as a young lawyer, James Boswell is credited with *A View of the Edinburgh Theatre during the Summer Season, 1759*, a faithful thrice-weekly report on and critique of the plays produced across that summer season (Scullion 1998, 107-108). From such fruitful ground, new Scottish plays like *Patriotism* (1763), a political farce in support of Prime Minister Bute by advocate John (James?) Baillie, emerged. Meantime, earlier in the century, interrelations within theatre as cultural crucible are seen in the development of a major play, Allan Ramsay's *The Gentle Shepherd*. McGavin, as already noted, has pointed to Haddington's dramatic vitality in earlier centuries: its schoolmaster from 1720 until 1731 was John Leslie, a friend of Allan Ramsay's. Through Leslie and Ramsay, the potential links between school drama, and professional playwriting and theatre become clear. *The Gentle Shepherd*, published first in 1725, was revised as a ballad-opera for Haddington Grammar School pupils' performance. This took place on 22 January 1729 in what was then Edinburgh's venue for professional theatre performance: Taylor's Hall. Such a clear link between different forms of drama, and also the continuity or re-emergence of drama in particular institutions and locales,[4] here between school and professional, suggests a complex and interactive sense of theatre in Scotland. Further, while plays in schools might be secular (though on classical subjects) – as early as 1600, Terence was played in Elgin under the auspices of the Master of the Grammar School – it is clear that by the 1730s plays performed by scholars might be not just secular, but contemporary. When in 1731 Leslie became Dalkeith's schoolmaster, Vanbrugh's *The Provok'd Husband* was performed there, only three years after its Drury Lane première. This is a more rapid move from West End to regional performance than is seen in much UK professional regional theatre today. As Morgan observed, "it won't do to say that the Scots are by nature undramatic or untheatrical" (Morgan E. 1999).

Despite Morgan's observation, however, it is true to say that after 1707 there was further cause for many Scots to suspect the role of professional theatre beyond its identification with expense and anti-Presbyterian values. When, very soon after the

---

4 I am grateful to Professor John McGavin for drawing my attention to this point and the following point about the production of Terence in Elgin. I owe him thanks for his most helpful comments on a late draft of this paper, as I do to Dr Trish Reid.

Union, learning to speak English became the fashion, a key part of the process, especially for the Edinburgh middle classes, was the speech training and teaching of anglicised pronunciation offered by actors from the English stage. The professional theatre in Scotland was for many years part of a conscious process of post-Union descotticisation, which I have called "The (Rule) Britannia Project" (Brown 2012, 4-5). This did not necessarily reconcile many Scots to the value of professional theatre; rather it made professional theatre an alien form. Leaving aside Ramsay's work, almost all the professional theatre texts, even on Scottish topics, until very late in the 18th century, were in English, still then largely an alien language in an alien artform. Even as late as 1821, in his novel *Annals of the Parish*, John Galt finds it possible to observe and gently satirise an attitude which he dates in his fiction to 1789:

> the elderly people thought his language rather too Englified, which I thought likewise, for I could never abide that the plain auld Kirk of Scotland, with her sober presbyterian simplicity, should borrow, either in word or deed, from the language of the prelatic hierarchy of England. (Galt 2001, 102-103)

Theatre was not only a crucible of change intellectually and politically; it might also provide a means of changing speech and language behaviour. And theatre was then employing "prelatic" language.

Despite some 18th-century reservations about the art form, one of the most famous moments in Scottish religio-political and cultural history was theatrical. Home's *Douglas*, already referred to, opened in Edinburgh's Canongate Theatre on 14 December 1756. Home was a member of the Kirk's relatively cosmopolitan Moderate wing, which included such leading church, university and Enlightenment figures as William Robertson, Hugh Blair, Adam Ferguson and Alexander "Jupiter" Carlyle. Ian Clark observes:

> The driving force in Moderatism was a mood of cultural liberation and optimism which made the Moderate clergy aspire to play not merely a national but a European role [...] [they] had no desire to see the Church of Scotland drawn aside by a narrow and sectarian spirit from the mainstream of Scottish life [...]. (Clark 1970, 204)

Already at the 1756 General Assembly, the Moderates had defeated an Evangelical attempt to excommunicate David Hume. They sought, in effect, the cultural liberation of Scotland: Robertson, university Principal, was a leading revisionist historian; Blair effectively invented the study of English Literature, holding the first Chair of its kind, Rhetoric and Belles-Lettres at Edinburgh, from 1762; Ferguson is the father of social sciences. All participated with Hume, who played Glenalvon, in a rehearsal of *Douglas*, Robertson reading Randolph, Carlyle Old Norval, Home himself Douglas, Adam Ferguson Lady Randolph and Hugh Blair Anna. Of that cast only Hume was not a minister. A decade after Culloden, *Douglas* explores the tragic results of civil conflict and hidden identity, but it has importance beyond theatre in marking a crucial challenge, seeking to change older ways of thinking. The local Presbytery responded, as was its wont, by censuring ministers, including Carlyle, who attended the play and approving on 5 January 1757 an *Admonition and Exhortation* declaring playhouses immoral. But it seems that by then the Kirk's rejection of theatre was losing force. Those censured mostly apologised, but stayed in post, generally seen in a sympathetic light; the *Admonition* itself had little or no practical impact. The Evangelicals were in retreat, while Home, as already noted, resigned his charge in June, heading off any discipline he faced and south to London where Garrick presented *Douglas* to great acclaim (see also Morgan M. 2012). The professional playhouse theatre had now established itself alongside other dramatic forms as a locus for challenge of existing ideas.

There remained, however, a variety of communal dramatic forms besides folk drama. Interestingly, as professional stage and text-based drama developed a more popular profile, one finds local plays like John Finlayson's *The Marches Day* (1771). Set in Linlithgow, and featuring the burgh's trades, vivid Scots dialogue, much banter and local references, it celebrates the town's annual festival (which still takes place) and may represent a pulling together of traditions of communal, folk and school plays. In another case, identified by Barbara Bell, we find "overt and immediate communal ownership of the localised source material as in the case of 'John O' Arnha'" (Bell 2001, 54).[5] This play adapted a short poem by George Beattie, a Montrose lawyer, featuring his contemporary, John Finlay, a burgh officer celebrated for tall tales. John, after a day's drinking at a fair and fighting another local worthy, meets supernatural beings on the way home. Local scenery for the performance included a central scene of Montrose High Street on the day of the Rood Fair. Such local drama complemented the National Drama about which Bell has written extensively (cf. Bell 2001). This form was highly successful in 19th-century Scotland, largely based on adaptations of Scott's novels, which for most of that century provided a locus of debate about, and examination of, Scottish cultural and political identities.

As railway travel became commonplace and industrial forms of touring out of London and Edinburgh took over from local companies, by the latter part of the 19th century both local and national drama were in decline on main stages. Scottish playwrights who wanted to develop their art, by and large, found themselves working within the structures of commercial theatre with its Mecca in London's West End. Popular drama continued, not least with the establishment of the Scottish Community Drama Association in 1926, but much of that amateur theatre came to reflect a cosier version of professional theatre rather than a distinct strand of theatre concerned with cultural change. There were exceptions like Joe Corrie's Bowhill Players, which presented some of his socially radical plays of the 1920s, before he succumbed to the need to write for the SCDA market, and the radical productions of Glasgow Unity Theatre in the 1940s. Nonetheless, it seemed that theatre in Scotland had become a branch of a more centralised professional theatre. Leading Scottish playwrights like J. M. Barrie and, to an extent, James Bridie seemed to mark a way forward through the West End for a Scottish theatre whose focus was less cultural change and more commercial success. Yet, the Unity experiment provided a seedbed that developed a range of performers like Russell Hunter, Andrew Keir, Roddy McMillan and Marjorie Thomson and playwrights like Ena Lamont Stewart and, again, McMillan (although both of those writers had difficulties being accepted on Scotland's main stages until the 'renaissance' arrived). It took time for their impact and that of their colleagues to work through the more centralised theatre systems of the first two-thirds of the 20th century, even when such companies as Glasgow Citizens (1943-) and Edinburgh's Gateway (1953-65) and Royal Lyceum (1965-) were established. Nonetheless, work through they did. It behoves us to remember the deep underlying Scottish theatre traditions that fed their energy. Given those traditions and this article's analysis of the

---

5 For a more detailed discussion, see Bell (2011, 54-57).

historic role of drama and theatricality in Scottish cultures, one should recognise that the recent 'renaissance' is less a surprising efflorescence and more a logical evolution from preceding, but not always legitimate, dramatic and theatrical traditions. These for a time had gone into apparent abeyance, but only it seems to erupt into vibrant activity with all the more force and politico-cultural impact in recent years.

It is a flaw of much recent writing about Scottish theatre that it has not properly taken account of the longer-term theatrical and dramatic traditions of Scotland, reaching back more or less continuously over seven hundred recorded years – and no doubt many more unrecorded – and their role in cultural change. Clare Wallace says:

> As work by Randall Stevenson, Ian Brown, Mark Fisher among others attests, with regard to theatre it is not until after World War II, and in particular the 1970s, that a radical and socially committed Scottish theatre begins to actively distinguish itself and to assert its own value and specificity. (Wallace 2011, 200)

I recognise this characterisation of a substantial part of my recent work on contemporary Scottish theatre and its renaissance. I do not repudiate the vitality of that renaissance nor the arguments I have set out for its cultural importance and impact. But I plead guilty to fostering an impression that "it is not until after World War II, and in particular the 1970s, that a radical and socially committed Scottish theatre begins to actively distinguish itself and to assert its own value and specificity." As this essay has made clear, radical Scottish theatre, "a crucible for cultural change," has a far longer, wider and deeper pedigree: "Arts first; politics later."

Works Cited

Anon. "Panto, Variety and the Scottish People." 2011. Staging the Nation. A Conversation about Theatre. 16 January 2012 <http://stagingthenation.com/panto-variety-and-the-scottish-people/>.

Bell, Barbara. "The National Drama and the Nineteenth Century." *Edinburgh Companion to Scottish Drama*. Ed. Ian Brown. Edinburgh: Edinburgh University Press, 2011. 47-59.

Brown, Ian. "Staging the Nation: Multiplicity and Cultural Diversity in Contemporary Scottish Theatre." *The Edinburgh History of Scottish Literature*. Vol. 3. Eds. Ian Brown et al. Edinburgh: Edinburgh University Press, 2007. 283-294.

—. "A Lively Tradition and Creative Amnesia." *Edinburgh Companion to Scottish Drama*. Ed. Ian Brown. Edinburgh: Edinburgh University Press, 2011a. 1-5.

—. "Public and Private Performance:1650-1800." *Edinburgh Companion to Scottish Drama*. Ed. Ian Brown. Edinburgh: Edinburgh University Press, 2011b. 22-40.

—. *"Our multiform, our infinite Scotland:" Scottish Literature as 'Scottish', 'English' and 'World' Literature*. Glasgow: Association for Scottish Literary Studies, 2012.

Carpenter, Sarah. "Scottish Drama until 1650." *Edinburgh Companion to Scottish Drama*. Ed. Ian Brown. Edinburgh: Edinburgh University Press, 2011. 6-21.

Clark, Ian D. L. "From Protest to Reaction: The Moderate Regime in the Church of Scotland, 1752-1805." *Scotland in the Age of Improvement*. Eds. Nicholas T. Philipson and Rosalind Mitchison. Edinburgh: Edinburgh University Press, 1970. 200-224.

Findlay, Bill. *A History of Scottish Theatre*. Edinburgh: Polygon, 1998.

Galt, John. *Annals of the Parish, The Ayrshire Legatees, The Provost*. Edinburgh: Saltire Society, 2001.

Graham, H. G. *Social Life of Scotland in the Eighteenth Century*. London: Black, 1937.
Lochhead, Liz. *Educating Agnes*. London: Nick Hern, 2008.
McGavin, John. "Drama in Sixteenth-Century Haddington." *European Medieval Drama* 1 (1997): 147-159.
—. *Theatricality and Narrative in Medieval and Early Modern Scotland*. Aldershot: Ashgate, 2007.
McKenzie, J. "School and University Drama in Scotland, 1650-1760." *Scottish Historical Review* 34 (1955): 103-121.
Maloney, Paul. "Entertainment and Popular Culture." *Changing Identities, Ancient Roots: The History of West Dunbartonshire from Earliest Times*. Ed. Ian Brown. Edinburgh: Edinburgh University Press, 2006. 142-181.
Morgan, Edwin. "Scottish Drama: An Overview." 1999. *ScotLit* 20. 16 January 2012 <http://www.arts.gla.ac.uk/scotlit/asls/Scottishdrama.html>.
Morgan, Megan Stoner. "Speaking with a Double Voice: John Home's *Douglas* and the Idea of Scotland." *Scottish Literary Review* 4.1 (2012). Forthcoming.
Newton, Michael. "Folk Drama in Gaelic Scotland." *Edinburgh Companion to Scottish Drama*. Ed. Ian Brown. Edinburgh: Edinburgh University Press, 2011. 41-46.
Pitcairne, Archibald. *The Assembly*. London: 1722.
Scullion, Adrienne. "The Eighteenth Century." *A History of Scottish Theatre*. Ed. Bill Findlay. Edinburgh: Polygon, 1998. 80-136.
Sorensen, Janet. "Varieties of Public Performance: Folk Songs, Ballads, Popular Drama and Sermons." *The Edinburgh History of Scottish Literature*. Eds. Ian Brown et al. Edinburgh: Edinburgh University Press, 2007. Vol. 2. 133-142.
Todd, Margo. *The Culture of Protestantism in Early Modern Scotland*. New Haven: Yale University Press, 2002.
Wallace, Clare. "Unfinished Business – Allegories of Otherness in *Dunsinane*." *Cosmotopia: Transnational Identities in David Greig's Theatre*. Eds. Anja Müller and Clare Wallace. Prague: Litteraria Pragensia Books, 2011. 196-213.

Canada und Irland – die neuen Themenhefte von Abi Workshop Englisch!

Zielgerichtet und erfolgreich auf das Abitur vorbereiten – auch mit den neuesten Themenheften gelingt das zuverlässig. Die Arbeitshefte mit CD-ROM bieten alles was der Oberstufenunterricht zu abiturrelevanten Themen verlangt und können ergänzend zu einem Lehrwerk oder völlig unabhängig davon eingesetzt werden.

Abi Workshop Englisch Canada
Schülerheft mit CD-ROM
978-3-12-601009-2 • 11,25 ☻
Lehrerheft
978-3-12-601019-1 • 11,95 ●△

Abi Workshop Englisch Ireland
Schülerheft mit CD-ROM
978-3-12-601010-8 • 11,25 ☻
Lehrerheft
978-3-12-601020-7 • 11,95 ●△

Alle Themen- und Methodenhefte zu Abi Workshop Englisch finden Sie unter www.klett.de

☻ Bei diesen Titeln erhalten Sie als Lehrerin oder Lehrer ein Prüfstück zum Prüfpreis mit 20 % Ermäßigung. Das Angebot gilt nur für Titel, die grundsätzlich zur Einführung geeignet sind. | ● Titel nur zum angegebenen Preis erhältlich | △ Nur mit Schulstempel erhältlich

Bestellung und Beratung bei Klett:
Ernst Klett Verlag, Postfach 10 26 45, 70022 Stuttgart
Telefon 0711 · 66 72-13 33, Telefax 0711 · 66 72-20 80
www.klett.de

GLENDA NORQUAY, Liverpool
Untying the Knots: Gender and Scottish Writing

Writing for *Scotlit*, the newsletter of the Association of Scottish Literary Studies, in 2011, Andrew Hook described his experiences of "Teaching Scottish Literature in the USA." While the newsletter focused on the importance of embedding Scottish literature in Scotland's education curriculum, Hook's article reflected on the process of selecting texts to teach for a student class at the Ivy League, Dartmouth College. His conclusion reinforces the journal's emphasis on the quality of Scottish literature available and the importance of its dissemination.[1] Considering the construction of a syllabus for "modern Scottish literature" (from 1900), Hook notes some choices were inevitable – *The House with the Green Shutters*, *Sunset Song* and *The Prime of Miss Jean Brodie*. But he admits to thinking "long and hard" about choosing another woman writer for a college where "Women and Gender Studies were big across the campus." In the end he selected Catherine Carswell's *Open the Door!* When, on course completion, students were asked to assess texts in terms of "Literary Merit, Enjoyment, Difficulty and Enlightenment," Hook notes that, despite his best efforts, this novel came out worst under all headings:

> In seminar discussion I came back again and again to the point of how challenging the book was, given conventional attitudes towards the role of women in Scottish society before the First World War – and how significant the author's friendship with D. H. Lawrence was in the composition of the novel. But the majority were unpersuaded […]. (Hook 2011, 11)

Having just finished editing *The Edinburgh Companion to Scottish Women's Writing* (Norquay 2012), Professor Hook's narrative elicited sympathy for the lack of success with Carswell, but also gave pause for thought. In the introduction to the *Companion* volume I consider whether Scottish women's writing demands separate consideration or has now achieved full integration within a body of "Scottish literature." The fact that Professor Hook felt the need to gesture towards the gender agenda by including two novels by women seemed, rather dismayingly, to suggest: that Scottish women's writing still occupies a peripheral role in thinking about the literary canon; secondly, the perception remains that only women writers can address gender issues; and thirdly, that the value of women writers – with the exception (almost always) of Muriel Spark – is in their representation of women's experiences. It is surprising, as we move into the second decade of the 21st century, that the work of challenging canon formations and notions of literary value, of questioning the construction of gendered identities, of recovering the work of neglected women writers or the body of work in masculinity studies, should not have advanced our gendered understanding of Scottish literature further than this.

This essay explores where we are in the gendering of Scottish literature, bringing together different critical approaches which might take us beyond the impasse de-

---

1 "I like to think that by the end of the course some enlightenment over both Scotland's past and present, joined to some appreciation of the achievements of modern Scottish novelists, had been gained by a group of young American students at Dartmouth College." (Hook 2011, 11)

scribed by Hook. Drawing on my experiences in editing the *Companion to Scottish Women's Writing*, it examines relationships between national and gendered identity formations and reflects on the value systems, critical hierarchies and assumptions which contribute to canon formation within Scottish writing. It argues that recent debates within Scottish literary criticism and work represented by the new *Companion* volume offer more fruitful ways of thinking about gender than tokens of representation, either numerical or experiential.

Gendered understanding of Scottish literature has its own narrative history. As Susanne Hagemann and others have noted, a feminist critical approach developed relatively late in Scottish literature. In a wide-ranging contribution to *The Edinburgh History of Scottish Literature*, Hagemann suggests it "did not happen until the early 1990s," citing as explanation a focusing on the quest for Scottishness in what she terms "a small-nation syndrome" (Hagemann 2007, 214). Caroline Gonda, in 1995, quoted novelist Ali Smith's assertion that "Scottish women's writing has only really been given a place [...] in the last ten years" (Gonda 1995, 5). Matt McGuire, surveying critical responses to 20th-century Scottish literature, notes that until very recently gender has remained a highly marginalized area. Yet while endorsing Hagemann's view of a formal opposition between "critical preoccupations with the nation and an interest in questions of gender" (McGuire 2009, 63), McGuire suggests the exuberance of modern Scottish literature might be attributed to "the long overdue arrival and recognition of writing by Scotland's women" (63, 65).

The landmark in that process of recognition is usually identified as Douglas Gifford and Dorothy McMillan's weighty *A History of Scottish Women's Writing*. Arguing the validity of a separate account of women's writing, the editors assert: if the collection "carves out more space to talk about women's writing then that seems good enough to be going on with" (Gifford and McMillan 1997, ix). Covering a wide range of writers (although, as later histories suggest, perhaps less comprehensive in its coverage of Gaelic culture), it surveys themes, and individual writers. This collection was, to an extent, a series of interpretations but, as the editors acknowledge, primarily an act of recovery, part of that early-stage feminist project.[2] There had, however, been earlier expressions of feminist discontent and exploration of tensions between gendered and national identities. McGuire, delineating the situation before the resurgence of women writers, cites a 1979 interview with Margaret Atwood in *Cencrastus* magazine in which William Findlay comments "there are and have been very few women writers in Scotland" (Findlay 1979, 2), and suggests Gifford and McMillan's 1997 collection shone a light into "the darkened rooms" (McGuire 2009, 66). However, a vigorous correspondence in subsequent issues between Findlay and Aileen Christianson and engagement in the pages of *Cencrastus* with gendered inflections of national identity – Anderson and Norquay's "Superiorism,'" argues the sexism of the Scottish intelligentsia, calling for gender-inflected readings of our literary culture (Anderson and Norquay 1984, 8-10) – evidences an earlier, active concern with feminism and nationalism.[3] Prior to Gifford and McMillan's collection, Marilyn Reizbaum theorized

---

2 Other important acts of recovery include Kerrigan (1991) and McMillan (1999).
3 Christianson responded to Findlay's question by suggesting women were busy addressing oppression in other areas (Christianson and Findlay 1984, 43). Findlay noted the policy of *Cencrastus* had been to adopt "a deliberative policy of attempting to elicit material both creative *and* analytical, from and about women in Scotland, with depressing results. With few expectations we were promised material

confrontations between gender and national understanding in "Canonical Double Cross Scottish and Irish Women's Writing" (Reizbaum 1992). Picking up on writer Joy Hendry's memorable image of "the double knot on the peeny," knots in the apron representing the dual restrictions of sex and nation (Hendry 1987, 36), Reizbaum articulates the double exclusion suffered by women writing in marginalized cultures, Scotland and Ireland, "where the struggle to assert a nationalist identity obscures or doubly marginalizes the assertion of gender, the woman's voice" (Reizbaum 1992, 165). Noting that "[w]omen have been traditionally excluded by the mainstream literary establishments in Scotland and Ireland in historical consonance with the exclusion of women's writing elsewhere," Reizbaum argues:

> Women have found themselves in a peculiar predicament, compelled to resist or challenge the demands of the nationalist imperative in order to clarify the terms of their own oppression, and consequently disregarded on the basis that their claims do not embrace the *more* significant issues of national self-determination. […] the nationalist struggle has been defined in patriarchal terms and has effectively excluded many women not only from a tradition of writing but from any identification with nationalist aims […].
> (Reizbaum 1992, 172)

Reiterating Hendry's phrase, coined in 1987, Reizbaum demonstrates that a feminist engagement with Scottish women's creativity and a tense relationship with existing literary paradigms were articulated some time before 1997.

Nevertheless, Gifford and McMillan's collection offered a robust response to processes of exclusion, demonstrating a wealth of writing by Scottish women. Two further volumes which intensified the focus on individual writers but applied a more specifically theorized feminist approach were Carol Anderson and Aileen Christianson's *Scottish Women's Fiction, 1920s to 1960s: Journeys into Being* (2000) and Christianson and Alison Lumsden's *Contemporary Scottish Women Writers* (2000). Both collections offered complex readings of lesser-known writers and resituated established figures such as Spark within a feminist context. As the subtitle suggests, *Journeys into Being* focused on self-development and gendered understanding in women's writing. The second volume, shaped by the idea of "alternative imaginings," presented highly women-centred perspectives, combining acts of recovery and interpretation to demonstrate the pleasing strengths of women's writing in the 20th century. These collections, along with Caroline Gonda's *Tea and Leg-Irons* (1992), are characterized by what McGuire terms a tone of "celebratory enunciation" (McGuire 2009, 72), and represent important challenges in thinking about female creativity.

Yet questions around the conflicting pulls of national and gendered identifications and their implications for both subjectivity and the nation state remained. Aileen Christianson's return to the subject in her influential "Debatable Lands and Passable Boundaries" evinces their continuing power. Deploying the Scottish image of "debatable lands" – borderline territories – she recognizes the value of occupying "in-between spaces" and argues for Scottish women's multiple and heterogeneous relation to gender and nation as a positive. By identifying Nan Shepherd's novels as critically marginalized and misunderstood because of their specificity – north-east, rural, female subject matter – Christianson interrogates the interpretation of literary texts as

---

but despite many reminders it never forthcame […]" (Christianson and Findlay 1984, 43). Petrie notes the importance of Anderson and Norquay's intervention (Petrie 2004, 65).

representing 'national' concerns. Urban and "masculine" fictions have too frequently assumed the role of embodying Scottishness (Christianson 2002, 72-73). Her argument connects with an increasingly lively engagement with masculinity and Scottish writing.

If Hagemann sees feminism coming slowly to Scottish literary criticism, Neil McMillan identifies a similar tardiness in masculinity studies:

> The specificities of what might constitute various types of Scottish masculinities have only just begun to be addressed by theorists, partly due to a resistance to theory, and in particular to men's studies, on the part of Scottish critics [...]. [T]hinking through the construction of hegemonic masculinities will always pose a problem for the Scottish critical tradition because it trades on the idea that to be a Scot, of whatever class, is always to occupy a marginal position. (McMillan 2003, 68)

Since 2003 significant work by Berthold Schoene – in *Writing Men*, in *The Edinburgh Companion to Contemporary Scottish Literature* and in various essays – work by Gill Plain exploring Scottish detective fiction and its paradigms of masculinity, and a monograph and essays by Carole Jones have all extended awareness of masculinities within the theorizing of gendered positions. Lea and Schoene's collection, *Posting the Male*, contained important contributions addressing contemporary models of masculinity in Scottish writing. As the editors note, the essay by Irene Rose on Jackie Kay's *Trumpet* (1998), in which "masculinity and femininity continue to clash quite alarmingly at the same time as they contrive to congeal harmoniously into one," most acutely demonstrates the impossibility of clear-cut demarcations within gender and literary studies (Lea and Schoene, 2003, 8). In their introduction, the editors confront the work of another influential Scottish critic, Christopher Whyte. Interrogating his view that

> the most effective way of fostering a solution to the crisis of (straight) masculinity is to move beyond it, and, quite simply, pay it less attention. For the doings of violent men neither merit nor repay the time so often spent in contemplating them. (Whyte 1998, 284)

they propose an agenda for "renouncing once and for all the monadic fixity of all traditional gender identities – be they masculine or feminine, straight or gay" and embracing a kind of gender "nomadism" instead (Lea and Schoene 2003, 16). In 2003 they are already arguing against essentialist identities and acknowledging the subtleties of literary engagements with gender.

Other studies by Schoene and Jones offer sophisticated readings of the complex politics dynamics of gender, nation and sexuality played out in contemporary Scottish fiction. Jones shows in analysis of a Welsh novel and a Barr play how camp/drag can function in ways which reassert phallic masculinity (Jones 2009a). Her work also demonstrates a keen awareness of race in systems of representation, examining James Kelman in a postcolonial context and reading McIlvanney's *Docherty* and Welsh's *Marabou Stork Nightmares* as deploying whiteness and abjection as shaping discourses in both masculine and sexual politics (Jones 2006). Wider theoretical debates again sharpen the nuances of specific interpretations of Scottish texts.[4]

Yet, while Scottish writing has not been seen as "a crucible of explosive and rebellious representation of gender" (Jones 2009b, 11), critical debates around the rela-

---

[4] See also Kasia Boddy and Berthold Schoene in Bell and Miller (2004).

tionship of gender and nation become increasingly volatile. This is most evident in criticism by poet, novelist and critic Christopher Whyte. Whyte's 1995 *Gendering the Nation: Studies in Modern Scottish Literature* worked to an important agenda, with essays extending a critical lens to lesbian writing and to homophobic representations in established fiction. Exposing assumptions made around both normative sexuality and models of masculinity, it demonstrated discussions of gender did not need to be consigned to women's writing but were central to understanding the whole of Scottish literature. Indeed Whyte argues that Scottish culture is "a privileged site for the study of gender and its interaction with other factors in the formation of identity" (Whyte, 1995, xvi). Whyte, however, becomes increasingly concerned with the implications of identity politics in a nationalist context and vice versa. In his influential 1998 essay on Scottish masculinities, a terrain explored further by Schoene, Plain and Jones, he raises a number of significant questions about the ways in which gender and literature interact. Presenting Scottish fiction in the context of its "representational pacts" – negotiations of subject, authorship, readership and politics – Whyte argues that urban fiction increasingly and explicitly assumed the burden of national representation; that prose likewise took over from poetry in this respect; and that consumers of 'hardman fiction' are unlikely to be hardmen themselves but often women and/or middle-class. He observes:

> [O]ne may posit a demand on the part of the Scottish middle-class for fictional representation from which it itself is excluded; a demand, in other words, for textual invisibility. (Whyte 1998, 275)

Refusing easy models of literary identification Whyte calls for a different perception of the subject matter, subject positions and systems of representation offered by contemporary Scottish literature.

He engages further with questions of canon formation in Bell and Miller's 2004 collection *Scotland in Theory* – "Queer Readings, Gay Texts: *Redgauntlet* and *The Prime of Miss Jean Brodie*" uses two canonical Scottish novels to offer another challenge to established modes of reading. Here Whyte suggests that texts may offer homoerotic readings without necessarily imputing sexuality to their author. The marrying of literary theory to Scottish literary criticism, Whyte posits, has been so difficult because of an inherent tension: "The theorist threatens to dissolve the very basis on which the nationalist has struggled to create a canon" (Whyte 2004b, 152). After discussing cross-dressing and triangulation in *Redgauntlet*, he expresses astonishment at the ways in which its positioning within a Scottish context had occluded the lesbian dynamics of Spark's novel: was this because of the importance attributed to the novel in Scottish canon formation (and, as Hook demonstrates) its popularity as a teaching text? Whyte may be right. While queer readings of Spark's work feature in Martin McQuillan's *Theorising Muriel Spark* (2001), neither his collection nor Whyte's essay seem to have had significant impact upon Scottish critical constructions of Spark: indeed the recent *Edinburgh Companion to Muriel Spark* appears to confirm Whyte's sense of an inherent tension between canon and theory.[5]

If Whyte's concerns are political they are also literary, problematising the ways in which specific texts are mined for their engagement with one issue or another. In words revealing the poet he is, Whyte's Introduction to *Modern Scottish Poetry* asks

---

5   For a critique of 'queer' readings, see Carruthers (2010).

whether we should assume that "individual poems will act like iron filings, leaping into place when the appropriate magnet (the appropriate historical or political narrative) is applied beneath the paper they are scattered across" (Whyte 2004a, 8). Calling for a re-evaluation of the literary by rejection of the 'representative,' he echoes Christianson's demand that our maps of the Scottish literary canons are reconsidered. As McGuire notes, critics such as Cairns Craig, Carla Sassi and Alan Riach assert that Scottish literature provides a unique artistic space "in which the politics of national identity are played out'" (McGuire 2009, vii), while Whyte perceives this notion of writing as an extended meditation on nation as "*the* most highly problematic aspect of Scottish criticism" (McGuire 2009, 30). Situating creative writing within a matrix determined by engagement with the nation is to crush textual subtlety, imposing a monolithic concept of what the nation might mean. Whyte's polemics raise important questions about configurations of gender, class, national and sexuality but also, in that image of the iron filings clustering around particular magnets, they register the value in nuanced models of the complicated dynamics between authors, texts, readers and readings.

Recent critical engagements with gender and nation have undoubtedly moved beyond the crude representationalism or nationalist agendas that concern Whyte. Carla Sassi, for example, in *Why Scottish Literature Matters*, draws attention to the work and life of long-neglected north-east writer, Lorna Moon, suggesting that in her shifts of identity Moon, like contemporary media icon Madonna, impersonates and parodies contrasting and clichéd identities, challenging their "essence" and exploring performativity (Sassi 2005, 157).[6]

An alternative, but equally imaginative approach, can be found in Maureen Martin, *The Mighty Scot: Nation, Gender and the Nineteenth-Century Mystique of Scottish Masculinity* (2009), which looks at representations of masculinity, in particular that of the "rugged Highlander," as deployed in narratives of national identity. Martin suggests that the figure of the highlander is difficult for lowlanders to draw on: just as the image of the contemporary hardman was consumed by a middle-class and female readership, allowing a deflective imagining of "representative Scottishness," so 19th-century embodiments of a national masculinity offered a satisfactory figuring for a wider British audience, but remained largely irrelevant for much of the home audience. As Lyn Abrams notes, Martin's work represents an important development: in foregrounding "the neglected construct of masculinity as a historical category [it] offers a thought-provoking commentary on conceptions of national identity" (Abrams 2010). Drawing attention to the gendering of debates around national identity and the gendered inflection of national narratives, it too calls into question assumptions about the 'representative.' Martin's work, as with Christianson's on marginality, Schoene's on masculinity and Whyte's on textual invisibility, suggests a more complicated model of texts and audiences, ideologies and subject positions. The metaphors of debatable lands, of nomadism, and of "border-making" – used by Carla Sassi – all suggest attempts to free spatial configuration from monolithic literary traditions or essentialist notions of being and belonging. Indeed Sassi transforms the stone-like presence of Grassic Gibbon's "Chris Caldeonia" into a figure occupying "borderline spaces" (Sassi 2009, 151).

---

6 For Moon's challenging juxtapostions of the social and the personal see Norquay (1990); on her writing in the vernacular, see McCulloch (2004) and Norquay (2004).

The vibrancy of critical and theoretical debates around national and gendered identities also inflects the *Companion to Scottish Women's Writing*. While the volume serves as an introduction to the subject, its fifteen essays go beyond simple models of recovery or celebration, advancing nuanced understanding of the gendered determinants of form, genre and market. Some chapters present a curious freeing from the concerns of the nation, others a more subtle engagement with it. The essays are less concerned with agonizing over the sex of their subjects or with their Scottishness, but instead address the specifics of historical or geographical location, the contexts of production and reception and the complexity of the writing itself.

One feature of the *Companion* volume is the ways in which literary categories and aesthetic constructs are reinvestigated. Suzanne Gilbert, for example, writing on "Orality and the Ballad Tradition," suggests female orality, conceptually and practically, challenges Romantic concepts of the voice. Arguing for ballad culture's influence on later women writers, she demands we rethink relationships between the continuity of literary tradition and the specificity of performance. Sarah Dunnigan, evaluating what spiritual writing affords women, individually and within communities, suggests that the mystic – in spiritual activism, as a source of eroticism or evidenced in life-writing – was a dominant imaginative structure for women's creativity. Offering a variety of subject positions, spirituality is traced in a range of writings, demonstrating points of affinity and difference. Addressing the conceptual challenges of a culture and creative tradition in which the accessibility of material and understanding of its transmission poses their own challenges, Anne Frater and Michel Byrne likewise demonstrate the need for critical complexity in analysing the different creative outputs of women in Gaelic society. The transgressive use of high cultural forms and vernacular engagements with women's daily occupation again show points of affinity but significant differences.[7] Reconsidering the place of women in the Scottish Enlightenment and their shaping contribution to wider cultural configurations, both national and intellectual, Pam Perkins identifies a significantly distinctive "mixed intellectual sociability." In another questioning of aesthetic and generic categories, she traces the merging of "sociable conversation" with "sophisticated literary play." Both Perkins and Aileen Christianson, on "Private Writing," demonstrate that apparent silences of Scottish women in published work during this period are not representative of their contribution to intellectual culture. Just as Perkins draws on gender as a way into questioning established understanding of the Enlightenment, so Christianson questions distinctions between public and private creative activity. Suggesting that 19th-century women writers worked in sophisticated negotiations of public and private writing, she argues that their awareness of genre, their implementation of artistic choice and their processes of revision, even in 'private' writing, demand a reappraisal of literary value systems.

While questioning our understanding of literary categories, essays in the volume also reveal women's conscious negotiation of genre boundaries. The complexity and sophistication of these maneuverings is another significant feature of the collection, offering more than the magnet under paper effect criticized by Whyte. Kirsty Macdonald, in "Writing the Supernatural," considers the power women writers gained through using the paradigm of supernatural, while, in a resituating of the domestic

---

7   There is still further work to be done in applying gendered perspectives to Gaelic culture; Watson (2011) draws more on postcolonial thinking than engaging with gender.

fiction by Mary Brunton and Susan Ferrier within sociopolitical debate over national identity, Ainsley McIntosh suggests the romance genre offered more than its conventional format might appear to allow. In my own chapter on "Genre Fiction," I consider detective fiction's power to challenge contemporary paradigms of female agency and knowledge.

The volume also suggests there is still much to reconsider in our canon formations. Florence Boos reveals the importance of working-class woman Janet Hamilton's contributions as memoirist and political commentator: while the views she articulated may not be explicitly feminist in tone, her presence and range of writing show her as a formidable exponent of ideas and a time in which both her class and gender worked against her. Even more striking is the emergence of Margaret Oliphant as a dominant figure in Scottish literary culture. She is significant in a number of areas: as Helen Sutherland demonstrates in "Margaret Oliphant and the Nineteenth-century Periodical Press," she could utilize a masculinised area of literary production to give her authority of a male voice and the disguise of a house style but still voice her own concerns as a woman writer; in her supernatural stories, as Macdonald argues, Oliphant negotiates the fine boundaries between madness and the semiotic; she is also a significant presence in Christianson's analysis of private writing, and Anderson's discussion of travel writing. This suggests not only the prolific nature of Oliphant's output but also her importance as a key reference point in 19th-century writing, presenting a significant challenge to our literary maps. Paradoxically, Oliphant's prolific output, in so many different areas, appears to have relegated her to a minor position within Scottish 19th-century fiction: while *Edinburgh Companion* volumes address the work of individual writers such as Scott, Stevenson or Spark, Oliphant's significance strains the boundaries of several chapters in this collection, suggesting a more appropriate recognition of her importance. As with Hamilton, Oliphant forces us to reconfigure our maps of the 19th-century Scottish canon. And other writers, sadly not addressed in the Companion, nudge the borders of our consciousness: Rebecca West should perhaps have had a place here; 18th-century Shetland poet Margaret Chalmers also merits attention (cf. Fielding 2008).

This is not to say that mappings of a specifically national terrain pass unacknowledged. Both Mary Brunton and Susan Ferrier, McIntosh argues, demonstrate sharp understanding of competing cultural discourses around landscape, national identity and power in their explorations of Highland life. For later writers geographic space, whether real or fictional, offers a means of questioning perceptions of home, rootedness, and dwelling. As Carol Anderson suggests, in "Writing Spaces," Nan Shepherd, Violet Jacob and Catherine Carswell use the matrices of rural life, small town and city to map out subjectivity. Literary and geographical decentring is given a more political resonance in chapters by Margery Palmer McCulloch and Eleanor Bell. McCulloch claims Carswell, Moon, Naomi Mitchison and Willa Muir contribute in important ways to the Scottish Renaissance but offer more nuanced articulations of national identity than their male counterparts. In the 1960s, Bell suggests, Mitchison and Elspeth Davie were situated uneasily within national literary and political configurations, while for other experimental women, such as Margaret Tait and Helen Adams, creativity took them beyond Scotland.

A geographical remapping, small but significant, is also suggested in terms of the difficult issue of 'representative' fiction. Both McCulloch and Anderson present Catherine Carswell's *The Camomile* as a great 'Glasgow novel.' As McCulloch observes, the novel pre-empts and challenges Duncan Thaw's complaint in *Lanark* that Glasgow as a city has no imaginative existence (Gray 1981). For Carswell the streets of Glasgow, so often understood as masculine and threatening urban spaces, offer a liberating function, just as those of London did for Virginia Woolf. Likewise the literary landscapes traced by Anderson make us rethink the contours of both the country and Scottish imaginations. The hugely successful historical fiction of Dorothy Dunnett, a figure absent from *The Companion to Twentieth-Century Scottish Literature,* also offers a challenging yet neglected locus for the exploration of national narratives. In its conflation of the politics of desire and the emergence of a nation state, Dunnett's "Lymond" series in particular demands a reassessment of cultural hierarchies within fictional forms. Its sophisticated gendering and manipulations of readerly pleasure again suggests an alternative to the contemporary, urban, realist or postmodernist models of fiction which conventionally embody 'Scottish' fiction. Dunnett's oeuvre, the vibrant body of work female crime writers and the domestic romances of a writer such as Isla Dewar all merit recognition as 'popular' negotiations of a country's identity and the construction of men and women within it.

While 20th-century women's writing offers, as McGuire notes, an invigoration of Scottish literature, here too absences and paradoxes remain. Although Monica Germanà suggests, in her chapter on "Contemporary Writing" the decentred self and a resistance to stable roots has become one of the most productive forces in contemporary women's fiction, in poetry, Rhona Brown argues, through a comparative analysis of Marion Angus, Liz Lochhead and Kathleen Jamie, the 20th century also saw an increasingly complicated tension between home and away. Brown suggests all three writers, drawing on traditional forms, exploring memories collective and individual, work on the boundaries of the general and specific. Through this they both challenge and validate the implications of their own Scottishness. If a resistance to fixity, combined with a detailed attention to the particular, characterizes contemporary women's writing in Scotland, it is also a shared feature of critical approaches in the *Companion* volume. In their different ways the essays show that writings by women address a whole range of experiences, some determined by gender, some by age, region, class, ethnicity. They demonstrate that the inflections of gender go well beyond the representational, energizing the dynamics of the literary marketplace, problematising subjectivities, complicating models of interpretation and interpretive communities. Indeed they shape our very understanding of such apparently simple terms as 'literary merit,' 'difficulty,' 'enjoyment,' 'enlightenment.'

Images for capturing Scottish literature's relationship to gender have moved from the tension and impasse implied by "the double knot on the peeny" and the antagonistic possibilities of urban 'hardmen,' to cluster around "debatable lands," "gender nomadism," and "border-making." Reflecting the influence of postcolonial thinking, they represent an openness to new maps based on nuanced understanding of the gendered dynamics of form and of audience. By avoiding easy paradigms of identification and 'experience,' seeing instead possibilities in deflection and displacement, these models offer new contexts for understanding Scottish writing. But these new modes of thinking will only be effective if they result in serious reconfigurations of the canon, informed by a recognition that literary genres carry with them their own traditions and assumptions around gender. Yet these ideas cannot remain as theoretical debates, but must be played out in the range, choice and situating of texts presented and taught as Scottish literature.

Works Cited

Abrams, Lynn. "Maureen Martin, *The Mighty Scot: Nation, Gender and the Nineteenth-century Mystique of Scottish Masculinity.*" *Victorian Studies* 52.4 (2010): 634-635.

Anderson, Carol and Aileen Christianson, eds. *Scottish Women's Fiction, 1920s to 1960s: Journeys Into Being*. East Linton: Tuckwell, 2000.

Anderson, Carol and Glenda Norquay. "Superiorism: the Sexism of the Scottish Intelligentsia." *Cencrastus* 15 (1984): 8-10.

Bell, Eleanor and Gavin Miller, eds. *Scotland in Theory: Reflections on Culture and Literature*. Amsterdam and New York: Rodopi Press, 2004.

Carruthers, Gerard. "Muriel Spark as a Catholic Novelist." *The Edinburgh Companion to Muriel Spark*. Eds. Michael Gardiner and Willy Maley. Edinburgh: Edinburgh University Press, 2010. 74-84.

Christianson, Aileen. "Gender and Nation: Debatable Lands and Passable Boundaries." *Across the Margins*. Eds. Glenda Norquay and Gerry Smyth. Manchester: Manchester University Press, 2002. 67-82.

— and Alison Lumsden, eds. *Contemporary Scottish Women Writers*. Edinburgh: Edinburgh University Press, 2000.

— and William Findlay. "Letters." *Cencrastus* 17 (1984): 43.

Fielding, Penny. *Scotland and the Fictions of Geography*. Cambridge: Cambridge University Press, 2008.

Findlay, William. "An Interview with Margaret Atwood." *Cencrastus* 1 (1979): 1-2.

Gifford, Douglas and Dorothy McMillan, eds. *A History of Scottish Women's Writing*. Edinburgh: Edinburgh University Press, 1997.

Gonda, Caroline. *Tea and Leg-Irons: New Feminist Readings from Scotland*. London: Robert Hale Ltd., 1992.

—. "An Other Country: Mapping Scottish/Lesbian Writing." *Gendering the Nation*. Ed. Christopher Whyte. Edinburgh: Edinburgh University Press, 1995. 1-24.

Gray, Alasdair. *Lanark: A Life in Four Books*. Edinburgh: Canongate, 1981.

Hagemann, Susanne. "From Carswell to Kay: Aspects of Gender, the Novel and the Drama." *The Edinburgh History of Scottish Literature: Volume 3*. Eds. Ian Brown et al. Edinburgh: Edinburgh University Press, 2007. 214-224.

Hendry, Joy. "The Double Knot on the Peeny." *In Other Words: Writing as a Feminist*. Eds. Gail Chester and Sigrid Nielsen. London: Hutchinson, 1987. 36-45.

Hook, Andrew. "Teaching Scottish Literature in the USA." *Scotlit: The Newsletter of the Association for Scottish Literary Studies* 41 (2011): 10-11.

Jones, Carole. "White Men on Their Backs – From Objection to Abjection: The Representation of the White Male as Victim in William McIlvanney's *Docherty* and Irvine Welsh's *Marabou Stork Nightmares*." 2006. *International Journal of Scottish Literature* 1. 18 June 2012 <http://www.ijsl.stir.ac.uk/issue1/jones.htm>.

—. "State of Transformation: Drag Queen Masculinity in Two Scottish Texts." 2009a. *Genders* 50. 18 June 2012 <http://www.genders.org/g50/g50_jones.html>.

—. *Disappearing Men: Gender Disorientation in Scottish Fiction 1979-1999*. Amsterdam and New York: Rodopi, 2009b.

Kerrigan, Catherine, ed. *An Anthology of Scottish Women Poets*. Edinburgh: Edinburgh University Press, 1991.
Lea, Daniel and Berthold Schoene, eds. *Posting the Male: Masculinities in Post-War and Contemporary British Literature*. Amsterdam and New York: Rodopi, 2003.
Martin, Maureen. *The Mighty Scot: Nation, Gender and the Nineteenth-Century Mystique of Scottish Masculinity*. Albany: SUNY Press, 2009.
McCulloch, Marjorie, ed. *Modernism and Nationalism: Literature and Society in Scotland 1918-1939*. Glasgow: Association for Scottish Literary Studies, 2004.
McGuire, Matt. *Contemporary Scottish Literature: Reader's Guide to Essential Criticism*. London: Palgrave Macmillan, 2009.
McMillan, Dorothy, ed. *The Scotswoman at Home and Abroad: Non-Fiction Writing 1700-1900*. Glasgow: Association for Scottish Literary Studies, 1999.
McMillan, Neil. "Heroes and Zeroes: Monologism and Masculinism in Scottish Men's Writing of the 1970s and Beyond." *Posting the Male*. Eds. Daniel Lea and Berthold Schoene. Amsterdam and New York: Rodopi, 2003. 68-87.
McQuillan, Martin. *Theorising Muriel Spark: Gender, Race, Deconstruction*. London: Palgrave, 2001.
Norquay, Glenda. "Dark Star Over Drumorty: The Writing of Lorna Moon." *Studies in Scottish Fiction: Twentieth Century*. Eds. Joachim Schwend and Horst W. Drescher. Frankfurt am Main: Peter Lang, 1990. 117-131.
—. "Finding a Place: the Voice of Lorna Moon." *Études écossaises* 9 (2004): 91-103.
—, ed. *The Edinburgh Companion to Scottish Women's Writing*. Edinburgh: Edinburgh University Press, 2012. Forthcoming.
Petrie, Duncan J. *Contemporary Scottish Fiction: Film, Television and the Novel*. Edinburgh: Edinburgh University Press, 2004.
Plain, Gill. *Twentieth-Century Crime Fiction: Gender, Sexuality and the Body*. Edinburgh: Edinburgh University Press, 2001.
—. "Hard Nuts to Crack: Devolving Masculinities in Contemporary Scottish Fiction." *Posting the Male*. Eds. Daniel Lea and Berthold Schoene. Amsterdam and New York: Rodopi, 2003. 55-68.
Reizbaum, Marilyn. "Canonical Double Cross Scottish and Irish Women's Writing." *Decolonizing Tradition: New Views of Twentieth-century 'British' Literary Canons*. Ed. Karen R Lawrence. Urbana and Chicago: University of Illinois Press, 1992. 165-190.
Rose, Irene. "Heralding New Possibilities: Female Masculinity in Jackie Kay's *Trumpet*." *Posting the Male*. Eds. Daniel Lea and Berthold Schoene. Amsterdam and New York: Rodopi, 2003. 141-58.
Sassi, Carla. *Why Scottish Literature Matters*. Edinburgh: The Saltire Society, 2005.
—. "The (B)order in Modern Scottish Literature." *The Edinburgh Companion to Twentieth-Century Scottish Literature*. Eds. Ian Brown and Alan Riach. Edinburgh: Edinburgh University Press, 2009. 145-55.

Schoene, Berthold. "Angry Young Masculinity and the Rhetoric of Homophobia and Misogyny in the Scottish Novels of Alan Sharp." *Gendering the Nation*. Ed. Christopher Whyte. Edinburgh: Edinburgh University Press, 1995. 85-106.

—. *Writing Men: Literary Masculinities from 'Frankenstein' to the New Man*. Edinburgh: Edinburgh University Press, 2000.

—. *The Edinburgh Companion to Contemporary Scottish Literature*. Edinburgh: Edinburgh University Press, 2007.

Watson, Moray. *An Introduction to Gaelic Fiction*. Edinburgh: Edinburgh University Press, 2011.

Whyte, Christopher, ed. *Gendering the Nation. Studies in Modern Scottish Literature*. Edinburgh: Edinburgh University Press, 1995.

—. "Masculinities in Contemporary Scottish Fiction." *Forum for Modern Language Studies*. 34.3 (1998): 274-285.

—. *Modern Scottish Poetry*. Edinburgh: Edinburgh University Press, 2004a.

—. "Queer Readings, Gay Texts: *Redgauntlet* and *The Prime of Miss Jean Brodie*." *Scotland in Theory: Reflections on Culture and Literature*. Eds. Eleanor Belle and Gavin Miller. Amsterdam and New York: Rodopi Press, 2004b. 147-165.

DONNA HEDDLE, Kirkwall
"The North Wind Doth Blow:"
A New Agenda for Northern Scottish Studies

1. The Background

The Orkney and Shetland Islands, along with Caithness on the Scottish mainland, are identified primarily in terms of their Nordic cultural and linguistic heritage. This was the rationale behind the creation of the University of the Highlands and Islands' interdisciplinary Centre for Nordic Studies (CNS) (with campuses in Kirkwall, Orkney, and Scalloway, Shetland), which provides a focus for an enmeshed holistic interdisciplinary approach to locative research and teaching. Its research and teaching ethos exemplifies the paradigm for a new area specific of Scottish Studies involving the Nordic heritage of Scotland, now known as Northern Scottish Studies. The CNS was founded in 2006 with a single staff member based in Orkney – myself, a Scottish literary, linguistic and cultural historian, who was appointed Director at that time. I had arrived in Orkney from the University of Edinburgh in 1999 with a vague remit to develop an undergraduate degree in Cultural Studies, and had realized very quickly that standard paradigms of Cultural or Scottish Studies would not reflect the locative and interdisciplinary focus essential to analyse and evaluate fully the lives of the communities where the programme was to be taught. I had also noted that there was no extant research centre for the study of Scotland's Nordic heritage, and that this area of study required valorising in general, and in the communities themselves in particular. There was, in fact, a gap in the market both literally and philosophically. A new holistic approach to learning articulated with location was needed, and proved very successful once implemented – the undergraduate degree won the Times Higher Education Supplement Award in 2005 for most imaginative use of distance learning. This was the forerunner for the new paradigm which ultimately led to the CNS development.

I was joined in June 2009 by an administration officer, Lynn Campbell, and in August 2009 by the full CNS team – historical archaeologist and Viking specialist Dr Alexandra Sanmark from Sweden and linguist Dr Ragnhild Ljosland from Norway, in the Orkney campus, folk historian and onomastic expert Dr Andrew Jennings from Shetland and North Atlantic Rim literature and cultural dialogue specialist Silke Reeploeg, originally from Germany but very much part of the Shetland community, in the Shetland campus. The CNS was officially opened on 17 June 2011 by Norwegian Ambassador to the Court of St James', Mr Kim Traavik. Since the CNS's inception, collaborative links have been established with the Universities of Oxford, Cambridge, Nottingham, Edinburgh, Aberdeen, Durham, Oslo, Vienna, Uppsala, Copenhagen, Lund, Western Australia, Bergen, the Faroe Islands and Newfoundland.

This unique project brings new research, cultural policy, community engagement, and teaching initiatives to the islands. It has developed a theoretical approach to this specific area of studies in both particular and general terms, by seeking to make connections between the living traditions and social structure of the Highlands and Islands region, its past and future, and by setting it into a European context. It has sought to make the theoretical research of practical benefit to the communities themselves by valorising the research area in order to create viable cultural products and new regional policies. The importance of interdisciplinary research, allied to community ownership and community involvement is central to the ethos and the strategic aims of the CNS. Its challenges lie in its geographical location and in building networks as a result of this.

First, a clear definition of the present discipline boundaries is required – an agreed standard from which to explore new methodologies and paradigms for studying specific cultures. Culture is the accumulated knowledge of all social, literary, artistic and collective activity that is passed on from generation to generation. Investigating a culture is both the study of the way we live and have lived, and the study of the way we communicate as social beings, looking at the underlying ideologies and assumptions of individuals and social groups, and explaining the manner in which these assumptions are shaped, produced and communicated generally. Having said that, Cultural Studies has always been a highly contested terrain. Over time the concept of Cultural Studies has evolved into a more generic term referring to an increasingly popular international cross-disciplinary and anti-disciplinary field, as well as to an intellectual movement based on transdisciplinary philosophy. Culture is therefore granted some independence, but at the same time it is emphasised that the practices and symbolic dimension of everyday life must not be treated in isolation from questions of power and politics. The newer field of European Studies, which has recognised synergies with Cultural Studies, exhibits this widening focus, while focussing on developments in European integration from a comparative perspective through a study of elements of political science, EU public policy, European history, European law, economics, sociology, European culture, European literature and European languages. 'Place' is a central concern for the national and regional perspective in European Studies, a concern which was also fundamental in shaping Northern Scottish Studies, a field which essentially lies at the Cultural Studies end of the European Studies parabola, and seeks global relevance beyond predefined geographical and disciplinary borders.

How does Northern Scottish Studies connect with the well-established and complex discipline of Scottish Studies? Scottish Studies came to prominence in the 19th century under the aegis of luminaries such as Sir Walter Scott, and was focused at that time upon the issue of origin – foregrounding an 'introverted' and multidisciplinary approach, involving history, ethnology, and literature, rather than a comparative and interdisciplinary one. Although Scott is often hailed as the father of European Romanticism, which itself gave birth to modern nationalism, what he established in his novels and poems was largely a backward-looking, parochial concept of Scottish national identity, identified and quantified in terms of its larger neighbour England. Scotland was the past, Britain was the future.

Scotland to Scott, and to the Victorians who followed, was a place that did not exist primarily in geographic or cultural terms, but in a static and a-temporal space of its own. The 19th-century romanticisation of the Celtic tradition, largely ascribed to Scott and his mythicisation of the Highlands and Gaelic culture (generating, for example, popular cultural icons such as tartan), paradoxically developed at a time when native Gaelic language and culture were repressed and marginalised, and at the expense of a more nuanced representation of Scotland's complex national identity. The Nordic culture of the far North of Scotland, among other regional expressions, remained largely invisible, although many writers, including Scott, flirted with the concept of Nordic values and used Old Norse motifs in their writing,[1] while Scotland's past came to be perceived as a 'golden age,' where society and the state were at one and where the culture had a certain cohesion, as exemplified by the vernacular literature of the Makars and, later, by Robert Fergusson, Robert Burns, among others (Wittig 1958; Craig 1996).

Literature was also the prime marker for the socio-cultural development of the 20th-century Scottish literary Renaissance, which was not exclusively Gaelic-centric, but allowed for expression in an indigenous mélange of dialects and old and new languages.

It is then true that Scotland has essentially settled for a 'Celtic' and by extrapolation Gaelic cultural identity definition and marker as a polar opposite of the Teutonic origin myth embraced by the English, or the Norse version prevalent in the Northern Isles. This meant, among other things, that the field of Scottish Studies became synonymous in the first instance with Celtic Studies, first taught as a discipline in Scotland at the University of Edinburgh in 1882. This explains the highly Gaelicised self-conscious presentation of modern Scottish identity, although the social anthropologist Sharon Macdonald notes that it was only in the second half of the 20th century that Gaelic was perceived as central to Scottish identity, despite the continuing decline in the number of Gaelic speakers in Scotland (Macdonald 1997, 6-7).

The nature of Scottish nationalism is as complex as the development of Scottish Studies as a discipline, as it combines differing peoples, all experiencing a problematic sense of identity, with the added dimension of the comparison to the larger construct of British identity. The mechanics of identity formation are therefore multidimensional, as the notion of 'Scottish' varies considerably depending on geographical and demographic contexts. This is reflected in the scope of the disciplinary field denominated Scottish Studies, which itself expanded as a discipline from Celtic Studies in the 20th century with the creation of research centres and curricula to study the culture through its literature, art, music, history, media, philosophy, politics, social issues and cultural theory, both in Scotland and abroad. The founding of the School of Scottish Studies at the University of Edinburgh, in 1951, created a particular disciplinary offshoot for the field in native traditional and folk culture, with a strong emphasis on the oral tradition.

Northern Scottish Studies is therefore an area-specific, interdisciplinary branch of a highly complex multidisciplinary tree. Within Northern Scottish Studies there is an imperative to bring together overlapping areas of Scottishness – to connect geographies and temporalities. The counterpoint of light and shadow may be a key Western aesthetic, but in the case of Scottish Studies there is a high degree of dappling and shading between the two.

---

1 See Walter Scott's version of *Eyrbyggia Saga* (1814), the first abstract in English of an Old Norse saga. Scott used Scandinavian material in *The Antiquary* (1816), *Ivanhoe* (1819), most obviously in his last narrative poem, *Harold the Dauntless* (1817), and in *The Pirate* (1822), set in the Northern Isles. See also James Hogg's *Queen Hynde* (1825) and R. M. Ballantyne's *Erling the Bold* (1869).

2. The New Paradigm for Northern Scottish Studies

The international landscape for language studies, linguistics and area studies is changing rapidly. Globalisation may be accelerating, but is increasingly counterbalanced by local and regional particularisms. Most European nations today have to reassess their own national narratives in the light of new global contexts and new interdisciplinary paradigms, allowing for new metaphysical locations and accounting for colonial and post-colonial effects and structures. This applies also to Scotland, which, in the 20th century, underwent fundamental demographic, territorial, and political changes, affecting how Scots looked at their world and their relationship to it.

Such changes in perspective in relation to notions of national identity were reflected in the concept proposed by Benedict Anderson of "imagined communities," in his text of that name first published in 1991. Anderson follows, with Ernest Gellner and Eric Hobsbawm, a school of nationalism in which nations are posited as modern products motivated by political and economic agendas – as Gellner notes in *Nations and Nationalism,* for example, "nationalism is primarily a political principle that holds that the political and the national unit should be congruent" (Gellner 2006, 1). Along similar lines, Hobsbawm's influential collection, *The Invention of Tradition* (1983), clearly posits the politicisation of tradition in opposition to the primordialist view, which states that nations have existed since the earliest times in human history. Imagined communities exist therefore as an aspect of social constructionism, along with what Edward Said termed "imagined geographies" (Said 1978, 39, 71), shedding light on the relation between perception of identity and the power of hegemonic interpretation.

The need for a self-conscious re-assessment of hegemonic perceptions of heritage and identity was key also in the reimagining of Northern Scottish identity. If "imagined geographies" can be a source of empowerment, then the re-creation of an existing, albeit marginalised, regional identity, combining altruistic motives of research, preservation and promulgation with the need of the communities for loci of power and influence, represents a very valuable opportunity both for the local communities and for researchers, and changes the very nature of academic research.

Territorial borders delimit privileged topographies often created and modified by external forces, such as the migration of people and ideas due to changing political and social landscapes. Borders are characterised by increasing complexity, taking on different meaning and value in different contexts. This also applies to disciplines themselves: as the borders between them have become more fluid, one can now easily interact with different communities of the mind. This has an extraordinary 'knock-on' effect for the researcher, who today can move from the traditional subject- , area- and time-specific close scrutiny of a component of a greater whole, often resulting in a necessarily limited range of outputs, to a more inclusive and holistic mosaic, aiming at creating one comprehensive 'big picture' out of all the different but complementary discipline components. It is quite literally an expansion of the researcher's consciousness. Academic identity allied to a specific discipline is more and more an outmoded concept in the context of the modern university system and the general move in thinking from the discipline-specific to the interdisciplinary.[2]

Once the concept of change and development in the researcher's focus was established at the CNS, a definition had then to be created to reflect the nature of the change. Language and nomenclature are subject to political and power struggles. The same goes for the very meaning of "Northern Scottish Studies." Any canonical definition of Northern Scottish Studies, in fact, would be the most ideological, the one that has gained a hegemonic position in the struggle to establish itself as a subject in its own right. It follows, then, that all descriptions and definitions of Northern Scottish Studies are a cultural construction, subject to change. As all cultural constructs, however, they are also instrumental in creating a sense of specific location and identity, allied to interdisciplinary concepts.

The CNS strategy has been to produce an ethnogenesis for the Scots with Nordic heritage – this is a process through which an amorphous social landscape develops ethnically distinct social groupings through self-conscious culture creation. The recognition of this process has fostered the questioning of generally accepted perceptions of origin and identity, very much in line with a wider, post-devolution questioning of monolithically conceived notions of Scottishness. Since the 1990s, in fact, the homogeneity of Scottish identity has come under fire from literary and historical scholars alike. Berthold Schoene, for example, remarks in *The Edinburgh Companion to Contemporary Scottish Literature*:

> Discontinuity and adaptability have become Scotland's cultural trademarks […]. From this powerful critical paradigm shift, which champions the cultural authenticity of the fragmented, marginalised, shadowy, and wounded over that of the allegedly intact, wholesome, and self-contained, Scottish culture has emerged as from a distorting mirror. No longer regarded, or led to regard itself, as exclusively Scottish and thus found or finding itself lacking, it becomes free to reconceive of itself in broader terms, with reference to other cultures (not just English culture), indeed as situated within a vibrant network of interdependent cultural contexts. (Schoene 2007, 9)

This weaving together of cultural contexts is now firmly established as the way forward for Scottish Studies as a discipline itself (see Carruthers et al. 2004, 15).

CNS researchers are not the first to focus on Nordic aspects of heritage either. As Julian D'Arcy points out comprehensively in the first three chapters of his groundbreaking *Scottish Skalds and Sagamen*, interest in Old Norse and Nordic literature has always been particularly strong in Scotland. However, D'Arcy makes the very valid point that, although research has been published on the Old Norse influence on specific writers such as Walter Scott and Thomas Carlyle, this "usually fail[s] to treat this influence from a specifically Scottish perspective, either literary or historical" (D'Arcy 1996, 4).

D'Arcy's literary perspective, along with that expressed by Schoene, was very much a component in the development of the CNS paradigm, which sought to reflect these same changes in perception, link them to location, and unite them across a wider

---

2   The issue was first addressed by Tony Becher in *Academic Tribes and Territories: Intellectual Enquiry and the Culture of Disciplines* (1989), revised in 2001 in collaboration with Paul Trowler. Becher, in the mid-1980s, analysed and evaluated the approach to research of well-established disciplines in high ranking HEIs in Britain and America, and the influence of knowledge structures on research practices.

range of disciplines. The fundamental concept of Northern Scottish Studies marks therefore a shift from a centralist to a poly-centric cultural and national model. Along similar lines, the new paradigm moves away from a concentration on literature and ethnology into the wider field of area studies, an interdisciplinary field of research and scholarship with a specific geo-cultural, national-federal/regional focus, encompassing both the social sciences and the humanities, particularly in terms of history, sociology, European and Cultural Studies.

The CNS is now concentrated on Northern Scotland's journey to identity, focussing on the cultural influences which shaped it, and not exclusively on where the journey began. It is also concerned with ways to promulgate research and knowledge to the widest possible audience. To this end, it embraces multimedia approaches and technologies as a means of circumventing the limitations of location, therefore moving from discipline-specific, book-based resources, to multimedia generic geocultural categorisations. Dissemination is not only done through multimedia platforms, however, but also more directly through teaching provision allied to a strong research strategy.

3. The Paradigm in Practice: Teaching and Research

The CNS teaching curriculum concentrates on postgraduate provision and community engagement. It approaches Northern Scottish Studies in a manner distinct to the dynamic interdisciplinary research focus of the CNS. The programme juxtaposes core concepts (mass and popular culture; cultural industries; ideology; power and discourse; subjectivity; cultural praxis; spatiality) with exemplary writings and case studies drawn from different periods in the development of the field. The curriculum traces selected methodological strategies (ethnography; discourse analysis; institutions and culture industries; cultural practices and everyday life; close readings and textual analysis) to produce a distinctive set of programmes which negotiate the traditional divide between Arts, Humanities and Social Science subjects. The programmes are centrally concerned with issues of representation, identity and cultural diversity. They are: MLitt Highlands and Islands Literature; MLitt Orkney and Shetland Studies; MLitt Highlands and Islands Culture; and MLitt Viking Studies. They are studied by students all over the world through technologies such as virtual learning environments and videoconferencing, and have proven extremely good recruiters. The applied approach to understanding identity and the range of soft transferable skills achievable has resulted in excellent student destination results. In terms of community engagement – local writers and historians feature as guest lecturers and a comprehensive range of evening classes, public seminar series featuring notable academics from across the world, summer schools, and training programmes (such as the STGA[3] Orkney Green Badge Tourist Guide course) have created local jobs and opportunities in culture and heritage.

The CNS research strategy, which created these programmes, promotes a conception of Northern Scottish Studies rooted in lived experience, adopting a broad-ranging view in an effort to produce a holistic viewpoint of the many facets surrounding the central 'truth' of cultural social constructions. The teaching curriculum embraces stud-

---

3 Scottish Tour Guide Association.

ies of culture in both specific and general terms, by seeking to make connections between the living traditions and social structure of the Highlands and Islands region and the region's past and future in the North Atlantic Rim. It also seeks to explore the tools, methods and validity of the study of culture worldwide through the application of universal concepts to an area-specific framework which combines four main interdisciplinary focussed strands: cultural history, practical skills and pure theory, language and literature. The research strategy is immeasurably strengthened by being taught in, by and to the communities it studies, and will ensure that the ownership of their cultural identity passes back to those communities, while placing and expressing that identity in a global context.

Language is a critical asset for authenticating and expressing ethnic identities. The diversity of the Scottish linguistic situation is a case in point. Gaelic has official status and a clear focus for study at Sabhal Mòr Ostaig, the Gaelic college on Skye, which is, like the CNS, part of the new University of the Highlands and Islands. The other indigenous languages of the Highlands and Islands – Scots, Orcadian and Shetlandic – did not have a locus for study until the advent of the CNS which has been able to influence the linguistic policies of the Scottish Government on such language variants, helped to raise awareness of the significance of these variants to the Highlands and Islands, and has conducted research into the area, resulting in unique teaching and research initiatives such as the MLitt Orkney and Shetland Studies and the CNS-led AHRC funded project on Orkney and Shetland dialect, which commenced in February 2012.

Such a research focus is an imperative for maintaining cultural identity in the Northern Isles as well as for placing it in its North Atlantic Rim context. For almost a thousand years, in fact, the language of the Orkney and Shetland Islands was a variant of Norse, known as Norroena or Norn. The distinctive and culturally unique qualities of what is now Orkney dialect and Shetlandic/Shaetlan spoken in the islands today largely derive from the sister languages of Faroese, which too developed from the Norse brought in by settlers in the 9th century, and from Icelandic, with a growing Scots influence from the 12th century onwards, when the see of Orkney was transferred from the Archbishopric of Nidaros in Norway to the Scottish church. The passing of the Orkney Earldom to the Scots line in 1329 and the 'Impignoration' of 1468, when Orkney and Shetland were passed to James III, King of Scots, by Denmark-Norway as part of a marriage dowry, saw a marked valorisation of Scots at the expense of Norn, as Scots became the language of commerce and government and Norn became devalued and ultimately fell into disuse by the end of the 18th century. Some aspects of Norn remained in the Orkney and Shetland dialects, however, and they are perceived prime cultural markers for the communities. These dialects have sustained a flourishing indigenous culture and have been used recently by local writers such as Robert Rendall, Christina Costie, Christine de Luca, Christie Williamson and Robert Alan Jamieson to create a non parochial literary output, which globalises the islands' local culture and which is celebrated in local archives and libraries as well as in Scotland and beyond.

There is a well-known relationship between knowledge and power: the CNS research agenda aims to empower the local communities by helping them make the leap from the theoretical to the practical, and indeed the practicable, use of their lived experience, as section four is going to illustrate.

4. Research Case Study: The Hjaltland Research Network

Diaspora and migration form a large part of area studies and there is an increasing focus on translocal, transregional, transnational and transcontinental study. It is this outward-looking factor which has contributed so strongly to the research philosophy of the CNS: aiming at applying global concepts in an area-specific context, envisaging new types of regionalisation in a world of globalisation and transnational integration and recognising that hegemonic formation must be countered and skills developed to empower communities.

A direct result of the CNS policy of having eminent researchers deliver free public seminars in Orkney and Shetland was the opportunity for communication and collaboration among scholars and local communities, which led to the emergence of the "Hjaltland Research Network" and its associated projects. These have generated a great deal of excitement across the North Atlantic Rim and illustrate the new paradigm for Northern Scottish Studies extremely well.

The Hjaltland Research Network, coordinated by CNS Shetland based team member Andrew Jennings, received £17,000 from the *Royal Society of Edinburgh* in 2011 to bring together national and international scholars of folklore, onomastics, linguistics, genetics, isotope research, archaeology and history from the CNS and the universities of Edinburgh, Lund and Copenhagen to pilot and develop a large-scale research project entitled "Mapping Viking Age Shetland" – Hjaltland being the Norse name for Shetland.[4] "Mapping Viking Age Shetland" seeks, through the digitising and mapping of the datasets of each discipline, to answer many of the unresolved questions about Shetland's Viking Age, such as: what happened to the pre-Viking population; the date of Viking settlement; the origins of the Norse settlers and the anomaly of the divergent origins of the male and female lines; the nature of Shetland's connections to the Celtic world; the intensity of settlement and the extent and duration of Norse pagan beliefs and folk traditions. "Mapping Viking Age Shetland" is a truly interdisciplinary approach to Viking Age research, applying the latest technological advances and innovative new research in the various scientific and technological fields, allowing for the teasing out of additional information from existing sources and the uncovering of new evidence – onomastic, genetic and isotopic – which looks likely to challenge long-held preconceptions of identity and lineage based on literary or historical sources alone. Scientific evidence, the new data-sets and the employment of new IT and cartographic technologies allied to tradition, folklore, literature and history are redefining human geography in a specific location and creating links which were previously unknown or unevaluated.

The project so far has involved the creation of elements which can be put together to build a mosaic of the Viking Age in Shetland through a spatially-enabled, multi-relational database and interactive multilayered maps. It therefore uses the very building blocks of society, the genes themselves, along with the environmental evidence, the words for people and places and the tangible and intangible cultural heritage, to put together a tessellation of integrated information – the 'big picture' of Viking influence in Shetland. This 'big picture' is enhanced by the NEST (Northern Encounters: Societies Transformed) transnational project, currently in development,

---

[4] More information on these linked projects can be found at the project website http://www.hjaltlandnetwork.com/.

and also an offshoot of Hjaltland (led by Peder Gammeltoft at the University of Copenhagen and involving CNS team members Andrew Jennings and Alex Sanmark), which will gather and evaluate data from the areas the Vikings raided, settled or traded from an interdisciplinary focus. The project aims at challenging established 'truths' and raise new questions about the nature of Viking activities in general, and will make this available to communities and academics alike through internet-based knowledge exchange activities such as peer-reviewed open-access books, commissioned reports, recorded seminars (available on a dedicated portal) and a bespoke map web-interface and a smart phone application. In line with the comparative and outward-looking focus of Northern Scottish Studies, "Mapping Viking Age Shetland" itself will be the pilot for a larger scale project, called MSGI: "Migration, Settlement and Genetic Inheritance: Mapping the Legacy of the Viking Age," which will continue the journey across the North Atlantic Rim to give an ever widening context for the cultural identity of Northern Scotland.

5. Conclusion

The research teams have been developing core scholarly outputs[5] for the emergence of a Northern Isles based academy – a region-based academy which is already having consequences for the vitality of an area of Britain peripheralised by institutional developments in the modern age, such as the gravitation of government to the south of England, but which has now new opportunities for renaissance in the new European and Scottish governmental structures. The CNS's location has not been a barrier to the development of networks and teaching linkage, in fact it has been an enhancement and a source of attraction to partners in a range of high value and high profile international projects and in conference hosting.[6]

Where next on the journey of discovery and development? In line with its own exocentric and non-parochial focus and its desire to reflect a changing and mutable society, the CNS is seeking to continue to develop social policy for the Highlands and Islands and to be a locus for research, teaching, community engagement and excellence in the area and further afield. Specific theoretical developments reflecting the CNS focus on area-specific studies of global concepts will include a firmer focus on Island Studies, in partnership with other island-based universities across the world, where islands are studied on their own terms and issues. Notions of 'islandness' and insularity, dependency, resource management (including culture and heritage) and connectivity will be explored through emerging theoretical approaches and affiliated discipline areas such as Small Island Studies.[7]

---

5   An exhaustive bibliography of CNS publications can be found at http://www.uhi.ac.uk/en/research-enterprise/cultural/centre-for-nordic-studies/publications.
6   Since 2006, the following conferences have been organised and hosted by CNS: *Voices of the West Minority Languages Conference*, in association with the Minority Languages Song for Europe competition (2008 and 2009); *Rognvald 850* (2008), commemorating the death of Earl Rognvald of Orkney; *Looking at Shetland Outside the Box: The Meeting of Nations and the Creation of Shetland Culture* in association with the Elphinstone Institute at the University of Aberdeen (2009); *2009 International Triennial Conference of the Forum for Study of the Languages of Scotland and Ulster*; *Inaugural St Magnus Conference* (2011). CNS will host the forthcoming *Women's History Network Conference* in Orkney in May 2013, and will also co-host the 3rd *Island Dynamics Conference* in Cyprus in 2013.
7   This emerging field is led by, among others, the University of Prince Edward Island, which has the world's first chair in Island Studies, see http://www.upei.ca/~iis/acad.htm, and by the International Small Islands Studies Association, see http://isisa.maui.hawaii.edu/.

The CNS has created a new way of integrating research and community engagement with economic and social viability and has put Northern Scottish Studies, Orkney and Shetland firmly on the map of international academic research. However, much work remains to be done, both in the direction of empowering local communities and in re-visioning a regional and trans-regional Nordic identity.

Works Cited

Anderson, Benedict R. O. G. *Imagined Communities: Reflections on the Origin and Spread of Nationalism.* London: Verso, 2006.

Becher, Tony. *Academic Tribes and Territories: Intellectual Enquiry and the Culture of Disciplines.* Milton Keynes: SRHE and Open University Press, 1989.

— and Paul Trowler. *Academic Tribes and Territories: Intellectual Enquiry and the Culture of Disciplines.* Buckingham: The Society for Research into Higher Education and Open University Press, 2001.

Carruthers, Gerard, David Goldie, and Alistair Renfrew, eds. *Beyond Scotland: New Contexts for Twentieth-Century Scottish Literature.* Amsterdam and New York: Rodopi, 2004.

Craig, Cairns. *Out of History: Narrative Paradigms in Scottish and British Culture.* Edinburgh: Polygon, 1996.

D'Arcy, Julian Meldon. *Scottish Skalds and Sagamen: Old Norse Influence on Modern Scottish literature.* East Linton: Tuckwell Press, 1996.

Gellner, Ernest. *Nations and Nationalism.* Oxford and Massachusetts: Wiley-Blackwell, 2006.

Hobsbawm, Eric and Terence Ranger, eds. *The Invention of Tradition.* Cambridge: Cambridge University Press, 1983.

Macdonald, Sharon. *Reimagining Culture: Histories, Identities, and the Gaelic Renaissance.* Oxford: Berg, 1997.

Said, Edward W. *Orientalism.* London: Penguin Books, 1978.

Schoene, Berthold, ed. *The Edinburgh Companion to Contemporary Scottish Literature.* Edinburgh: Edinburgh University Press, 2007.

Trowler, Paul, Murray Saunders, and Veronica Bamber. *Tribes and Territories in the 21st-Century: Rethinking the Significance of Disciplines in Higher Education.* London: Routledge, 2012.

Wittig, Kurt. *The Scottish Tradition in Literature.* Edinburgh and London: Oliver and Boyd, 1958.

ALAN RIACH, Glasgow
What Good is a Canon? The Case of Scottish Literature

On 25 January 2012, the main front page story in *The Herald* newspaper in Glasgow told readers that the Scottish government had decided that Scottish literature would be a required subject in all schools in Scotland (Denholm 2012). It must seem strange that a nation's literature has been so neglected in that nation's schools, yet the case of Scottish literature is singular. After the Union of Crowns in 1603 and the Union of Parliaments in 1707, from the 18th century on, establishment of English literature as a subject for study in education, especially in the 19th and 20th centuries, coincided with the expansion of the British Empire. The central authority of London as economic power and English as the language of authority prized English literature, and later American literature, as most valuable in education. These are broad generalisations, but they serve to introduce the current condition, which must be unfamiliar and decidedly unusual to readers internationally. Since 2006 I have been involved in numerous meetings with the Scottish government, the Scottish Qualifications Authority, the Association for Scottish Literary Studies and others, in the negotiations for the establishment of Scottish literature as a required subject in the curriculum, an entitlement to which everyone should gainfully be introduced.

Sometimes these negotiations have been vexed because of the historical and cultural contexts for the long-standing relationship between Scottish and English literatures and the institutional silencing of Scottish literature in education. The situation is changing, but the argument still has to be made. Since January 2012, two concerns have repeatedly been raised in formal meetings and casual conversations, and they form a Catch-22 problem. The first concern is: how are teachers to identify what is meant by the term 'Scottish literature'? If you have never studied the subject, how do you know what it is or is not? Many schoolteachers of English in Scotland have studied 'English' literature in their undergraduate degrees, and many will have read American, Irish and postcolonial literatures, and some have encountered Scottish texts. Many, however, will have no acquaintance with Scottish literature. Until recently, fine teachers might introduce Scottish literature to schoolchildren with deep knowledge and contagious enthusiasm, but the provision was optional. Many other teachers might have no interest in teaching the literature of the country and have not been required to do so. The new government directive could thus be welcomed as a wonderful opportunity, or it might be resisted as an imposition. The second concern, arising from the idea that it is an imposition, is the desire to keep the options as open as possible, to oppose the very idea of a defined or prescribed canon of 'Major Texts' or a 'Great Tradition of Scottish Literature.' To exclude the resource of a canon leaves your options open but generates self-doubt and a lack of confidence about what is agreed, while to insist upon a canon is coercive. Catch 22.

The canon is always up for debate. At its most essential, it is something to build from, not to be reduced to. In his magisterial yet contentious study, *The Western Canon* (1994), Harold Bloom lists his own selection of major works from world literature – as far as he can – and includes seventeen Scottish authors: William

Dunbar (*Poems*); James Boswell (*Life of Johnson*; *Journals*); Tobias Smollett (*The Adventures of Roderick Random*; *The Expedition of Humphry Clinker*); Robert Burns (*Poems*); Sir Walter Scott (*Waverley*; *Old Mortality*; *The Heart of Midlothian*; *Redgauntlet*); Lord Byron (*Don Juan*; *Poems*); John Galt (*The Entail*); James Hogg (*The Private Memoirs and Confessions of a Justified Sinner*); Thomas Carlyle (*Selected Prose*; *Sartor Resartus*); James Thomson/"Bysshe Vanolis" (*The City of Dreadful Night*); John Davidson (*Ballads and Songs*); Robert Louis Stevenson (*Essays*; *Kidnapped*; *Dr Jekyll and Mr Hyde*; *Treasure Island*; *The New Arabian Nights*; *The Master of Ballantrae*; *Weir of Hermiston*); George Macdonald (*Lilith*; *At the Back of the North Wind*); David Lindsay (*A Voyage to Arcturus*); Edwin Muir (*Collected Poems*); Norman Douglas (*South Wind*); Hugh MacDiarmid (*Complete Poems*).

The values that inform this list are clear: these are recognised classics most English-speaking readers would acknowledge, even though there are some surprises (such as George Macdonald and David Lindsay). Still, it would be wrong to say it is sufficient: for example, it does not admit any Gaelic literature and there are no women. Yet even if we revised and expanded this list paying attention to these two major components, the result would still be arguable. Nowhere should it be suggested that a canon should include the *only* names you need to know. What the present article will argue, however, is that any student of Scottish literature should know *at least* certain authors and works, why they are important and what they are good for, and the historical sequence in which they lived and wrote. It is, after all, what every one of us does in university teaching, when we select a list of set texts for a course we wish to convene.

Let me offer a canon of Scottish literature in twenty authors, as an example, paying attention to certain criteria: there must be representation 1. of what we could demonstrate as literary merit; 2. of the experience of women as well as that of men; 3. of the three languages in which most of Scottish literature has been composed – Gaelic, Scots and English – even if we can only approach the work through translations or with a glossary; 4. of Scottish people, or of Scotland, and the variety of identities that constitute those terms (geographical, historical, industrial, rural, residents and travellers, exiles and tradition-bearers); 5. of accessiblility and difficulty (some authors present more problems than others and contemporary readers may find the language of Dunbar, the narrative longeurs of Scott or the political extremism of MacDiarmid particularly challenging). The twenty authors could thus be: Robert Henryson, William Dunbar, Mark Alexander Boyd, Sileas na Keppoch, Jean Elliot, Robert Burns, Duncan Ban MacIntyre, Alasdair McMhaighster Alasdair, Walter Scott, James Hogg, John Galt, Mary Macpherson, R. L. Stevenson, Margaret Oliphant, Hugh MacDiarmid, Lewis Grassic Gibbon, Neil Gunn, Sorley MacLean, Edwin Morgan, Liz Lochhead.

Like any list, this is already contentious. However, if you contend that there should be no canon at all, no 'set texts,' no assured list of authors who might be said to constitute a trajectory of major work in Scottish literature, and if you want to keep the list absolutely open, then you might include George Orwell's *1984*, because it was written on the Isle of Jura, or Joseph Conrad's *Heart of Darkness,* because it was first published in Edinburgh in *Blackwood's Magazine*, or Shakespeare's *Macbeth,* because it is – apparently – about Scottish people. Indeed, these claims could be made by someone who believes a canon is necessary, but need only be defined by very flexible criteria. Willy Maley's *100 Best Scottish Books of all time* (2005) included some of these texts in a controversial contribution to the debate. Along similar lines, if you say that Scottish literature must be about Scotland and Scots, must you exclude Walter Scott's *Ivanhoe*, R. L. Stevenson's *Jekyll and Hyde* and *Treasure Island*, Hugh MacDiarmid's "On a Raised Beach" and *In Memoriam James Joyce*, Edwin Morgan's science fiction poems, Janice Galloway's *Clara*?

Scotland is a subject many writers deal with directly, and the anthology *Scotlands: Poets and the Nation* (2004), which I co-edited with Douglas Gifford, gathers poems which explicitly engage with questions of national identity, but there are many Scottish writers whose work deals with other things, such as John Henry Mackay, and many others, such as Walter Scott and MacDiarmid, who write sometimes about Scotland and sometimes about different subjects, but who are remembered in Scotland mainly through their Scottish work.

It will help to consider a different, yet related context. In India, on 26 January, one day after *The Herald* announcement in Scotland, *The Telegraph Calcutta* described a situation that had flared up at the Jaipur Literary Festival: Salman Rushdie had been invited, was warned of threatened violence, had agreed to appear by video link, but his appearance had been eventually cancelled by the organisers because of the potential for disruption by protestors. Liberal thinkers insisted that the right of free speech in a secular context should be upheld by law, but the religious and political context was bearing down on the idea of such a right. In the lead article on the editorial page of *The Telegraph Calcutta*, "Making a Tradition: Why the Idea of Indian Literature Needs Salman Rushdie," Ananya Vajpeyi asked what is indeed the central question in canon-formation: "[…] which works of art – which novels, paintings, films and music – will stand the test of both historical time and political change? In 2047, when India turns one hundred, will Salman Rushdie's stories still sit on our bookshelves [...]?" (Vajpeyi 2012). This takes us to the heart of the question raised by the title of the present article – what good is a canon?

Clearly, there are literary, artistic and cultural values that cannot be constricted to political and religious priorities. Secular priorities of free speech and non-violence are reciprocated by works of literature and art. This is true even of literary and artistic works of political and religious determination and bias. *Paradise Lost* may have its intentions in politics and religion, but its literary quality is what keeps it valuable and readable. Hugh MacDiarmid's three "Hymns to Lenin" may be dedicated to a political leader who is no longer regarded as a hero, but the poems still offer challenges and affirmations beyond their historical moment.

Arguments over the value and validity of canonisation have polarised literary studies since at least the 1970s, with key references including Colin McCabe's *James Joyce and the Revolution of the Word* (1978), the essay "The Crisis in English Studies" by Walter Jackson Bate for *Harvard Magazine* (1982) and Terry Eagleton's *Literary Theory: An Introduction* (1983), but the case of Scottish literature raises particular issues. The central question is the simplest: when does the assertion of canonical value act as progressive resistance, rather than reactionary constriction?

Resistance to the authorities that insist upon a canon is surely necessary when such insistence is limiting, distorting or misguided. Yet a counter-proposal introducing different priorities and preferences is effectively another canon. Canonicity itself is not dissolved or removed. My revision of Harold Bloom's list given above demonstrates this. The understanding that priorities themselves have their own historical moment might help here, but perhaps the only way to reject any idea of canonicity would be to surrender the power of determining priorities and preferences altogether. Problematically, this practice always gives power to other decision-makers.

In India, the case of Salman Rushdie just cited indicates the value of cultural authority confronted with the threat of sectarian violence. The decision to exclude Rushdie was made in response to this palpable threat, and the value of a canonical secular authority in literature itself was being put forward in *The Telegraph Calcutta* in preference to religious determination, political pragmatism or cowardice. Claiming Rushdie as a figure in a lasting literary history, whose value must be maintained against such violent foreclosures, shows clearly how a literary canon engages with and repudiates the assertions of power and the threat of violence. The moment was hot, but the same power-struggle can continue over centuries in a cold, dispassionate way. Thus, arguing for a distinct canon of Scottish literature is equally an attempt to help defend the authority of cultural values, in opposition to the values of bigotry and prejudice. A space needs to be agreed on, where a canon might be set up and its value demonstrated, and its openness to revision maintained, without the threat of foreclosure. While the Indian example is possessed of its own distinction, the analogy with Scotland is helpful.

This is the case, to a greater or lesser degree, in most countries I know. On the grounds of my experience teaching Scottish literature in New Zealand from 1986 to 2000, and delivering guest-lectures on the subject in China, India, France, Romania, Singapore, Ireland, the United States, as well as in Scotland, where I currently hold the established Chair of Scottish Literature at the University of Glasgow (the only such institutionally-established Chair in any of the Scottish universities), I would point out that a multi-faceted approach to Scotland's literary and cultural history should not neglect the definition of a canonical 'spine.' Approaches that lead into hitherto unexplored or less well-established areas of the Scottish literary tradition, theoretical approaches that intellectualise the subject at the expense of popular access, specific emphasis on writers or texts that demonstrate the value of particular achievements, equal representation of work by particular identities, defined by gender, class, language, religion, sexuality, ideological orientation and disposition of one kind or another – all these remain live possibilities and some certainly require encouragement and redress in the face of neglect. The dynamics of the situation are always in play. Yet, given such a quantity of possibilities, what co-ordinate points may be relied on? This is the central question.

The historical trajectory of what I have called the 'spine' of the subject, its full articulation and its supple interconnectedness, may be emphasised at particular points by regenerative moments of revaluation and revivification of past tradition. Allan Ramsay in the 18th century and MacDiarmid in the early 20th century deliberately set out to re-introduce older traditions of Scottish literature to their contemporaries, regenerating a longer view. The resurgence of creative work in the 1980s and 1990s in Scotland coincided with a comprehensive revaluation of cultural production in literature, art and music through the same period. The purpose of having this depth of understanding is to provide something essential for 'vertebrate' identity – only by such understanding can the subject be compared and valued alongside other literatures.

In the 21st century, the context of cosmopolitanism and trans-national economies defines the historical location in which the political and personal – the most public and the most intimate – aspects of literary work are at their most valuable. This is our context, especially since the inauguration of the position of National Poet for Scotland – established in 2004 with the appointment of Edwin Morgan, who was succeeded in 2011 by Liz Lochhead. While the public prominence of such figures is valuable, the commercial disposition of celebrity culture brings its own cost, and a 'laissez-faire' attitude to literature may lead to the neglect of work that should be noticed more widely. Elizabeth Burns's collection, *Held* (2010), for example, is one of the most remarkable books of poetry published in recent years, but it went relatively uncelebrated in the mass media, too easily giving space to more familiar names. Literary appreciation may be distorted by political or religious preference, by commercial priorities and by newspaper editors who underestimate their readers' abilities and appetites. There will always be a need for preference and choice to be demonstrated, but there must be an agreed space open for that demonstration. For *Held* not to be widely reviewed is a form of marginalisation while for Rushdie not to be permitted to engage in a conversation with others is a form of censorship, but in both cases we need to pay attention, for critical redress is always going to be required.

In his essay "The Study of Scottish Literature" (2003), Ian Duncan observes how bizarre it is "that the study of Scottish literature should require a defence in Scotland in this day and age," although he admits that he knows "from experience that the case needs to be made elsewhere" and that he himself, when working as a young scholar, once asked the critic and editor Thomas Crawford whether it made sense "to think about Scott in the light of a Scottish – as distinct from an English or British – literary tradition." Duncan wryly reports: "With what I now recognize to have been heroic forbearance, he [Thomas Crawford] replied that such a point of view might indeed prove quite fruitful" (Duncan 2003, 1). Unfortunately, the case still has to be made. Duncan's essay draws to its conclusion with the speculation: "Perhaps the last thing Scottish literature needs is the unifying forcefield of a 'Great Tradition'" (4). There is uncertainty there, however. "Perhaps" some "unifying forcefield" might sometimes actually help.

Carla Sassi concludes her important and valuable book, *Why Scottish Literature Matters* (2005), by affirming that Scottish literature does matter: "this is beyond doubt – but it will have to be explained in other languages and to other cultures in order to survive" (182). Why has it not been explained as comprehensively and confidently as other literatures – American, Irish, English, Australian or New Zealand literatures, say? The reasons bear scrutiny.

The National Library of Scotland, the Scottish Poetry Library, the Mitchell Library in Glasgow and Scotland's university libraries generally, are vast storehouses of under-examined and inter-connected treasures. A great deal of work has been done, especially since the 1980s, but a great deal more remains to be done. For example, there are in 2012 at least six histories of Scottish literature available from eminent publishers, some in multiple volumes, containing scholarship of the highest calibre, and the resources for teachers available from the Association for Scottish Literary Studies are extensive and growing. But the subject still needs to be more widely known and discussed with more confident curiosity. Interviewed on BBC2's *Newsnight* programme on 29 November 2011, I was asked, "Is there such a thing as

Scottish literature?" Staggered by the inanity, I was grateful when the novelist A. L. Kennedy replied:

> Is there such a thing as English literature or Irish literature or American literature? You don't want to claim any literature for a country because it's international and has to do with the commonality of human experience, but Scotland exists, as a cultural entity, as an historical entity [...]. I want somebody to be able to sit in a Scottish school and think, I can succeed, being myself from my country, using the language that I use, being the person that I am, and that's very difficult to do if you don't see images of your country in movies, if you don't see them on television in a widespread, meaningful and powerful way, if you're not reading Scottish texts or hearing the Scottish voice as a voice of success, and if you don't understand your history you're just going to keep on, as everybody says, repeating your mistakes. [*My transcription*]

In specific areas, authors, works and details, Scottish literature probably remains the most under-researched major subject within what might broadly be called 'English Studies.'

Within this complex context, there are specific areas that remain opaque to this day. Chapter 6 of Sassi's book begins with a warning: "It should be noted that the 'Renaissance' [of the 1920s] has been and remains very little explored outside Scotland" (Sassi 2005, 104). There are various translations of MacDiarmid, Lewis Grassic Gibbon and Neil Gunn, particularly in Germany and Italy, but it seems that there is relatively little widespread appreciation internationally of the modernist movement towards cultural assertion of national self-determination that MacDiarmid led in the 1920s. Why, then, is there no adequate, brief, accessible and thus translatable account of it that is widely known and generally accepted? And how great is the gulf between what Scottish readers and critics familiar with the writers, works and the movement as a whole, know of it, and the general sense of its value outwith Scotland?

In Scotland, criticism of the latter half of the 20th century has redressed the situation of undervalued women writers of the first half, especially Violet Jacob, Marion Angus, Catherine Carswell, Willa Muir, Nan Shepherd and Lorna Moon. That critical revaluation itself, especially in the 1980s and 1990s, owed a great deal to the thrust of the Scottish Renaissance Movement of the 1920s. Prominent among the critics and literary historians of the era is Margery Palmer McCulloch, whose *Modernism and Nationalism: Literature and Society in Scotland, 1918-1939* (2004), *Scottish Modernism and its Contexts 1918–1959: Literature, National Identity and Cultural Exchange* (2009) and *Scottish and International Modernisms: Relationships and Reconfigurations* (2011) are crucial. Conversely, little concentrated and systematic effort has been invested by the British cultural establishment to recognise and promote Scotland's national cultural movement of the 1920s. Indeed one might argue that some effort has been made in the opposite direction. A canon of Scottish literature submerged within a canon of British or, more pointedly, English literature inevitably erases national or local expressions of difference, irrespective of the aesthetic value of the literary work. This is one reason why there is no Gaelic literature in Harold Bloom's list noted above. It is also why the infectiously sharp, punchy and witty accounts of Modernism written by Hugh Kenner focus on America, in *A Homemade World* (1975), Ireland, in *A Colder Eye* (1983) and England in *A Sinking Island* (1987), but hardly mention Scotland at all. Indeed, the latter book begins by stating that the word 'English,' until recently, "implied the culture of an island called England" (Kenner 1987, 3).

Of course, discussing canon-formation in the 21st century involves the consideration of specific demands and issues. The continuities of critical revaluation may be seen in the context of a diversity of literary work, so that it is not only possible but necessary to keep the canon open. In this respect, a Scottish literary canon is a composite tradition, intrinsically different from other national traditions when they are defined as monolithic. If an essentialist definition of national tradition requires continuity, organic wholeness and an ancient and uninterrupted line of development, Scottish literature exists in defiance of such a conservative validation of a unitary tradition. In itself it offers a rich range of alternative values, of material for comparative criticism, as it includes more than one tradition, more than one language. So the balance has to be to recognise the distinctiveness of a national literature and also, at the same time, to understand its open value in universal human terms, as far as that is possible. If the distinctive national literature may be indicated by reference to languages, historical events, geographical characteristics and political struggle, the universal aspects of that literature might be indicated with reference to their general application in the context of education.

It is perhaps worth considering briefly the impact and role of canon-formation on academic curricula, and thus in the information directly presented to generations of students. Some years ago, the educational jargonistas were enthusiastic about the notion of 'Transferable Employability Skills:' university teachers of literature were required to identify and describe what these 'Tranferable Skills' might be. This relates to the fundamental purpose of our teaching provision: the fundamental purpose is to help students towards further education, which implies *an attitude towards experience*, as opposed to training, which implies *a learned ability in specific skills*. Within the furtherance of education, specific transferable skills may be acquired through training and students will be exercised in ways to make use of them in literary study. These might include ability in critical analysis, logical reasoning, articulate verbal argument and clear, direct writing, understanding of subtlety and nuance, resistance to the mechanical excesses of systematic meaning and so on. However, our teaching is primarily intended to help provide an education. Training is part of the education. To reverse that order and suggest that education should be at the service of training would be regressive.

In education, all literature has an essential value in helping to understand the various attitudes towards experience people have and have had. So anyone who can should be encouraged to read authors such as Herman Melville, Wole Soyinka, Emily Bronte, Bertolt Brecht, Gustave Flaubert, George Eliot, Shakespeare, Rabelais or Dante, and as widely as possible, but nobody should undervalue the literature of their own people, written in languages close to their own, and with reference to people, places, things and events that are familiar and local. In fact, one should never undervalue any literature – ironically, for generations, Scottish literature may have been valued more internationally than by Scots in Scotland. This is the situation that the current Scottish government and a number of interested parties are attempting to change.

I should put my own cards on the table now. Let's revise and expand on the lists above, but give ourselves fifty names. I would say that these are authors every student of the subject should be familiar with to some degree, some of the writers to be recommended because each of them gives something necessary: John Barbour, Blind

Harry, Robert Henryson, William Dunbar, Gavin Douglas, David Lyndsay, Mark Alexander Boyd, William Drummond, Thomas Urquhart, the (anonymous) Ballads, Mary MacLeod, Sileas na Keppoch, James Macpherson, James Boswell, Tobias Smollett, Alasdair MacMhaighster Alasdair, Duncan Ban MacIntyre, James Thomson, Allan Ramsay, David Hume, James Hutton, Robert Fergusson, Burns, William Ross, Jean Elliott, Byron, Scott, Hogg, Susan Ferrier, John Galt, Margaret Oliphant, Thomas Carlyle, Mary Macpherson, James ('B. V.') Thomson, John Davidson, R. L. Stevenson, George Macdonald, J. M. Barrie, David Lindsay, Norman Douglas, George Douglas Brown, Edwin Muir, Hugh MacDiarmid, James Bridie, Norman MacCaig, Sorley MacLean, Robert Garioch, Iain Crichton Smith, Edwin Morgan, Liz Lochhead.

Why do these writers matter? Each one could be the subject of deep study and would repay, and indeed have repaid scholarly enquiry, but collectively they open the door to a more extensive, diverse and complex terrain: the authors named all write of things that cannot be found elsewhere but also, each one might prompt further reading that would complement and relativise their own centrality and status. The diversity characteristic of Scottish literature is evident in language (Gaelic, Scots and English), form (poems, plays, fiction), representation of experience of women and men, religious and political commitment, regional predilection and choice, epochal significance in the international context (Medieval and Renaissance, Enlightenment, Romanticism, Modernism); different cultural sensibilities, and so on. Thus the list expands upon those lists offered above, with the specific agenda that there should be a balance between the representation of experiences specific to Scotland and the literary distinctiveness of their expression, or transnational literary tenets. This agenda both confirms and questions conventional canon-formation.

In any national canon, there are distinctive themes. In American literature, they are well-known: the frontier, the non-conformist *isolatos* (Huck Finn lighting out for the territories, Ishmael and Ahab, Holden Caulfield in *The Catcher in the Rye*), or the American dream and its failure (the foundational myth of the egalitarian society, and the pathos of its impossibility in F. Scott Fitzgerald's *The Great Gatsby*) – to name a few. Similarly, other literatures have their own preoccupations.

'English' literature describes a colonial and imperial history with its attendant notions of the good society and its discontents. Consider the line from Shakespeare's history plays and *The Tempest*, with its island-native Caliban and imperial magus Prospero, and John Donne, describing his lover's body as "my America, my new-found land," to the small-town worlds of Jane Austen and George Eliot, ultimately troubled by the romantic lovers, serious artists and committed political individuals, who cut across social proprieties and families with property to protect, whether in the shape of the famously "single" man Darcy in *Pride and Prejudice,* or Ladislaw in *Middlemarch,* or the title character in *Daniel Deronda*, who opens little England to a Europe that threatens to overwhelm her. Consider the novels of industrial England, where Dickens's London is the heart of an empire from which comes tainted benefit. In the 20th century, consider D. H. Lawrence's working-class miners and their very specifically English society. And internationally, in Rudyard Kipling's *Kim*, consider the depiction of the imperial exploitation of wealth in an exotic context, and consider, in the transitional work of Joseph Conrad, in *Heart of Darkness* and *Lord Jim*, how we read the imperial, colonial, racist world of the 19th century and read forward into the postcolonial world, in works that offer a depiction of imperialism that implies its own critique. In this respect, critical attacks on the canonical status of English literature that have come from postcolonial, feminist, radical political stances, and others, may be seen as inherent or implicit in the work of its very authors.

African literature in English has also its own major themes. Chinua Achebe's novel *Things Fall Apart* describes a human tragedy specific to the Nigerian colonial clash, while South African literature, from Alan Paton's *Cry the Beloved Country* to the poetry of Dennis Brutus, deals directly with the matter of Apartheid and the need for freedom from racist oppression.

When David Dabydeen and Nana Wilson-Tagoe, in *A Reader's Guide to West Indian and Black British Literature* (1987), entitled one chapter "Selected Themes in West Indian Literature," they listed: Anti-imperialism and Nationalism; The Treatment of Race; The Theme of Childhood; The Treatment of Women/Women Characters; The Theme of Migration; The Rastafarian Theme in West Indian Literature; Post-independence Critiques; Carnival; Calypso. What this list makes clear is that some themes might be explored comparatively in any literature – for example, the representation of women or of children or indeed of men – but there are themes which arise specifically from a particular history (Rastafarianism, Carnival and Calypso), and there are themes which, while they have a universal reference, are going to be represented differently in different cultures at different moments in history (such as the treatment of race, or the themes of migration, anti-imperialism and nationalism). Some are more important, more urgently in need of address in some nations and at certain times rather than in others.

What might be similarly major themes distinct to Scottish literature? Consider these: 1. The Matter of the Nation: the unfinished business of home; 2. The Idea of Kinship: a sense of communication across difference, a common purpose between different people, people who speak different languages, or who come from different geographies of place and imagination; 3. Resistance and Freedom: a sense of self-determination or independence, the call for 'Freedom!' with, from one point of view, its exaggerations of nationalist euphoria and exceptionalism and, from another, its initial self-defensive assertion of the need to redress injustice; 4. Egalitarianism: the idea that education should be a birthright and not a privilege of money or class, the ideal of equality of opportunity; 5. Voice and Languages (Gaelic, French, Latin, Scots and English): an optimistic curiosity about the linguistic variety and the voices of the people of Scotland; 6. Geography: the specific terrain and locations of Scotland in their contrasts; 7. Humour and Austerity: the comic exuberance of Urquhart, the gameplaying of Morgan, the sympathetic understanding of Burns and Scott and the severities and extremities of compassion in Henryson, MacDiarmid, Lochhead.

At the heart of these themes are ideals of community and the question of national identity. This is nothing to be complacent about. The other side of a positive sense of diversity is a negative sense of difference: sectarianism, racism, violent separations of identity that are as rife in Scotland as in England, Ireland, America, Africa, the Caribbean or elsewhere. Yet the potential in these recurrent themes is real. The questions they raise recur in ways that distinguish Scottish literature from other national literatures.

A canon is a form of cultural empowerment. At times this power can be used badly, closing off options and limiting possibilities. At times it can work as effective resistance to such foreclosure and oppression. It is therefore always to some degree both an empowerment and a limitation. It can give form to identity, and form can give power. Yet power is always negotiated by position. To agree on co-ordinate points that allow a canon to be a prompt for further exploration and critical understanding would be to resist monolithic, unchanging authority, but at the same time to affirm cultural qualities and values that should be maintained. The balance is crucial. A canonical understanding of Scottish literature ought to help counterbalance three centuries of institutional neglect, and it should also enable confident self-determination in channels of cultural transmission, both within and outside of Scotland.

Works Cited

Bate, Walter Jackson. "The Crisis in English Studies." *Harvard Magazine* 85 (1982): 46-53.
Bloom, Harold. *The Western Canon: The Books and School of the Ages.* New York: Harcourt Brace, 1994.
Dabydeen, David and Nana Wilson-Tagoe, eds. *A Reader's Guide to West Indian and Black British Literature.* London: Hansib Books, 1988.
Denholm, Andrew. "Pupils Told They Must Study Scots Literature." *The Herald* (Glasgow) 25 January 2012: 1.
Duncan, Ian. "The Study of Scottish Literature." *Scot Lit* 28 (2003): 1-4.
Burns, Elizabeth. *Held.* Edinburgh: Polygon, 2010.
Eagleton, Terry. *Literary Theory: An Introduction.* Oxford: Blackwell, 1983.
Gifford, Douglas and Alan Riach, eds. *Scotlands: Poets and the Nation.* Manchester and Edinburgh: Carcanet Press and the Scottish Poetry Library, 2004.
Kenner, Hugh. *A Homemade World: The American Modernist Writers.* London: Marion Boyars, 1975.
—. *A Colder Eye: The Modern Irish Writers.* Harmondsworth: Penguin Books, 1983.
—. *A Sinking Island: The Modern English Writers.* Baltimore: The Johns Hopkins University Press, 1987.
Maley, Willy. *100 Best Scottish Books of All Time.* Edinburgh: The List, 2005.
McCabe, Colin. *James Joyce and the Revolution of the Word.* London: Macmillan, 1978.
McCulloch, Margery Palmer, ed. *Modernism and Nationalism: Literature and Society in Scotland, 1918-1939.* Glasgow: Association for Scottish Literary Studies, 2004.
—. *Scottish Modernism and its Contexts 1918–1959: Literature, National Identity and Cultural Exchange.* Edinburgh: Edinburgh University Press, 2009.
— and Emma Dymock, eds. *Scottish and International Modernisms: Relationships and Reconfigurations.* Glasgow: Association for Scottish Literary Studies, 2011.
Sassi, Carla. *Why Scottish Literature Matters.* Edinburgh: The Saltire Society, 2005.
Vajpeyi, Ananya. "Making a Tradition. Why the Idea of Indian Literature Needs Salman Rushdie." *The Telegraph* (Calcutta) 26 January 2012: 14.

MICHAEL MEYER, Koblenz

Antonia S. Byatt's Intermedial "Art Work:" The Empire Knits Back

Critics have developed various sophisticated hypotheses about the specific relationships between Byatt's *Matisse Stories* and its reproductions of Matisse's art. Gabriele Rippl (2005, 275-280) and Silvia Bigliazzi record the numerous ekphrastic parallels between Matisse and Byatt. Silvia Bigliazzi appreciates the "mise en abyme strategy of intertextuality" (Bigliazzi 1999, 194) in the hybrid "patchwork," but she states somewhat disappointedly that the reproductions primarily serve as accessible and decorative illustrations of the texts – with one exception that I will come back to (192, 195, 198). Catherine Mari even goes further when she states that Byatt's static, evocative descriptions imitate Matisse: "adoptant les priorités esthétiques de Matisse, ces nouvelles se font l'écho de la conception de l'art de ce peintre, 'un art d'équilibre, de pureté, de tranquillité'" (Mari 1997, 32). While it is true that visual description forms a central feature of Byatt's stories, I would seriously question that Byatt endorses balance, a sense of complacency à la Matisse, or any notion of transparent or 'pure' ekphrasis. Isabel Fernades comes to the convincing conclusion that the feminist stories invite new perceptions of Matisse (Fernades 2006, 201). Laurence Petit takes into account both the ekphrastic and the feminist features of Byatt's book in comprehensive and balanced readings (Petit 2005; 2006; 2008). I would like to considerably expand these approaches to the story "Art Work" and take a closer look at its multiple intermedial relationships from the perspectives of literary criticism *and* art history, the latter of which critics of Byatt's short fiction often neglect. "Art Work" deals not only with some of Matisse's particular works but also with the qualities of and relationships between painting, sculpture, crafts, design, photography, and writing. Byatt explores the influence of gender, race, and class on the production and the reception of art, work and art, and especially its critical evaluation and market value. In opposition to Mari and Bigliazzi, I consider the fictitious feminist work of art delineated in detail towards the end of the story, not Matisse's art, as an imaginary correlative to Byatt's story *and* as a subversive supplement to the pictures by Matisse that frame the story.

In spite of her feminist detachment from Matisse's *erotics*, Byatt seems to have chosen the modernist painter as her subject matter for his complementary *aesthetics*: Matisse regarded painting and drawing as a visual language, and Byatt uses writing for visual effects. Matisse's line drawings form the middle ground between painting and writing in literal and metaphorical ways. According to Matisse, drawing is "plastic writing" (Matisse 1995b, 131). Line drawing, Matisse continues, "contains [...] my possibilities of synthesis, the different points of view that I could more or less assimilate through my preliminary study" (131). Byatt, who positions the line drawings between the coloured reproductions of his pictures on the cover of the volume and the text of her stories in the volume, seems to unfold these different points of view suggested in the pictures, but also adds perspectives omitted or repressed by Matisse.

Matisse's self-reflexive drawing on the work of art, *L'artiste et le modèle reflétés dans le miroir* (1937), which reveals the gendered process and product of drawing, serves as an appropriate preface to the self-reflexive story.

L'artiste et le modèle reflétés dans le miroir, 1937

Fig. 1: Henri Matisse, *L'artiste et le modèle reflétés dans le miroir* (1937; The Baltimore Museum of Art: The Cone Collection), in Byatt (1994, 29).

In the foreground, the drawing shows a nude as a decorative object (with a bracelet and a necklace) in a relaxed, voluptuous pose with an ambiguous gaze that seems to be directed at the observer of the picture. However, it is questionable whether she sees the observer, since her eyes are looking "as if in a mirror, turning away from us into themselves" (Elderfield 1992, 41). Her back is reflected in the mirror, so that the observer obtains a view of the front and the back of her body, which is, albeit, only a white surface with an outline, a space for the projection of male fantasies. The nude in the foreground is opposed to the reflection of the artist's upper body, wearing rather formal dress. Behind him, we see decorative fronds and more sketches of decorative nudes, mirroring each other and the present scene in their sinuous lines. John Elderfield is certainly right when he remarks that the "model dissolves into her reflection" but less so when he observes that the drawing is "a reverie on female beauty with the artist himself looking on" (27). It is important that the mirrored artist looks at his easel outside of the picture rather than at his model, suggesting his absorption in art and his detachment from an erotic interest in the model, a view that is endorsed by his formal dress. However, the deflection of his gaze is belied by her pose and position in the foreground, exposed to the voyeuristic view. As Elderfield stresses, Matisse exposes the fact that the models are silent, preoccupied, and theatrically positioned, and that the (imaginary) union is delayed or the "consummation held in suspense" (41). This picture perfectly translates Matisse's aesthetics of a double interest in the erotic body and in the beauty of his composition, which is, as he himself admits, "perhaps sublimated voluptuousness" (Matisse 1995b, 132). The art historian Marcia Brennan lucidly explains how masculinity and aesthetics dovetail in Matisse's work and life via a dialectical relationship with women: "Matisse's artworks presented an implicitly male audience with a privileged, if ultimately fictive, opportunity to access the sensual aspects of the female body while simultaneously preserving the option of intellectual detachment" (Brennan 2004, 11). The story "Art Work," as opposed to the "The Chinese Lobster" in Byatt's collection, offers no direct female response to Matisse's erotic art but a creative feminist expression of the female body and work. The ramifications of gender in the production and appreciation of art form the link between the drawing discussed above, the reproduction and ekphrastic description of Matisse's *Le silence habité des maisons* (1947), and the story itself.

"Art Work" starts with an ekphrastic description of a rather poor black and white reproduction of Matisse's *Le silence habité des maisons* in Sir Lawrence Gowing's book on the artist and his enthusiastic praise of the painter's "sumptuous" (Byatt 1994, 31)[1] colors and "extraordinary virility" (32), an assessment which is somewhat qualified by the colored reproduction of the painting on the cover of the book. We can see that Byatt's description of the formal composition is quite precise. However, instead of the large array of luminous colors, which, according to the narrator, we "may imagine" (32) upon Gowing's account we find that the picture reproduced in color on the cover is dominated by black and shades of bluish grey, painted over bright yellow shining through. The dark walls of the interior frame and set off the window with a view on a tree in bright light outside. Thus, the colors suggested by Gowing and Byatt's narrator represent the picture only with a difference – as does the reproduction in black and white. This self-reflexive intermedial juxtaposition throws doubt upon the question of the appropriate reproduction of art, adequate ekphrastic description, gendered aesthetic value judgements, and the necessary but hardly controllable imaginative readers' responses to all of the above. Byatt's ambivalent introduction raises awareness for the problems of ekphrasis and prepares the reader for the 'colorful' descriptions to come, asking him or her to use their imagination in order to generate color from the black signs of printed words on the white pages. Byatt has Matisse's colors 'speak for themselves' (with a difference in the colored reproduction), but uses very evocative language in order to convey the colors of the imagination and the fictitious works of art in the story.

In view of the feminist story, the two pictures seem to complement each other: the male artist at work on a nude (his potential lover?) in his studio corresponds to his absence in the domestic sphere of his home, where a mother (his wife?) and a child

---

[1] Further references to the short story will be indicated by page numbers in parentheses.

are sitting at a table with a book. The situation suggests leisure time, but not necessarily harmony or silent bliss. In the upper left corner on the wall, the enigmatic outline of a head could represent the trace of the absent father or/as a dark mirror. We could re-read Matisse's picture as the 'silencing' of the wife and child under the surveillance of the patriarchal ruling spirit, a still life that turns the domestic space into something like a mausoleum. The somber interior is set off against the bright space outside the figures turn their backs to. However, the open white book on the table may provide an escape. The book is empty as the faces, and as Laurence Petit aptly states, they invite us to fill their blanks and to tell the story of the picture:

> This "painted" book thus becomes the locus of an interesting double mise en abyme, wherein the pages turned by the child potentially contain the transcription into words of the imaginary world around them and are, at the same time, the very pages of the short story "Art Work" that we are just about to begin. (Petit 2008, 399)

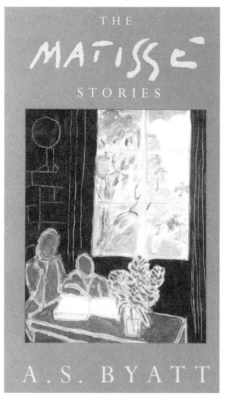

Fig. 2: Henri Matisse, *Le silence habité des maisons* (1947; Bridgeman Art Library, London), as reproduced on the cover (excerpt) of Byatt's *Matisse Stories*.

Possibly, Silvia Bigliazzi hints at a similar point when she writes: "[W]hat kind of book is this? Is it an autonomous object in Matisse's painting, or is it a pictorial equivalent of Byatt's book?" (Bigliazzi 1999, 198). The implied answer seems to be that it is both. Bigliazzi concludes that here, the relationship between picture and text becomes irony and turns into "an uncontrollable semiotic machine" rather than "a coherent compound of images and words" (198), but she does not analyze the ekphrastic complications Byatt explores towards the end of her story.

The story celebrates colors and pays homage to Matisse (Petit 2008, 399-400), but it does so with tongue in cheek, I would add. Laurence Petit convincingly states that "the three artist figures that this short story stages, namely Robin the painter, Debbie the illustrator, and Mrs. Brown the sculptor/decorator, represent three modes of expression favored by Matisse over the course of his long career" (Petit 2008, 398). However, the story reflects both of the framing pictures with irony and negotiates gender in art. Byatt's intermedial quotation defamiliarize Matisse. The story makes the reader aware of Matisse's influence on the design of objects but also of his reduction of women to passive objects (Fernades 2006, 205): Robin and Debbie's daughter, reclining on her bed, looks like in one of Matisse's portraits, and the design of her bedspread imitates Matisse's picture *Jazz*. Matisse's *Silence* is ironically juxtaposed to the plethora of noises in the house, from the stereo and the hoover, the washing machine, and other household gadgets. Matisse's portraits of naked and passive women exclude all the household chores women took care of in order to maintain his comfort and his carefree life, as is the case with Robin Dennison: their work is devoted to art, effacing the women's work which forms the backdrop of their career. In addition, Byatt "is indirectly calling attention to the differences between her own medium – sounds and words – and Matisse's art of colours, lines and forms" (Fernades 2006, 203). The story tells us how the male artist's absolute devotion to his art leads to his alienation from his family.

Byatt's narrator raises a question but does not answer it directly: "Who is the watching totem under the ceiling" (32)? Later, the narrator presents us with the narcissist and neurotic artist Robin Dennison, the 'madman in the attic,' who is obsessed with colors and collects "fetishes [...] of glossy, very brightly coloured solidity" (62).[2] Byatt's elaborate ekphrastic descriptions of these objects betray both her fascination with colors and a certain self-reflexive irony, implying a distance from the perfect mimesis Robin aims at in his version of neo-realism. Robin's neo-realist art, "just this side of kitsch, then and now" (52), displays two extremes: bare surfaces and tiny hyperrealist objects. He seems to be possessed by the colors of things rather than displaying his possession of things through artistic representation in the sense of Matisse (Matisse 1995c, 156). Robin does not only stand "for the intellectual, cerebral, rational, spiritual, purified, and dematerialized pole of Matisse's approach to light and color" (Petit 2008, 398). He exaggerates and reduces this approach to a rigid system, a "caricature" (Fernades 2006, 207) that Matisse himself would have scorned (cf. Matisse 1995a, 41). Robin is fascinated by the "pure sensuousness" and "power" (56) of Matisse's *Luxe, calme et volupté*, a patriarchal fantasy of an island arcadia with a clothed motherly figure and several naked beauties (cf. Elderfield 1992, 33-36). The only male figure in the picture is a boy on the verge of his initiation into sexuality. Robin resembles a petulant boy rather than a man, and fails in his imitation of Matisse's style (56-57). Sometimes Robin paints the shadow of a toy soldier into

---

2 Laurence Petit develops a relevant alternative reading that compares the totem to Mrs. Brown's position as a cleaner, who has superior insight into the Dennisons' family life and their household, and seems to weave herself into her soft sculpture of an interior (Petit 2008, 408). Petit's interpretation would support the change of real power from the male head of the family to the female 'underdog' that Robin seems to despise for her apparent filthiness and ignorance, an attitude that betrays discrimination of race, class, and gender.

crowds of other things in his pictures (62), a self-effacing remnant of a dated masculinity, which recalls the virility attributed to Matisse in a satirical manner that works both ways (cf. Fernades 2006, 209).

Byatt's story can be read as an allegory of the (real or desired) decline of the domination of fine art by bourgeois men and the rise of women in adverse circumstances. The minor male artist is confronted with three women who represent the gendered change in the art market: the Irish-Jamaican Sheba Brown, an underprivileged lower-class cleaner who turns out to be an innovative artist, Dennison's own wife, the critic (cum artist), and the self-confident gallery owner Shona McRury.

Robin's wife Debbie (temporarily) gave up her ambition to become an illustrator and designer for the more immediately accessible and remunerative career of a design editor for *A Woman's Place*, implicitly not restricted to the home (36). In spite of Debbie's and Shona's interest in Robin's art as defamiliarizing the perception of trivial objects (Debbie) and raising an awareness of the littleness of our lives (Shona), both women are more intrigued by the "amorphous" (68) feminist art which does not aspire to "the 'authority' of 'artworks'" (68-69). This feminist art would represent everyday things that male artists neglect, and "the interior cavities of women, not the soft fleshy desirable superficies explored/exploited by men" (69), an obvious critique of Matisse's nudes.

Whereas Robin Dennison's art is his life (as was Matisse's), the cleaning lady Sheba Brown turns her life and work into art against all odds, or rather with the odds and ends other people discard, parts of upholstery, strands of wool, bits and pieces of all sorts of fabrics. Matisse was also an eager collector of textiles, starting out "as an art student, spending tiny sums he could not afford on frayed scraps of tapestry from Parisian junk stalls," and even continuing to pick up discarded rags when he could buy expensive embroideries and carpets from Africa, Arabia and Persia (Spurling 2004, 15). Ms. Brown's strange and innovative combinations of color are not only based on her intuitive and subjective aesthetic sense but also on the vast variety of colors she happens to come across over the years of her domestic service. She is closer to Matisse in her independent development than Robin, who consciously tried to emulate the great master but gave up. Matisse stipulated that the "knowledge of color depends upon instinct and feeling" and goes beyond any theory of colors (Matisse 1995a, 41). Petit argues perceptively that there is a parallel between Matisse's composition with color, Byatt's weaving of color into her text, and Brown's weaving of colors into her network of fabrics (Petit 2008, 407-408). Sheba is a "travesty" (Fernades 2006, 209) of Matisse: the 'colored woman's' version of an *arte povera*, using the traditional female crafts, is juxtaposed with Matisse's luxurious and bourgeois paintings and sculptures. Matisse sometimes seems to have adapted his female models to the decorative textiles he draped them in, but Mrs. Brown re-creates the image of women by the very textiles they used. Her stunning, colorful installation or assemblage of wall-hangings, crochetings, weavings, stitchings, and knittings in combination with a collection of everyday items and furniture exceeds comprehension – it is truly an expression of the female Other missing in both Matisse's and Robin's art: The Empire knits back.

In spite of her indulgence in optimistic, lively colors, Sheba does not present the joy of women but includes what Matisse ignored (Fernades 2006, 209). There are creatures which could be furniture, animals, or women, both recalling and confusing the images of women as objects of use or pleasure and creatures of nature (78-79). In the center of the cavern, a soft, almost organic interior, we find a defamiliarizing and inverted version of an arch-patriarchal motif: a dragon, a chained lady, and a knight. The 'dangerous animal' is "a Hoover and a dragon, inert and suffocating" (80), representing the household chores that fetter women to the domestic sphere. The woman's body is broken and twisted, chained by "twisted brassières and demented petticoats, pyjama cords and sinister strained tights" (80). The composition recalls images of sexual violation. It is disturbing that the woman's eyeholes are cut out and "stitched round with spiky black lashes" (80), as if to expose her reduction to a sexual object of the male gaze.[3] The tiny knight is an even poorer version than Robin Dennison's and totally incongruous to the situation: "a plastic knight on a horse, once silver, now mud-green, a toy soldier with a broken sword and a battered helmet" (80). Sheba Brown ridicules traditional expectations of masculinity, an ironic echo of Gowing's comment on Matisse's 'virility,' which seems to be of as little use to women as the toy soldier or real men, as Sheba knows from her own experience with the abusive father of her children.

The golden letters of Mrs. Brown's name and the title "WORK IN VARIOUS MATERIALS 1975-1990" (81) on a washing line recall both her colored skin and her work (Petit 2008, 408-409), Byatt's use of colored letters, and her ekphrastic description of Sheba's fictitious work of art. In spite of Byatt's rendering of Sheba's installation in very evocative language, Sheba's work can neither be described nor interpreted exhaustively in writing due to its complex and transgressive features and the medial differences between visual and verbal representation. Of course, the information given in the story is 'sufficient' and each reader is free to conceive his or her version of the imaginative and imaginary work.

Next to the letters, Debbie finds the photograph of an amused Mrs. Brown: "Her skin has come out duskier than it 'really' is, her bones are sculpted, she resembles a cross between the Mona Lisa and a Benin bronze" (81). The observer, Debbie, views the photograph from a double perspective, redolent of Roland Barthes's theory, which roughly locates photography between an analogous inscription of reality without a code and art as a coded sign (Barthes 1982, 19). The reference to reality is put in inverted commas: Debbie knows that her object of correspondence is not reality as such but her perception of reality. Nevertheless, she finds that the photograph represents 'reality' only with a difference, which paradoxically adds an artistic touch to the picture reminiscent of a three-dimensional sculpture. Ironically, it is helpful to understand the mimetic mis-representation by the photograph through the reference to the arts, in other words by ekphrasis in the story.[4] In this case, the invocation of the European Mona Lisa and the African mask from Benin, both expressions of beauty, mystery, and ultimate artistic accomplishment, do not aim at the exact mimetic representation of the hybrid Irish-Caribbean artist, but at an elaborate appreciation

---

3   Matisse also painted women with empty or blackened eyes, a feature that could be read as a sign of closed painted eyes or as a way of reducing them to puppets – either interpretation is disturbing and disconcerting to the voyeuristic gaze.
4   The reflection on photographic misrepresentation brings us back full circle to the beginning of the story because the inadequate but interesting photograph echoes Gowing's reproduction of Matisse in black and white. In both cases, the ekphrastic description requires both the reader's imagination and knowledge of the cultural context in order to generate both visual quality and verbal meaning.

that adds to our understanding of her in a larger cultural context. The ekphrastic periphrasis reveals an ironic and self-reflexive postmodern combination of writing, traditional and modern African and European arts. The multiple ekphrastic representations of the photograph in words, in terms of a painting and a sculpture, help to make sense but also complicate our understanding because the intermedial semiotic process foregrounds both the Derridean "différance" (cf. Derrida 2004) of any representation and the otherness of its subject.

Mrs. Brown immediately attracts the attention of the media. Ironically, the critic in a woman's magazine does not value her art as a work of her own, but compares her "intricate woven backgrounds" (83) to the paintings of the mad and violent Victorian artist Richard Dadd, and her "luxurious innovations" (83) to those of the Anglo-American Kaffe Fasset, who has actually appropriated and successfully marketed the "decorative" female crafts of knitting, needlepoint, and patchwork (cf. Kaffe Fasset Studio 2011). However, Sheba Brown's creative and disturbing re-knitting of the male images of women invert and subvert Kaffe Fasset's commercial and conservative designs for upscale comfortable homes. The fact that Richard Dadd killed his father is not mentioned in that critique but may form a subconscious motif of the critic's comparison of Dadd and Sheba, alluding to the rise of the woman artist over '*his* dead body.' Thus, the parochial article places Sheba Brown in a tradition of deviant white male artists that she most likely has never even heard of, and neither in Matisse's tradition nor in the more appropriate tradition of women's arts and crafts. Sheba admits to having turned into art what she learned about and from the Dennisons. In turn, she inspires Debbie to return to making book illustrations and Robin to paint in weaving patterns and new colors. Debbie's exotic fairies have the "haughty face of Sheba Brown" (89), but Robin paints Kali the Destroyer in a dark and terrifying, "simplified travesty of Sheba Brown" (90). His vengeful misrepresentation inverts her creative power. Robin's new picture vilifies the woman artist in spite or rather because of her influence on him. The image of Kali is the very opposite of Matisse's silent beauties and stereotypically represents women as monsters, mothers, or maidens. These misogynist stereotypes fly into the face of Sheba Brown's complex, ambiguous and inexhaustible web of textures, colors and meanings, which forms an intermedial correlative of Byatt's moderately feminist "Art Work," without collapsing the differences between the fine arts and the art of language, Brown's intuitive style and Byatt's intellectual and highly self-reflexive style. Thus, the story and the imaginary installation form the vision of a new kind of the '*sister* arts,' which criticize the masculine tradition of the gendered arts and the international art market, which highly prizes Matisse's many masculine and decorative pictures.

Works Cited

Anon. "Dadd, Richard." The J. Paul Getty Museum. 24 October 2011 <http://www.getty.edu/art/gettyguide/artMakerDetails?maker=281&page=1>.

Barthes, Roland. "The Photographic Message." *Image-Music-Text*. Ed. and trans. Stephen Heath. Glasgow: Fontana, 1982. 15-31.

Bigliazzi, Silvia. "'Art Work': A. S. Byatt vs Henry Matisse, or the Metamorphoses of Writing." *Textus: English Studies in Italy* 12.1 (1999): 185-200.

Brennan, Marcia. *Modernism's Masculine Subjects: Matisse, the New York School, and Post-Painterly Abstraction*. Cambridge, MA: MIT Press, 2004.

Byatt, Antonia S. *The Matisse Stories*. London: Vintage, 1994.
Derrida, Jacques. "Différance." *Literary Theory: An Anthology*. Eds. Julie Rivkin and Michael Ryan. Oxford: Blackwell, 2004. 278-299.
Elderfield, John. "Describing Matisse." *Henri Matisse: A Retrospective*. Eds. John Elderfield et al. New York: Museum of Modern Art, 1992.13-78.
Kaffe Fasset Studio. London, 2011. 24 October 2011 <http://www.kaffefassett.com/>.
Fernades, Isabel. "Matisse and Women: Portraits by A. S. Byatt." *Writing and Seeing: Essays on Word and Image*. Eds. Rui Carvalho Homem and Maria de Fátima Lambert. Amsterdam: Rodopi, 2006. 201-210.
Mari, Catherine. "De Tableau en Histoire, d'Histoire en Tableau: Le Lecteur-Spectateur dans *The Matisse Stories* de A. S. Byatt." *Etudes Britanniques Contemporaines: Revue de la Societé d'Etudes Anglaises Contemporaines* 12 (1997): 31-40.
Matisse, Henri. "Notes of a Painter, 1908." *Matisse on Art*. Revised ed. Ed. Jack D. Flam. Berkeley and Los Angeles: University of California Press, 1995a. 30-43.
—. "Notes of a Painter on His Drawing, 1939." *Matisse on Art*. Revised ed. Ed. Jack D. Flam. Berkeley and Los Angeles: University of California Press, 1995b. 129-132.
—. "The Role and Modalities of Color, 1945." *Matisse on Art*. Revised ed. Ed. Jack D. Flam. Berkeley and Los Angeles: University of California Press, 1995c. 154-157.
Petit, Laurence. "'Truth in Framing': Medusa's Defeat or the Triumph of the 'Framed' Self in A. S. Byatt's Medusa's Ankles." *Images and Imagery: Frames, Borders, Limits: Interdisciplinary Perspectives*. Eds. Leslie Boldt-Irons, Corrado Federici and Ernesto Virgulti. Studies on Themes and Motifs in Literature 74. New York: Peter Lang, 2005. 117-136.
—. "Textual and Pictorial Distortions: Sublimity and Abjection in A. S. Byatt's 'The Chinese Lobster'." *Etudes Britanniques Contemporaines* 31 (2006): 117-126.
—. "Inscribing Colors and Coloring Words: A. S. Byatt's 'Art Work' as a Verbal 'Still Life'." *Critique: Studies in Contemporary Fiction* 49.4 (2008): 395-412.
Rippl, Gabriele. *Beschreibungs-Kunst. Zur intermedialen Poetik angloamerikanischer Ikontexte (1880-2000)*. München: Fink, 2005.
Spurling, Hilary. "Material World: Matisse, His Art and His Textiles." *Material World: Matisse, His Art and His Textiles. The Fabric of Dreams*. Eds. Anne Dumas et al. London: Royal Academy of Arts, 2004. 14-33.

Anglistik

Universitätsverlag
WINTER
Heidelberg

SEEBER, HANS-ULRICH
Literarische Faszination in England um 1900
2012. 368 Seiten,
10 Abbildungen. (Anglistische Forschungen, Band 426)
Gebunden € 58,–
ISBN 978-3-8253-5996-6

Das aus dem Lateinischen stammende, im Englischen zunächst selten gebrauchte Wort 'Faszination' bedeutet ursprünglich Behexung mittels Augenzauber (‚böses Auge'). Heute ist das Wort zu einem unverzichtbaren begrifflichen Instrument der Umgangssprache, der Werbesprache und der Literaturkritik geworden. Welche Gründe hat das? Kann man sagen, dass die klassische Ästhetik seit etwa 1900 von einer Ästhetik der Faszination abgelöst worden ist? Die Studie konzentriert sich auf die Zeit um 1900, in welcher der Begriff zum ersten Mal in den Mittelpunkt des Interesses rückt (u. a. in der Suggestionspsychologie). Nach einer Erörterung der Wissenschaftsgeschichte des Begriffs erprobt die Arbeit in Fallstudien (Oscar Wilde, Henry James, u. a.) seine interpretatorische Ergiebigkeit. Um die epochen- und kulturübergreifende Relevanz des Begriffs nachzuweisen, geht die Studie ergänzend auch auf Autoren (u.a. William Shakespeare) aus einer anderen Epoche oder einem anderen Kontext ein.

D-69051 Heidelberg · Postfach 10 61 40 · Tel. (49) 62 21/77 02 60 · Fax (49) 62 21/77 02 69
Internet http://www.winter-verlag.de · E-mail: info@winter-verlag.de

RENATE BROSCH, Stuttgart

Third Space in Rohinton Mistry's "Swimming Lessons"

In writing about narrative space the proliferating metaphors of in-betweenness, liminality or third space immediately come to mind. Following the work of Henri Lefebvre, Edward Soja and Michel de Certeau on the socially constructed nature of space, the concept of third space expresses a new quality of encounters between the self and its environment. As part of a pervasive struggle in cultural criticism to find alternatives to dualistic ways of thinking, the notion highlights transgressive qualities and a potential for liberation and emancipation in spatial practices. In postcolonial studies especially, the potentialities of third space have acquired leitmotif status. As a traditional locus of initiation, liminal spaces are predestined for the expression of certain theoretical positions fundamental to postcolonialism, in particular the notion of hybridity as imagined by Homi Bhabha (2000, 1). In consequence, such in-between places are often invested with emancipatory or subversive possibilities in providing the background for resistant or creatively reconstructive practices, which temporarily liberate characters from restraints. In the following article I attempt to substantiate a reading of narrative space by supplementing these metaphorical interp retations of third space with a detailed analysis of the space *in* the text as well as the space *of* the text. Using Rohinton Mistry's short story "Swimming Lessons" as a model case for the narrative construction of space in short stories, I propose that space plays a more significant role in short stories than in longer narratives because the genre favours semanticized spatial contrasts which are resolved into an emergent third at the end. Thus the short story's triadic structure functions on several levels to generate a sense of binary oppositions overcome.

Following sociological and geographical studies of place as a dynamic, shifting, socially constructed and experiential concept ("the spatial turn"), narratological analysis has in recent years also become more attentive to literary constructions of space. Traditional models of storytelling understood narrative space primarily in terms of description of setting and hence as a static impediment to the temporal succession of narrative. By contrast, critics nowadays reject this concept of fictional topography as an inert container, where story happens. Instead they see it as an active force that pervades the literary field and shapes its plot (Friedman 2005, 194). In this view, narrative continually marks out boundaries and bridges them, creating a complex and dynamic network of differentiation and combination in which the spatial trajectories actively enable narrative by establishing frontiers and borders which mark difference and produce conflict or linkages (194). This dynamic understanding of narrative space requires a shift in approach towards a more experiential interpretation of literature. For the reader, place is always implicitly necessary for every action performed by a character, even if there are no separate segments of text devoted to information about space (Bal 2004, 140).

Textual elements like perspective and deictica create the reader's sense of place through evocation of quasi-corporeal involvement in its spatial environment. In mental processes of visualization the reader maps out the textual references and relationships and responds to the "experiential iconicity" of the space *of* the text (Wolf 2001, 325). The feel of the fictional environment is usually commented on in terms of atmosphere and mood for want of more precise categories for the reader's imaginative response. Certainly, experiential aspects of narrative space are the most difficult to investigate and therefore neglected by most theorists; some even claim that their inclusion lacks scholarly viability (van Baak 1983, 3). But to disregard them is to ignore that narrative space is not only part of the story world but performed in a related mental operation by readers as well, who connect the processing of text with their own physical-mental experience of being-in-the-world. I propose that the short story's poetics of brevity is predicated on a spatial dimension which informs the narrative as well as pertaining to the particular reading process demanded by the genre. Hence, an important concern of such an investigation must be to discover the way in which the spatial features of the text produce certain imaginative responses in readers, whose mental imagery in turn depends on individual as well as cultural predispositions and conceptualization.

The experience of reading is of paramount importance in interpreting the genre of the short story. Because short stories need to appeal to the reader's imagination in such a way as to cause some sort of mental engagement and be remembered in spite of the brevity of the reading experience, they tend to make use of strategies which promise cognitive and affective impact.[1] To consider the short story in terms of the literary experience it offers, rather than as a text with a set of determinate generic characteristics, means to enter the border land between story and audience, between interpretive communities and texts. The approach allows us to look at organizational acts which depend on both the structure of the text as well as on the cultural input by the reader.

By taking into account reading experiences, the achievements of postcolonial criticism in relating literature to social and political power structures past and present can be supplemented with a consideration of the context of reception. Only by including reading practices can we adequately judge the cultural work literature performs. Thus the inclusion of reading processes into the analysis of texts is not meant as an erasure of the need for an ethical position in postcolonial studies. To think of storytelling as performative, or in anthropological terms as "communication-based social action," makes clear its privileged function in community construction (Brydon 2007, 41).

Short stories are a genre that involves readers in reaching out beyond its confined borders, inviting them to make connections with intertexts and cultural memory as well as with other readers. Instead of offering large views of the world, which contain their own value systems, they can speak to the reader's need to make connections, to discover similarity in difference in a "webworking creative act" (Stafford 2001, 8). Like the anecdote, a proximate genre, they have to presume the cultural currency of their larger framework.

---

1 The views on the specificity of short stories expressed here are taken from my monograph *Short Story: Textsorte und Leseerfahrung* (2007). In this book I argued that the genre can only be defined as an aesthetic experience. The genre typically offers a challenge in the form of two apparently opposite but in effect complementary mental activities: visualisation and projection. "Visualisation" refers to the visual images created in the mind of the reader in response to the features of a literary text (Esrock 2005, 633), and "projection" or "projective blending" designates the extrapolation of meaning beyond the frame of the text and/or the fictional world, which takes place in the reader's attempt to come to terms with recalcitrance (cf. Turner 2006, 96).

As Susan Ferguson points out "setting is a more significant factor in the modern story than in the nouvelle and novel in terms of proportion of discourse space allotted to it" (Ferguson 1994, 226). Why should space be such a determining factor? We know that elaborate descriptions of scenery are not the short story's particular domain. Like all narratives, short stories respond to the primary interest of readers in character and plot development; but since their own curtailed space does not allow large development of either, they make amends through other appellative strategies in which narrative space can play a part. Particularly, conflict, which is an important means of producing attention, can be effectively and economically presented via spatial semantization. Moreover, space is an appeal to visualization, as any narrative element that evokes external reality is easily imagined and therefore makes an effective appeal to the reader; and because places contain multiple cultural semantizations they can function allegorically and/or metaphorically to expand the meaning of the narrative and thus to take the reader into a shared realm of myth.

Because of these narrative functions, I would argue, short stories favour a relatively static composition of contrasting or opposed narrative spaces which is then resolved into a third space as an "emergent blend" at the end.[2] This frequent spatial design in short stories is most effective when several textual aspects collude: firstly, a proportionally extensive treatment concentrating on a particular binary of setting, secondly, the use of symbol or allegory in the semantization of places so that the spatial dichotomies reverberate with wider meaning, and thirdly, the "spatial form" of the narrative in which the formal structure of the text mirrors the spatial setting. For the investigation of narrative space we should therefore distinguish between a) thematized space in the text, mostly in descriptions of places and locations, b) spatial values that emerge from the codes and multiple semanticizations which certain places have acquired in cultural memory, and c) spatial form, by which I understand all the verbal and medial strategies that create the space of the text.

A sense of place and the feel of a setting is, of course, a large part of a story's visuality. On the most obvious level, story space is established through local colour. But clearly, it is not only the descriptive content that influences our cognitive mapping of story space. According to Aleida Assmann, places are to be distinguished from abstract space in being marked by face to face encounters, by having a personal history, not unlike an individual (Assmann 2009). Place is the focus of human experience, memory, desire and identity. Representations of places, therefore, are fictional constructions that target emotional investment. Fiction enables the reader to perform a doubling structure in reading, i.e. to imagine worlds other than the one we are in and to feel as another person would. In other words, literature, when it succeeds in engaging our imagination, does this most powerfully when we overcome the restrictions of textual perspective and shift (even if only momentarily) to a more comprehensive one. And this experience in the act of reading is not just interpretive

---

2   According to Mark Turner, blending is a concept that designates something that is going on all the time, whenever we process information. We are constantly blending the old with the new, alternative viewpoints with previous ones, adjusting our opinions and modifying them to accommodate alterity with prior belief and knowledge systems. In processing a sophisticated literary text like the short story, blending means not a complete fusion of images and ideas, but a simultaneous awareness of different possibilities, from which a "blend" results with "emergent properties that are not possessed by the input views" (Turner 2006, 96).

or evaluative at the end of a reading act as a tagged-on hermeneutic act; it is a reading experience that is visual as well, an act of visualization.

Since space is socially and culturally constructed, as recent critics argue, it is not only material geography and the environment that operate as determining influences upon the interpretive consciousness, but also place and location that are attributed meaning by being written, narrated and interpreted (Brookner 2005, 5). These cultural codings of space influence the writing and reading of spaces. In a complex web of intertextuality, narratives of places are grounded in and feed into the cultural memory, thus creating an ongoing discursive formation around these locations. Texts like the short story that depend on achieving density through compression must rely to a large extent on a framework of knowledge which allusions to other texts and cultural articulations evoke. These intertextual and contextual signals may allude to literary pretexts, recalling canonical topoi like the pastoral, or the city or the road; in doing so they have recourse to a common storehouse of images providing some idea of a place, even for readers who have never been there.

For postcolonial short stories the division into contrasting spaces is an obvious choice because of their ability to reflect the clash of cultures, which is a primary topic, as well as certain theoretical positions fundamental to postcolonialism. The ruptured condition of colonial and postcolonial societies not only finds expression in literary representations but is part of the expectations informing the reception of the literary text. Accordingly, the postcolonial must be perceived as a mode of reception, as "a matter of complex reading, complex listening, whereby the plethora, the multitude of voices can be heard" (Punter 2000, 188). The orientation towards the marginalized and incomplete as well as the effort to detect relations between local particulars and larger general concerns which feature in postcolonial short stories can also be found among the preferences of current readerships so that a tendency on the production side may meet with a favourable disposition on the audience side.

Rohinton Mistry's story "Swimming Lessons" (SL) calls for a postcolonial reading from the start. It is the finely balanced final story of Kersi, a character we have met in some of the previous stories in the collection. This story takes him to his new home as an immigrant in Canada, discussing – as is often the case in postcolonial short stories – the implications of place for character (Davis 2001, 328). Mistry's short story offers a sophisticated example for the binary construction of narrative space, ultimately transcended by an emerging third space. It is structured on principles of polarization in terms of the space in the text as well as the space of the text.

The first thing we notice in approaching the story is its alternating print. This difference in the typographic quality of layout and formatting alerts us to two different parts of the story. On the one hand, there is Kersi's experience, on the other, the speculations of his parents on their son's well-being in the foreign country. The division goes so far as to exhibit different modes of narration: while the son's story is recorded in the present tense of a diary or journal, the parents' experiences are told by a third person narrator in the more usual fictional past tense. The structural binary is further borne out in the division into the contrasting settings (Canada and India), making the reader accommodate imaginative shifts between two countries and cultures literally worlds apart. In imaginative leaps from Bombay to Toronto and back again, we become familiar with different corresponding protagonists, residents of their respective neighbourhoods.

Though my description so far suggests difference on every level between the two story strands, the reader does not experience them as unconnected. The textual movements between the two locations prompt deft parallels between the lives in both multicultural urban settings. Kersi is trying to deal with loneliness and racism in his new home by creating analogies between the residents he encounters in his apartment complex and their Indian counterparts. Through his focalization, the petty, sad and comic personalities in both cities appear increasingly and comfortably similar. Moreover, the two places are part of the same plot: while the Canadian episodes recount Kersi's migrant experience, each episode in India gives us the parents' reactions to communications from him. In this way both focus on the cultural adjustment of the immigrant protagonist who is the subject of his parents' fearful and hopeful conjectures. Thus, the story emphasizes the dialectics informing the situation of diaspora.

For the production of a sense of 'spatial form' as defined above, SL employs a remarkable feature that impacts on the reader's response. Two contrasting forms of narration serve the purpose of structuring the compositional binary: Kersi's parts of the story are written in the first person and in the present tense, the parents' parts of the story are written in the more conventional third person and in the past tense. In spite of its current popularity with authors, present tense narration is still a slightly more difficult form for the reader than the past tense. Past tense narration makes it extremely easy to navigate the fictional world; all the other tenses follow naturally and logically from an initial deixis which locates us firmly in space and time, thus granting easy access to times before and after the narrated moment (Le Guin 1998, 73). The advantage of the past tense is its illusionary quality, resulting from the commodious arrangement the reader's imagination makes within the fictional world. The choice of the past tense in the Indian parts suggests that they are already fictional material for the budding author. It also implies that his relation with his Indian past is being transformed and fictionalized by memory.

One of the reasons why contemporary writers often prefer the present tense is that they shun the facile illusion of the traditional past tense because they have rejected the idea of *grands récits* and wish to make their readers aware of minor, neglected, marginalized perspectives. The present tense in narrative is more focussed than the past tense; "it sacrifices the larger time-field to achieve keen, close focus" (Le Guin 1998, 73). The present tense is therefore ideal for postcolonial purposes: it makes narration episodic, leading from one moment to the next and excluding global temporal reference. Because of its suspension of temporality, present tense narration approaches spatial form more closely than does a past tense narration. In this case it increases the uncanny effect of doubling in our reading experience of the experience of Kersi, the author.

The view through Kersi's eyes which the reader shares is a radically marginalized perspective characterized by perceptual distance. His view of Canada is that of an outsider, and visual spectatorship is his main mode of experience in the foreign country. Distance is stressed in his desiring observation of two women in bathing suits who appear unattractive on closer view. His few verbal exchanges with other residents in the apartment complex consist mostly of small talk hampered by intercultural misunderstanding. While Kersi observes Canada as an often disappointing visual event from the security of his flat, the reader must necessarily recreate this distance to the Canadian world in his/her visualization.

"What all exiles have in common is distance from a place of connection, a distance that affords a view from outside, unperturbed by proximity or participation" (Evelein 2009, 16). In this formulation the experience of displacement is not solely one of loss, but also one of enrichment since the outsider's view it enforces can transform perceptions creatively. This takes place in the imaginative space of the hero's memory, where in contrast to the bleak Canadian prospects India is reconstructed in vivid and colourful detail. Such a reconstruction of "imaginary homelands" (Rushdie) is a typical feature of diasporic writing; the homeland is imaginary because of distance from the present conditions in the mother country as well as from the past remembered. The images thus created help overcome the problems and disadvantages of life in the diaspora.

The central role of the swimming pool is indicated by multiple semanticization. The place where Kersi takes lessons is a space of terror because of his dread of water, but also a space of temptation where he spies pubic hair on female swimmers, a space of frustration where he becomes the object of racist insults, and ultimately a space of acculturation where he makes his peace with his new home. Trips to the swimming pool for lessons are virtually the only times he ventures out of his voluntary confinement in the apartment complex. This singularity in movement through fictional spaces suggests that this place is marked out for special meaning. It is no coincidence that the metaphorical leitmotif of the story has to do with water and swimming. Learning to swim stands for a process of acculturation as well as an initiation into literary writing as a self-protective activity. Water or rather an immersion in water carries connotations of rebirth and *rite de passage*. These symbolic meanings come into full play in the end when Kersi overcomes his dread of water, immerses himself in the bathtub for the first time and decides to take up swimming lessons again: "The world outside the water I have seen a lot of, it is now time to see what is inside" (Mistry 1999, 281). The image of water as a solution to the problems grounded in two places prompts metaphorical transfer from space to experience and invites associations of fluidity, stability and uncontainability. Thus the reader's visualization foregrounds qualities which are the very characteristics of the response to diaspora through which the migrant can shape and adapt his identity to produce a more dynamic and mixed version of the self.

The main character ultimately liberates himself from his mental and spatial confinement. In terms of thematized space, the description emphasizes confinement in both settings. Both parts of the plot are acted out in enclosed spaces – the parents in their apartment block in Mumbai, the son in his apartment complex in Canada. Synthesis on a surface level of content and plot resolution occurs when Kersi finds his feet in his new home country through becoming a writer. At the end of the story he sends his first publication to his parents. The collection mother and father then proudly read is entitled *Tales from Firozha Baag*, like the volume that contains the story SL. Kersi's fashioning of a new identity emerges from his writing; it is a third space of enunciation which readers can experience in the making. In terms of the construction of space this solution can be read as the third space of hybridity which the main character creates in answer to his diasporic dilemma. In a postcolonial literary text hybridity is an important characteristic which does not imply a denial of the traditions from which it springs, but rather focuses on a continual cross-fertilization. Ethnic identity is "a matter of 'becoming' as well as of 'being,' [it] belongs to the future as much as to the past [...] identities are the names we give to the different ways we are positioned by, and position ourselves within, the narratives of the past" (Hall 2003, 236).

Since we are informed that the third space of imaginary homelands made up by Kersi eventually finds its way into a published book, we must feel that the most important result is being withheld, especially when we read how much the parents relish and cherish the stories. For the reader the effect is almost uncanny: we map out a third space in the imagination as a response to an over-conspicuous absence in SL between the two stories of a) the hero's subjective impressions of Canada and b) his parents' divided response to his stories about India. In asking us to imagine the stories Kersi writes, SL asks us to replicate his effort in creating a hybrid world made up of elements from both locations.

The story invites the reader to participate in the process of signification by its necessarily elliptical form. Encountering fictional readers' responses to unknown stories is a strange experience for the actual reader and surely intended to be so by the author, or in Wolfgang Iser's more sophisticated terms, the indeterminacy is a textual instruction for the implied reader. The difference between the compassionate mother's emotional reading and the father's rational explication of the texts increases the indeterminacy and creates an experience of dissonance in the reader's mind. The divergent ways mother and father react to the stories make us wonder what they are supposed to like. Some clues to the stories' content are provided in the parents' discussion and in the recurrence of Parsi characters from the suburb of Mumbai where Kersi grew up and where his parents still live. More than these bits of information the title of the fictional collection, *Tales from Firozha Baag*, suggests that all the previous stories in the collection we are reading can now be redefined as the fictional author's production. The last story's thinly veiled autobiographical protagonist thus retrospectively claims authorship for the story cycle. The previous narratives become a multilayered composite portrait of a remembered society which we can now attribute to an identifiable narrative voice. SL thus asks us not only to modify our previous experience of the stories (demanding a flexibility of judgement that is a mainstay of the migrant's survival) but also to perform a metaleptic reading of this one in responding to its meta-narrative incentive.

The short story raises questions about self-representation by interrogating the narrative form itself. The manner in which the fictional writer Kersi appropriates the cycle in order to enact re-presentation becomes "a metaphor for the complexity of ethnic lives, the articulation of subjectivity and the process toward self-identification, asserting the flexibility of the creative consciousness and the intertextual process constitutive of contemporary Asian American and Asian Canadian fiction" (Davis 2001, 26). Thus the structure of the text and the imaginative processes it necessitates help generate a feeling of empathy or identification with the protagonist's situation of displacement. At the very least it depends on actively participating in imagining that which allows the protagonist a sense of release from the pains and pressures in migrant life.

As readers of Mistry's cycle *Tales from Firozha Baag* we are placed in a strategic position, charged with determining meanings – ethnic, racial, or cultural – by imaginatively bridging textual insularity. As readers of its last story SL, we insert the stories experienced in the past into a present and differently located narrative about someone caught between the frying pan and the fire, i. e. racism and marginalization in Canada and poverty and conformism in India. In performing this act of remodeling our previous reading, we are responding creatively to a situation similar (on a small scale) to the central character's, who finds an outlet for his frustration in writing. Since the composite portrait of India is retrospectively attributed to the single Asian-Canadian voice of Kersi, an ambivalent combination of cycle polyvocality and individual articulation results. Rather than providing closure, the emerging blend alerts us to the creative potential inherent in transience and mutability.

Writing the stories about India into the last story about Canada triggers an interaction between reader and text in which a third is generated that possesses no space in the narrative. This third space of interaction is outside both the fictional world and the real one from which we derive our understanding of it. Because in this case third space there is an emergent blend, an act of imaginative creation on the part of the hero, the reader is flattered to suppose that his or her mental processes resemble the fictive ones of transformation and growth. This sort of meta-narrative analogy is a highly satisfying conclusion to a literary text.

The short story as a literary form much constrained in length to a significant degree seems to possess an impulse towards overcoming that very limitation. This tendency shows most obviously in the formation of loose sequences and more tightly organized cycles, hybrid forms between short and long narratives which have proven attractive for postcolonial voices. Postcolonial literature has seen a proliferation of short story cycles and sequences which provide an "illustration of the general process of multiethnic literature toward plurality, multiplicity, polyphony, and fragmentation as it tends to favour the multi-voiced text" (Davis 2001, 17). In story cycles the movement from one story to the next "necessitates constant reorientation and the uneasy reciprocity between part and whole conditions the ongoing determination of meaning" (Kennedy 1988, 14). "As such, the act of amalgamation required for the understanding of the short-story cycle mirrors that needed [sic] for the consolidation of the ethnic subjectivity portrayed" (Davis 2001, 22). A cycle challenges the reader, obliging him or her to abandon the self-contained world or situation of one story before entering the next independent story (Kennedy 1988, 16). Beyond these ordinary complications of cycles, SL and its preceding stories impose new strategies of reading, as its retrospective modification hints at overarching connections through a play of differences.

The example of SL appears to prove that it is not only the cycle as an obvious hybrid between short story and novel, but the short story itself which is peculiarly appropriate to expressions of postcolonialism. This appropriateness is evident in the production of narrative space from a conflicting binary into an emergent third space. Short stories appeal to the human desire for transgression, since they normally encourage the reader to go beyond the borders of the text in some way, for instance in demanding a projection of meaning beyond what is written out, but also – as in this case – when metalepsis changes our perception in retrospect. The genre's preference for hybrid characters and borderline situations, moreover, makes it perfect for portraying transcultural issues. It is therefore no wonder that it turns out to be a favourite form of expression for authors with a postcolonial agenda. It promotes transgressive communication not only across cultural, national and class borders within the fictional world but also in terms of communicative appeal to its readers (Brosch 2007, 202). As Michael Fischer contends,

[t]he characteristic of contemporary writing of encouraging participation of the reader in the production of meaning [...] or using fragments or incompleteness to force the reader to make the connections [...] is not merely descriptive of how ethnicity is experienced, but more importantly is an ethical device attempting to activate in the reader a desire for *communitas* with others, while preserving rather than effacing differences. (Fischer 1986, 232-233).

In promoting the sharing of reading experiences with other readers interested in postcolonialism, literary texts exhibit their true social and political value (Hunter 2001).

Works Cited:

Assmann, Aleida. "Geschichte findet Stadt." *Kommunikation, Gedächtnis, Raum: Kulturwissenschaften nach dem Spatial Turn.* Eds. Moritz Csáky and Christoph Leigeb. Bielefeld: Transcript, 2009. 13-27.

Baak van, J. J. *The Place of Space in Narration: A Semiotic Approach to the Problem of Literary Space with an Analysis of the Role of Space in I. E. Babel's "Konarmija."* Amsterdam: Rodopi, 1983.

Bal, Mieke. *Narratology: Introduction to the Theory of Narrative.* Toronto: University of Toronto Press, 2004.

Bhabha, Homi K. *The Location of Culture.* London: Routledge, 2000.

Brookner, Peter, and Andrew Thacker. "Introduction: Locating the Modern." *Geographies of Modernism: Literatures, Cultures, Spaces.* Eds. Peter Brookner and Andrew Thacker. London: Routledge, 2005. 1-5.

Brosch, Renate. *Short Story: Textsorte und Leseerfahrung.* Trier: WVT, 2007.

Brydon, Diana. "Storying Home: Power and Truth." *Tropes and Territories: Short Fiction, Postcolonial Readings, Canadian Writings in Context.* Eds. Marta Dvorak and W. H. New. Montreal: McGill-Queen's University Press, 2007. 33-48.

Davis, Rocío G. *Transcultural Reinventions: Asian American and Asian Canadian Short-Story Cycles.* Toronto: TSAR, 2001.

Esrock, Ellen. "Visualisation." *Routledge Encyclopedia of Narrative Theory.* London: Routledge, 2005. 633-634.

Evelein, Johannes F. "Traveling Exiles, Exilic Travel – Conceptual Encounters." *Exiles Traveling: Exploring Displacement, Crossing Boundaries in German Exile Arts and Writings 1933-1945.* Ed. Johannes F. Evelein. Amsterdam: Rodopi, 2009. 11-31.

Ferguson, Suzanne C. "Defining the Short Story: Impressionism and Form." *The New Short Story Theories.* Ed. Charles May. Athens: Ohio University Press, 1994. 218-230.

Fischer, Michael M. J. "Ethnicity and the Post-Modern Arts of Memory." *Writing Culture: The Poetics and Politics of Ethnography.* Eds. James Clifford and George E. Marcus. Berkeley: University of California Press, 1986. 194-233.

Friedmann, Susan Stanford. "Spatial Politics and Arundhati Roy's *The God of Small Things.*" *A Companion to Narrative Theory.* Eds. James Phelan and Peter J. Rabinowitz. Malden, MA: Blackwell, 2005. 192-205.

Hall, Stuart. "Cultural Identity and Diaspora." *Theorizing Diaspora: A Reader.* Eds. Jana Evans Braziel and Anita Mannur. Malden, MA: Blackwell, 2003. 233-246.

Hunter, Lynette. *Literary Value / Cultural Power: Verbal Arts in the Twenty-First Century*. Manchester: Manchester University Press, 2001.
Kennedy, J. Gerald. "Toward a Poetics of the Short Story Cycle." *Journal of the Short Story in English* 11 (1988): 9-25.
Le Guin, Ursula. *Steering the Craft*. Portland: The Eighth Mountain Press, 1998.
Mistry, Rohinton. "Swimming Lessons." *Colonial and Postcolonial Fiction: An Anthology*. Ed. Robert L. Ross. New York: Garland Publishing, 1999. 265-282.
Punter, David. *Postcolonial Imaginings: Fictions of a New World Order*. Edinburgh: Edinburgh University Press, 2000.
Rushdie, Salman. *Imaginary Homelands: Essays and Criticism 1981-1991*. London: Granta, 1992.
Stafford, Barbara Maria. *Visual Analogy: Consciousness as the Art of Connecting*. Cambridge, MA: MIT Press, 2001.
Turner, Mark. "The Art of Compression." *The Artful Mind: Cognitive Science and the Riddle of Human Creativity*. Ed. Mark Turner. Oxford: Oxford University Press, 2006. 93-114.
Wolf, Werner. "The Emergence of Experiential Iconicity and Spatial Perspective in Landscape Descriptions in English Fiction." *The Motivated Sign: Iconicity in Language and Literature*. Eds. Olga Fischer and Max Nänny. Amsterdam: John Benjamins Publishing Company, 2001. 323-350.

ALBERT-REINER GLAAP, Düsseldorf

Palace of the End by Judith Thompson – A Canadian Playwright's View of the Iraq War

Palace of the End, premiered in 2007, deals with the situation before and after the US-led invasion of Iraq. It is not a play in the conventional sense but a trio of monologues, spoken by three different individuals. One of these characters, a female soldier, took part in the abuses of Iraqi captives at Abu Ghraib prison and is awaiting trial for the maltreatment of prisoners. In the next monologue, a British weapons inspector is sitting against a tree in the woods a few hours before his death. And the third vignette is spoken by a courageous woman who describes how she and her son were viciously tortured under Saddam's regime but survived.

Judith Thompson's play is not concerned with a specifically Canadian event. Its theme is one of worldwide concern. The three pieces together reflect a personal view of the outrages of a misbegotten war. *Palace of the End* haunts and moves. (Coulbourn 2008)

Canadian playwrights and the Iraq War – how do these get together? Why should a prominent Canadian playwright write about the Iraq War?
The main target of Canadian theatre in the 1970s was to present a vision of contemporary Canadian society and thereby shape a Canadian national mythology. Many of the plays in those days were historical or social portraits of people from different geographical and class backgrounds. In the 1980s and '90s regionalism had gone out of fashion in favour of multiculturalism, which was increasingly being mirrored in stage plays. Changes in Canada's cultural set-up led to a new concept of diversity, which means that there is not just one type of Canadian theatre, but plays by Native authors and by writers of Asian or African descent, and others which are also Canadian plays. In the course of the past ten to fifteen years, the canvas has widened even further: it is not taken for granted anymore that plays written by Canadian authors are concerned with specifically Canadian topics, although they are still uniquely Canadian. Judith Thompson's *Palace of the End* (2007) is a striking example. Why should she – one of the most important contemporary Canadian playwrights – write about Iraq under the regime of Saddam Hussein? Her own answer to this question will be quoted later.

The title *Palace of the End* is a reference to what used to be a royal palace until it became Saddam Hussein's torture chamber. *Palace of the End* is not a play in the conventional sense, but a trio of vignettes, of three monologues spoken by three different individuals, each of whom has lost a life and/or a career. Ultimately, the play is three in one, the linking element being the situation before and after the US-led invasion of Iraq. The three characters are Soldier in the first monologue, which is titled "My Pyramids," Dr. David Kelly and Nehrjas Al Saffarh in the second, "Harrowdown Hill," and the third, "Instruments of Yearning," respectively. The three are not fictional characters, but based on real people: Soldier on Lynndie England, who was prosecuted for the maltreatment of prisoners at Abu Ghraib; Dr. David Kelly on the late British weapons inspector, who informed the press that Tony Blair's government had exaggerated the military threat posed by Saddam's regime; and Nehrjas Al Saffarh on the Iraqi dissident, a member of Iraq's communist party, who was tortured (together with her children) and arrested in the initial phase of Saddam Hussein's regime when it was still being backed by the US. The titles of the three monologues set the tone for what is to follow. "My Pyramids" is a reference to Lynndie England's way of having prisoners form human pyramids. "Harrowdown Hill" points to the woods near Dr. Kelly's Oxfordshire home where he is believed to have committed suicide. And "Instruments of Yearning" is a weird euphemism for Saddam Hussein's secret police.

Soldier (alias Lynndie England) is awaiting trial for military malpractice. She is pregnant with her soldier-boyfriend's baby and admits that she took part in the abuses of Iraqi captives at Abu Ghraib prison to impress her male colleagues. She thinks that what she did is no different from the bullies she experienced as a child. Audiences, when listening to her story, will be reminded of the notorious photographs of the American soldier making a thumbs-up gesture in front of naked Iraqi captives in Abu Ghraib. If she is sent to prison, she will lose everything, including custody of her baby.

In the second part of the play, we see Dr. David Kelly (Thompson 2007, 59) sitting against a tree in the woods a few hours before his death. In a government inquiry he was criticised and harangued for what he had told the BBC. Here he is sitting now with a bottle of water contemplating the conspiracy theories that he expects to follow his death. He recalls the events – a thwarted human being who bleeds to death from self-inflicted wounds.

He met his tragic end in Oxfordshire in 2003. Certainly, one of Dr. Kelly's statements that will be remembered by those having listened to this monologue is the following: "I'm beginning to think that it's the greatest sin of our time. Knowing, and pretending that we don't know, so that we won't be inconvenienced in any way" (Thompson 2007, 21).

The third monologue is a powerful testimony of an Iraqi woman, Nehrjas. Her story is set before the first Gulf War. She is a most courageous and beautiful woman. She relates her personal experiences at the time when she and her sons tried to hide from Saddam's regime where her husband, leader of the Communist Party, could be found. They were therefore viciously tortured by the secret police whom they finally survived.

Theatre critic Johnnie Walker writes: "It is very difficult to listen to her describe how her children were tortured before her eyes, but it's also one of the most honest and powerful moments you're likely to see on stage this year" (Walker 2008). "Instruments of Yearning" is the most powerful and shocking of the three monologues. Whereas the preceding two miniatures have counterparts in the real world, Nehrjas' story is not well-known. According to Martin Morrow, Judith Thompson says that "she learned about the Saffarh family's ordeal from her Toronto neighbours, Dr. Thabit A. J. Abdullah, an Iraqi history professor at York University, and his wife, Samara. Nehrjas' monologue is based on a written account of her experience, which Samara Abdullah translated from Arabic" (Morrow 2008). Jeremy Kingston asserts that Nehrjas "represents the countless Iraqis who watched their children tortured to death in front of them" (Kingston 2009).

In reality, Lynndie England was sentenced to three years in a military prison because she participated in the abuse of prisoners, though under orders. As regards Dr.

David Kelly's death, the question remains if he actually committed suicide. But there is no doubt that Nehrjas Al Saffarh lost most of her family when Saddam was in power, and she herself died in an air raid during the first Gulf War.

As mentioned before, this play is not a play in the conventional sense. It is not just one monologue after another; the three sections are linked with each other. "You have a perpetrator-tool, you have an observer, and you have a victim," said Judith Thompson in an interview I conducted with her. "They all take different positions: Lynndie England is the weapon, the hand; David Kelly is the mind; and Nehrjas is the heart."[1] In the CanStage Berkeley Street Theatre production in Toronto, the three characters were all on stage at the same time: Lynndie England in a swivel office chair with a desk and a lot of papers; David Kelly on a hill under a tree where he was dying; Nehrjas was not on stage from the beginning and had just a little chair, table and oriental carpet. The director did not let the actors move while one of the others was talking. The linking element is the Iraq War, but also an ethical question. Should we despise Lynndie Engalnd, is it she who is culpable or her superiors at the Pentagon who made her their tool? "She was brought up in a violent and sexist world, as a person of no privilege, no currency, not even beauty. She is constricted to violence, as it were," says Judith Thompson, and asks, "Is she responsible? How much are we responsible for people like her in our society?" David Kelly, although he knows that something is wrong, takes a long time to finally speak up, and he then risks everything. He is like most people these days. They see what is happening but let it happen lest they lose their standing and their position. David Kelly is closest to us. We see what happened to him, whether he committed suicide or was killed.

And how do we feel about Nehrjas Al Saffarh, whose intelligence, wit and humour we admire, while we cannot fathom why she allows a child to die, rather than give up the name of her husband? Judith Thompson's comment on this reveals both her personal feelings and her expectations towards the audience:

> I can't imagine that giving up the name of one person could cause hundreds of thousands of children to die. I don't understand that, but I am trying to force myself as a writer, and therefore my audience, to wrap their minds around that and grapple with it. To me, that's what good theatre does: it provokes questions like that, so that you leave unsure, wanting to talk about it.

What would I do? would be the big question that ends with the audience also asking: Where do I situate myself? How have I betrayed my ethics? Have I ever taken a risk for my morals? Or do I sit back?

The title of Thompson's play is *Palace of the End*. To her, it means 'Palace of Death:'

> The end is the end of our lives. I think most of us want to know then that we were the person that we believed ourselves to be. We hope to leave a legacy for our children. What legacy does Lynndie leave? David Kelly leaves a legacy of courage. He was a hero, in the end, because he did risk everything. And Nehrjas? She took a gamble, she really didn't think they would kill a child.

---

1 All further unreferenced quotations of Judith Thompson are taken from the interview conducted with her by Albert-Reiner Glaap in Toronto on June 02, 2011 (unpublished).

Palace of the End was performed in North Hollywood, California, in 2007, a production which was followed by stagings in Toronto, New York, Vancouver, Edmonton, Manchester (England), at the Edinburgh Festival, at the Arts Festival in Galway (Ireland), in Madrid, Italy and South America. And what were the theatre critics' responses? Here are just four examples from the reviews. Romina Oliverio writes about Alumnae Theatre's production:

> The strength of the play invariably […] lies in Thompson's exceptionally raw and powerful material. Thompson is a master of excavating the recesses of the human psyche. [This production] has derived from Thompson's work a piece of theatre that will haunt and move you. (Oliverio 2008)

Palace of the End received its New York premiere at the Peter Jay Sharp Theater on June 23, 2008. Reviewers use two yardsticks against which the production is measured: the extent to which the play is shocking and haunting, and the assumed predisposition of US-American theatregoers who have been confronted, or even 'overfed,' with detailed information and news about the Iraq war. Frank Scheck writes: "The most shocking thing about Judith Thompson's *Palace of the End*, about the horrors of the Iraqi war is, how not shocking it is." And: "Despite the fine, admirably restrained performance and powerful writing, *Palace of the End*, fails to lift itself into the realm of the truly haunting" (Scheck 2008). Neil Genzlinger asserts:

> The territory has been pretty thoroughly worked over in plays, documentaries, books and articles of all sorts. That's not to say that examining the war and its effects is no longer important; just to warn that this intense hour and 40 minutes may, to American viewers who have already taken in a lot of this stuff, start to feel like self-flagellation (or perhaps like being flogged by a neighbor; Ms Thompson is Canadian). (Genzlinger 2008)

In The Epoch Times, Diana Barth writes: "Wars have always been with us, and their components are always the same. Good people suffer needlessly. They lose their property, their sanity, their lives. Unfortunately, no remedy is offered" (Barth 2008).

In the Manchester production, which also transferred to Galway Arts Festival in July 2009, Eve Polycarpou played the role of Nehrjas, no doubt the hardest of the roles in the play, as Nehrjas details her hardly bearable inhumane treatment at the hands of Sadam's police. Polycarpou grew up in Brighton, being of Greek Cypriot descent. She started her career in the arts, became a singer, composer, scriptwriter and actress. In 2008, she was unexpectedly confronted with a medical crisis – a benign pituitary brain tumour was diagnosed – and had to undergo medical treatment by radiation. It was in that phase of her life that director Gregory Hersov offered her the chance to appear in *Palace of the End*. "I wasn't sure if I'd even be fit enough to read the script let alone perform in the play," Polycarpou says, "but I asked my consultant for his opinion and he said it was important to have an optimistic attitude" (McBride 2009). The six weeks between the end of her course of therapy and the beginning of rehearsals, she says,

> gave me time to get my strength up for the play. One of the things I find amazing about doing the role is that performing it was part of my own process of recovery yet I am telling the story of this woman who suffered incredibly at the hands of the Saddam regime. Relating her tale certainly made me feel very humble and thankful for my own life. (McBride 2009)

Palace of the End is set in a country far away from Canada, its theme being one of worldwide concern. "But what made a Canadian playwright write about Iraq under Saddam Hussein?" was the question put at the beginning of this paper. Judith Thompson initially found it hard to write this play. In the interview, I asked her what had motivated her to write this play – as a Canadian playwright. She argued:

> We are all global citizens. Borders have dissolved with the internet in many ways. This is a concern to all of us. Whether or not we are there – we are in the pocket of America. The play is not just specifically about Iraq. I am convinced it will be done in 20 or 40 years, because it's all about war. It is about ethical decisions. Each character grapples with very complicated ethical choices. It could be Bosnia, it could be the war of 1812. It doesn't matter that it is Iraq.

Still, the question remains, if *Palace of the End* can be considered a *Canadian* play What makes it Canadian? Thompson gives her answer:

> It doesn't have to have a Canadian name or a Canadian location. We watch, perhaps as observers, as peace-keepers. The play *is* Canadian, and I will tell you why: three wildly divergent voices are used to state a single sad truth, each of which is inspired by actual people and their suffering. (emphasis original)

In his review of a production of Thompson's play, Martin Morrow quotes a statement by the playwright:

> Two hundred people are dying every day in Iraq. [Canadians] have to do something about it, in terms of aid or accepting more refugees. Here we are as privileged Westerners, living on the tip of this iceberg that's in an ocean of blood. We can see the iceberg and the blood, but we are just dancing on the tip. (Morrow 2008)

In the published version of *Palace of the End*, Thompson encourages readers of the play to donate to the Iraqi Alannal Association, a charity. Her royalties from the sale of the book are also going to this charity. The general lack of attention basically is what Thompson complains about, but the emotional component of her play will make audiences more aware of the situation in Iraq and other similar situations in the world.

Works Cited

Barth, Diana. "Theatre Review: 'Palace of the End.' Three fierce views of the Iraqi war." *The Epoch Times* (24 June 2008). 9 January 2011 <http://www.theepochtimes.com/news/8-6-24/72336.html>.
Coulbourn, John. [Review]. *Toronto Sun* (19 January 2008).
Genzlinger, Neil. [Review]. *The New York Times* (24 June 2008).
Kingston, Jeremy. [Review]. *The Times* (2 and 10 February 2009).
McBride, Charlie. [Review]. *Galway Advertiser* (9 July 2009).
Morrow, Martin. [Review]. *www.cbcnews.ca*. (16 January 2008).
Oliverio, Romina. [Review]. www.broadwayworld.com (2008).
Scheck, Frank. [Review]. *New York Post* (30 June 2008).
Thompson, Judith. *Palace of the End*. Toronto: Playwrights Canada Press, 2007.
Walker, Johnnie. [Review]. *Culture, Events* (23 January 2008).

Seaing through the Past

Postmodern Histories and the Maritime Metaphor in Contemporary Anglophone Fiction

Joanna Rostek

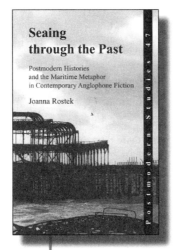

From Daniel Defoe to Joseph Conrad, from Virginia Woolf to Derek Walcott, the sea has always been an inspiring setting and a powerful symbol for generations of British and Anglophone writers. *Seaing through the Past* is the first study to explicitly address the enduring relevance of the maritime metaphor in contemporary Anglophone fiction through in-depth readings of fourteen influential and acclaimed novels published in the course of the last three decades. The book trenchantly argues that in contemporary fiction, maritime imagery gives expression to postmodernism's troubled relationship with historical knowledge, as theorised by Hayden White, Linda Hutcheon, and others. The texts in question are interpreted against the backdrop of four aspects of metahistorical problematisation. Thus, among others, Iris Murdoch's *The Sea, the Sea* (1978) is read in the context of auto/biographical writing, John Banville's *The Sea* (2005) as a narrative of personal trauma, Julian Barnes's *A History of the World in 10½ Chapters* (1989) as investigating the connection between discourses of origin and the politics of power, and Fred D'Aguiar's *Feeding the Ghosts* (1997) as opening up a postcolonial perspective on the sea and history. Persuasive and topical, *Seaing through the Past* offers a compelling guide to the literary oceans of today.

Amsterdam/New York, NY
2011. 363 pp.
(Postmodern Studies 47)
Bound €72,-/US$108,-
E-Book €72,-/US$108,-
ISBN: 978-90-420-3381-8
ISBN: 978-94-012-0079-0

USA/Canada:
248 East 44th Street, 2nd floor,
New York, NY 10017, USA.
Call Toll-free (US only): T: 1-800-225-3998
F: 1-800-853-3881

All other countries:
Tijnmuiden 7, 1046 AK Amsterdam, The Netherlands
Tel. +31-20-611 48 21 Fax +31-20-447 29 79
Please note that the exchange rate is subject to fluctuations

REVIEWS

Peter Erlebach. *Natur und Spiritualität in der englischen Literatur- und Geistesgeschichte*. Heidelberg: Universitätsverlag Winter, 2011. 197 pp.

In a heated academic exchange between Arthur O. Lovejoy and Leo Spitzer in 1944 about whether Romanticism and Hitlerism are "held together by a certain *Geist*" (Spitzer, 192), Spitzer famously contended that "not analytical History of Ideas but only *Geistesgeschichte* [...] can explain historical events" (191).[1] In his reply, Lovejoy challenged Spitzer's conception that historians must apply an "organistic method" (207) and remain at the level of "mutually exclusive climates" (212) and argued instead that we must examine individual, and sometimes incompatible ideas in order to understand a particular period.[2] Peter Erlebach has chosen the contested term *Geistesgeschichte* for his diachronic survey of nature and spirituality in English literature but it should be noted that he follows in Lovejoy's footsteps rather than Spitzer's. While claiming that the concept of *natura spiritualis* permeates all canonical literary works ("die zentralen Werke der englischen Literatur," 155), Erlebach does not construe a particular *Geist*. Instead, he sets out to identify the manifold literary appropriations of the notion that nature is imbued with spirituality. Moreover, he does not claim that the concept *natura spiritualis* is the be-all and end-all of English literature. When discussing 19th-century novels, for example, Erlebach concurs that naturalism, grounded in empiricism, and realism, inherently critical of spirituality, prevailed. Erlebach identifies the roots of a sustained link between nature and spirituality in Pre-Socratic thought, which established a pantheist perspective and thus invested nature with spiritual qualities. According to Erlebach, this nexus then provided the productive model for conceptions and representations of nature as diverse as the pastoral, 19th-century exoticism or *fin de siècle* vitalism. At the cost of ignoring counter narratives, Erlebach presents a *grand récit*: while spirituality may have been marginalized in the arts at certain periods, the concept of *natura spiritualis* never quite disappeared. In a sense, then, Erlebach construes the idea of spiritual nature not as a prevailing *Geist* but as a residue that authors can always turn to for their literary expressions.

With his broad concept of spirituality, Erlebach manages to align paradigms of nature that seem quite disparate: authors of Gothic novels are akin to Chaucer who projected the psychological turmoil of his characters unto the seasons and the landscape; landscape gardens share qualities of surprise and wonder with Shakespeare's Athenian forest. It is the book's greatest achievement, in my view, that it urges us to see order in variety. Erlebach's argument is astonishingly, and refreshingly, positivistic: Erlebach has no ambitions to pre-empt counter arguments, his *Geistesgeschichte* is delivered with conviction. The positivistic stance ties in with aesthetic judgements. Erlebach maintains in passing, for example, that *Sir Gawain and the Greene Knight* is undoubtedly the best verse epic (30).

The close readings certainly bring to the fore that the motif Erlebach investigates allows for a fascinating perspective on literary history. More often than not, however,

---

1 Leo Spitzer. "*Geistesgeschichte* vs. History of Ideas as Applied to Hitlerism." *Journal of the History of Ideas* 5.2 (1944): 181-203.
2 Arthur O. Lovejoy. "Reply to Professor Spitzer." *Journal of the History of Ideas* 5.2 (1944): 204-219.

he moves too quickly from one text to the next, remaining at the level of plot, character and imagery at the expense of probing more deeply into stylistic features and generic constraints. Style and generic choices are important, however, if we wish to understand changing ideas with respect to language as an appropriate tool for representing or conjuring up spirituality. Obviously, Erlebach's *grand récit* must be selective to establish a coherent narrative, and due credit must be given to the author for pressing his argument without digressions. However, I would have wished that Erlebach had paid more attention to Anglo-Saxon texts which explore the evil side of nature and investigate the destructive power of natural forces. Erlebach briefly refers to the description of Grendel's haunt (28) but he does not explore nature's dark side which is evoked so vividly in *Beowulf* or *The Wanderer*. Instead he postulates that Grendel's mere reflects the hero's anxieties, and that negative attributions only serve as a contrast to highlight persistent notion of the *locus amoenus*. What is missing, too, are poems, plays or novels by 20th-century and contemporary authors who attempt to realign secular perspectives with bioethical positions. Goethe is conspicuously absent in this study while a whole, albeit short, chapter is devoted to Emerson and American Romanticism.

Academic readers will have issues with this study. Primary sources are not properly listed so that it is impossible to tell which edition or print Erlebach used for his interpretation. This blemish points to the level of abstraction that this *Geistesgeschichte* advocates, and it corroborates the criticism that the texts discussed in this survey are conceived of as monolithic. Moreover, recent scholarship that has fundamentally changed our view of literary encounters with nature, for example in the field of Darwinism, is not consulted. Nearly two-thirds of the scholarship referred to is German, which in itself is not a point of criticism. Erlebach's *Geistesgeschichte* displays the range of the German philological tradition but there are undoubtedly fields that have been explored more comprehensively elsewhere. Despite its 829 footnotes, Erlebach's book is very readable, essayistic at times but delightfully 'jargon-free,' and it will certainly appeal to readers who are interested in English literature and the nexus of spirituality and nature.

Hamburg   FELIX SPRANG

Wendy Marie Hoofnagle and Wolfram R. Keller, eds. *Other Nations: The Hybridization of Medieval and Insular Mythology and Identity*. Heidelberg: Universitätsverlag Winter, 2011. 248 pp.

Against the backdrop of recent studies on the postcolonial Middle Ages as well as on medieval nationhood, the editors of this essay collection set out to "trace the complex processes of mythologizing (and hybridizing) identities in the British Isles throughout the Middle Ages" (2). With the eleven essays in this collection, the editors bring together an extremely rich and varied collection of studies, covering almost one thousand years (from the Danelaw to the second half of the 17th century) and ranging from name studies to discussions of literary texts of different genres and languages. The contributions are sorted chronologically and according to topic within the individual periods (e.g. the discussions of the Welsh materials appear close to one another as do the two contributions on Gawain). This underlines the connections between the individual articles and provides the book with a degree of coherence that many essay collections lack.

The opening contribution by Shannon Lewis-Simpson stands out in two ways. Not only is it the only essay in the book treating Anglo-Saxon/Scandinavian cultural contacts (while many of the others focus on Anglo-Saxon/Norman or Anglo-Norman/Welsh contacts) but it is also the only purely linguistic contribution. It is a carefully executed and well-structured study of Anglo-Saxon and Norse names as well as of mixed forms and of the ways in which these names can be interpreted in terms of the hybridization of the different cultures. Importantly, Lewis-Simpson states that "names are signifiers of ethnic identity and do not signify ethnicity per se" (19). She further points out that name choice, while it may be an expression of identity, is also sometimes just one of fashion and individual whim. Nevertheless she contends that "[t]he notion that social attitudes are reflected by naming is key" (22). Lewis-Simpson treats the names in four subchapters, looking first at Old Norse names that are unattested elsewhere and concluding that the culture of the Scandinavian settlers was not a stagnant but a vital one. Second, she claims that Old English and Irish names were scandinavized to better suit the settlers' pronunciation and, third, that Old Norse names were Anglicized predominantly in the Southern Danelaw where Anglo-Saxon exerted more influence on Scandinavian than the other way round. Fourth, she analyses hybrid compounds containing both Old English and Old Norse elements, which are unique to the Danelaw and cannot be found in any other areas of Scandinavian influence. This attests to the fact that the "influence of contact was of enough significance to affect the naming patterns" (29). It is clear from these findings that the two cultures did not live in isolation and that the dialogue between them in fact started fairly early (31). The hybrid names, Lewis-Simpson states, may even "constitute evidence of a deliberate hybrid strategy" (32).

The highly recommendable essay by Wendy Marie Hoofnagle looks to William the Conqueror's castle building as providing a symbolic landscape for Anglo-Norman writers such as Geoffrey of Monmouth on which to base their literary constructions of a 'New Troy' as a parallel to Charlemagne's 'New Rome.' She begins her discussion at the Ostrogoth Theoderic's highly symbolic rebuilding of ruined Rome and continues with Charlemagne's Carolingian palace, his use of Roman *spolia,* as well as his building layout strategies to demonstrate not only his imperial claims but also simultaneously his independence from Rome (49-50). Upon arriving in England, the Normans were the first to erect secular stone buildings (while the building of stone churches on formerly Roman sacred sites had been practiced before in Anglo-Saxon England). Hoofnagle then returns to Gordon Hall Gerould's 1927 statement that Geoffrey of Monmouth "formed Arthur in the image of Charlemagne" (58) and that the Anglo-Normans aligned themselves with both of these powerful rulers. Geoffrey of Monmouth, she claims, "neatly sidesteps Rome as an imperial ancestor by inventing a parallel, rival empire in Britain to the one created by Aeneas in Rome, that of a 'second Troy' established instead in London, rather than simply reproducing Rome in an Insular [sic] context" (60). For example, Geoffrey provides the white tower, William's original construction, with Trojan antiquity by claiming that it was in fact built by Belinus. This ancestry predates and consequently bypasses that of Rome. The Britons, however, have now become the barbaric other and are presented as the 'Welsh,' no longer fit to rule. The Normans thus rightly assume lordship (60). Hoofnagle concludes that "the Anglo-Normans exploited their hybrid legacy […] to create an enduring image of themselves as emperor-kings with Britain as the center of their empire" (64) and thereby supported their appropriation of both the symbolic and the real Anglo-Saxon landscape.

Brenna Mead's contribution works on two levels: First, it focuses on literary and historical hunting accidents that connect Trojan, Roman, and British history. Ascanius as presented in the anonymous French *Eneas*, Brutus as presented in Wace's *Roman de Brut*, Marie de France's Guigemar and William Rufus all have hunting accidents that can be read as turning points, leading to war, exile, new foundations and new rulers respectively. According to Mead, it is Marie's use of the verb *traire* that connects this level to the second one, that of Marie's "genre critique" (84). Marie plays with the genres of history and romance by "openly disavowing and then tacitly engaging in the field of history writing" (65). Mead argues that "*estoire* and *lai* are not genres that fulfill and complete one another" but that the "moment between *estoire* and *lai* is a suspension, a hybrid world in which opposed constituent elements coexist but also reveal their mutual incompletion" (68). This is a very interesting article, especially due to its two levels, but unfortunately, the connection between the literary hunting accidents and the historical one involving William Rufus remains rather underdeveloped. The overall argument would certainly have profited if this had been given a bit more space than just the last half-page of the article.

Robert R. Edwards' article engages with the uncanny in Walter Map's work as a way of "unwriting the rhetoric of continuity and integration" (87) prevalent in the project of post-Conquest national history of the Normans. Like Marie de France, Walter Map chooses a genre that is not among the dominant ones such as historiography, romance or religious writing. Instead, he includes in his narrative marvelous, hybrid and monstrous elements. Edwards points out that the England of Map's lifetime was not just a postcolonial one but also itself engaged in colonial projects (Wales, Scotland and Ireland) and he argues that the "marvelous stories […] serve as figures to express the structural tensions of these colonial-postcolonial arrangements" (96). The uncanny offers "a framework in which alterity is understood to be internal, constitutive, and asynchronous" (96). Edwards exemplifies this claim with the story of Herla, in which the association of Herla's eternally vagrant troop with the decentered court of Henry II serves as a *translatio imperii*. The story of Hameric, in turn, "demonstrates Map's capacity to unwrite institutional history by summoning the alterity it seeks to consolidate" (102). In all of Map's Welsh tales, Edwards concludes after his discussion of them, "the uncanny emerges as the repressed secret that finds its way into the social sphere and into lines of descent," which means into history (107). In this way, Map brings "popular and folk traditions into the orbit of high literary culture" and shows that "they are already present as the repressed memory within the official narratives of nationhood and identity" (107).

Kristen Lee Over takes up this thread of Welsh tales in her discussion of the *Historia Peredur vab Efrawc*. Against the background of the fact that Anglo-Saxons and Anglo-Normans were coalesced "into a collective identity of 'the civilized' English while simultaneously differentiating the Welsh and others as British barbarians" (110), she discusses Chrétien de Troyes' literary Welshman Perceval in his Welsh transformation in the *Historia Peredur vab Efrawc*. This tale, she argues, turns "the failed civilizing project on its head and [infuses] the literary Welshman with positive cultural value" (112). Perceval-turned-Peredur here becomes the perfect warrior and champion who corrects the faulty behavior of Arthur's court and ultimately helps Arthur to "reemerge as an effective leader incorporated with Peredur into a larger collective of familiar Welsh warriors" (118). Arthur's world, Lee Over claims, learns from Peredur about the true martial values. Achieving this, she concludes, the tale "intervenes in colonial discourse in a way that contests the surety and stability of Anglo-Norman, English norms" (124).

The article by Erich Poppe and Dagmar Schlüter turns to the hybridization of national and regional identities in the Irish *Togail Troí,* an early translation of the Troy myth according to Dares into Irish. This is surprising because, as the authors point out, "the Irish did not derive their origins from Rome and Troy" (127). Tracing the different Irish origin myths, most prominently the *Lebor Gabála Érenn* which synchronizes the Gaels with the Israelites, but also those connecting the Irish language with Greek, they come to the conclusion that the Troy myth had a very particular function in medieval Ireland. They suggest that "the confrontation between Ulster and the larger, remaining provinces of Ireland [...] could easily have been perceived by some medieval Irish *literati* as mirroring the political situation of the Trojan War, namely, a large power, Greece, at war with a smaller one, Troy" (135), The Trojan myth thus served as a foil for the understanding and interpretation of the *Táin Bó Cúailnge*, a lengthy narrative about early Irish history contained in the same manuscript.

Peter Larkin's contribution continues the thread of 'non-English' literature by focusing on the Latin *De Ortu Waluuanii* in which Gawain is constructed not as a British but as a Roman knight. The unusual features of the text (Latinity, presentation of Rome) must be seen in relation to Geoffrey of Monmouth's vision of history. In Geoffrey's version, Arthur's victories over Rome "illustrate the renewal of British culture" (149) and Gawain, "[t]hough educated and knighted in Rome [is presented] as thoroughly British and far superior to Roman knights" (150). This, Larkin points out, is quite different in *De ortu Waluuanii*. Here, the hero is invested with a Roman identity. Quintessential rites of chivalry such as knighting are Romanized (152f.). In stark contrast to this, a people of transgressive dwarfs that Gawain encounters "on the periphery of the Muslim world [...] resemble the Britons of Isidore and Geoffrey" and "this resemblance indirectly implies that the Britons are a fallen and degenerate race" (161). *De ortu* is even more explicit in the depiction of Arthur and his queen, here untypically named Gwendolena, a name that holds an association with Wales. Accordingly, Gwedolena is invested with the characteristics of a Welsh witch. Gawain, in this context, appears as a better knight than Arthur, first in the queen's visions and later also on the battlefield. Arthur and his men are portrayed as "a fallen race in the need of renewal" while Gawain comes to serve "as an agent of *translatio imperii*" (163).

Susan Carter's highly recommendable article again focuses on Gawain, with a special emphasis on gender aspects. She starts out by stating that the heroic acts which define the hero as such often happen in cultural borderlands, with the defining monster being a creature of the other side. In both *Sir Gawain and the Green Knight* and *The Wedding of Sir Gawain and Dame Ragnelle*, the monstrous other is female agency. Morgan and the lady challenge Gawain's identity and Ragnelle, as the loathsome lady, "must be embraced and pleased in a testing of the hero" (166). In both tales, Carter notes, "female sexuality is a dire if un-chivalric threat to masculine identity and survival" and "the thrill of this threat activates identity crises in social areas" (173). She comments on further parallels between the two texts; both are 'border texts' in which challenges to the Arthurian court arise with figures associated with the borderlands. Also, both texts markedly cross gender boundaries: Ragnelle asks Gawain to kiss her for Arthur's sake, the Green Knight insists on Gawain giving him the kisses he earlier acquired, thereby forcing him into a feminized position (179-180). Both tales end on a happy note, with Gawain having successfully negotiated with the monstrous other. Carter concludes that the surprisingly happy endings show that "outlandish cultural aliens can be bedded, wedded, and brought into the social framework to strengthen it with their exogamous alterity" (184).

Wolfram Keller's article focuses on hybridity in Chaucer's *House of Fame* as a locus of adaption of the Troy story for the making of English nationhood. The crucial question raised by the Troy story, he claims, is "how to synthesize selves and nations" (185). Keller explores Benoît de Sainte-Maure's Old French *Roman de Troie* as well as Guido delle Colonne's *Historia destructionis Troiae* in terms of a number of dichotomies such as the opacity and transparency of the characters' identities and he claims that Chaucer, in contrast, unhinges such dichotomies. In doing so, Chaucer "illustrates that identity's masks can be to varying degrees opaque or transparent" (187). To imagine "narrative selfhood beyond the Guidoan dichotomy of opacity and transparency" in such a way, Keller argues, makes the self become "translucent" (190). He demonstrates how hybridity serves this aim in his discussion of the dreamer Geffrey's combination of Ovidian and Virgilian elements in the presentation of Dido, in the presentation of the House of Fame as a "meeting place for narratives" of different provenance and in the blank page on which the poem closes. This last element, Keller argues, serves to "engage both Geffrey and the audience in a hermeneutic process of re-writing, of de- and re-mythologizing" (204).

Lindsay M. Jones' contribution on linguistic hybridity and identity in early English drama is a very intriguing one in that it discusses the negotiation of "the terms of what it meant to be an English speaker" (208) in view of the breakdown of both the traditional triglossic situation (Latin, French, English) and the feudal system in the 14th century. Jones claims that the "early English dramatic tradition advanced a strong argument that the English language was essential to the formation of an English nation, by demonstrating the ways in which a standardized English language might usurp the institutional power of Latin and the regnal authority of French" (211). She exemplifies this with striking passages. With the Latin-speaking Herod of the Towneley *Processus Talentorum* who first needs to translate his own speech into English to be understood, Latin is marginalized. The scene thus serves as a warning for the institutional powers of England who "must convert to a vernacular authority, or risk suffering the same impotence" (215). The character of Tutivillus, "one of the most frequent abusers of the Latin language on the early English stage" (215), collects Latinate phrases dropped by careless preachers. With this character, Jones shows, the "Towneley *Judgement* play criticizes not only English-Latin hybridity in Middle English, but also the aural authority which Latin had been granted in medieval England" (217). Finally, she discusses the example of Herod which presents French speakers as "tyrannous, scandalous, and often ostentatious members of the aristocracy" (220). In the Chester Vintner's Play, Herod is presented as a French speaker whom the Magi, in an adaptive gesture, approach speaking French. The game that Herod plays with Christ is a linguistic one, too, in which "the frivolity of the French court" is conflated "with the malevolence of Herod's treatment of Christ" (223).

The closing contribution by Bernadette Smelik returns both to an Irish work and to Arthuriana, and in this way provides a continuation of this predominantly medieval collection into Early Modern literature. In her discussion of the *Eachtra Mhelóra agus Orlando,* she focuses on the anticipation by readers who were probably familiar with Ariosto's Italian *Orlando Furioso.* This familiarity, she claims, opens a rift between "text-specific anticipation and the initial anticipation of the reader" (230). The expectation that the piece is in the context of an Italian romance rather than an Arthurian one is the first to be revised by the readers, the second one, namely that this is a knightly quest, then has to be revised in favor of it being a love story. Next, Merlin turns out to be a villain and finally, it is Melóra, dressed as a knight, who undertakes the quest for the magic objects that will save her beloved Orlando. This, Smelik points out, is a reference to woman warriors in native Irish literature (238). This hybrid of Arthurian, Italian and Irish traditions foregrounds the concept of surveyability in that it illustrates differences between initial and text-specific anticipation and demonstrates how certain elements steer the anticipation of the audience (240-241).

This is a very recommendable collection that provides many new insights into questions of hybridization and identity formation. There are two points that I would like to criticize and both were probably not in the editors' hands. First, as with so many essay collections, especially if they were developed from conference sessions, one would wish that the articles that are closely related in terms of topic or sources would comment on each other in some way. There are in this collection, for example, several articles on Welsh materials, as well as several that treat Arthuriana. It is a pity that the general pressure to publish usually does not allow for that kind of internal discussion. Second, I caught myself several times leafing to the end of the book in search of a general bibliography. The inclusion of one, in contrast to the inclusion of an internal discussion, would not have taken much time and would certainly have helped to further underline the connections between the individual articles.

Bern   NICOLE NYFFENEGGER-STAUB

Christian Huck. *Fashioning Society, or, The Mode of Modernity. Observing Fashion in Eighteenth-Century Britain.* **Würzburg: Königshausen & Neumann, 2010. 358 pp.**

In the course of the 18th century, fashion in Britain became fashionable. Wearing the right clothes and possessing fashionable goods became important means of displaying cultural status and negotiating identities. Social positioning, class, and gender relations were acted out in and through fashion. While the role of fashion in the formation of social identity is by now well documented, Christian Huck's study *Fashioning Society, or, The Mode of Modernity* extends this line of research by examining the multifaceted relations between fashion and modernity: that fashion makes 18th-century society modern is the key premise of this fine and richly interdisciplinary study.

In contrast to many previous, largely historical studies, Huck's book is less concerned with actually worn dress, but with representations of fashion. Fashion, according to Huck, is located at the interface between individual experiences and social structures and it is an imaginary idea as much as a material, visual thing. Hence, the book essentially examines the knowledge conveyed by discursive, media and material contexts conveyed about dress, fashion and style. To gauge the complex interrelations between fashion, media practices and 18th-century British society, Huck draws on an admirably broad spectrum of media, ranging from newspapers and conduct books, novels and prints, to trade manuals, handbills and engravings. The book proceeds from the assumption that such representations of fashion were crucial to producing a "second reality" (14) that shaped the self-organisation of society and propelled the creation of an imaginary normality. Representations of fashion allowed people to adjust their modes of behaviour according to this new, second reality, ultimately transforming historical contingencies of observation into normality. Fashion, as Huck convincingly argues, is therefore less a means of displaying one's identity "but a mechanism to make (aesthetically) perceivable which parts of a mass-mediated reality one has (momentarily) selected" (262).

Modernity, in Huck's study, is understood in terms of Niklas Luhmann's systems theory, i.e. as a form of a society that is constituted by "observation of observations" (25) and is experienced as the result of an open development. According to Huck, the specific contribution that fashion made to modernity lies in the facilitation of observations and the ensuing experience of contingency. 'Observing' fashion thus has a double meaning as it refers to both looking at clothes and following the "mode" (9), i.e. the imaginary, culturally circulating idea of fashion. The emergence of fashion was driven by a number of factors characteristic of 18th-century British society, most notably the society of London: the development of an urban society, which offered new possibilities of observation and increased the possibility of meeting strangers, who were primarily assessed by their dress; the expanding economy and the enhanced availability and affordability of clothes; an increase in social mobility and the possibility, but also obligation, to find one's own position in society; new media technologies, which enabled a pervasive circulation of printed documents and visual representations that codified new modes of observing and regulated dress codes. Principally, in "this modern sartorial regime" (21) people's clothes can be observed as meaningful choices, i.e. as expressions of beliefs, intentions and cultural distinctions. Fashion allowed people to position themselves in society and, at the same time, it required them to learn how to see fashion and how to observe observers. The fashioning of society was therefore intricately related to new practises of observation and went along with "an explosive rise in the reciprocal observation of fellow individuals" (12).

Accordingly, and this is certainly one of the most intriguing lines of argumentation, Huck locates fashion within 18th-century visual culture and scrutinizes new modes of observing, i.e. new scopic regimes (*sensu* Jonathan Crary), related to fashion. This new mode of observing, which was able to come to grips with fashion, is epitomized by a spectator who occupies an almost paradoxical position: The observer stands outside his own world and "manages to come close to his objects without [...] being seen himself" (96). In the course of detailed and persuasive interpretations, Huck demonstrates that this ideal of a "visible invisible observer" (99) is embodied most perfectly by Joseph Addison's Mr Spectator. Rambling around London, Mr Spectator observes others while remaining curiously invisible in the midst of society. The uninvolved observer position, emerging as a result of the new development of mass media, had a potentially disciplinary effect (although also opening up possibilities of evading it): It was not only instrumental in perpetuating a gendered and class-based dress code but also in connecting individuals to society. Huck argues that, although the position of the unobserved observer is commonly defined as a male privilege, it was not restricted to men but could also be occupied by females. Though certainly an interesting argument, I find it not fully convincing: Even if females (Huck refers to Mrs Prattle, the apparent author of the *Parrot*) did claim to occupy this position, this claim would certainly have challenged conventional notions of femininity in ways that deserve closer attention.

The study elaborates the relation between fashion, visuality, economy and gender in intriguing interpretations of selected novels, with special emphasis on Samuel Richardson's *Pamela*, Daniel Defoe's *Moll Flanders* and Eliza Haywood's *Fantomina*. The novel, according to Huck, was the first literary genre that uses "clothes under the aegis of fashion" (188), meaning that representations of fashion were now primarily used for the individualisation of characters. Individuality, under the tutelage of fashion, is no longer "an ontological given" (219; but was it ever?) but is constituted in an open and performative process of self-fashioning. At the same time, fashion allowed individual protagonists to enter a broader discourse and thus to be recognized in and through society. To the extent that representations of fashion made it possible for different readers and protagonists to direct their desire towards a shared object, namely fashion, the novel worked against the distancing and disembodying effect generally ascribed to the culture of print. I find this conceptualization of fashion as both a means of individual self-realization and social interpellation convincing as it challenges the conventional understanding of the female figure as being fully defined and reified by the new 'sartorial regime' of 18th-century consumer society.

All in all, there are numerous, innovative insights to be gleaned from Huck's study and there is no doubt that the book makes a very readable, timely and pertinent contribution not only to 18th-century studies and the bourgeoning field of fashion history but also to cultural and media studies. The interpretations of various texts and images are multifaceted as much as cohesive. The book's thorough engagement with theory, most notably with systems theory, is inspiring and gives rise to important qualifications of concepts and models that structure much research on 18th-century British culture. But it probably would not be the good book that it is if it did not beg some questions. One of these concerns the relation between representations of fashion and constructions of cultural otherness, a relation that the study only touches on briefly. As is well known, representations of fashion in 18th-century texts and images were frequently mobilized to denigrate national others, most notably French aristocrats and, by implication, the frenchified English gentlemen, who were thus portrayed as effeminate, irrational and weak. What is more: Fashion in 18th-century discourses is time and again explored in the context of the various imperial projects of the age. To understand the emergence of modernity more fully, it would surely have been interesting to gauge the ways in which representations of fashion were exploited for stabilizing the imperial ideologies and new patterns of consumption. But this is a minor qualm that steps back behind the fact that this is a study that is theoretically engaging, wide-ranging and thought-provoking.

Passau   BIRGIT NEUMANN

Dirk Schulz. *Setting the Record Queer: Rethinking Oscar Wilde's* **The Picture of Dorian Gray** *and Virginia Woolf's* **Mrs. Dalloway. Bielefeld: transcript Verlag, 2011. 274 pp.**

Hard to believe but true: Dirk Schulz's *Setting the Record Queer* is the first book-length comparison of Wilde's *The Picture of Dorian Gray* (1891) and Woolf's *Mrs. Dalloway* (1925). Aligning itself with a recent and thriving methodological tradition, the study concentrates on the two canonised novels' queer potential, that is, the unruly textual/sexual energy through which they criticise the heteronormative order. Heteronormativity, queer studies have taught us, installs, protects, and seeks to prolong the structuring influence of two asymmetrical dichotomies located at the very basis of society: 'male' vs. 'female' and 'homosexual' vs. 'heterosexual.' Every artefact or practice which resists, irritates, destabilises, questions, parodies or otherwise undercuts this double dichotomy, every argument or approach, which generally exposes it as artificial, performed, culturally constructed or historically contingent, can rightfully claim to have a queer dimension or interest. Schulz sets out to demonstrate that Wilde's and Woolf's classics participate in chipping away at what props up heteronormativity. Yes, fair enough: somehow, we have always known, felt or suspected this. But forget about the status of 'gay classic' for Wilde's novel and the hints at Mrs. Dalloway's lesbian desire, for this is not what Schulz is after. Rather, he is interested in how the novels unfold their queer potential through textual strategies. Surprising, perhaps, but spot-on, is the insight that three out of four recent re-writings of *The Picture of Dorian Gray* and *Mrs. Dalloway* fail miserably as heirs to their predecessors' queer quality. Declaring Michael Cunningham's *The Hours* (1999) the exception, Schulz's consecutive analysis makes a compelling case against Jeremy Reed's *Dorian: A Sequel to The Picture of Dorian Gray* (1997), Will Self's *Dorian: An Imitation* (2002) and Robin Lippincott's *Mr. Dalloway: A Novella* (1999). Forcefully revealing what the original novels deliberately leave in the dark, clarifying what Wilde's and Woolf's texts take great care to keep ambiguous, these rewritings may boast openly gay content, but queer they are not. Impossible? Well...it is not, actually. Granted, as 'queer' has become an umbrella term for everything LGBTTI[1], queer studies are commonly deemed interested in anything not heterosexual. According to this definition the rewritings by Reed, Self and Lippincott could be considered queer. In a stricter, more radical sense, however, it is not enough to be not-heterosexual to qualify as queer. For that, fundamental issue needs to be taken with the heteronormative. Schulz makes use of this latter, analytically more useful definition to sound out the queer spaces created by the six texts he analyses. What he finds is this: At the point beyond which heteronormativity itself, its myth-making and essentialist creed, are to be criticised, the narratives by Wilde, Woolf and Cunningham go ahead. The three other rewritings, however, stay behind, merely reaffirming where they should be subverting and, thus, setting the originals' queer record disturbingly straight once again.

Given the parallels between them, a joint examination of *The Picture of Dorian Gray* and *Mrs. Dalloway* was long overdue. Both narrations, Schulz argues, are overshadowed by their authors' mythologised ('homosexual') biographies; both stage an

---

1 The acronym stands for lesbian, gay, bisexual, transsexual, transgender, intersexual.

interest in the replacement of authenticity/essentialism by performance; both use "distortions, gaps and absences" (40) as narrative techniques; both counter truth-effects with de-mythification; both deconstruct the opposition between depth and surface, signified and signifier, while being obviously aware of the problematic nature of linguistic representation; both hold that it is impossible to disentangle literature and life; both display a marked "resistance to either/or readings" (33), generally shunning categorisation, labelling and narrative closure, while valuing and protecting vagueness, ambiguity, contradiction and semiological play; desire, especially, is portrayed by both narratives as an instable energy; and both – this is one of Schulz's main points – expose "the concurrent peril and allure of unequivocal signification, and of the heteronormative ordering of the symbolic stabilised through reiterative performativity" (10). Both Wilde's and Woolf's novels have, of course, been previously discussed by myriads of scholars, and a fair share of their articles touches upon same-sex desire. In a chapter on recent critical reception, which specifically targets articles that claim to sail under the flag of queer studies, Schulz demonstrates why most of these publications are rather more committed to classical gay/lesbian identity politics and their issues (biographism, hagiography, canonisation, essentialist homosexual attributions).

If there were a patron saint of queer studies, it would be St. Michel. Schulze's book, thus, cannot avoid drawing on Foucault, when he states that "sex and sexuality can be seen as *the* sites where the discourses on the interconnection of the body and the word, nature and nurture, biology and sociology seem to find their climactic locus" (48). The main sources for his study's theoretical backdrop, however, are Roland Barthes and Judith Butler. This choice, too, comes as no surprise to readers who are aware that importing poststructuralist semiotics into gender studies helped shape queer studies' theoretical skeleton just as much as Foucault's writings, and probably more than lesbian/gay identity politics did. Specifically, Schulz uses Barthes's writings on myth, truth-effects, and textual performativity, and Butler's concept of gender performativity as a foundation of his literary analyses. Both Wilde's Lord Henry Wotton and Woolf's eponymous protagonist, he argues, "question the factuality of commonly accepted truth" (53). Mainly through these characters do the two novels share the "contempt for the naturalising processes of a symbolic ordering that distort rather than represent history while presenting themselves as self evident" (53) which, decades later, was going to be described by Barthes as the mythologizing process. Much like the Foucauldian understanding of the body as discursively produced, Butler's smashing of the naturalised links between sex, gender and sexuality, which underlie the "heteronormative pact" (63), is a *sine qua non* for any queer project. Perhaps due to the all-pervasive familiarity of her theory of gender performativity Schulz only invokes Butler briefly, stressing that "the enemy of queer theory is *not* any 'other' sex, any 'other' gender or any 'other' sexuality but their essentialised and naturalised dichotomies" (66). In later chapters, both Dorian's erotic fascination with Sibyl Vane's theatrical (cross-)gender performances, and Mrs. Dalloway's awareness of her own and others' perpetual staging of emotional and sexual identities as "always potential and never essential" (128), are read by Schulz with reference to Butler's concept.

The central section of *Setting the Record Queer* unfolds the comparison between *The Picture of Dorian Gray* and *Mrs. Dalloway*. A little repetitive at times, both interpretations offer solid arguments and deliver true insight when they converge. One case in point is when Schulz traces the semiological reasons for the death/survival of the novels' characters. For him, Wilde's text underscores that there are only two ways to escape from the vice-like grip of all naturalised meaning: Lord Henry Wotton's path of witty paradox and ambiguity, in which a "playful resistance to and mistrust in its mythologies" (82) surfaces that ensures his survival, and Dorian's path of death. Schulz argues that, in the novel's logic, it is the young man's misreading of his mentor's queer refusal of all essentialised forms of common sense which condemns him to death. Moreover, the "looking for the essential truth by means of mythologies and [...] narcissistic identification" (77) and the "longing for ultimate meaningfulness" (84) prove to be fatal to all characters who share it with Dorian. In Woolf's novel queer energy is generated by refraining from fixing meaning and by portraying it instead "as a constant process of interpretation" (99). Clarissa who, like Lord Henry, "resents definition and categorisation" (124), is the prime medium through which readers of *Mrs. Dalloway* encounter how the text "lays bare the performative constructedness of textual and sexual identity" (125). Clarissa consciously stages herself as the perfect hostess, the perfect wife. Although she struggles against social restrictions to keep available her "manifold potentialities" (129), her refusal to buy into the ideology which claims that surfaces mirror authentic core identities guarantees her survival.

Schulz's judgment on the rewritings by Reed, Self and Lippincott is severe. All three are found guilty on the charge of betraying the original novels' queer politics by, one way or another, naturalising the heteronormative order. Filling in the gaps (of gay sexuality) deliberately left open by Wilde's novel, Reed's *Dorian: A Sequel*, set during the *fin de siècle*, "presents gender ambiguity as a trait of decadence and aberrance" and "adheres to essentialist notions and traditional oppositions" (141). By robbing Lord Henry Wotton of everything that defines him in the original, and by, moreover, underscoring the very binarisms *The Portrait* disavows, Reed's text, Schulz maintains, clearly favours confirming Wilde's status as gay icon over attempting to emulate his narration's destabilising power. Will Self's *Dorian. An Imitation* is set in the 1980s of Thatcherite Britain. As Schulz's analysis proves, this novel, too, goes against a central narrative strategy of *The Portrait,* by presenting the negative version to the original's positive outlook on performativity: "Whereas [Wilde's novel] transfers the notion of textual performativity to a possibility of individual resistance and subversion of the heteronormative matrix of the bourgeoisie, its self-proclaimed imitation posits murderous shamelessness and perversion as the reason for and outcome of deceitful performance" (161). In contrast with Reed's un-queer but harmless tale, however, Self's narration is shown to have a worryingly homophobic edge. It partly derives from depicting Lord Henry, Wilde's queerest character, as a "self loathing homosexual" (202), and partly from the novel's reactionary portrayal of AIDS. Going back to Susan Sontag's *AIDS and its Metaphors*, Schulz traces how Self's novel transmogrifies the disease from a medical to a cultural condition, presenting the virus as "the symptom and symbol of society's increasing corruption" (174). Just like Reed and Self, Lippincott is in the business of undoing ambiguities of importance to the novel he rewrites. Similarly to *Dorian. A Sequel, Mr. Dalloway* comes out of Schulz's analysis as a fairly innocuous and simple coming-out story, "built upon essentialist, teleological and representational terms" (225), and told in the mode of a confession. From a gay studies perspective, there is nothing wrong with this. From the point of view of a study interested in a rewriting's handling of its original novel's queer legacy, however, it is problematic. While Woolf keeps her readers guessing what combination of desires may be the reason for the Dalloway's estrangement, Lippincott's outing of

Clarissa's husband puts an abrupt end to all ambiguity. By 'correcting' this alleged 'flaw' in Woolf's text, Schulz argues, *Mr. Dalloway* becomes a sad example of how easily 'gay' can become the opposite of 'queer.' In living up to the legacy of *Mrs. Dalloway* as a narrative on the instability, incongruousness, incoherence and fluency of identity, the inscrutability and indeterminacy or ambivalence of desire and the unavoidability of gender as a performance, Michael Cunningham's *The Hours* stands alone in keeping the record left by *Mrs. Dalloway* queer. In tracing the semiological codes of the flowers, the kiss and the party, first introduced by Woolf, through the rewriting's three narrative strands, Schulz shows his interpretative skill to full advantage. Barthes's death of the author is put to good use in showing how Richard's suicide can put an end to mythologising knowledge and liberate Clarissa's interpretation of herself and Laura. The concept's evocation is less convincing in connection with Virginia's final escape from the voices in her head.

It is the strength of studies like Schulz's that they make us see what, once we *have* seen it, should always have been obvious. *Setting the Record Queer* succeeds in making a double point: that the comparison of *The Portrait of Dorian Gray* and *Mrs. Dalloway* can deliver new insights; and that queer reading offers the method to help us understand these classics' critical legacies better. While there is no denying that the texts by Reed, Self and Lippincott are not as subversive as those by Wilde and Woolf, it seems methodologically at odds with poststructuralist articles of faith to judge rewritings by their 'faithfulness' to their originals. Obviously, this is where queer theory is more political than poststructuralist semiotics. Incidentally, the three un-queer novels are also badly written. Schulz never actually says so, and one suspects that he refrains from all aesthetic judgment of this kind for feasible reasons. (After all, we do not want to risk falling back into believing that great literature is the only kind of writing worth scholarly attention.) The problem with *not* discussing that *The Hours* is altogether a better text is that readers might link queer potential in general directly to literary quality. While it may be true that complex or ambitious texts are more likely to be able to unfold a deconstructive power, not every text of literary quality professes a critical attitude towards heteronormativity. It would not have hurt to spell out at some point that it is not the aesthetic quality *per se* which makes *The Hours* a queer text, and that it is not the lack of literary skill which makes the other three rewritings fall short of Wilde's or Woolf's novels' destabilising potential.

Berlin   SYLVIA MIESZKOWSKI

Bernfried Nugel and Jerome Meckier, eds. Aldous Huxley Annual. A Journal of Twentieth-Century Thought and Beyond. Volume 9 (2009). Guest Ed. James Sexton. Münster: LIT Verlag, 2011. vi + 240 pp.

Aldous Huxley Annual. A Journal of Twentieth-Century Thought and Beyond is based on the assumption of Huxley's significance for the present as "novelist, essayist, philosopher and holy man" (v). The volume under review comprises a new miscellany arranged and commented on by guest editor James Sexton, nine lectures from the Fourth International Aldous Huxley Symposium in Los Angeles in 2008, two paintings and a poem presented there by Carolyn Mary Kleefeld and a contribution by Brian Smith, the winner of the Peter Edgerly Firchow Memorial Essay Prize.

The topics of rather unknown or so far unpublished Huxley vignettes and essays as well as poems, ranging from contemporary architecture to literary figures and curiosities, reflect his widespread interests and intellectual activities. Witty in tone and concise in style, he captures individual idiosyncrasies and anthropological constants like middle-age hypochondria, self-delusion or female vanity in the glimpses and impressions typical of the modernist writer and poet. Much to the delight of the recipient, the poetry segment also includes Huxley's undated holograph of "The Lady & the Pug," probably composed for Lady Ottoline Morrell's little daughter, reminding the reader of T. S. Eliot's *Old Possum's Book of Practical Cats*, and the facsimile of "Soap" from his 1912 Sketchbook with a drawing in pencil and colour. While the literary reviews and essays on rather 'marginal' subjects like Lorenzo da Ponte, Mozart's librettist, or Walter Savage Landor, Milton's contemporary, both first published in *The Athenaeum,* entertain by virtue of their Autolycus manner or mannerism, it is the architectural journalism that provides deeper insight into Huxley's modernist views. As editor and reviewer of the magazines *Vogue* and *House & Garden,* he wrote numerous pieces between 1920 and 1930 stating his skepticism towards Ruskin's Gothicism and his preference for newer aestheticians represented by the members of the Bloomsbury Group, Roger Fry and Clive Bell. In this context he pleads for a synthesis of the Renaissance classical and an unpretentious English style, a synthesis already convincingly achieved by Inigo Jones and Christopher Wren. In "The Architecture Club Exhibition" he states:

> That English architecture has vastly improved within the last thirty years is a fact that we can record with certainty [...]. From the beastly slough in which Ruskin contrived to plunge it, our architecture has manfully climbed [...]. There is no likelihood of its ever plunging again into that bog of details and features, into that sham Gothicism, pseudo-peasantry and quaintness from which it has just emerged. (55)

The manifold references to architecture and their frequently metonymical connotations in his fictional work, like *Antic Hay* or *Point Counter Point*, make these editorials even more valuable.

Focusing on Huxley's various metaphysical inclinations in general and their manifestations in his dystopian and utopian literature, the lectures contribute further approaches to the relationship of Christian and Buddhist mysticism in his philosophical and fictional œuvre. Bernfried Nugel expresses his regret about the author's revisions of the Old Raja's "Notes on What's What" in his final version of *Island* by quoting long passages of the latter's original philosophical conjectures, a striking synthesis of Western and Eastern concepts culminating in "a thorough criticism of culture" (79). These concepts are also discussed in Gerd Rohmann's "Matters of Life and Death" which drafts an inspiring amalgam of Montaigne's reflections, religious thinking and the various personal experiences with the phenomenon of death and dying. Through awareness, dying, considered as "our great liberation from individual, mostly destructive, personal life-time" (101), has lost its terror. It is the biblical interpolations Guin A. Nance analyses in Huxley's *The Perennial Philosophy*, pointing out "the doctrine of the oneness of all" according to which "God within and without and all capable of partaking of God and his kingdom" forms its centerpiece (105f.). Again, it is the yearning for awareness that transcends the borders between religions and unites Eastern and Christian notions, although Huxley's adaptation of the biblical ductus emphasises his own tendency towards Western thinking. Other scholars, like Valery Rabinovitch, concentrate on the writer's utopian fiction. The examination of the interdependence of *Brave New World* and *Island* leads to the conclusion that, after thirty years, Huxley has finally reached an "ideal of a synthesis of different values" (184), a syncretism simultaneously uttered in philosophical terms.

Brian Smith's essay "Jeffersonian Reminders: Aldous Huxley on Property, Happiness, and Freedom" is more than just another contribution. "[No] positive philosophy," according to the Suffolk University professor, "has featured more consistently [...] as a necessary part of (de)constructing utopias than that of Thomas Jefferson" (205). On the level of discourse, *Brave New World*'s dystopian concepts of uniformity and manipulation mirror the philosopher's anxieties while "a practicable social philosophy" can emerge from the concept of theocentrism in *Island* (221), thus giving way to a "nuanced 'human potentiality'" (224) – an attainable utopia?

All in all, Volume 9 of the *Aldous Huxley Annual* is highly recommendable, not only for connoisseurs of the novelist and thinker, but also for recipients more generally interested in the interrelatedness of the manifold facets of modernism.

Greifswald ANDREA BECK

Joachim Frenk and Christian Krug, eds. *The Cultures of James Bond*. Trier: WVT, 2011. 288pp.

Documenting a conference held at the University of Saarbrücken in June 2009, Joachim Frenk's and Christian Krug's collection *The Cultures of James Bond* has lined up an impressive array of scholars and topics. As Christoph Lindner demonstrates in his perceptive overview on both the past and the future of Bond criticism placed at the end of the volume, Ian Fleming's Cold War hero has been promoted to attracting a vibrant scene of "transdisciplinary, transhistorical and transcultural" (271) studies of popular culture. Lindner affirms what the editors sketch out in their introductory remarks: the arguably "global turn" (271) of serious Bond criticism responds to the fact that the 007 franchise has reached the status of a cultural myth recognized around the world, reinforcing its consistency by effectively fusing repetition and variation, generalization and specification, stabilization and subversion.

To account for the cultural memory, the intertextual references and the semiotic complexity activated by the Bond formula (2), Lindner's reflection on the critical routines of Bond scholarship would have been a productive point of departure. Not all of the contributors reflect their critical practice as thoroughly as Lindner, though. As a consequence, some of the essays do not fully realize the opportunity to address significant gaps in Bond research, to examine emerging and new sides and branches of the Bond franchise, and to demonstrate a motivated use of theoretical approaches and methodological tools. This partly holds for James Chapman's essay on the different versions of *Casino Royale*. It does certainly make sense to place this eminent Bond scholar's piece on Fleming's seminal first novel at the beginning of a collection which in many respects keeps coming back to Daniel Craig's controversial relaunch in the 2006 film *Casino Royale*. Even though Chapman presents an informative overview on the different adaptations and appropriations of Fleming's portrait of the agent as an emerging spy, his outline remains firmly tied to unfolding a conventionally cultural critical emplotment. This is geared towards a "big, brash, loud extravagant, spectacular and highly commercial" (22) reincarnation of the agent, but it refrains from explaining any of the political and formal implications of the reinvention of *Casino Royale*.

Chapman's reluctance to theorize is not surprising, as he belongs to what Lindner identifies as the "historical" school of Bond criticism. Next to this essay, the collection presents two contributions whose employment of theory appears at least as problematical as Chapman's penchant for a fact-driven historical reconstruction. In "M Stands for Mother," Abigail De Kosnik subjects Craig's performance to an orthodox psychoanalytical treatment, diagnosing the agent's "developmentally stunted psyche" as frozen in eternal childhood with M as the ersatz mother of a Freudian family romance (145). Unfortunately, de Kosnik's examination of Bond's developmental deficiencies stops short where it could have been used to account for the serial energies mobilized by the Bond formula: if the agent's family romance indeed "goes on and on" (157), it might have been interesting to compare the compulsive repetitions of different serial heroes and also to consider how successful serialized narratives are currently feeding on popular notions of therapy. In her essay on the tourist locations in Bond's universe Susanne Schmidt enlists recent theories of space to reconsider how movie audiences are invited to enjoy the films' lavishly excessive display of interchangeable holiday venues. Implying a strongly generalizing notion of spectatorship Schmidt fails to address the possibility of local responses to Bond's globalized pleasure grounds. Her fairly arbitrary application of concepts such as Foucault's "heterotopia" and Augé's "non-spaces" also yields unintentionally comic effects when applied to the toilet in the spoof version of *Casino Royale* (1967), whereas her remarks on Bond's vehicles and tourism in the agent's footsteps merely add a few impressionistic observations sprinkled with further theoretical name-dropping.

Luckily, the volume does contain a considerable number of essays which demonstrate that the topics of travel, tourism and space are well worth exploring. Kirsten Sandrock undertakes a comprehensive reading of Ian Fleming's hitherto underestimated travelogues *Thrilling Cities Part 1 & 2* (1963), offering material for further study of the Bond formula's nexus of travel and adventure as well as the "*bondification*" of the author's own life (212). Joyce Goggin contributes a dense case study linking the economic development of Las Vegas' entertainment industry to *Diamonds are Forever* (1971). As a counterpart to Schmidt's essay Claus-Ulrich Viol's text on "Spatial Desire" provides a positive example of theorizing Bond criticism, drawing on Deleuze's and Guattari's notion of "smooth" and "striated" spaces as well as on their concept of "desiring machines" (187). Viol succeeds in reconsidering Bond's manifold movements as productive energies both affirming and subverting the eponymous flows of a globalized economy. His consistent and differentiated application of Deleuze's and Guattari's less pathologizing version of psychoanalysis appears more apt to do justice to the serial pleasures of following a hero whose "constant becoming" and "lack of a substantive identity" cannot be sufficiently explained as a sustainable naturalization of an understated amalgamation of machismo and Englishness.

This is not to say that aspects of gender and class can no longer play a productive role in Bond scholarship. In her essay on Daniel Craig's acts of revamping the agent Claire Hines opens up the promising field of cross-marketing the Bond formula in British men's lifestyle magazines. In a related piece, Dan Ward analyzes Craig's anxious body-building and its promise of psychological depth in the context of so-called "masculine epiphany" film narratives such as *Fight Club* and *American Beauty*. The deviant quality of the last two Bond movies is also at the centre of Alessandro Catania's considerations of Jim Collins' concept of "high pop" (97). Like many other contributors Catania returns to Umberto Eco's canonical structuralist analysis of the formulaic constituents of the Bond myth. To produce a more sophisticated and dynamic account of the evolution of the Bond film series, Collins' notion of "high pop" has to be slightly modified: instead of a high cultural commodity successfully borrowing blockbuster marketing techniques, the Craig films maintain their mass cultural appeal while simultanenously generating an effect of quality and sophistication targeting new and more differentiated audiences. Needless to say, this "remystification of the aesthetic" allowing "for the return of prestige" (99) has infuriated a substantial part of the Bond fan community. Catania convincingly explores how cultural capital can be mobilized by a strategic reorientation of narrative strategies and in doing so encourages us to link the latest Bond films to the rich field of so-called "quality" series in American and British television. How much can be gained from a comparative perspective is impressively demonstrated by Georgia Christinidis' contrastive examination of the Bond stories and the English cult television series *Dr. Who*. Combining approaches from sociology and media studies Christinidis produces a richly layered explanation of the question why James Bond has proved to be so much more exportable than Dr. Who: while the latter series relies on narrative continuity and effects of verisimilitude satisfying science fiction fans in particular, the Bond films employ a reservoir of formulaic elements uniting even Bond's different actors; while Dr. Who celebrates a middle-class Englishness characterized by quotidian domesticity, Bond's stylish carelessness masks the social origins of his charismatic authority and thus turns him into an exportable hero with much more ambiguous class associations (84).

Christinidis draws on Bourdieu's concept of the habitus to no longer condemn but analyze the agent's "superiority without substance" (85). The productivity of such transdisciplinary approaches is further affirmed by Barbara Korte's remarks on the evolution of Bond's heroism, by Monika Seidl's phenomenological close reading of the Bond silhouette as a creatively shifting emblem, and by Cordula Lemke's innovative take on Bond's emotions as embodied by his different actors. In terms of the transmedial range of the contributions collected by Frenk and Krug, a clear focus still lies on the relationship between Fleming's novels and the film adaptations, whereas the rich field of digital media, marketing and fan communication is only partly covered in Hans-Joachim Backe's informative overview of Bond games and comics. When, finally, it comes to the transcultural and transnational dimension envisioned by the editors as well as by Lindner, the collection mainly illustrates that much work remains to be done. Nevertheless, this volume of Bond scholarship does not only take its object convincingly seriously, but is also likely to inspire attractive courses on a topic highlighting and challenging the study of popular culture.

Frankfurt am Main   JULIKA GRIEM

Jan Rupp. *Genre and Cultural Memory in Black British Literature.* Trier: WVT, 2010. 204 pp.

Genre criticism has experienced a remarkable revival in the German academic debate of the past decade, with research in English studies focusing on the redefinition of the historical novel. Writers such as Marion Gymnich, Ansgar Nünning, and not least Astrid Erll have re-charted the field and thus revised the poststructuralist position which subsumed genre writing as a declining practice under the term intertextuality. Jan Rupp's *Genre and Cultural Memory in Black British Literature*, which originated as a PhD thesis at the University of Gießen, ties in with the growing body of research that has recently been published in the field. Rupp reads a body of recent Black British novels on the background of genres such as *Bildungsroman*, crime novel, and historical novel and identifies both a decisive change within the genre of Black British writing and a change within the genres informing Black British writing. His intention is to both put forward the Black British genre as redefining the perception of cultural memory and the new notions of cultural memory as redefining the idea of generic writing, as well as to prove both positions in a close reading of a choice of recent novels.

Rupp places himself in the tradition of Stein and Sommer and their decisive and well-devised work on Black British fiction. In contrast to Stein and others, however, who tend to use the term "Black British fiction" as a loose generic description or rather as a common denominator of a group of texts, Rupp emphasizes the generic identity of Black British writing. When repeatedly referring to the "*genre of* and the *genres in*" Black British writing in his extended discussion of genre criticism and memory studies (chapters 1 and 2), the "*genre of*" Black British writing is described as increasingly restrictive and reductive because of the preconceptions connected with it regarding author, content, and narrative position, whereas the use of "*genres in*" Black British writing is valued as opening up new options for Black writers to position themselves in a different literary context. Rupp discusses the "self-reflexive engagement" (38) of authors such as Mike Phillips or the "possibility [of the genre of Black fiction] to review its own tradition" (35). Much emphasis is also placed on the genre-focused marketing of Zadie Smith's first novel *White Teeth* which shows the force of genre definition for other writers (14-15). Insightful and knowledgeable as the study of the chosen examples is, it does not fully convince the reader of the importance of this double generic approach.

The focus of Jan Rupp's work, however, lies on another level of discussion, where the author manages to present a thoughtful discussion of the dialogical relationship between genre and cultural memory. Playing with several dimensions of this relationship (such as genre memory, genres as sites of cultural memory, genres as scripts or cognitive schemata which structure both individual experience and the understanding of history), and referring to iconic texts of recent literary and cultural theory as sources and reference points of this discussion, Rupp presents a *tour d'horizon*, moving from Nora to Nünning, Bakhtin to Halbwachs, Bourdieu to Assmann, and Ricoeur to Zapf. The scope referred to in this survey, however, raises the question whether such a daunting task can be met in a 180-page PhD format.

In his third chapter, which examines nine examples of Black British fiction published between 1997 and 2004 both on a formal and a contextual level, Rupp sets out to discuss how "genres shape and influence the construction of cultural memory"

(58). In his analyses, he repeatedly refers to notions discussed in the preceding chapters, whereas the argument structure builds on an adaptation of Zapf's notion of discursive procedures (60-61). Rupp's case studies aptly illustrate these adapted procedures. The reflection of established memorial discourse(s) (61), which Rupp calls "alternative cultural memory" (70), shows in the narrative multiperspectivity of Fred D'Aguiar's *Bethany Bettany*, the satirical and picaresque re-writing of the imperialist *Bildungsroman* in Harry Kunzru's *The Impressionist* and a rhetoric of dissociation in Caryl Phillips's *A Distant Shore*. A second procedure of actively and "imaginatively recover[ing] counter-memories" (61), which Rupp names "cultural memory in crisis" (70), is illustrated with Bernadine Evaristo's *Lara*, Zadie Smith's *White Teeth* and Monica Ali's *Brick Lane*. Here, shared practices and objects of commemoration are called into question or satirized, such as the reference to the middle passage as founding myth, the validity of a re-writing of imperial and migration history, or the gendered notion of migration. In his last group of novels, put under the heading "constructing new myths" (70), Rupp discusses the procedure of reshaping existing memory structures by the addition of marginalized memories (61). Thus, in Mike Phillips's *A Shadow of Myself*, the notion of a Black Europe is set up in contrast to the Black Atlantic, in Andrea Levy's *Small Island*, the myths of the Windrush and of the Blitz experience are "filtered through the lens" (155) of the West Indian war effort and participation in the Battle of Britain. In Diran Adebayo's *My Once Upon a Time*, finally, the format of the hard-boiled urban crime story with its analogy in Black street culture is added to and reframed by African mythology, romance structures and pastoral.

The rather short conclusion manages to complete the line of argument put forward in the introduction, but remains sketchy as to the implications of the research results. Thus, the relationship between memory studies and genre studies will need much further attention, while the necessity of proposing a strong notion of Black British writing as genre still remains disputable. In spite of these limitations, this ambitious study is a must-read for researchers in the fields of recent Black British fiction, genre fiction, and cultural memory studies.

Karlsruhe   DORIS TESKE

Silke Stroh. *Uneasy Subjects. Postcolonialism and Scottish Gaelic Poetry.* **Amsterdam and New York: Rodopi, 2011. 378 pp.**

Silke Stroh's study is both timely and challenging. The theoretical and empirical territory that she carefully maps – the intersections between Scottish literature and postcolonialism – has been explored by a number of scholars in recent years, and yet this stands out as an important and extremely useful addition to a field of investigation which seems to be gaining momentum on both sides of the disciplinary border. Because academic disciplines do have borders – in the form of set practices, conventions, world-views, at worst even of 'creed' and entrenched conformism – and like all borders, even these may reward generously those who travel through them, at their own peril. Stroh's study provides ample evidence of this.

The border separating Scottish studies from Postcolonial studies is in fact a particularly contested one: unlike Ireland, which quickly and on the whole smoothly integrated into the first-wave postcolonial paradigmatic status of 'victim' of English/British imperialism, Scotland remained too conscious of its role of 'coloniser' – first as an independent nation and then, after the Union of Parliaments in 1707, as a partner of the British Empire – to embrace unconditionally postcolonialism, as much as postcolonialists, for symmetrical reasons, remained for a long time reluctant to investigate Scotland's cultural and political predicament. With the gradual problematisation of the postcolonial paradigm, however, the border has become less daunting, and fruitful exchange between the two areas has begun to take place. If postcolonialism, in fact, has been recently marked by a trend "towards dismantling traditional binarisms and towards paying more attention to ambiguities and complexities" (26), similarly, post-devolutionary Scotland has also started to emerge slowly from a long-standing entrenched cultural antagonism with England which, in the course of the 20th century, often narrowed the scope of literary criticism to a defensive 'nationalist' practice. And while it is not appropriate to reclaim a 'pure' postcolonial status for Scotland, there are many important intersections between the two fields, an awareness of which may indeed contribute towards a timely and needed gauging of disciplinary paradigms for both areas, as Stroh observes and indeed goes a long way to demonstrate in her study.

Another disciplinary border effectively challenged in *Uneasy Subjects* (a border most English studies specialists outside Britain will not be aware of), is that running between 'Celtic studies' and 'Scottish studies' (with the latter focusing exclusively or mainly on Scots and English language expressions) – a compartmentalisation largely deriving from the Gaidhealtachd's history of cultural marginalisation within Scotland itself, and still fostered by the current academic set-up. Once more, it is in post-devolutionary Scotland that this border is being questioned systematically for the first time by scholars who have started revising the Scottish literary canon along wider and more comprehensive lines. The introduction of a Gaelic editor/advisor for the *Edinburgh History of Scottish Literature* (2006) or for the *Edinburgh Companions to Scottish Literature* series, among other possible examples, is indicative of a significant change in perspective. Recent scholarship has also revealed how in imperial Britain internal national/ethnic affiliations were complex and often multiple: indeed, as Stroh puts it, "various allegiances could not always be balanced with ease – their negotiation frequently occasioned discursive tensions, elisions and conflicts even for texts or authors who did attempt to strike a balance" (78).

As a scholar who has engaged in both Scottish and postcolonial studies, as well as – even more exceptionally – in the study of Scottish Gaelic language and literature, Stroh seems uniquely endowed to face the above challenges. It is indeed the rare combination of the author's specific competences, matched with a keen critical eye and a serious and wide-ranging work of research, that make this work so valuable, and in many respects pioneering.

Structured in ten tightly-packed chapters, *Uneasy Subjects* charts the development of Gaelic poetry from the Middle Ages to the present day, deploying postcolonial and comparative tools of analysis – the central assumption (exhaustively discussed in its theoretical implications in chapter 1 and further gauged and illustrated in the following ones) being that such an approach can be regarded as useful and legitimate on the grounds of the history of political subordination, otherisation, cultural marginalisation suffered by the Gaels at the hands of the Anglo-Scottish centre. Stroh is, however, cautious and attentive in her deployment of postcolonial theory, and takes into account, for example, Highland involvement in the imperial enterprise, thus avoiding the simplified representation of the Gaels as a consistently oppressed Other. She also goes a long way to chart exchange and hybridisation between 'Celts' and 'Anglo-Saxons', thus debunking myths of 'purity.' The very title of her study, in fact, consciously conveys the difficulty and indeed the ethical 'uneasiness' of applying postcolonial theory to this specific context, warning the reader that s/he is going to be faced by critical questions whose answer may not be straightforward. Stroh's cautious attitude is indeed mirrored in the chapter titles, as four out of ten bear a question mark, such as the title of chapter 2, which opens with the question "Colonial beginnings?" Stroh is on the whole more assertive than one might expect in this same chapter, where she aptly reminds us how in antiquity "Celts were often regarded as the most savage barbarians of all. Thus, Celticity has always been inextricably connected to discourses on 'barbarian' Others and colonization" (44). Question marks here signal complexities and definitional problems that cannot be reduced to simplified postcolonial categories. They represent a challenge more than a strategy to defuse dissenting voices from both sides of the postcolonial/Scottish border.

Uneasy Subjects has several merits beyond critical border–crossing and a comparative approach: the first is possibly its breadth. Encompassing several centuries of cultural and literary history, it provides us with invaluable insight into what is indeed a complex territory. It also represents a systematic, solidly theoretically grounded discussion of the interrelations of postcolonialism and Scottish studies: by effectively summarising and discussing all previous contributions to this field, it establishes itself as an invaluable resource for future researchers in this field. Finally, by engaging with the cosmopolitan language of postcolonialism it allows Scottish literature to enter into dialogue with other world literatures, while, by displacing postcolonial theory onto an unfamiliar territory, it fruitfully strains and challenges its limits and stakes.

Verona   CARLA SASSI

Joanna Rostek. *Seaing through the Past: Postmodern Histories and the Maritime Metaphor in Contemporary Anglophone Fiction.* **Amsterdam and New York: Rodopi, 2011. 363 pp.**

In the past decade, numerous books in literary and cultural studies have tackled the problem of history and how it is narratively constructed. Historiography and postmodern theory have laid the ground for a discussion of history as stories that follow generic and narrative conventions. It is this notion of history as a set of stories and a range of discursive practices that forms the basis of Joanna Rostek's study. The book can therefore be categorised as belonging to the area of historiography, and the theories and names that she works with, among them Hayden White, Linda Hutcheon and Michel Foucault, are well-known.

However, the study connects this well-established approach with a metaphor that has always played a decisive role in English literature and culture: the sea. Shakespeare, Defoe, Coleridge or Conrad are only a few of the famous writers whose works testify to the long-standing concern with this metaphor. It is the interesting and innovative feature of Rostek's book that it neither concentrates on such well-researched writers nor exclusively focuses on historiography. In spite of claims that the maritime metaphor has lost its relevance in an age of air travel, Rostek shows how contemporary Anglophone literature uses the sea to ask how history is constructed and deconstructed. The study's thesis is that "in a notable proportion of contemporary Anglophone fiction, the past and history are metaphorically conceived of in terms of the sea" (17). The sea as well as the past are seen as sharing central ambivalences. Both are beyond control, unpredictable and boundless, yet humans want to possess, narrate and confine them.

The corpus of the study spans the Anglophone novel of the last three decades with a focus on the 1990s and 2000s. The earliest novel is Murdoch's *The Sea, the Sea* (1978), while Lessing's *The Cleft* (2007) and McEwan's *On Chesil Beach* (2007) are the latest books considered. All in all, the study includes an impressive fourteen novels, mainly by authors from Britain, but also from Ireland, Canada and South Africa.

After an introduction that gives an overview of the study's topic, novels and aims, the book begins with a theoretical chapter that presents findings from postmodern theories of history as well as literature to then address the maritime metaphor. The forms and functions of the sea and related metaphors like ships, sea voyages and storms are presented in terms of their literary, artistic, philosophical and socio-historical relevance. These chapters already show that the book's choice of combining the question of historiography with an analysis of the maritime metaphor in contemporary novels is well-thought-out. The authors chosen do not simply continue an outdated, even nostalgic tradition of writing about the sea. Instead, they contest national, colonial and traditional versions of the sea and thus question the knowability of the past via a creative reworking of this established motif.

The subsequent chapters document this combination of continuity and contestation for four related areas of postmodern histories: auto/biographical writing, personal trauma, discourses of origin and power, and postcolonial histories and retellings. The chapters combine two to four novels, which are arranged chronologically, and each is preceded by a brief theoretical outline and concluded by a summary. This clear structure makes it easy to compare the chapters in terms of the overarching question of the sea as a means to question the accessibility of the past and the objectivity of history.

Chapter 3 and 4 address how individual pasts are constructed in fictional biographies and autobiographies and how traumatic events are remembered and confronted. Both chapters again substantiate the ambivalence that the sea and history share. The protagonists and auto/biographers of Murdoch's *The Sea, the Sea*, McWilliam's *Debatable Land*, Swift's *Last Orders* and McEwan's *On Chesil Beach* long for life stories in their entirety, wholeness and truth, and the traumatised protagonists of Martel's *Life of Pi* and Banville's *The Sea* struggle for a voice and narrative that articulate their past and its traumatic events adequately and truthfully. History is desired in the sense of an access to the past, i.e. the real events that shape the present. On the other hand, all of the protagonists are aware of the impossibility of a clear distinction between past, present and future, an impossibility which is outlined by the novels' rejection of linear narrative, causality and reliability. In both chapters, the sea combines these features by destabilising geographical, temporal and personal boundaries and liquefying the hope for the real.

Chapters 5 and 6 then move from individual histories to the collective dimension by discussing the connection between origins and power in Barnes's *A History of the World in 10½ Chapters*, Winterson's *Lighthousekeeping*, Lessing's *The Cleft* and

Unsworth's *Sacred Hunger*, and by analysing postcolonial histories and their disavowal of the ideological assumptions behind colonial history in Coetzee's *Foe*, Warner's *Indigo, or Mapping the Waters*, D'Aguiar's *Feeding the Ghosts* and Kneale's *English Passengers*. Both chapters again show how unattainable the protagonists' and narrators' desires for origins, foundational myths and a unified past really are and how the fluid nature of such histories is reflected in motifs of sea voyages, diving, floods and drowning. Here, a special emphasis is put on the question of colonial misconceptions and representations in postcolonial rewritings. Rostek fittingly states that this approach "reclaims the drowned" (317).

What this study therefore convincingly shows is how time and space converge in one of the oldest metaphors of human language and literature and how it comments upon our desire for unity and history, which is unfulfillable. The highly readable, well-structured book interprets a corpus of texts that is, in this combination, innovative, and combines it with an approach to a metaphor that still yields an enormous imaginative power. *Seaing through the Past* thus indeed "offers a compelling guide to the literary oceans of today," as the dust jacket says.

Mannheim SARAH HEINZ

Marie-Hélène Gutberlet and Sissy Helff, eds. *Die Kunst der Migration. Aktuelle Positionen zum europäisch-afrikanischen Diskurs. Material – Gestaltung – Kritik.* **Bielefeld: transcript Verlag, 2011. 370 pp.**

Contemporary literary and visual expressions of migration reveal the vital relationship between art, social sciences and cultural studies. This edited anthology focuses on the medial, literary, architectural, and artistic reflections of African-European migration. The collection consists of essays, interviews, portraits of writers and artists, including artists' manifestos – all of which engage with the task of uprooting the binary discursive practices that generally depict African-European migration in terms of hunger and war and other atrocities pertaining to migration (e.g. living in asylum). The anthology is not only genre-bending in terms of its interdisciplinary and transcultural approaches to the "art of migration," but it often transgresses the generic boundaries imparted by the very term anthology. The contributions are presented not in a chronological but in thematic order. They explore research interests, biographical, medial, visual and artistic issues pursued by the writers, filmmakers and critics. The anthology is not strictly based on African literary studies; the contributions concurrently transgress fictional, medial and visual aspects of a diverse range of writers, artists and filmmakers across the African continent. The introduction sets a commanding conceptual tone for the collection, followed by three main thematic chapters with the first section consisting of five, the second section nine, and the third section ten contributions respectively. In the first thematic chapter, "Filmische Parallaxen," the five essays focus on the genre of film and on the visual arts, with a close attention to the strategy of voice-over in Ousmane Sembene's *Broom Sarret* (1966), A. R. Hayman's *Leopoldsville* (1946) – a colonial contrapuntal documentary – and Djibril Diop Mambety's *Contras' City* (1968). In his essay "Meine Filme, meine Orte: Gedanken eines schwarzen Filmemachers im Exil" Idrissou Mora-Kpai, a black film director in exile, explains why the theme of migration has inspired his work in a multifaceted way, while Marie-Hélène Gutberlet's essay on the notion of change of place ("Ortswechsel") focuses on trans-Saharan and trans-Mediterranean travels in contemporary movies. Julien Enoka Ayemba focuses on the exile movie *Heremakono* (2009) by Abderrahmane Sissako, concentrating on the film director's means of representation and subversive strategies.

In the second thematic chapter, entitled "Grenzen in Visual Culture" (a German-English neologism), five out of nine essays engage with digital blackness and cyberspace (Sissy Helff), and computer games (Soenke Zehle). This chapter includes a German re-print of Florian Schneider's essay "Enclaves, Exceptions and the Camps as a Counter-laboratory," which deals with the night of 29 September 2005 in the Spanish enclave Ceuta, a military outpost in Morocco, when 215 men and women tried to get across a barbed wire, an action which was video-taped; this chapter also includes an essay on the topography or heterotopy of migrant camps in video art installations (Brigitta Kuster). Other essays in this thematic chapter contain Kerstin Pinther's article on architecture and migration, and the idea of the migration of architecture in an African context; Ulf Vierke's essay on contemporary African art in Germany focuses on issues of home, homelessness, and a search for cultural identity in the realm of arts.

In the third thematic chapter, "Mobile Narrative," the essays address the representations of Africa in Europe in various artistic forms; two essays and an interview focus on the Congolese Berlin-based writer Winfried N'Sondé and his novel *Le cœur des enfants léopards* (*Das Herz der Leopardenkinder*) (2008). In addition to a 'manifesto,' this section presents several poems by Nigerian poet Uche Nduka. Other essays address Abdulrazak Gurnah's novels (Eva Ulrike Pirker), Ugandan writer Goretti Kyomuhendo's novel *Waiting* (2007) (Doreen Strauhs), and the London-based Pakistani artist Rasheed Areen. The latter focuses on the notion of the "Mediterranea" as a space where Africa, Asia and Europe meet.

All essays address the way the authors, artists and critics create and employ images and distinctive and contrasting views of the particular migratory experience under discussion. Accordingly, Gutberlet's and Helff's main trajectory is concerned with a whole range of African-European transnational, trans- and intercultural expressions and representations in the field of African and European studies, ethnology, cultural anthropology, visual arts, art history, philosophy, as well as postcolonial and transcultural literary, cultural and film studies.

While I was happy to encounter some familiar and unfamiliar names and writings in this selection of African art, literature, and the media, I found that the use of the term 'anthology' required more elaboration.

Overall, the volume is finely edited and the selection of the essays reveals richness of academic and artistic material on the migratory experiences from the African subcontinent (and Europe). In this regard, it is a useful academic/artistic resource for readers interested in African arts, literature, and the media who have previous knowledge in this field of study. In sum, the essays in this volume offer thoughtful and nuanced reflections on African-European migration and make a compelling case for why we must continue to explore literary and visual representations from Africa in/and Europe. By focusing on the theme of migration, this volume displays the potential of literature and the visual arts to soften the boundary between 'us' and 'them' and to promote awareness and contrasting views of particular historical and geopolitical issues pertaining to migratory perceptions.

Chemnitz   CECILE SANDTEN

Ellen Dengel-Janic. *'Home Fiction.' Narrating Gendered Space in Anita Desai's and Shashi Deshpande's Novels*. Würzburg: Königshausen & Neumann, 2011. 226 pp.

Literature by Indian authors writing in English is booming and has increasingly entered the global literary mainstream, for example in the form of recent award-winning bestsellers such as Kiran Desai's *The Inheritance of Loss* (2006) or Aravind Adiga's *The White Tiger* (2008). Not surprisingly, this has also triggered a rising interest in critical studies on Indian literature. Literary and cultural analyses of the works of the renowned Indian author Anita Desai, in particular, have surged over the last few years, with Hena Ahmad's *Postnational Feminisms* (2010), Elizabeth Jackson's *Feminism and Contemporary Indian Women's Writing* (2010) and Sujatha Rao's *Postmodernist Approach to Anita Desai* (2011) as the latest contributions.

In her study, Ellen Dengel-Janic aims to show how Anita Desai and Shashi Deshpande, who can be regarded as two of the most famous contemporary Indian authors writing in English, construct the private space of the home and thereby engage with topics of gender, national history and the construction of identity in a postcolonial context. As Dengel-Janic summarizes in her introduction, 'home fiction' encompasses literary representations of women within the gendered space of home. Her interdisciplinary approach, which focuses on both literary and social constructions of space, draws on an extensive theoretical framework, including Henri Lefebre's influential theory of the social production of space, Judith Butler's concept of performativity, and the construction of national identity.

Chapter 1 looks at the conceptualization of 'home' in Indian culture and history, paying particular attention to 'Mother India,' a term widely used for the nation state of India in a process of gendering national consciousness. The chapter also investigates the status of 'woman' as metaphor for the mythic place of home and takes a look at the historical development of that metaphor, from 19th-century Indian English literature to the National Movement and Gandhi's highly problematic concept of 'pure femininity.'

The second chapter is concerned with English prose by Indian authors up to the late 1930s, a survey intended to provide the backdrop for approaching the 'gendered spaces' in Desai's and Deshpande's novels. Dengel-Janic claims that these early works, although mainly situated within the framework of a traditional encoding of womanhood, also offer subversive readings that question these traditional concepts, as, for example, in Cornelia Sorabji's collection of short stories *Love and Life Behind the Purdah* (1901), R. K. Narayan's *The Dark Room* (1938) and Raja Rao's *Kanthapura* (1938).

In the third chapter of her study, Dengel-Janic shows how Desai, through both the means of narrative strategies and narrated space, emphasizes the constructedness of gender and questions the validity of the 'gendered space' of home. Desai's first novel *Where shall we go this Summer?* (1975) can be read as a biting critique of male-centered versions of Indian national history, apparent in the use of spatial imagery that implies ideological representations of the nation and in the opposition of the gendered home space and the utopian space of the island where the protagonist Sita grows up. The protagonist's refusal to conform to the traditional concept of womanhood entails, as Dengel-Janic argues, a sharp social critique of the 'Mother India' image, which the study links to Indian politics of the 1960s and 1970s, and to Indira

Gandhi's use of this image. Desai's novel *Fire on the Mountain* (1977) deals with spaces of enforced exile and also incorporates spatial remnants of India's colonial past, the summer residence of the British Raj in particular, so that the novel's construction of space negotiates the complexities of colonial and postcolonial history. In her analysis, Dengel-Janic looks at the concept of 'colonial nostalgia,' the Gothic as well as the role of violence, in order to illuminate the construction of space in the novel, and she points out convincingly how the main female characters in the novel are located outside the normative and gendered space of home. Their marginal position within Indian patriarchal society leads to an 'inner exile' that also finds its expression in terms of physical space. Desai's most successful novel *Clear Light of Day* (1980) is primarily concerned with conflicts within the private space of home, and, by using several narratives, emphasizes the diversity of versions of home space. *Clear Light of Day* focuses on the theme of diaspora and, in portraying diasporic identity and the spatial separation of the family, discloses the fragmentation of home space and the myth of the nation and the home as an imagined whole in an increasingly globalized and culturally disparate world.

The fourth chapter of the study explores the role of home in the novels of Shashi Deshpande. The main argument of this analysis of several of Deshpande's novels is that the construction of home space in these texts cannot be restricted, as other critics have attempted to do, to showing women as chained to the private spaces of home, but that home space is much more ambiguous and shifting, so that stable identities (even that of the victimized, fenced-in woman) within the home remain elusive. In *The Dark Holds no Terrors* (1980), Deshpande's first novel, the traditional home of the protagonist Saru's childhood is juxtaposed to a newer version of the nuclear family in 1970s Bombay. Portraying inter-marital rape, the text sheds light on one of the great taboos within Indian culture and thereby disrupts notions of home as a domestic idyll. Dengel-Janic incorporates trauma theory to investigate the rendering of rape on both the level of the plot and that of narrative strategies. *The Long Silence* (1988), which deals with a woman writer and her dissatisfaction with her duties as a mother and wife, is mainly concerned with the tension between private and public space. The analysis is augmented by Deshpande's own reflections on the process of writing and her status as a woman writer, as well as the contestable terrain of women's writing in general. This rather extensive journey into the fictionalization of the process of writing and its gendered implications, however, somehow seems to lead away from the analysis of spatial characteristics. In Deshpande's novel *A Matter of Time* (1996), home space is mediated through a diversity of male and female narrators. As Dengel-Janic argues, rewarding insights into the meanings of gendered home space can be provided by looking at narrative technique instead of following a mere mimetic, plot-centered approach. Thus, different focalisers and alternations between first and third person narrative show the plurality of conceptions of home space within the families and thereby accentuate the disintegration of the home as the text's central theme, and they also expose the creation of the unified, homogeneous home space of Indian nationalist mythology as an illusion.

The conclusion summarizes the main arguments concerning Desai and Deshpande's particular explorations of home space. The problematic field of 'women's writing' is addressed again and set in relation to classic feminist discourse. The conclusion also surveys more recent novels by female Indian authors, such as Githa

Hariharan and Manju Kapur, and their conceptualizations of gendered spaces within a cultural climate influenced by globalization and the rise of the Hindu Right. Whereas Desai and Deshpande's home space is not primarily concerned with class, the younger generation of writers also looks at the class-based construction of home by, for example, including lower-class protagonists and their perception of home space. As Dengel-Janic concludes, the rendering of home space in Indian literature written in English remains an effective strategy to comment on the abstract myth of the home as authentic national space.

One of the great strengths of Dengel-Janic's approach lies in her continual focusing on both plot-centered and aesthetic strategies, which greatly enriches the analysis. Her preoccupation with aspects of the position of women's writing and with the extensive exploration of family conflicts, however, at times tends to marginalize aspects of space. Moreover, space is often treated in broad structural oppositions of settings (such as traditional vs. modern home or home vs. exile) which are then taken as a point of departure for discussing familial relationships and their dynamics. This approach is surely valuable, as apparent in Dengel-Janic's profound investigations of the gendered existence of Indian women in these texts. However, what can be seen as missing in a study explicitly concerned with literary representations of 'lived space' is a more in-depth and nuanced reading of how that space is constructed from its physical details, and how these depictions shape or echo the protagonists' experiences as well as more general cultural and social trends. Moreover, Dengel-Janic's emphasis on subversion, particularly in early Indian literature written in English, should perhaps be treated with more caution, mirroring the typically postcolonial approach of unearthing strategies of resistance in colonial 'native' texts so as to emphasize their progressive quality. However, this is not to diminish the merits of this extensive, well-researched and coherent study, which can be unreservedly recommended to scholars of Indian literature in English.

Kiel   OLIVER LINDNER

Mark Aronoff and Kirsten Fudeman. *What is Morphology?* **Chichester, West Sussex: Wiley-Blackwell, 2010. 312 pp.**

What is Morphology? is an introductory book to the study of linguistic morphology that targets undergraduate students with minimal background in the general study of language. It introduces the reader to the basic issues in morphological description and analysis from a theory-independent perspective, with a focus on the fundamental questions that equally concern all theories of morphology. This second edition incorporates revisions resulting from feedback to the first edition, including an online answer key to the exercises, and an additional chapter on experimental and computational methods in morphological analysis.

The book is organized in eight chapters that introduce general notions like morphological analysis, morphemes, words, lexemes, but also address some details about morphological processes as well as the main questions concerning the interface between morphology and phonology, syntax, semantics, and the lexicon. A welcome innovation of the book is that, besides the usual theoretical presentation with examples from various languages and the related set of exercises, each chapter contains a section that introduces a particular aspect of the morphological system of Kujamaat Jóola, a language spoken in Senegal. This idea stems from the authors' conviction that the morphological system of a language can only be understood as a whole. The structure of the chapters is very convenient both for the student and the lecturer: it allows a direct application of the theoretical matters to an unknown language, thus making the content more exciting for the student, and at the same time providing a handy and stimulating means for the lecturer to evaluate the student's understanding.

The first chapter, "Thinking about Morphology and Morphological Analysis," introduces the notion of morpheme, the main principles that are at play in morphological analysis, and the authors' basic theoretical assumptions, such as the idea that morphology cannot be reduced to other grammar components. Chapter 2, "Words and Lexemes," presents a few theoretical considerations with respect to basic morphological terms like (syntactic, phonological, function vs. content) words, lexemes, inflection, derivation, and the lexicon. These two preparatory chapters are followed by five chapters that are concerned with the interaction between morphology (or morphological processes) and the other components of grammar: phonology, the lexicon, semantics and syntax. "Morphology and Phonology" discusses, among others topics, allomorphy as illustrated by the English past tense suffix /d/ with the three forms [d], [t] and [əd], language-specific phonotactic constraints (e.g. minimal word constraints in various languages), and the role of phonology in the distinction between primary and secondary affixes as, for instance, the prefixes *in-* and *un-* (see *irréparable, irrévocable* vs. *unrepáirable, unrevókable*). "Derivation and the Lexicon" addresses the compositionality question with respect to word formation and how this determines whether a derived word must be part of the mental lexicon or can be interpreted solely on the basis of morphological rules. "Derivation and Semantics" continues this discussion on compositionality by bringing forward various instances of polysemy in the case of zero-derivation, agent nouns derived with *-er* in English, or the suffix *-ei* in German (e.g. *Bäcker* 'baker' - *Bäckerei* 'bakery' vs. *plaudern* 'to chat' - *Plauderei* 'chat'). The sixth chapter, "Inflection," compares this morphological process with derivation, and gives an inventory of inflectional morphological types: affixation and stem alternations, apophony/ablaut, root-and-pattern morphology as in Semitic languages, reduplication and suppletion. A typological sketch is also provided that classifies languages between analytic and synthetic: at one end are isolating languages like Vietnamese, which has no inflection or derivation, but only compounding, then come inflective languages, whether agglutinative like Hungarian or fusional like Latin, and at the other end, we have polysynthetic languages often spoken in North America, where complex words can be built to express what in English would be full sentences. "Morphology and Syntax" describes the difference between morphological and syntactic thinking with respect to words and inflection, and illustrates a number of syntactic alternations that involve morphological means: passive, antipassive, causative, applicative constructions, and noun incorporation. The last chapter, "Morphological Productivity and the Mental Lexicon," presents some examples of experimental studies on a recurrent question in the book, namely, whether derived words are accessed by speakers from the lexicon or via morphological rules. A key concept in these approaches is morphological productivity, which ties into the compositionality issues raised earlier in the book.

What I find most appealing about the book as teaching material is the way it approaches the readers. I shall limit myself to just two general aspects here. The first one is the informal presentation, despite the well-documented theoretical ideas behind it. Instead of a prescriptive approach, the authors opt for a dynamic style with few definitions and mostly inductive reasoning: examples from every-day life are analyzed and lead to generalizations about morphology. Various little tasks are assigned throughout the presentation, something that students will find most appealing.

Another aspect is the objective viewpoint with respect to content, as the book does not pretend to offer 'the one and only truth' about morphological analysis. From the very beginning it promotes an attitude of 'skeptical realism:' "you should always believe that what you are looking for is God's truth, but [...] you should consider all that you have found so far as hocus-pocus" (12). It thus makes the student aware that scientific truth is a matter of argumentation and deeper investigation, and a change of perspective can always challenge well-established ideas. This characteristic of the book particularly recommends it for teaching, as it is often the case that undergraduate students are reluctant to engage in argumentation and favor prescriptive contents. This book manages to lure the student into thinking and arguing rather than learning definitions.

Stuttgart   GIANINA IORDĂCHIOAIA

Andrea Cabajsky and Brett Josef Grubisic, eds. *National Plots: Historical Fiction and Changing Ideas of Canada.* **Waterloo, Ontario: Wilfrid Laurier University Press, 2010. 252 pp.**

"If some countries have too much history, we [i.e. Canadians] have too much geography." Cited as an epigraph to the concluding essay in the present collection, this saying by former Canadian Prime Minister William Lyon Mackenzie King is subverted by all the contributions to this volume as they analyze renderings of Canada's multifacetted past in the country's historical fiction. Resting on the conviction that historical fiction always reflects the needs of the present (according to Herb Wyile, one of the foremost critics to have written on Canadian historical novels and a contributor to the present volume, historical novels are "historically situated representations with contemporary motivations and concerns" (126)), the essays address the function of historical fiction as a vehicle for expressing changing assumptions about the nation and about 'Canadianness.' Theoretically informed and with great interpretative sensitivity, they illustrate how Canadian historical fiction often reveals a tension between skepticism or even relativism on the one hand, and a yearning for continuity and an identification with place on the other. These tensions, it appears, are particularly resonant in a nation which, according to Robert Kroetsch, had to 'uninvent itself,' i.e. deconstruct frames of definition established by others (British, American), in order to construct a sense of national identity. The concerns of nation-building have also included a revisionism that has given voice to the marginalized, as is evident for instance in Rudy Wiebe's novels about the troubled history of European settlement in the Canadian West. As the essays in the present volume make clear, however, new historical novels critically engage with the revisionist model, aiming at a re-appraisal of the function of historical fiction "in an increasingly post-national era critical of national metanarratives" (34).

The forms of Canadian historical fiction, and the ideological questions pursued by the genre are succinctly discussed in an introduction by the editors ("Historical Fiction and Changing Ideas of Canada" (vii-xxiv)). Due attention is paid to the meta-narrative element that is a hallmark of recent historical fiction from Canada (indeed, it seems appropriate that the term 'historiographic metafiction' was coined by a Canadian critic, Linda Hutcheon), and theoretical contexts of the genre are delineated with much critical acumen. The 13 essays which follow are divided into three parts, offering new readings of 'classics' and of works which may be seen as representative of developments in the genre in the first section ("A Noble Past? New Questions, New Directions"), while discussing texts dealing with the marginalized in the second ("Unconventional Voices: Fiction versus Recorded History") and works connected with Canada's cultural-historical regions in the third section ("Literary History, Regional Contexts"). References have been compiled and appended at the end, and – unusual for a collection of essays, but the more welcome – there is an index. The 'historical fiction' discussed includes novels, short stories and fictionalized historiography, and there is a balance of essays devoted to the in-depth analysis of individual works and of more comprehensive pieces. All of them, however, are methodologically stringent and united by their endeavor to read texts against the grain of earlier interpretations, especially with regard to views on history and on how history and the past have proved functional within the national framework.

Opening part one of the collection, Kathleen Venema deals with the question of historical fiction's 'ambiguous' status using the example of a novel on the fur trade (Fred Stenson, *The Trade*, 2000) which is indebted to documentary sources and to patterns of Gothic fiction at the same time. As Venema shows, the latter become problematic especially with regard to the novel's portrayal of Métis characters, and the book thus raises questions as to "[w]hat responsibilities, to the past and to the future […] writers take on when they reframe history" (6). Cynthia Sugars's essay on Aimée Laberge's *Where the River Narrows* (2003), a Quebec novel written in English (it should be noted here that the volume deals exclusively with English language writing), shows how the author establishes a "foundational genealogy" (22), aligning family history with national history in order to exclude questions of colonial occupation. Emphasizing the settler-ancestors' connection with the land, Laberge's novel, according to Sugars, subscribes to a romantic nationalized version of Quebec history. Dealing with historical and literary portraits of Thomas Scott, who was executed as an opponent of Métis leader Louis Riel in 1870, Albert Braz shows how genre may determine the portrayal of a controversial historical figure, and how the "Canadian desire for self-indigenization" (50) may account for the fact that Riel has mainly been portrayed as a national hero. In an article on *Barometer Rising*, Hugh MacLennan's 1941 novel on the Halifax explosion of 1917, Robert David Stacey convincingly argues that, contrary to established readings which hold that in the novel the explosion marks a caesura, a violent awakening from colonial dependence to national history, the present of the novel's events (Canada's involvement in the First World War) is really repeated in 1941, when Canada was again fighting on the side of the British. Tracy Ware's illuminating essay on the ambivalences created by the narrative voice in Alice Munro's short story "Meneseteung" (*Friend of My Youth*, 1978), which is set in 19th-century Ontario, concludes the section.

With one exception, the essays in part two are concerned with two important groups within the Canadian ethno-cultural spectrum, the First Nations and Black

Canadians. Joseph Boyden's *Three Day Road*, a novel about the participation of Native Canadian soldiers in World War I and thus a significant addition to a substantial body of contemporary Canadian novels about that war, is analyzed by Herb Wyile, who emphasizes Boyden's interpretation of the war in terms of aboriginal culture. In particular, Wyile focuses on how Boyden represents the monstrosity of the war by referring to the cannibalistic Windigo of Native mythology, a concept which also provides him with an interpretative frame for the harshness and sexual abuse which were rife in Canada's residential school system (Wyile might have referred here to similar images in Tomson Highway's *Kiss of the Fur Queen*). Wyile's essay is in some ways complemented by Shelley Hulan's on a 19th-century historiographical work by a Native writer, George Copway's *Traditional History and Characteristic Sketches of the Ojibway Nation* (1850). As Hulan states, Native-authored works are marked by a strong fictional element which produces a resemblance to orature. This is also the case, as Pilar Cuder-Domínguez shows in her discussion of novels by Lawrence Hill, Mairuth Sarsfield, and George Elliott Clarke, in works rendering the experience of Black Canadians, a group which is very diverse in itself, comprising the descendants of Black Loyalists and recent immigrants from Africa and the Caribbean. In both cases, their history is under-represented and largely absent even from recent monographs and collections on Canadian historical fiction. Concentrating on aspects of gender rather than race, Aritha van Herk's "Turning the Tables" concludes this part. Discussing, among others, Robert Kroetsch's novel on the Klondike Gold Rush, *The Man from the Creeks* (1998), van Herk's inspired essay shows how women characters in historical fiction tend to subvert the 'master narratives' of which they are part by invading 'male spaces' and thereby escaping categorization.

Focusing on regional contexts, the essays in the third part seem to bear out Maurice Carless' contention that "the true theme of the country's history in the 20th century is not nation building but region building" (157). Claire Campbell attributes the fact that Western Canadian writers like Wiebe, Margaret Laurence, Kroetsch, or Guy Vanderhaeghe have frequently turned to historical fiction to a self-consciousness on the part of these writers as to the potentially ahistorical image of Western Canada, and to a desire to counter the stereotype of the West as a "frontier free from history" (151). Different premises apply when it comes to Newfoundland, one of the oldest British colonies on North American soil and the youngest province of Canada (1949). Using the example of Wayne Johnston's *The Colony of Unrequited Dreams* (1998) and Michael Crummey's *River Thieves* (2001), novels about the province's controversial first Premier Joe Smallwood and the extinction of Newfoundland's Native inhabitants respectively, Paul Chafe demonstrates that in these novels about an "Old Lost Land" (167) the emphasis is in fact on the loss of major identity factors in the course of the island's history. Owen Percy's essay on "Imagining Vancouvers [!]" discusses two outstanding representatives of historiographic metafiction from the 1980s (George Bowering's *Burning Water*, 1980; Daphne Marlatt's *Ana Historic*, 1988) and their rendering of de-centered and fragmented rather than comprehensive histories of the West Coast, as manifested in their reliance on experimental narrative techniques. The final essay by Dennis Duffy, the second in the collection on Munro's "Meneseteung," explicitly engages with Canada's presumed lack of history with the help of Munro's text. Taking the story as a point of departure, Duffy reviews Munro's work with regard to her creation of a fictional history of the "Munro Tract," as he calls the writer's Huron County, showing how the stories construct a continuum to become pieces of a *roman fleuve* on the area.

With the exception of occasional misprints (xiii, 151, 153, 156, 157), this is a carefully edited collection which succeeds in capturing the diversity of English-Canadian historical fiction as well as providing valuable categories for structuring this wide field, besides fresh and insightful close readings. *National Plots* will thus be indispensable reading for anyone interested in the ongoing and significant contribution of historical fiction to a Canadian sense of identity.

Graz   MARTIN LÖSCHNIGG

Stefan L. Brandt and Astrid M. Fellner, eds. *Making National Bodies: Cultural Identity and the Politics of the Body in (Post-)Revolutionary America.* **Trier: WVT, 2010. 164 pp.**

The book under review is the latest volume in the Mosaic series "Studien zur amerikanischen Kultur und Geschichte." A timely contribution to the study of Revolutionary and Post-Revolutionary America, *Making National Bodies: Cultural Identity and the Politics of the Body in (Post-)Revolutionary America* is edited and with an introduction by Stefan L. Brandt and Astrid M. Fellner. It fruitfully introduces current debates in cultural studies on corporeality and embodiment into the field of early American history and discourses of nationhood. *Making National Bodies* explores the aesthetic and ideological implications of historical discourses of self-fashioning in which the dimension of the corporeal becomes instrumental to negotiations of individual and collective identity.

Combining eight essays and a programmatic introduction, the collection is divided into three thematic parts, each exploring aspects of American corporeality and early nationhood: A first section on foundational mythmaking, "The Politics of the Body and the Making of America," consists of an essay on emerging figures of American motherhood in light of a patriarchal rhetoric by Timothy K. Conley, Astrid M. Fellner's study of the gendered national body in early American iconographic tradition, and Gabriele Pisarz-Ramírez' analysis of Christopher Columbus' role as pillar saint in early American poetry that documents attempts to situate the new nation in a hemispheric context. In section two, "The Body and Discourses of Medicine and Sexuality," essays by Thomas Clark and Jörg Thomas Richter sound the relevance of contemporary medical and sexual discourses for moral and political considerations of the new citizen. Finally, "Embodiment and National Self-Fashioning" addresses questions of literary genre with regard to ethnicity and early American plays (Zoe Detsi-Diamanti), gender and the epistolary form (Christian Quendler), and aesthetics of the body in Charles Brockden Brown's *Edgar Huntley* (Stefan L. Brandt). While all contributions merit closer attention, only a few can be discussed in detail and may serve as illustrations of the volume's overall project and range of study.

Astrid Fellner traces the politics of the body in revolutionary America by outlining changes in its representations and uses in early American iconography. She pays particular attention to the female body as a site of contestation and as a carrier of revolutionary potential. She convincingly shows how the close linking of woman, body, nature, and American national identity shifted from the intricate power relations of the colonial triangle (consisting of the trinity of land, native, and Europe, as characterized by Peter Hulme in his 1984 study *Colonial Encounters*) to a binary relation.

Fellner discusses how the newly particularized body required a reinterpretation during the revolutionary period in order to control the unruly ambiguities of its rebellious potential and gendered identity.

Thomas Clark's contribution, "'...to convert men into republican machines': Rush, Foucault, and the making of virtuous bodies," is one of the highlights of the collection. Combining historical detail with concise theoretical argument, Clark's study investigates Benjamin Rush's emphasis on bodily dimensions in the creation of the good citizens of the republic. While the correlation with Foucault's work on biopolitics and his interest in the modern production of governable bodies seems evident, Clark seeks to counter this response; he highlights the fundamental differences in Rush's agenda in order to extricate Rush's thought from the genealogy of the liberal state and its subject. Identifying Rush's idea of the good subject as primarily virtuous rather than autonomous, Clark argues how Rush's notions must be read as "die-hard classical Republican" (63) and as incompatible with the liberal state's strategy of casting its governable subjects as autonomous individuals.

Stefan Brandt's concluding essay, "Exploring the 'Heart of the Wilderness': Cultural Self-Fashioning and the Aesthetics of the Body in Charles Brockden Brown's *Edgar Huntley, or, Memoirs of a Sleep-Walker*," traces Brown's reflections on a poetics of effect to an aesthetics of affect through a strategy of 'visceral writing.' Brandt investigates the argument that in the context of the post-revolutionary period, Brown's writings are to be read as negotiations of an American body politic for the new nation and shows how its aesthetics signal a struggle with an early but profound distrust of Reason on the premises of which the new Nation understood itself to be founded. Brandt's study methodologically reflects on the question of relating social dimensions and literary text without simplistic mimetic conflation or disregard of aesthetic implications. Brandt shows how *Edgar Huntley's* complex aesthetic structure creates rich metaphorical spaces of "trackless wilderness," and how traumatic encounters with a terrifying Other embodied by the "savage Indian" also function as the gothic *doppelgänger* of a darker self. Brandt's differentiated discussion of aspects of social and literary practice and the aesthetic potential of the novel in processes of social communication, self-imagination, and constitution of identity results in an elucidating reading of Brown's text, which compellingly exemplifies the volume's overall endeavor.

The collection is a welcome contribution to the field of early American studies, and it signals well beyond its range of historical interest the productiveness of an intersection between a growing field of studies of the body in its discursive and material implications and a distinctly American studies approach heedful of historic and methodic specificity.

Erlangen   KARIN HÖPKER

Waldemar Zacharasiewicz, ed. *Riding/Writing Across Borders in North American Travelogues and Fiction*. Wien: Verlag der Österreichischen Akademie der Wissenschaften, 2011. 394 pp.

Riding/Writing Across Borders is a collection of essays based on papers delivered at a 2009 symposium in Vienna. Composing conference papers into an intellectually coherent and stimulating ensemble can be a challenge, but Waldemar Zacharasiewicz has succeeded magnificently. Not only did he assemble some of the most eminent experts of travel writing at the original event, but he has also produced a book that is consistently enlightening and stimulating to read. The majority of contributions pursue a clearly identified set of research questions that probe both the stereotypes perpetuated by the genre and those that have been attached to it. Other essays – such as Gudrun Grabher's analysis of ekphrasis in Jorie Graham's poetry – read the "riding/writing" of the symposium title primarily as a metaphor, but these discussions too are effective as poetic digressions, complements, and counterparts.

The contributors are British, American, Austrian, Swiss, and German scholars of English and American literature and of cultural studies, but as is inevitable with travel writing the essays also venture into geography and mapping, the history of transport, the dynamics of settlement, and many other subjects. Aritha van Herk sets the multidisciplinary tone in a thought-provoking riff on literary suitcases that ranges widely through autobiography, family history, immigrant history, philosophy, film, and fiction. Equally rewarding is Christopher Mulvey's essay "Nathaniel Hawthorne's Wondrous Stream Riding the Borders of Antebellum Experience" which analyses the effect of the Erie Canal on transport, settlement, and identity formation. His reflections take their time to get to Hawthorne, but the wait is well worth it. Another contribution preoccupied with questions of transport, James Schramer's "Paved with Good Intentions: Eisenhower, the Interstate High-Way System and the American Road Trip," intersperses detailed readings of Jack Kerouac and John Steinbeck with brief comments on the sections of the Interstate high-ways that feature in *On the Road* and *Travels with Charley in America*.

The "matched set of ladies' luggage" evoked by van Herk instantly made me think of the matched set Sylvia Plath brought with her to Cambridge, to the everlasting scorn of her British friends, and of the fastidious set of suitcases spied through the open door of Mary Richards' walk-in closet. Several essays investigate material questions of travel and gender, but none is more interesting than Michael O'Brien's study of Louise Catherine Adams. O'Brien opens up a field of research that has so far been relatively neglected, possibly because of a scholarly prejudice against the "relevance" of the experiences of privileged travellers such as diplomats, their families, and their entourage. This essay also illustrates particularly well that research questions may be appropriate for one social class of women travellers but not necessarily for another, and it is not surprising that the theories he has culled from the "scholarly literature about gender, women, and travel in the decades adjacent to [Adams's] 1815 journey" are not always applicable to her "Narrative of a Journey from Russia to France 1815." For example, O'Brien correctly points out that while the middle-class traveller may indeed have begun to dominate 19th-century travel and tourism, Adams and other travellers with complex identities like hers cannot be accommodated under that heading. New parameters of discussion will also have to be developed for travellers like Stephen Leacock and Marshall McLuhan whose journeys were – as discussed in David Staines's essay – variously motivated by promotional, academic, philosophical and patriotic concerns, and not by those of an average middle-class tourist.

Adams's narrative of dangerous travel through post-Napoleonic Europe evokes Guy de Maupassant's celebrated story "Boule de suif" of a French company of travellers after the Franco-Prussian War, and several of the essays are recommended background reading for stories that use the coach, car or railway ride as a structural motif to highlight historically fraught subjects and moments. One such contribution is Sherrill Grace's sensitive reading of Canadian literary texts inspired by the two world wars. Another is Gary Totten's superb "Geographies of Race and Mobility in Carl Rowan's *South of Freedom*" in which complex critical vistas are coincidentally opened up for Flannery O'Connor's "A Good Man is Hard to Find" or Toni Cade Bambara's "Gorilla, My Love," both of which radically undermine the assumption that mobility can automatically be equated with freedom.

In Rowan's case, contradictions are part and parcel of the narrator's everyday persona, but other essays document such inconsistencies by investigating the dissenting voice of a travel companion. The letters of German topographer Georg Carl Ludwig Preuss, for example, provide an observant and often sardonic counterpoint to those of Colonel John Charles Frémont, "America's 'Great Pathfinder'." As related by Arno Heller in "German Scientists and Artists Exploring the Trans Mississippi West," Preuss's letters to his wife did not come to light again until a hundred years later when a descendant sold them to the Library of Congress. (Robert Sayre's essay on "Moreau de Saint-Méry's Voyage" suggests that it is not only such original papers that may require scholarly archeology, but also the popular historical fiction – such as Kenneth Roberts' – inspired by it). These texts provide important emendations to their more famous companion pieces, but the Native people in Rudy Wiebe's *A Discovery of Strangers* formulate a completely different perspective on the Franklin expedition, as discussed in Heinz Antor's spirited "Border-Crossings, Inter-cultural Encounters, and the Negotiation of Otherness in Rudy Wiebe's *A Discovery of Strangers*."

Two dozen essays are too many to do justice in a brief review, but these comments may give an overview of this warmly recommended volume.

Vancouver   EVA-MARIE KRÖLLER

Stefanie Schäfer. "*Just the Two of Us:*" *Self-Narration and Recognition in the Contemporary American Novel*. Trier: WVT, 2011. 230 pp.

Schäfer's book "*Just the Two of Us:*" *Self-Narration and Recognition in the American Novel* looks at the creation of a "narrative identity, the depiction of remembrance, the uses of metanarrative commentary, and the stimulation of reader judgment by narrative progression" (200). The book consists of an introductory chapter with the title "The Self Examined in Contemporary American Literature," followed by "Self-Narration and Ethics" and the chapter "Reading Autodiegetic American Novels," which provides close readings of five 21st-century American novels.

The first chapter initially focuses on autobiography, establishing how a self is created and conveyed in an autobiography, which successfully illustrates the weak boundaries that separate autobiography from the novel, making fictional autobiography a worthy subject of study. Schäfer addresses "Fictions of Identity in contemporary American literature" next, claiming that self-narration is of utmost importance in American literature, "self-scrutiny and the story of individual struggles" being central and stabilizing in regard to identity (12), which is illustrated very well by the examples in chapter 3.

While these discussions, along with "Aims, Method, and Corpus" make up the first chapter, a second and extensive one is given to ethics (Schäfer emphasizes the importance of "'the ethical turn, '" 47), dealing with the telling itself, followed by the interaction between teller and reader; this chapter is crucial since the author claims that the teller has to work harder than in autobiography to make the reader accept the protagonist's experiences as convincing. This point is well illustrated and well developed.

Many different strands that illuminate the debate are expertly woven together, giving a fascinating insight into contemporary discussions, ranging from the autobiographical pact to the importance of identity in American fiction, the establishing of identity to literary period to ethics to the Other. Some of these ideas would be interesting to pursue further: most prominently, the question of how to classify these novels. Some sentences and footnotes give hints as to that: they are post-postmodern, as the author claims (for example in the conclusion), since they employ closure while the postmodern novel refuses to do so. Schäfer refers to Dorothy J. Hale in arguing that "[i]n proposing a procedural and narrative concept of self, the autodiegetic novels analyzed are harbingers of a new, post-postmodernist branch of self-representation in literary texts that might form the kernel of a new 'ethical theory' of the novel'" (207). A footnote mentions other novels that represent a similar narrative situation while distinguishing them from novels by authors such as Jonathan Franzen, who are seen as New Realists, claiming that the narrative situation is different here, that the latter authors "work with various focalizers and a covert narrator" (17). Does that maybe determine their belonging to New Realism? In contrast, are the five novels discussed in this book transitional because of the narrative situation? This would give the narrative situation a decisive role in the classification of novels, but unfortunately Schäfer does not pursue this any further. Likewise, the fact that she considers 9/11 "a historical watershed" (17), as she writes in another footnote, should also lead to a more extensive debate of its influence on the decade in which the five novels are set, as well as how the narrator-reader relations are influenced by this.

Five contemporary American novels are analyzed in chapter 3, namely Geraldine Brooks' *March*, Curtis Sittenfeld's *Prep*, Benjamin Kunkel's *Indecision*, Marisha Pessl's *Special Topics in Calamity Physics*, and Jeffrey Eugenides' *Middlesex*. All these novels were published between 2002 and 2006. The order in which they are analyzed is not chronological, but instead "determined by the narrative scenario and function of the self-narrative along the scale between the confessional (in which the reader represents witness and judge of the narrative), and didactic example (which aims at making readers see things differently" (57-58), showing again the importance the study sees in the reader's contribution to the creation of a text. While the first two of the selected novels are confessional, *Indecision* is seen as "the middle ground" (204), while *Special Topics in Calamity Physics* and *Middlesex* are on the didactic side of the spectrum; the latter three novels enlist the reader for a political agenda, educate him or her, or ask for the consideration of society's role in the creation of truth. (The chapter, however, only mentions the spectrum; the detailed explanation is not given until the conclusion.) The analyses insightfully comment on contemporary culture and discourses and on how much the narrators are caught up in fixed prior narratives themselves.

The selection of the novels is very good; the author has chosen challenging works, and her interpretations are detailed and insightful, showing a good understanding of the genres these novels belong to and how they comment on those genres, what the narrators try to convey and what the novels say about them. The very complex narrative situations are skillfully dissected. The conclusion very successfully brings the novels together; it illuminates some of the issues again, but also shows that some clarifications would have been helpful earlier, as stated above.

The book shows some minor inconsistencies in spelling and formatting. These, however, are easily offset by the quality, insightfulness, originality and scope of the close readings. The fact that the novels are so recent makes these analyses even more impressive.

München   ANNA FLÜGGE

Greta Olson, ed. *Current Trends in Narratology*. Berlin: Walter de Gruyter, 2011. 367 pp.

In the last two decades the field of narrative research has undergone a process of theoretical and methodological renewal. A number of publications – beginning with David Herman's seminal *Narratologies* (1999) – have attempted to survey, assess and specify these developments. One of the most recent contributions in this tradition is the volume *Current Trends in Narratology*, edited by Greta Olson and based on a conference, which took place in Freiburg in 2007. The book, which is well placed in de Gruyter's Narratologia series, contains a substantial introduction by Monika Fludernik and Greta Olson, which outlines the conception of the volume against the backdrop of recent studies in the field. The authors of the introduction distinguish two "divergent tendencies in current narratological projects at large" (2): revisions of the models and concepts of 'classical' narratology on the one hand and attempts to open up new ways of doing narrative research by either applying the old categories to new objects or developing completely different models of narrativity, on the other hand.

Among the "current trends in narratology" referred to in the volume's title Fludernik and Olson have identified three major trends with "far-reaching implications for the future of narratology" (3). It is hardly surprising to find 'cognitive narratology' and 'transmedial/interdisciplinary narratology' in this group of three, since they are arguably at present the most visible areas of postclassical narrative research. In contrast, the third trend identified by Fludernik and Olson is a more unusual choice because it is as yet "without institutional foundation" (4): diachronic assessments of various local and national contributions to narratology. The volume's 13 chapters, which are conveniently preceded by abstracts, are grouped into three sections representing the three major trends identified in the introduction. The chapters within each section present quite dissimilar realizations of the respective narratological trends; the trends, therefore, come across as multifaceted rather than homogenous.

The first two chapters in the volume's section on "Narrative and the Mind" provide, for example, an elucidating illustration of how different disciplinary perspectives persist in interdisciplinary endeavours and demonstrate why they can complement each other precisely for this reason: While both Richard J. Gerrig and Uri Margolin look at the intersection of narratology and cognitive psychology, they do so from opposite vantage points. Gerrig, a cognitive psychologist, provides a "dual-process account of literary reading" (37) which distinguishes between conscious and unconscious processes in a reader's mind and suggests that narratologists who take such findings into account can gain a more precise understanding and description of the reading process. In the following chapter Uri Margolin puts this theory into practice by borrowing terms from cognitive psychology to use as "a toolkit or instrumentarium for narratological description and theorising" (76) in order to more accurately describe the literary representations of failures of perception. In the cognitive section, Monika Fludernik also provides a systematic description of *you*- and *we*-narratives, which illustrates "the flexibility of cognitive categories" (122). (For anyone interested in continuing the research on either of the two text types the typologies as well as the appended bibliographies of literary *you*- and *we*-narratives will be very helpful.)

The second part of the volume contains a detailed discussion of potential benefits and pitfalls of the transmedial expansion of narratology (Werner Wolf) as well as a linguistic study of narrative elements in early scientific writing (Irma Taavitsainen). The majority of the chapters in this part, though, is concerned with the application of narratological categories to literary genres other than narrative: Eva Müller-Zettelmann, for example, advocates the application of narratological concepts to the genre usually considered the least narrative one of all: lyric poetry. With regard to dramatic texts Ansgar Nünning and Roy Sommer distinguish between mimetic narrativity – "the representation or a temporal and/or causal sequence of events" (206) – and diegetic narrativity, which occurs whenever characters in a play function as narrators. While they focus on the latter by describing the forms and functions of dramatic storytelling in Shakespeare's plays, Brian Richardson's discussion of different types of dramatic endings presupposes a conception of narrativity that requires no narrator.

While the volume as a whole sets out to provide a synchronic survey of current trends in narratological research, its third part consists of diachronic surveys of specific narratological traditions, which are regarded by Fludernik and Olson as forming "the basis for a future comparative narratology" (5). Wilhelm Schernus looks at the codification of narratological knowledge in Germany. Eyal Segal outlines the specifics of the Tel Avivian school of narratology, which is characterized by a combination of rhetorical orientation and an interest in questions of function. Both Sylvie Patron and John Pier survey narratological research in France: Patron reconstructs and critically assesses a 'French speciality,' the linguistic tradition of enunciative narratology, and recommends a "double reorientation" (332) to redress theoretical shortcomings of both enunciative and structuralist narratology; John Pier argues that although, strictly speaking, narrative theory in France did not participate in the postclassical turn, there is still "a body of research within the Francophone sphere that can be qualified as postclassical narratology" (349).

All in all, *Current Trends in Narratology* considers such a wide range of approaches to the study of narrative that most readers will discover something of interest to them, while the volume as a whole can be recommended to anyone with a general interest in the field of narratology.

Wuppertal SANDRA HEINEN

Christoph Bode. *The Novel: An Introduction*. Translated by James Vigus. Chichester, West Sussex: Wiley-Blackwell, 2011. 287 pp.

Christoph Bode's *Der Roman: Eine Einführung* was first published in German in 2005 and was reviewed in this journal (among others) by Annegret Maack in March 2007. A second edition was prepared by Bode in 2009, and last year *The Novel: An Introduction* was published in English. This publishing history seems to speak for itself, and the reviews the study has received so far are unanimous in their praise. I shall attempt to suggest where I see the value of this English version, but first I want to speak about the achievement of the translator, James Vigus. Bode's study is not easy to translate, although it does not use an overly academic style and although his line of argument is clear in each instance and usually immediately convincing. However, Bode deals with complex theoretical issues, especially in identifying types of narrative situations, including multiperspectivity and the so-called "unreliable narrator," and he comments extensively on some difficult narrative theories, predominantly those of the Austrian literary critic Franz K. Stanzel and the French structuralist Gérard Genette. Translating Bode's text and additional texts by various theoretical thinkers and many novelists is a daunting challenge, and Vigus has met it superbly. He even captures, in admirable fashion, Bode's seemingly laid-back, tongue-in-cheek-style, which makes the book a pleasure to read, and he hardly ever needs to interrupt the flow of the text by adding a translator's note. Thus, although translated from the German, *The Novel* does not read like a translation – which is probably the highest compliment a reviewer can pay the translator of a book.

The most important thing that can be said about Bode's study is the fact that it not only attempts to describe and define the structural features of the European (and American) novel and the way they function as instruments to generate sense and meaning for the reader, but that Bode's own stylistic devices present a concrete example of the designing and processing of the content they convey. This becomes most obvious in the first ("Beginnings: *What Do You Expect*") and the last ("The End of the Novel and the Future of an Illusion") chapters of the book. Of course Bode has in mind the beginnings and the endings of individual novels, the importance of their entering and exit points – from "Call me Ishmael" (*Moby Dick*) to, say, the famous ending of James Joyce's *Ulysses*. He wants to demonstrate that the end and purpose of a narration must be developed consistently from the beginning and that it must be possible to see the ending as the fulfillment of that purpose. However, as even the titles of the first and last chapters indicate, "beginning" and "end" are also forms of metalanguage: each novel, as it is being read, becomes an allegory of a self-contained meaningful experience for the reader. Therefore, Bode's first chapter logically needs to include a discussion of the difference between reality and fiction (illuminated by a brilliant analysis of Wolfgang Hildesheimer's *Marbot: Eine Biographie,* for example), the difference between *histoire* and *discours*, and, finally, the meaning of the "I" in autobiography. "The End of the Novel" must, by the same token, also be a commentary on the discussion of the end of the novel as a genre, and it must, eventually, refute that fate, because the modern novel arose precisely in order "to make sense of epochal, new experiences, to thematize the experience of innovation and novelty" (261). And new experiences will of course continue to need framing.

The bulk of the book is taken up by an analysis and interpretation of Stanzel's Typological Circle and Genette's Narrative Theory. This presents a problem to my mind, because although the study's subtitle is *An Introduction*, and although especially graduate students can certainly profit from the study of the tradition and the function of the "narrator" in fiction, the present-day approach to literature seems to be a different one. We no longer seek to understand a novel as a communication model, comprising the triad of author, text, and reader, but – following the lead of poststructuralism and the New Historicism – we rather seek to find or adduce homologies between various aspects of literature and its cultural context. Nevertheless, that said, one can still read *The Novel: An Introduction* as an interesting narrative about the history of how novels have been read and understood, and Stanzel and Genette are clearly very perceptive readers of novels.

Bode's sympathies seem to lie with Stanzel's categorization of the various narrative stances we can observe in the novel from its beginnings (*Don Quixote de la Mancha*) to the present. Bode especially admires Stanzel's ability to read texts closely, and he appreciates that the Typological Circle can accommodate most narrative stances – at least until the advent of Postmodernism and metafiction. "Metafiction" seems to presuppose at least two narrative levels, the language on the "upper" level referring to, and reflecting upon, that on the "lower" one. (What the term "meta" might exactly mean in this context is discussed at length by Bode in chapter 7: "Who Speaks? – Voice"). Stanzel's Typological Circle cannot be applied in this case, because different narrative levels have no systematic place in his theory. Here, the application of Genette's structuralist theory seems called for, at least according to Bode, unless one would rather follow the lead of the philosopher and writer William H. Gass, who introduced the idea of metafiction into critical discourse in the first place. The term, as Gass uses it, is taken directly from logic: metalanguage, that is, language about language. In logic, when a word is *used* it is in language, when it is *mentioned* it is in metalanguage. Any fiction or any part of a fiction that is about fiction in a similar way is metafiction. It is fiction looking at itself. Thus, the way in which Gass uses the term "metafiction" does not call for any spatial association at all; rather it connotes simultaneity with a difference. Bode's discussion becomes very useful, however, when he criticizes Genette's take on narrative embedding. For Genette, an inset narrative is a "metadiegetic narrative," and a narrative embedded into that narrative is a "meta-metadiegetic narrative." Genette himself concedes that the prefix here is opposite to the way it functions in logic; for him, a metanarrative is one recounted within a narrative, that is, a framed narrative. Here, as Bode demonstrates, the identification of different narrative levels does indeed become extremely important, especially when one wants to explain the effect that occurs when a narrative does not keep its levels distinct from each other and instead intentionally blurs them.

Since *The Novel* is conceived as an introduction to the interpretation of novels and to narratology, Bode presents all the narratological instruments of the genre, and he also explains how the modern novel can only be understood from a historical perspective. Important chapters are devoted to the concepts of time, character, and space, and apart from discussing established literary theories, Bode presents many in-depth analyses of individual novels – which often astound and fascinate by their clarity and freshness of perspective. For instance, Bode treats Franz Kafka's *The Castle* as a prime example of a figural narrative situation, distinguished by the appearance of a reflector-character, as defined by Stanzel. Bode's close reading of the beginning of the novel reveals that this narrative situation is better suited than others for presenting circumstances which are as yet not transparent and which the reader needs to unravel within the fictive medium of a consciousness. In the case of Kafka's novel, this amounts to a highly claustrophobic reading experience that continuously points to the puzzle at the heart of the novel, K.'s unresolved relationship to the castle. Another case in point is Bode's interpretation of Ian McEwan's novel *Atonement,* in a chapter which he pointedly calls "The Novel as Atonement." Bode shows that the mixture of a "figural narrative situation with the perceptible, sometimes even obtrusive presence of an authorial narrator" (according to Stanzel), or the "variable internal focalization with a heterodiegetic narrator" (according to Genette) can both be illuminating. The main character of McEwan's novel, who also acts as an author, wants to maintain absolute control, and this is "a reason for the incompleteness of an act of atonement" (196). For the reader realizes – precisely by understanding this mixture of narrative stances – that we can only believe in something like true atonement as long as we subscribe to just one narrative version.

Within the realm of literary theory, Bode does present-day criticism a real service by moving us decisively beyond Wayne C. Booth's concern with the *reliable* or *unreliable* narrator as markers for an *implied author* who represents the system of values and norms in a text (*The Rhetoric of Fiction,* 1961). Bode manages to demonstrate conclusively that Booth's presupposition – that the author, as implied author, is always irreducibly present in the text – only serves his own fundamentalist conviction that all narrators are unreliable who do not share *his* value-judgments and normative system. For Bode, "unreliable narration is narration that triggers reasonable doubts and in which credibility gaps become apparent" (207). Judgment and expectation are pragmatic qualities of distrust arising in the reader, rather than purely textual ones. Thus, as the narrative situation in *Atonement* reveals, the reader is much better off without having to assume an implied author, from whom he cannot distance him- or herself.

In addition to an extensive list of "References" and an "Index of Authors and Critics," Bode also offers a useful list of "Further Reading" materials containing titles on narratology and literary criticism in general, as well as information on literary and cultural theory. Thus, Bode's *The Novel: An Introduction* is a highly readable, at times quite amusing, very learned and extremely well researched study of the most important literary genre of modern times.

Stuttgart   HEIDE ZIEGLER

Isabell Ludewig. *Lebenskunst in der Literatur. Zeitgenössische fiktionale Autobiographien und Dimensionen moderner Ethiken des guten Lebens*. **Mannheimer Beiträge zur Sprach- und Literaturwissenschaft 78. Tübingen: Narr, 2011. viii + 229 pp.**

How do we lead a good life? What is a life we can say 'Yes' to? How do we achieve happiness when traditional value systems no longer hold and we have to come up with our own criteria for it? These questions are being mulled over by an excess of popular self-help literature, but like many such phenomena, they do indicate a real need for adequate answers and serious engagement. In this light, Isabell Ludewig's published dissertation is a timely contribution to a highly topical debate, and it goes a long way towards restoring philosophical depth. Taking its cue from the ethical turn or turn to ethics in the humanities, it sets out to make a case for the power of contemporary literary texts, especially fictional autobiographies, in answering our questions about the good life.

The canonical texts of the ethical turn, by J. Hillis Miller, Wayne C. Booth, and Martha C. Nussbaum, now date back a good twenty years. Their work has been followed, as Ludewig points out, more by individual and collective article publications than by monographs. Ludewig criticizes Booth and others for their widely differing and sometimes vague notions of ethics, and for the differing degree to which they place the literary text at the centre of their analyses. But she argues for maintaining the general thrust of ethical criticism, and for a return of the meaning-making and ethically-engaged individual where theories of poststructuralism have tended to reduce the subject to an effect of discourse and the play of signs. To remedy the shortcomings of earlier scholarship, she proposes to adopt as a frame of reference a concrete ethical theory – Wilhelm Schmid's *Philosophie der Lebenskunst* (1998) – and to consider not selected but all aspects of the literary text – form, content, and reception.

This approach is applied to three fictional texts – John Braine's *Room at the Top* (1957), Margaret Atwood's *Lady Oracle* (1976), and Kazuo Ishiguro's *The Remains of the Day* (1989). These are looked at using various aspects of Schmid's thinking, and certainly they confirm the view that ethical issues have currency not only in philosophy and public debate but also in literature. 'Lebenkunst' no longer denotes a normative ethics, as in the Aristotelian sense of the good life; instead, it compellingly demonstrates the ongoing relevance of ethical concern today, now directed at the question of care for ourselves and others, of how we are able to develop a viable sense of self, and of how the choices we make influence our own lives and those of others. In what are very precise and careful, or indeed 'caring' readings themselves, Ludewig reconstructs closely how the protagonists in the three fictional autobiographies live up to these challenges. She certainly achieves her goal to cast a deeper and more understanding eye on the protagonists and their accounts, tracing their life stories in close dialogue with Schmid's ideas. At various points, she is able to correct or extend existing scholarship, by reading Joan Foster's fragmented self-narration in *Lady Oracle* not as a sign of failure, for example, but as a life-affirming act – as a testimony of the continuous challenge to narrate one's life and, if need be, to start anew.

If the study sets out to pay equal attention to aspects of form, content, and reception, it is the latter two aspects on which it seems to concentrate most. It convincingly stresses the value of fictional autobiographies in creating alternative models of the world, of the kinds of lives people live and the decisions they take. As a matter of its non-pragmatic discourse, literature is defined as a privileged medium of ethical reflection – both on the level of the text, where fictional characters retrospectively take stock of their lives, and on the level between text and reader, where we are given an opportunity to reflect not only on the characters' but ultimately on our own life stories as well. This degree of reflexivity, constituted between 'narrating I' and 'experiencing I' in the autobiographical account, and between text and reader in the reception process, is placed at the centre of the ethical implications of literature. It persuasively demonstrates the practical relevance of literature, and the return of a more 'human' element in literary theory.

Fictional autobiographies no doubt make for highly pertinent source material, with the protagonists probing very similar questions about a life worth living as practical philosophy. As for the examples discussed, readers interested in fictional autobiography as a genre might perhaps have wanted to know more about the selection criteria of the three texts, how representative they are or what the overall development of the genre has been. Of course, this is as much a study of contemporary fictional autobiography as of its potential to engage with a specific set of philosophical questions. Ludewig proceeds on the assumption that studies in literary ethics should be equally based in literary and in ethical criticism, and part of her purpose is to illustrate and render plausible Schmid's theory of 'Lebenskunst.' This is a well-written and cogently argued book, which will be fruitful for further discussion in the area of literature and ethics.

Heidelberg   JAN RUPP

Stephanie Waldow, ed. *Ethik im Gespräch. Autorinnen und Autoren über das Verhältnis von Literatur und Ethik heute.* **Bielefeld: transcript Verlag, 2011. 182 pp.**

Emblematic of the recent turn to ethics in the humanities, Stephanie Waldow's collection of interviews, short literary pieces and essays about ethics in writing and speaking lives up to the *double entendre* of its title: *Ethik im Gespräch* lays out both a series of conversations about ethics and an ethics of social interface per se. Questions in this context inquire, for instance, what contemporary authors aspire to achieve, how they address their audience, what forms they use in doing so, or which themes pertain to ethics and morals in culture and society.

Published in 2011 in the transcript "Lettre" series, the small volume *Ethik im Gespräch* offers a state of the art take on the issues of authorial articulation and reader response. The editor, who is assistant professor of contemporary German literature at the university of Erlangen-Nuremberg, assembles pieces by contemporary German-speaking authors that range across the whole literary realm, from the aspects of writing as self-articulation to the features of the contemporary German-speaking literary industry at large. Readers may perceive at first glance that the volume's thematic interest provides the scaffolding for its structure: Within the framing provided by the editor's introduction, a panoply of (literary) encounters enfolds, featuring interviews with authors as well as short literary pieces. In the introduction, the editor assesses ethics as a 'linguistic encounter with the Other' ("sprachliche Begegnung mit dem Anderen" (8)) and distinguishes two aspects of literary application, the textual/narrative and the authorial/professional. The contributions included oscillate between these categories. Markus Orths takes the cultural habit of critically evaluating each and every text as a starting point for his exploration of identity work: He argues that each 'I' needs a 'you,' refining the role of the reader as author (of the meaning she discovers in the written) and of the author as reader (of her own work). In two interviews, Matthias Politycki and Juli Zeh comment on recent developments in German literature, reiterating, respectively, the relationship between ethics and aesthetics in what has been dubbed the "Neue deutsche Lesbarkeit" ('new German readability' (35)), and the quest for a new authorial narrative stance.

Zeh talks about postures she assumes while writing ("Schreibhaltungen" (56)) and distinguishes between ethics as the feasible and morals as its theoretical equivalent (cf. 61). This interview also showcases what might be perceived as a minor shortcoming of the volume: The discussion between Zeh and the editor hinges on reformulations by the latter. While this strategy is clearly vital for discussing the issues raised in the introduction, the technique here makes more room for interpretations on the inteviewer's part than for explanations by the interviewee. A minuscule weakness in this generally intriguing exploration of the ethics of literary discourse, this phenomenon highlights the multiple facets of encounter on display. While form (as interview) follows content (as inquiry) in some contributions, the literary pieces are all the more remarkable for illustrating the opposite: In Ulrike Draesner's lyrical essay or Georg Klein's magic-realist autobiographical story, readers will discover the potential of form for (re)creating content. These two essays are especially notable for their subtle, yet metareflective dealings with the Other as one's authorial persona (Klein) or as cultural Other in place, space, and experience, all capsized by the (un)translatability of language (Draesner). Translation and intercultural identities are also at the core of the interviews with German-Hungarian writer Terezia Mora and Doron Rabinovici. The interview with the latter forms the middle part of a tryptich on memory, remembrance, and narrative on the Holocaust: Alois Hotschnig writes about the ethics of remembering from an Austrian perspective, Rabinovici comments on storytelling as the kernel of memory-making, and Eva Menasse uses her family's own reception of her family history novel *Vienna* (2005) to illustrate the need for stories to fill in the gaps where historiographic documentation fails. The essays by Christoph Peters about language's inherent energy and the abstract category of aesthetic power and Norbert Kron about possibilities of resistance towards commercialization as "Feudalkapitalismus" round off the scope of the volume. Especially Kron's self-proclaimed guide for reinventing the artist persona as callboy exemplifies the overall transgressive interest of the book in renegotiating the implications of the ethical turn.

Academic readers from various disciplines will find this book versatile for its play on the nature of conversational encounter; the agenda, as posited in the introduction, is to invite readers to position themselves in response to the reading, and this indeed may represent the collection's most aspiring achievement. This projected reader response is aided by a set of tools, such as the biographic information about contributors or the references provided at the end of the interviews. The latter bear witness to the volume's theoretical basis, among which Judith Butler's *Kritik der ethischen Gewalt* (2007), a collection of her Adorno Lectures that ties in with her earlier *Giving an Account of Oneself* (2005), figures prominently. Waldow also draws from Levinas' publications on the topic and from Foucault's epistemological criticism, but she equally groups late modernist writings by Walter Benjamin about the narrator alongside Barthes' eponymous postmodernist death-of-the-author postulate. These theorems present adjacent and sometimes conflicting views of authorship, writing, and reading. However, the volume's aesthetically infused interest in ethics and the literary neglects other branches of the ethical turn in postclassical narratology, rhetoric and reader response criticism, and narrative identity: These have explored the nexus between self-narration and remembrance (which touches upon the workings of creative writing), as well as the workings of recognition in identity formation (which encapsulates the concept of Otherness employed in all interviews). Hence, a reading from an English and American studies perspective allows for an additional, cross-disciplinary assessment of the response to the ethical turn in German language studies.

Ethik im Gespräch is an insightful addition to the multifaceted discussion around ethics and the literary that builds on a performative agenda for making its point: It not only blends various forms of literary encounter by utilizing interviews, essays, and prose; it also allows for a selective, and literally discursive, reading that allows readers to pause and think about their own reading preferences.

Jena STEFANIE SCHÄFER

Stefan Horlacher. *"Wann ist die Frau eine Frau?" "Wann ist der Mann ein Mann?" Konstruktionen von Geschlechtlichkeit von der Antike bis ins 21. Jahrhundert*. Würzburg: Königshausen & Neumann, 2010. 292 pp.

It surely is no exaggeration to declare *"Wann ist die Frau eine Frau?" "Wann ist der Mann ein Mann?" Konstruktionen von Geschlechtlichkeit von der Antike bis ins 21. Jahrhundert* an ambitious book. The volume brings together twelve articles that address – combined from various historical and disciplinary perspectives – the bold questions of "when is a woman a woman" and "when is a man a man." As Stefan Horlacher makes clear in his introduction the rationale behind the breadth of approaches, disciplines and examples gathered in this anthology is not to aim for completeness. Rather the diverse temporal and discursive angles are believed to arrive at a more accentuated and – despite the given spatial limitations – more representative engagement with gender constructions and deconstructions. The volume after all comprises articles ranging from gender attributions in ancient Rome, Elizabethan England as well as France in the Early Modern Period to the very recent canon revisions in musical history on the one hand – where for a long time women's contributions were overlooked or negated – and the supposedly current crisis of masculinity on the other. The referenced discourses through which gender constructions and their subversions are approached in the anthology comprise historical, literary, musical, psychological, sociological and philosophical concerns. The collected essays therefore amount to a diversified and insightful read and this review can by no means do justice to any of them.

The wide scope of this collection speaks of careful circumspection and the willingness to account for the subject's complexity. By means of its interdisciplinary and diachronic prisms the multitude of discourses and media that shape particular gender conceptions appears to be taken into account. But in the reviewer's opinion, while the breadth and multiperspectivity of the volume is remarkable and most essays individually bring relevant aspects and very particular insights to current gender debates it is the aspiring premise of *"Wann ist die Frau eine Frau?" "Wann ist der Mann ein Mann?"* on the whole that rather draws critical attention to its "elisions." The most striking one is that non-Western perspectives on the subject hardly figure. At most they are mentioned in passing despite a subtitle that reads: *Konstruktionen von Geschlechtlichkeit von der Antike bis ins 21. Jahrhundert* (gender constructions from antiquity to the 21st century). The general uneasiness with the book's incentives thus is evoked through an underlying assumption of its asserted representative value rendering the Western-/ Eurocentric view on gender and sexuality even more dubious.

In his introduction Horlacher argues that the aim of this assemblage of essays is to show that the unsettling and unsettledness of gender concepts is – historically speaking

– not a new, but rather an ongoing and culturally encompassing phenomenon. While the contributions for the most part indeed provide convincing "evidence" for this assumption, two questions are raised all the same, namely: who still *needs* to be convinced of the timelessness of cultural negotiations of sex and gender norms and the fragility of sexual difference in the first place? And why does Horlacher *nevertheless* think it necessary to provide a sequential, historical tracing of what he believes to be important historical periods and names leading up to the current prevailing ideas informing gender norms and their confusions? Despite Horlacher's articulated discomfort with notions such as "master narratives" and "objective knowledge," he nevertheless provides a framing for this volume that reiterates rather than challenges a forward-moving, author-oriented and Eurocentric approach. Whereas an overall leaning towards poststructuralist considerations is discernible and most essays in the anthology at least mention Judith Butler's gender troubling and Michel Foucault's thwarting of a steadily growing "liberalisation" of sexuality as influential points of reference, it is an overall adherence to binary, heteronormative gender/sexuality conceptions as well as a conception of history as "progressive" that at times runs counter to the volume's own theoretical framing.

There is an apparently felt need to defend the theoretical and socio-political grounds of "(New) Men's/Masculinity"- and/or "Women's Studies." But the book's extensive borrowing from more gender inclusive and thoroughly deconstructive ideas makes the argument in favour of a gender-distinctive approach rather more confusing than consistent. How is it possible and why is it necessary to (re)claim to "speak for/from" decidedly gendered perspectives and at the same time argue for arbitrary or at least uncertain signifying possibilities? The title of the volume already is indicative of this conceptual predicament since its covering of only two attributive possibilities seems to underwrite rather than undermine a dichotomous idea of sex and gender. Whereas possible multiplications and complications of gendered and sexual positionings are mentioned in Horlacher's own as well as in most other contributions assembled here, the question remains why such concerns are then relegated to seemingly marginal realms and do not become the common ground from which binary and heteronormative conceptions can and need to be challenged. It is the continued assertion of a non-essentialist approach, the admittance of the constructedness and mutability of gender identities and the concurrent insistence on apparently universal gender- (or would it, in this context, be more "accurate" to say sex-)specificities that render the proposition of the volume as a whole dubious. Queer theoretical interventions pervade the articles, but do not surface as more encompassing interrogations of dichotomous structures. Trans* perspectives are completely missing, adding to the void of non-European contributions and thereby lines are drawn which the otherwise asserted fluidity of gender positionings would make impossible.

As stated before the critique here is not targeted at individual articles, of which several come up with very nuanced and convincing findings. Particularly Elisabeth Tiller's "Zeitsprünge: Judith Butler und *gender performance* bei Michel de Montaigne und Ambrose Paré" and Kerstin Stüssel's "Erzählte Familien und familiäres Erzählen im 'bürgerlichen' Realismus" provide insightful and challenging analyses by tying up particular historical conditions and narratives with very recent concerns. The contribution of Annette Kreutziger-Herr and Gesa Finke, "Studies in Music History:

No/More Gender?," also deserves special mention as it demonstrates the asynchrony in different academic disciplines and points out the requirement of contextual analyses and methodologies within gender studies. After all, whereas the admittance of gender ambiguities and strategies of denaturalisation counter a reiterated and naturalised concept of sexual difference, an alleged gender-*blindness* historically has often contributed historically to secure "man's" authorial position.

Horlacher's basic aim with this volume does not become clear in this regard. To argue for steadily diversifying discourses rather than the newness of "gender trouble" surely is an argument that Foucault – among others – has brought to scholarly attention. Does the editor then argue in favour of maintaining gender-specific positions or does he want to blend in with queer/deconstructive stances, in which case some of his explanations in the book appear self-contradictory. His musings and survey sketches of the "state of affairs" exhibit competence and care but would gain much more force if they were not caught up in the concurrent effort to argue for gender-specific – sometimes even to be regarded as universal – "realities" and representations on the one hand and their deconstruction on the other, without providing plausible arguments for the necessity or benefits of such a stance. Despite such remaining questions regarding the plausibility of amalgamating distinctively gendered and poststructuralist approaches, the volume offers a variety of interesting perspectives on manifold narratives, times and places and therefore is recommended to and should find a wide readership.

Köln   Dirk Schulz

Friedrich Balke and Marc Rölli, eds. *Philosophie und Nicht-Philosophie: Gilles Deleuze – Aktuelle Diskussionen.* **Bielefeld: transcript Verlag, 2011. 338 pp.**

In his stimulating study *French Theory*, the French intellectual historian François Cusset seeks to elucidate what he calls the American invention of French theory.[1] As he makes clear, the recomposition of French theory in the U.S. led to the production of a new radical discourse on the basis of these French texts. As Cusset maintains, many of these French philosophers would not have recognized themselves in the new American arguments and positions. In the second part of his book, "The Uses of Theory," Cusset discusses the use of French theory for radical political purposes in the 1980s, trying to explain the crucial role French theory played for identity politics, gender studies, queer theory, cultural studies, and subaltern and postcolonial studies. The role of Gilles Deleuze in this context can hardly be overestimated. The Deleuzian notion of micropolitics, or molecular politics, was enthusiastically received inside and outside of academia. However, reactions to Deleuze's thinking have always been highly idiosyncratic. While some contend that he is nothing but an overrated poseur, others think that he is not only the most important 20th-century philosopher of immanence and becoming who urges one to appreciate philosophy as a creative activity, but that it is moreover impossible to fully grasp the significance and complexity of the

---

1   Cusset, Francois. *French Theory: How Foucault, Derrida, Deleuze, & Co. Transformed the Intellectual Life of the United States*. Minneapolis: University of Minnesota Press, 2008.

tradition of French anti-Hegelianism, as Nietzscheanism, without considering the multilayered work of Deleuze.

The volume edited by Friedrich Balke und Marc Rölli seeks to offer a new perspective on Delueze's œuvre. While Balke already discussed the relation between philosophy and non-philosophy in his *Gilles Deuleuze zur Einführung*,[2] this collection analyzes the significance of non-philosophy from a variety of angles. The book is divided into an introduction and four parts. In the introduction the editors comment on the idea of non-philosophy as follows:

> Mit dem Begriff der Nicht-Philosophie wird signalisiert, dass sich die Philosophie nicht selbst genügen kann. Vielmehr wird sie genötigt, diese ihre Nichtselbstgenügsamkeit zu reflektieren und sich auf diesem Weg zu transformieren. (7)

Later they summarize the goal of this collection thus:

> Die Beiträge des vorliegenden Bandes praktizieren auf jeweils eigene Weise dieses Denken, das sich der Kontingenz der Begegnung mit einem Nicht-Philosophischen verdankt, das "vielleicht tiefer im Zentrum der Philosophie als die Philosophie selbst" ist. Dabei machen sich einige von ihnen die Einsicht zunutze, dass auch das Denken Deleuzes bestimmten Zwängen und Begrenzungen unterliegt, die dem philosophischen Diskurs entstammen oder eine bestimmte inzwischen historisch werdende Konfiguration reflektieren, die es nötig erscheinen lässt, die "dunkle Zone" dieses Denkens weiter zu entfalten, statt es lediglich in gelehrten Kommentaren zu bekräftigen oder zu widerlegen. (19)

Part 1, "Philosophische Interventionen," consists of three articles: Marc Rölli, "Gilles Deleuze – Philosoph der Immanenz;" Maria Muhle, "Zweierlei Vitalismus: Überschreitung – Normativität - Differenz;" and Stéphane Nadaud, "Deleuzianischer Nietzsche und nietzscheanischer Deleuze." The second part, "Kino nach Deleuze," consists of the following pieces: Oliver Fahle, "Der Film der zweiten Moderne oder Filmtheorie nach Deleuze;" Hanjo Berressem, "Was ist Philosophie? Gilles Deleuze, Was ist Kino? Werner Herzog;" Friedrich Balke, "In der Abwesenheit des Menschen: Über Lager, Landschaften und Geister in Philip Scheffners Halfmoon Files." The third part, "Übersetzung, Wiederholung, Verkettung," begins with a conversation between Antonia von Schöning and Hanns Zischler concerning their work on the Abécédaire, and continues with articles by Kurt Röttgers ("Es wiederholt sich") and Mirjam Schaub ("Das Wörtchen 'und:' Zur Entdeckung der Konjunktion als philosophische Methode"). Part 4, "Aspekte der Nicht-Philosophie," consists of the following four pieces: Ralf Krause, "Menschen – Körper – Sensationen: Deleuze zur Malerei von Francis Bacon;" Clemens Pornschlegel, "'Notre frère à tous:' Zur Insistenz der Figur Christi bei Deleuze;" Sjoerd van Tuinen, "Leibniz und die Psychophysik des Gehirns;" and Alexander Kluge/Joseph Vogl, "Was heißt Denken nach dem Ende des Durchblicks?: Zum Tod von Gilles Deleuze."

The articles collected in *Philosophie und Nicht-Philosophie* are for the most part illuminating, elegantly argued, and theoretically sophisticated. While some of them lack a critical edge, the majority offer new and challenging perspectives on this French philosopher. However, for Americanists and English studies scholars this

---

2   Balke, Friedrich. *Gilles Deleuze zur Einführung*. Frankfurt: Campus, 1998.

volume might be useful only to a certain degree since what they consider the most virulent questions regarding Deleuze's work are only mentioned *en passant*. I wish to call attention to three of those questions. The first concerns the role of *Anti-Oedipus* and above all *A Thousand Plateaus* for Hardt and Negri's *Empire*, *Multitude*, and *Commonwealth*. Undoubtedly, there have been numerous texts dealing with this relationship, yet this volume almost completely ignores it (only Muhle at least mentions Hardt and Negri). Second, the role Deleuze and Guattari's notion of minor literature can play for postcolonial literature and postcolonial studies is not discussed in this volume. Finally, and this is probably the most important point, Balke and Rölli's volume also refrains from discussing the relationship between Deleuze's transcendental empiricism and American pragmatism. Particularly in a volume dealing with nonphilosophy this omission is deplorable. Rölli makes a few interesting remarks about William James, but does not offer an in-depth analysis. As far as I can see, a detailed discussion of the relationship between Deleuze and pragmatism is still a desideratum.[3] In what way does Deleuze's philosophy of immanence, praxis, and multiplicity, his quasi-Emersonian aversion to stasis, as well as his radical antifoundationalism, antiessentialism, and antirepresentationalism, help us in the attempt to appreciate the contemporary significance of pragmatism? Furthermore, it is not only tempting to regard Deleuze as a Rortyan strong poet, but one should also see that both thinkers strove to make the idea of a genuinely postmetaphysical culture look attractive.

Eichstätt-Ingolstadt   ULF SCHULENBERG

Maria Eisenmann, Nancy Grimm, and Laurenz Volkmann, eds. *Teaching the New English Cultures and Literatures*. Heidelberg: Universitätsverlag Winter, 2010. 235 pp.

This volume contains 14 original contributions, all but one of which are written by EFL-teaching scholars established at English departments at German universities. On the surface, this seems hardly surprising given the subject matter of a publication that specifically targets traditional learning aims in EFL teaching at German secondary education institutions. Its explicit objective is the desire to expand the field of research (TEFL = Teaching English as a Foreign Language) by transcending the Eurocentric focus, e.g. the privileging of topics from British and North American studies, in order to challenge conventional parameters of curricula formation.

Divided into two parts, the volume presents case studies each of which focusses on areas of cultural and literary production that are recognized as having previously been excluded from the canon. Part I opens with Sabine Doff's article "Beyond Beavers and Bilingualism" (title abbreviated) in which she convincingly argues how Canada's linguistic and cultural diversity might enhance "teaching (about) English language, Anglophone literatures and cultures" (3). Her teaching suggestions incorporate guiding questions towards a critical reading of two literary texts, one an indigenous folktale, the other a short story by the Chinese-Canadian writer Garry Engkent.

---

3 For an exception, see Paul Patton, *Deleuzian Concepts: Philosophy, Colonization, Politics*. Palo Alto: Stanford University Press, 2010.

Taken together, the two narratives successfully encompass historical (e.g. the life and culture(s) of Canada's indigenous populations and the waves of migration to Canada) as well as contemporary perspectives (e.g. revisiting present-day debates on the status of multiculturalism). To some extent, Nancy Grimm's article takes a similar stance, seeking to overcome the cultural stereotyping and reductive preconceptions that are prominent in existing EFL-teaching materials on Australia and New Zealand. She adds an intertextual/intermedial approach to her selected teaching suggestions (songs/visual images/sports) and concludes each segment with a close reading of two feature films, both of which deal with the legacies of colonial settlement as experienced by the respective indigenous populations. Moving on to contemporary South Africa, Gisela Feurle introduces a course that aims to explore the (self-) representations of young people in a selection of South African literary texts, including "nonfictional texts and other media, such as photos, films, cartoons and music" (45). Although Feurle's intention to utilize the positive effects of the close proximity in age (producers and recipients) appears plausible, depoliticizing historical events by excluding the legacies of colonialism and apartheid as a system of racial segregation in contemporary South Africa misses the systemic nature of oppression. Oliver Lindner's innovative two-fold approach to intercultural learning in the classroom (Bollywood cinema and strategies of India's self-fashioning via the Internet), Michael Mitchell's fascinating outline of how to raise students' intercultural awareness through teaching primarily but not exclusively the English-speaking Caribbean and Rüdiger Ahrens' examination of specific linguistic features of the English language and the current status of English in all its complexities in South-East Asia and the South Pacific conclude the chapter "New English Cultures."

The eight contributions of chapter 2, "New English Literatures," by Albert Rau, Maria Eisenmann, Albert-Rainer Glaap, Nancy Grimm, Laurenz Volkmann, Mechthild Hesse, Göran Nieragden and Peter Freese, skillfully arranged to correspond with the various regions discussed in chapter 1, give a more detailed account of how literary/visual texts from an astonishingly wide range of the English-speaking world can be experienced rather than learned in the EFL classroom. Such inter- and transcultural encounters, combined with a growing awareness of the commonalities of the human experience, will perhaps in time diminish the importance of difference, and nurture mutual respect for the "Other" – so often referred to but so rarely critically commented on. More than any other subject-related discipline, TEFL contributes uniquely to the process of shaping the consciousness of young people from various ethnic and cultural backgrounds living in Germany. Thus its obligation goes beyond the more general educational purposes towards what Chambers and Gregory term the development of "civic responsibility and [...] moral and ethical thoughtfulness."[1] The academic reader of this publication as learner and teacher is therefore presented with a commendable endeavor combining the rapidly changing debates on transculturality, transnationality as well as the ever increasing objections to viewing the global community as postcolonial with the challenges of teacher training methodology and schoolteachers' daily teaching practices. In 2010, the editors claimed this collection of

---

1   Chambers, Ellis and Marshall Gregory. *Teaching and Learning English Literature*. London: Sage, 2006. 2.

articles was "the first publication in Germany of a full-volume book on teaching the so-called New English Literatures and Cultures" (vii), a statement partially eclipsed by the publication of various essays under the heading of "Focus on Teaching English" in the preceding issue of the present journal. In addition to the evident vibrancy of TEFL, the adjective "new" signifies here an increasing awareness of the necessity to incorporate those cultural expressions that are by no means "new," but rather ought to be made visible and heard. By doing so, it also reflects the current tendencies to restructure higher education course programs in English departments in Germany to accommodate the shifting nature of the discipline. Each entry of this volume is accompanied by a well-considered selection of electronic resources for either independent or guided study. The collection should prove a very useful and practical supplement for teacher trainees in Germany.

Bremen   JANA NITTEL

Peter Fenn. *A Student's Advanced Grammar of English.* **Tübingen: A. Francke Verlag, 2010. 581 pp.**

This Grammar of Modern English is designed to provide a comprehensive but concise treatment of the use of grammatical forms and their functions in Modern English. It is also a contrastive pedagogical grammar that aims at helping readers improve their skills in the use of English and avoid making common mistakes. As such, it has been particularly written for German students of English. Despite its pedagogical character it is not to be considered a prescriptive grammar since it tries to present British English as it is used with reference to various stylistic levels and communicative situations. The book does not assume any detailed prior knowledge of English linguistics to understand the descriptions. For that reason the author gives a very eloquent account of basic linguistic terms and concepts at the beginning of the book.

The book contains 14 chapters: 1. Introduction, 2. Nouns, 3. Pronouns, Determiners and Quantifiers, 4. Adjectives, 5. Adverbs, 6. Prepositions, 7. Conjunctions, 8. Verbs: Basic Features, Syntax and Forms, 9. Verbs: The Present and the Past Tenses, 10. Verbs: The Perfect Tenses, 11. Verbs: Future and Conditional Meaning, Indirect Speech, the Passive, 12. Verbs: Modal Verbs, 13. Verbs: Non-finite Verbs, 14. Phrase and Clause at Complex Level.

In the first section (1-26), Peter Fenn provides a short introduction to the concept of grammar, gives an overview of the history of English and its major types of variation, presents the various fields of language study, and briefly describes the basic grammatical categories in terms of form, function and use. Everything is well illustrated with clear examples.

The second chapter (27-72) begins by discussing the main grammatical and semantic features of nouns, then deals with plural formation (including spelling and pronunciation rules) and discusses details of use related to countability issues in a very systematic manner. His classification of nouns in that respect is especially interesting and very convincing. Two further parts of the chapter are concerned with the genitive case and with aspects of word formation. Although the author's theoretical approach to the grammatical categories and constructions is one of the great strengths of the book, there are, nevertheless, some minor points that I cannot agree with, such as his concept of the "double-head" in compounds (63). Furthermore, it is not clear why 'blendings' are listed under "Old Words – New Meaning," and 'acronyms' under "New Words – New Meanings."

Chapter 3 (73-140) looks at the main grammatical and semantic features of pronouns, determiners and quantifiers, also providing a distinction between their individual subtypes. Although it should be appreciated that the author tries to create a suitable communicative situation to explain deictic relations with regard to personal pronouns, the descriptions themselves seem quite confusing to me. Most other explanations in the book, however, are presented in a very clear and well-arranged way. Particularly helpful are references to and exemplifications of special regional or formal vs. informal uses. An interesting concept, which absolutely makes sense, is that of the 'pronoun *s*-genitive' (78).

The fourth chapter (141-187) refers to the position and function of adjectives, including their use as pre- and post-modifiers, identifies the most important semantic subtypes of adjectives (quantity, sequence, intensifiers, degree, etc.), describes adjective phrases functioning as clauses, addresses issues on word formation (typical prefixes, suffixes) and deals with comparison of adjectives. As in every chapter, the author gives a good systematic summary at the end, recollecting the most important key issues.

In chapter 5 (188-220), Peter Fenn first explains the difference between adjectives and adverbs before, as in the section on adjectives, discussing different kinds of adverbs (adverbs of time, frequency, etc.). It should be appreciated that he also includes in his set of adverbs such types as adverbs of focus, connective adverbs, or adverbs of comment, and that the distinction between form and function, i.e. between adverb and adverbial, is made very clear for the reader.

Chapter 6 (221-245) includes information on prepositions and prepositional phrases, as well as on individual prepositions and their usage, often in contrast to their German equivalents. The author does not only show the difference between particles and prepositions, but he also lists various idioms and figurative phrases with individual prepositions. Chapter 7 (247-272) is similarly structured. It begins with a distinction between prepositions and conjunctions and continues with a minute description of the use of individual English conjunctions, referring to stylistic features as well as to German equivalents and contrasts.

The following six chapters on the verb begin with a section on basic features, syntax and forms (273-310). Verbs are characterized as central units of sentences, expressing the predication. The description of the forms of verbs is a bit confusing to me since it comprises word formation patterns as well as the formation of grammatical variants of a word or a construction, such as non-finite forms, progressive constructions, as well as passive and perfect constructions.

In chapter 9 (311-339) present and past are treated as primary tenses in contrast to the secondary tenses in chapter 10 (340-370). The theoretical background to this distinction, taking into account the different points of orientation and the action point itself, is absolutely convincing. Both primary and secondary tenses are discussed with respect to simple and progressive aspect in a very clear and comprehensive way. Schematic visualisations help to give the reader a very clear picture. Explanations of the uses include important references to information structure and communicative situations.

In contrast to the straightforward contents of chapters 9 and 10, chapter 11 (371-429) is quite heterogeneous, since it comprises information about future tense, conditional clauses, reported speech, and passive voice. Nevertheless, future meaning is systematically related to all possible formal expressions. Conditional clauses are presented in very much detail with regard to different subtypes and variants. The concept of indirect speech is explained with the help of clear usage examples. Even in interrogative sentences with embedded reported speech, the syntactic and semantic relations can be easily understood by the reader due to suitable examples and graphic explanation. And finally the passive voice is described with respect to information structure and syntactic properties. The latter include even the passive formation of non-finite verbs and catenatives.

In the next chapter (431-458), the author discusses the modal verbs from an onomasiological point of view, thus starting from the respective types of modality (ability/capability, speculation, permission, directives, other modal usage) with their subcategories, and describing their linguistic expressions. Also included are, of course, issues of negation as well as pragmatic metaphors and aspects of politeness. Common errors made by German learners of English are exemplified and theoretically explained.

The final chapter on the verb (459-531) is devoted to non-finite forms. Infinitive and participle constructions, as well as the gerund are presented with regard to the tense and aspect forms they can express. The author provides a very detailed outline of possible structures: the distinction between *to-* and bare infinitival complements; catenative + object + infinitive; adjective + infinitive, etc. The use of non-finite verb constructions in subject position is discussed in contrast to alternative constructions with extraposition. Summaries and overviews in the form of tables help the reader to focus on the main points. What should be particularly emphasized is the fact that Fenn's grammar, in contrast to many other English grammars, draws a clear distinction between gerund and present participle with regard to their meaning and function.

Finally, chapter 14 (532-581) presents a thorough description of complex phrases and clauses. Fenn defines complex phrases as those that contain clauses. This section includes the formation and the use of restrictive and non-restrictive relative clauses, preposition stranding ('discontinuous prepositional phrases'), appositions, etc. Unfortunately, syntactic relations are not represented in the form of tree diagrams, but rather in flat structures. The use of slants and brackets needs getting used to.

To conclude, this book is a valuable addition to the many grammars of English already existing. It can be highly recommended especially for advanced German learners of English as well as for German university and school teachers of English. It is most obvious that the author has a lifetime of experience in teaching English language and linguistics in German higher education. Throughout the whole book the author highlights major contrasts between English and German usage and makes the reader aware of possible sources of error. Rules and explanations are always clear and supported by examples. If there are alternative options available, preferences are suggested with regard to contextual or situational factors. Important key concepts or terms are visually highlighted. What may be criticized, however, is the lack of an index, which would have made it much easier to look up specific items.

Potsdam   ILSE WISCHER

Jörg-U. Keßler and Anja Plesser. *Teaching Grammar*. Paderborn: Schöningh/ UTB, 2011. 271 pp.

Although most of the work in foreign language research and teaching methodology, over the past three to four decades, has drawn a very disadvantageous picture of grammar teaching and its impact on learners' developing linguistic proficiency, practicing teachers, for various reasons, have never stopped believing in the positive functions of teaching grammar. In most of the more recent state curricula for English in Germany, perhaps as a result of foreign language research, the role of grammar has now officially been reduced to fulfilling an auxiliary function in language teaching, which means, amongst other things, that grammatical knowledge and competence are not dealt with in exams any more. At first sight, a new book on teaching grammar may thus come as a surprise. However, the book under review does not propagate a return to 'traditional' grammar teaching since it is explicitly stated that neither grammatical categories and functions nor rules about how sentences can be constructed are focused on. Hence, it is not the contents and mediation of grammar that the authors are interested in; their aim is rather to "propose new attitudes and approaches to the actual teaching of grammar in the EFL classroom," and this is attempted by basically giving "an introduction to an SLA-based approach to grammar teaching based on major empirical findings in international studies" (11).

After the introduction (chapter 1), the book consists of four parts: I. Background, II. Second Language Acquisition Research and Grammar Teaching, III. Grammar Teaching in the EFL Classroom, IV. Service Section. Part I provides some relevant background information relating to definitions of grammar, Standard English and different types of grammar such as prescriptive, descriptive and pedagogical as well as the interlanguage approach, which is central to the concept of grammar and grammar teaching in this book. In addition, this part provides a useful account of the historically dominant language teaching methods, covering such topics as grammar translation method, direct method and audio-lingual method, as well as the communicative approach. Most of what the authors have to say is straightforward. However, their position on the teaching of Standard English and on prescriptive grammar seems ambivalent. On the one hand, they claim that prescriptivism "degrades dialectal variation" (39), and they criticize textbooks for being prescriptive and for not taking into account that there are various versions of Standard English (33). On the other hand, quite rightly, they point out the merits of prescriptive grammars which "provide L2 learners with a guideline to speak and write homogeneously in that they can modify their output toward a narrower range of the standard version of the target language, e.g. American English and British English" (39). Undoubtedly, there is a place for prescriptivism in language teaching because it is an indisputable and effective means to cope with the complexity and heterogeneity of a language in a pedagogical context.

Part II, which brings together SLA research and grammar teaching, constitutes the central part of the book. It expounds the concepts of interlanguage, teachability and processability from a psycholinguistic and an applied classroom perspective. The terms teachability and processability are very much related to the work of Pienemann,[1] who can be seen as the progenitor of the book at hand. In line with the concept

---

1 Cf. for example, Manfred Pienemann. *Language Processing and Second Language Development: Processabilty Theory*. Amsterdam and Philadelphia: John Benjamins, 1998.

of interlanguage, the idea of grammar and grammar teaching advocated is that a learner's grammar "develops gradually from an initial state towards the target language variety – ideally" and that "the learner's interlanguage follows a universal development path every learner of any second language goes through" (75). From this, it is concluded that "factors such as attitude, aptitude or any other external factors in SLA are, at best, secondary" (75), a corollary which is very much in contrast to a (more) social and sociologically inspired approach to (foreign) language teaching and learning. In processability theory, six stages in a learner's acquisition of their morphological and syntactic target language structures are distinguished. These stages are assumed to be acquired successively and in a particular order (cf. table 3: Processability hierarchy for English, 86-87). Following the teachability theory, it is not possible to skip a stage or alter its sequence by instruction. Learners have to be "developmentally ready" (155) in order to acquire a specific grammatical structure. The following two sentences, both uttered by a stage 3 EFL learner, are used to illustrate this point: (1) Peter go home, (2) He Tarzan (112). Since the acquisition of the "3rd Sg. -s" only takes place in stage 5, grammar teaching in the form of corrective feedback would be futile in this case, because the learner is not "ready" for its acquisition yet. For sentence (2), it is argued that "the underlying structure to be processed by the learner is SVO" (112), which is acquired in stage 2. Thus, the learner is able to process the SVO structure in sentence (2). In principle, this line of argumentation is plausible. Furthermore, it is pointed out that grammar instruction can be helpful if it focuses on a structure from the next stage, and thereby paves the way for 'smoother' acquisition. However, to postulate an SVO structure for sentence (2) is counterintuitive because the omitted verb is most likely not a full verb, but a copula ("He Tarzan, me Jane").

In Part III, the authors' concept of grammar teaching is applied to more recent developments in foreign language teaching such as focus on form, task-based learning, immersion programmes and grammar teaching, course books as well as the diagnosis of learner progress. Part IV consists of a glossary of useful terms and a comprehensive bibliography, which fails to list two titles by Piepho (1974; 2001), which are mentioned in the context of communicative language teaching (58), and by Larsen-Freeman (2003), referred to on p. 23.

The authors have succeeded in consistently applying the concept of processability in SLA to classroom application. They have also presented a technical, yet comprehensible introduction to some of the basic tenets and research results of SLA. The content progression and the didactic format of the book, in particular the insertion of study questions, recommendations for further reading after each chapter and the inclusion of a glossary recommend it for use in seminars and for self-study. Even critics of a psycholinguistically biased approach to SLA will admit that second and foreign language teaching have benefited from it. However, Lightbown's criticism that the teachability hypothesis only deals with a "tiny fraction" (105) of what goes on in the classroom (and outside) cannot be dismissed "empirically by studies" alone (15f.), but should be taken seriously because there is never a theory that can account for the total complexity of a phenomenon, and this also applies to foreign language teaching and learning.

Braunschweig   CLAUS GNUTZMANN

Holger Schmitt. *Phonetic Transcription: From First Steps to Ear Transcription.* Berlin: Erich Schmidt Verlag, 2011, 183 pp.

This volume offers a detailed account of phonetic transcription from a linguistic point of view, more than 80 exercises relating to different levels of difficulty including solutions, practical tips with respect to common difficulties as well as links to online solutions and websites from which computer tools such as phonetic fonts and applications (IPA sounds) can be downloaded. It is thus much more than just a practical guide to transcription, as the title might suggest.

The book is divided into four parts: the foundations of transcriptions and the three independent, self-contained practical sections on "basic transcription," "advanced transcription" and "transcribing actual speech." Furthermore the book is supplemented with lists of abbreviations and notation conventions, exercises, IPA symbols, the standard lexical set introduced by Wells (1982)[1] and a survey of pronouncing dictionaries.

The section on "Does transcription matter?" is a very strong, detailed and well-structured claim on why not only students of linguistics but also EFL teachers and students should learn to transcribe, as "[y]ou cannot afford to (or at least should not) teach English in a school setting [...] using words whose pronunciation you are not sure of" (19), and thus one has to be able to look up the pronunciation of words in a dictionary. Secondly, transcribing helps the development of an awareness of the pronunciation of English and an understanding of one's own pronunciation and thirdly, for many linguistic disciplines such as phonetics and phonology, morphology, language acquisition, clinical and forensic linguistics, sociolinguistics, varieties of English, etc. "transcription is not a luxury but an essential tool" (20). This section should be compulsory reading for all those authorities who would like to abolish phonetics and phonology as part of the undergraduate curriculum. The following sections on "Transcription outside linguistics," "Spelling vs. sound" and especially "What is phonetic transcription" are valuable contributions, written in such a way that they can be understood by lay persons and undergraduates without prior knowledge of phonetics and phonology. They supplement the statements made in the first section. The sections on "The International Phonetic Alphabet" provides some useful internet links to downloadable IPA fonts and sound files. "Choosing a pronunciation dictionary" might not be very relevant to undergraduate students but offers some help to lecturers in reaching a decision on what dictionary or what transcription system to apply in their courses. The same is probably true for the outline of the two reference accents, Received Pronunciation (RP) and General American (GA), which are both covered in the practical sections.

Each of the three following sections consists of a background part and a practice part. Section A, "Basic transcription," explains the phonemic principle, the "major principle in transcription" (35), starting by introducing Wells' (1982) Standard Lexical Set, supplemented with the [i] sound as in happY and the [u] sound as in inflUence. The table given on page 38 is so important that it should have been entered in an appendix or together with the other lists. As this set only covers the vowel sounds, a reference

---

[1] Wells, John. *Accents of English.* Cambridge: Cambridge University Press, 1982.

to Pullum and Ladusaw's (1986) *Phonetic Symbol Guide*[2] would have been useful. In the subsection on "The choice of symbols" Schmitt in a linguistically sound way justifies his decisions on which symbols he uses. However, the text is beyond any student who is untrained in phonetics and phonology. Although Schmitt's decisions are understandable, I would have preferred him to have stuck to one of the three major pronouncing dictionaries and referred to the differences given on page 29. I know from experience that the slightest deviation from the dictionary they use confuses the students.

The best and most useful part is "Some practical advice," which covers all major difficulties students have when starting to learn how to transcribe phonemically. I trust that if they follow the points mentioned, they will make rapid progress. The 37 exercises given in the practice section gradually lead the students from the transcription of single vowel phonemes to the phonemic transcription of words, including homophones and homographs. Apart from the exercises themselves, there is a characterisation in phonetic terms, typical graphemic representations as well as less common spellings for every symbol. Additionally, detailed explanations are given for the transcription of inflectional affixes (-s and -ed) and the dental fricatives, which are very useful, especially for German speakers.

Section B, "Advanced Transcription," deals with the broad phonetic transcription of sentences and texts. The difference between the three types of transcription is explained in great detail in the background part. However, the text presupposes advanced knowledge in phonetics and phonology and might not be easily accessible to students. The sections on "transcription conventions and transcription tolerance" as well as the one on weak forms, including the table given on pages 85-88, on the other hand, are very useful, even for beginners. The following 35 exercises again lead the student from simple sentences to more difficult texts, always commenting on the problems that might be encountered.

Section C, "Transcribing actual speech," mainly deals with ear transcription, i.e. transcribing actual speech, and is meant for very advanced students. The background section explains how relevant phonetic knowledge is for ear transcription, what factors influence auditory perception and how to analyse unfamiliar sounds or unknown languages and how to interpret data. It provides a rough overview of different areas of phonetics and phonology and their relevance for transcription, but the respective knowledge has to be acquired elsewhere. The 12 exercises in this section are mostly based on actual speech samples which are downloadable from the web. If a student is able to do these exercises, s/he will be very advanced in using and applying transcriptions on all levels and for different purposes.

This volume is not meant as a text book for a course in transcription but, as the author states, it "is meant to be a companion throughout your life as an undergraduate or even graduate student" (15). It might be relevant at different stages and in different settings, and thus I think that it belongs on the reference shelf of anyone involved in linguistics.

Zürich JÜRG STRÄSSLER

---

[2] Pullum, Geoffrey K. and William A. Ladusaw. *Phonetic Symbol Guide*. Chicago: University of Chicago Press, 1986.

Anne Schröder. *On the Productivity of Verbal Prefixation in English. Synchronic and Diachronic Perspectives*. Tübingen: Narr Verlag, 2011, 375 pp.

The monograph under review, which is based on the author's *Habilitationsschrift*, defended at the University of Halle-Wittenberg in 2008, deals with the diachronic history and present-day status of verbal prefixation in English. The central question raised by the author is whether the derivation of verbs by means of the prefixes *down-, up-, under-, over-, on-, off-, out-, in-* (e.g., *to downcast, to upgrow, to underact, to overcome, to onsell, to offload, to outreach, to inbreathe*), which used to be a fairly productive verb-forming pattern in Old and Middle English, has become unproductive in present-day English.

Having formulated this and other related research questions in a brief introduction (25-28), the author proceeds to a discussion of the notion of morphological productivity in chapter 2. This chapter, which comprises pages 29 to 61, dwells on the following issues: Is productivity a matter of the language system or the language use? Is it necessary to distinguish between rule-governed productivity and analogy and creativity? What are the limitations of morphological productivity? How can productivity be measured and quantified? As far as the last question is concerned, the author argues for "a multi-method approach […], which combines the various approaches to productivity measurement" (60). These include dictionary- and corpus-based measures of productivity as well as elicitation tests.

Before presenting the results of her investigation, the author contrasts prefix verbs (*to upbear, to down-lie*) with particle verbs (*to bear up, to lie down*), which can be seen as products of a rival verb-forming pattern. Chapter 3 elaborates on structural, diachronic, stylistic, morpho-syntactic, semantic, cognitive, and pragmatic differences between the two constructions. For example, the prefix verb construction is a synthetic means of verb formation, whereas the particle verb construction is an analytic means of verb formation; the analytic particle verb construction is believed to have weakened the synthetic prefix verb construction from the Middle English period onwards; prefix verbs are more typical of formal registers and written language, while particle verbs are more typical of informal registers and spoken language; etc. A good summary of similarities and differences between prefix verbs and particle verbs is provided in table 2 on p. 96.

The core of Anne Schröder's study is represented by chapters 4, 5, and 6. Chapters 4 and 5 are concerned with actual words that came into existence via verbal prefixation by means of *down-, up-, under-, over-, on-, off-, out-, in-*. In these two chapters the author attempts to measure the productivity of the word-formation pattern under investigation by counting the number of verbs containing the aforementioned prefixes. In chapter 4 the author presents a dictionary-based account of the productivity of verbal prefixation. The dictionary consulted by the author is, not surprisingly, the Oxford English Dictionary (to be more precise, the OED on CD-ROM). The central finding is that with the exception of *down-*, all prefixes have been productive since the Old English period (143). In addition, it appears that the prefix verb construction was not weakened by the particle verb construction during the Middle English period. On the contrary, the productivity of the eight prefixes under study increased during the Late Middle English and Early Modern English periods (143).

Chapter 5 presents a corpus-based account of the productivity of verbal prefixation. Section 5.2.2 discusses the type and token frequencies of the eight prefixes under analysis in the British National Corpus. With regard to type frequency, the most productive prefix is *over-*, while the least productive prefixes are *on-* and *off-* (151). With regard to token frequency, the most productive prefix is *in-*, while the least productive are *down-* and *on-* (152). In addition to counting the overall BNC frequencies of forms containing the prefixes under study, the productivity of an affix can also be established by counting the number of hapax legomena containing that affix. With regard to this productivity measurement, the most productive prefix is *over-*, while the least productive is *off-* (156). Section 5.3 compares the BNC frequencies of prefix verbs beginning with *over-* and *under-* and particle verbs ending in *over* and *under*. While the particle *over* is more productive than the prefix *over-*, the particle *under* is less productive than the prefix *under-* (192). Section 5.4 compares the frequencies of prefix verbs beginning with *over-* and *under-* and particle verbs ending in *over* and *under* in the BNC and the Lampeter Corpus of Early Modern English Tracts. On the basis of data from these two corpora, the author again argues that the analytic particle verb construction did not weaken its synthetic rival. Thus, while the productivity of the particles *over* and *under* has indeed increased over time, there has been no decrease in the productivity of the corresponding verbal prefixes (192). Finally, Section 5.5 analyzes the stylistic distribution of the eight prefixes under study in the BNC. The conclusion drawn by the author is that the prefix verb construction "fills an intermediate position between formal register Latinate or Romance loanwords and informal register verb-particle combinations" (193).

Chapter 6 focuses on potential words containing the eight prefixes under investigation. Section 6.4 discusses the acceptability of invented verbs like *to upplay*, *to overcharacterize*, *to downchat*, etc., which are not attested in either the OED or the BNC. 238 participants in an online survey – both native and non-native speakers of English – were asked to evaluate verbs like these on a scale from "normal English words" to "definitely not English words" (199). According to the author, native speakers "are rather reluctant to accept new words" (240). Also, it appears that "PhD holders and younger informants are slightly more tolerant towards new words than BA holders and older informants" (241). Section 6.5 presents the results of a coinage test. Of 238 participants in the online survey mentioned above, 189 agreed to invent five new words containing the prefixes *over-* and *under-* and then to explain what these invented verbs could mean (227). This test yielded 727 possible words beginning with *under-* and 673 possible words beginning with *over-* (227, 327-358). The most productive verb-forming patterns (i.e., those which were most frequently exploited by the participants of the coinage test) are a) prefix + simple verb (e.g., *to under-sit* "to sit down") and b) prefix + complex verb (e.g., *to over-criticize* "to criticize someone too much") (229).

Chapter 7 summarizes the central findings of chapters 4, 5, 6 and suggests areas for further study (e.g., measuring the productivity of verbal prefixation with the help of the World Wide Web). The last three chapters of the book comprise references (257-273), an appendix (275-368), and a verb index (369-375).

Anne Schröder's monograph can be recommended to anyone who researches the productivity of verbal prefixation in English as well as to any student of morphological productivity (not only in English but in other languages). In addition to showing that verbal prefixation has never ceased to be a productive verb-forming pattern, the author has also demonstrated that the formation of new prefix verbs is not blocked by fully-synonymous and fairly frequent particle verbs (232). As argued by, e.g., Rainer,[1] English lacks the word *stealer* because the meaning "a person who steals" is expressed by the fairly frequent word *thief*, i.e., the existing word *thief* blocks the derivation of the potential word *stealer*. However, as I have argued elsewhere,[2] the word *stealer* has existed in the English language since 1508. According to the OED, *stealer* was originally a full synonym of *thief* (which has existed since the Old English period),[3] but in the course of time has undergone semantic narrowing and come to signify "one who steals something specified." The derivation of the fully-synonymous *stealer* in 1508 was thus not blocked by the existing word *thief*. Similarly, the results of Anne Schröder's coinage test show that the fairly frequent particle verbs *to hit over*, *to make over*, *to talk over*, etc. do not block the derivation of the fully-synonymous prefix verbs *to over-hit*, *to over-make*, *to over-talk*, etc. (232).

As the author acknowledges, the study under review "clearly leaves space for further investigations" (254). Indeed, the synchronic productivity of verbal prefixation can also be studied with the help of the 425 million word Corpus of Contemporary American English (COCA). In addition, neologism collections such as, for example, Word Spy (http://www.wordspy.com/) and Webster Open Dictionary (http://nws.merriam-webster.com/opendictionary/), which contain mainly non-established words, can be taken into account.

The few points of criticism concern the editing of the book. The missing index of key terms (there is only the index of examples used in the study) and the header providing the number and the title of the chapters would definitely make the book more reader-friendly. Some pages (e. g., 45, 67, 69, 77, 102, 112, etc.) are fairly difficult to read because there are too many footnotes on them.

Düsseldorf   ALEXANDER TOKAR

Tanja Rütten. *How to Do Things with Texts. Patterns of Instruction in Religious Discourse 1350-1700.* Frankfurt: Peter Lang, 2011. 248 pp.

Tanja Rütten's book *How to Do Things with Texts. Patterns of Instruction in Religious Discourse 1350–1700* is a text linguistic, corpus-based study on three religious instructional genres, namely sermons, treatises and catechisms from the late medieval to the early modern period. Of these three genres, sermons and treatises occur both before and after the Reformation; catechisms, however, represent a new genre, which in this form originated from the Reformation. The topic is fascinating since the period between 1350 and 1700 is vitally important in cultural, literary and religious history. During this period major changes affecting text production took place, including the Reformation and its impact on Christian thought, instruction and religious practices, the changing relationship between Latin and vernacular learning, and the change from manuscript production to printing.

---

1 Rainer, Franz. "Constrains on Productivity." *Handbook of Word-Formation.* Eds. Pavol Štekauer and Rochelle Lieber. Dordrecht: Springer, 2005. 335-352, 337.
2 Tokar, Alexander. *Introduction to English Morphology.* Frankfurt am Main: Peter Lang, 2012. 47, 95-96.
3 *Oxford English Dictionary.* 06 June 2012 <http://www.oed.com/view/Entry/189467>.

As Rütten frames it, the aim of her study is to "explore how things are done with texts." She states that this can most comprehensively be done by concentrating on text functions, which form the middle level between single speech acts and the high-level discourse function. This approach gives valuable information on how genres work and evolve in all their complexity. While the individual genres may share the same discourse function, e.g. in this case religious instruction, they may differ significantly in regard to their text functions. By analysing these, specific genre profiles can be created and the shifts within and between the genres assessed. This allows comparison between the genres and points out differences and similarities which would otherwise go unnoticed. Rütten's study is welcome since, so far, genres have mainly been studied from the point of view of individual genres either on the discourse function level or on the level of speech acts.

For her analysis, Rütten has chosen five text functions typical of religious instruction. These are exposition (instructing by expounding), exegesis (interpreting the Bible), narration (instructing by telling a story, e.g. from the Bible), argumentation (instructing by discussing objections and opposing views) and exhortation (instructing by direct commands or requests, divided into "exhortation proper" and "exhortative acts"). All these have their representative illocutionary structures expressed through typical speech acts. Rütten traces the occurrence of these text functions and their co-occurrence patterns in different genres through the centuries. Her corpus contains works from three genres written between 1350 and 1700. The corpus is divided into four periods (14th, 15th, 16th and 17th century), and the three genres are divided into subgenres. Sermons include single and cycle sermons; treatises are divided into doctrinal, contemplative, controversial and exegetical treatises; catechisms are divided into plain and mimetic groups.

Rütten has compiled an electronic corpus, which relates to the *Corpus of English Religious Prose* project, and she has annotated it according to the five text functions. Rütten explains her criteria for identifying and tagging text functions clearly and, in general, it seems that various text functions can quite straightforwardly be distinguished from each other with the help of the typical illocutionary structures. However, identifying text functions is not mechanical, but is based on interpretations, and Rütten herself admits that there are cases where the boundaries between text functions in a particular text are not self-evident. This raises the question whether text functions can in some cases be identified and interpreted in different ways by different scholars. Since the analysis is, at the end, based on identifying text functions, the results of the study depend on the decisions made by the scholar.

The actual analysis and empirical results of the study are presented in chapter 5, which proves the usefulness of Rütten's comparative approach. First, Rütten shows that exposition and exhortation are the basic text functions of religious instruction, especially in the Middle English period. They occur in all genres throughout the study period. Argumentation, narration and exegesis appear to be more period specific, and they are preferred by certain genres. Argumentation appears typically in treatises while exegesis and narration are typical features of the sermons. Several interesting aspects and developments can be traced. For example, Rütten shows that early modern catechisms adopt the combination of text functions typical to medieval sermons and treatises (exposition and exhortation) while the genre profile (i.e. the typical combination of text functions) of these two traditional genres changes.

According to Rütten, this implies that the catechisms take the place of sermons as the means of primary religious instruction. Other interesting general trends include the increase of argumentation in all genres during the early modern period and the spreading of exegesis into treatises in the 16th century, although it generally is a feature typical to sermons.

Rütten also analyses the co-occurrence patterns, the typical text function combinations, within individual texts and genres across time. She argues and shows that those genres which exploit many text functions simultaneously are more flexible and adapt to changes more easily. Sermons appear to be the most flexible genre with normally four variable co-occurrence patterns. Rütten's analysis shows that different types of sermons have different patterns, but the flexibility of the genre also leaves room for the individual preferences of the preacher. Treatises seem to be a more homogeneous genre from the point of view of co-occurrence patterns: texts only involve two or three co-occurring functions and, usually, there is a major function supplemented by minor functions. Generally, Middle English treatises favour exposition while early modern ones prefer argumentation. The genre has several subtypes (e.g. doctrinal or contemplative treatises), which differ from each other in their aims and contents and thus accordingly favour different kinds of co-occurrence patterns. The third genre, catechisms, totally lack exegesis and narration and form a very stable genre applying two or three functions depending on the subgenre (plain or mimetic). According to Rütten, this confirms their role as basic instruction.

Rütten combines the overall quantitative data with analyses of individual text samples, which gives a very detailed picture of individual genres (and subgenres) and their developments. In the last part of the analysis chapter Rütten concentrates on interaction between text functions and on the ways they work together. This expands the discussion to the level of illocutionary structures. The structure of the book is extremely clear and straightforward. This makes the research process transparent to the reader and Rütten's argumentation is easy to follow. For example, chapter 5 proceeds from general results (the overall occurrence of text functions) to more specific ones (results on genre level and the level of speech acts).

In the last chapter of the book, Rütten places her results in their socio-historical context. This discussion is extremely interesting and gives new insights into the results obtained from the linguistic analysis. Indeed, many of Rütten's findings can be backed up by what we know about the religious culture of the era. For example, Rütten shows that contemplative treatises practically vanish after the Reformation. This phenomenon corresponds with the theological emphases of the Reformation. Similarly, the shift from sermons and treatises to catechisms as the major form of basic religious instruction, or the rise of exegesis and argumentation in the early modern period, are all features that can be further explained with text-external reasons, such as theological controversies. Although Rütten's main aim is to contribute to domain-based genre studies and to text linguistics, her approach and study can also be useful to scholars from other fields, such as historians and theologians, since it gives detailed data on the text and genre level. This can be exploited by those doing mainly qualitative text analysis without specifically linguistic interests.

Although Rütten takes the socio-historical issues into account, they could have been analysed even further. The interplay between texts and context could be discussed more clearly throughout the book since the texts relate to specific social and historical settings. For example, while discussing literacy in the late medieval and the early modern period, the different levels and concepts of literacy could have been taken into account in more detail, since the increase of vernacular religious texts is linked to the growth of lay literacy as well as to the relationship between Latin and vernacular. Could some of the diachronic changes within and between genres be explained by the fact that topics previously limited to Latin texts began to appear also in the vernacular ones? Late medieval literacies have been studied more and more in recent years and exploiting the findings of this research would have supplemented the conclusions made in chapter 6 where the division into mainly illiterate laity and literate experts in the context of late medieval period seems somewhat outdated.

In summary, Rütten's results are fascinating and from the point of view of a historian, this study provides valuable insights into contextualising linguistic data and the ways this can be used in explaining the development of religious texts. Rütten gives convincing answers to her research questions and the book meets the expectations it raises. Rütten shows that shifts in texts functions and co-occurrence patterns and the degree of popularity of genres relate to changing religious practices and thought styles. The study manages to show that the level of text functions can indeed reveal an extensive amount of information regarding the development and interaction of genres in a specific discourse domain.

Helsinki   LEENA ENQVIST

Marco Schilk. *Structural Nativization in Indian English Lexicogrammar.* **Amsterdam and Philadelphia: John Benjamins, 2011. 182 pp.**

This book investigates structural nativization in Indian English focusing particularly on collocations and complementation patterns of the ditransitive verbs *give*, *send*, and *offer*. The study is based on the Indian and British components of the International Corpus of English (ICE), the newspaper section of the British National Corpus (BNC), and a specifically compiled 110-million word corpus of Indian English derived from the online archive of the *Times of India* (ToI). The data indicate nativization processes in the collocational and complementational domains as well as an interaction of these domains (172).

After a brief introduction in chapter 1, chapter 2 sketches the development of Indian English from its beginnings to the present-day before discussing the currently most influential models of World Englishes as well as factors potentially influencing structural nativization, such as Angloversals, superstratal and substratal effects.

Chapter 3 introduces the basic theoretical concepts, assumptions, and statistical models on which the subsequent analyses are based, after which two major conceptions of collocations are offered, i.e. the quantitative concept of collocation on which this study is mainly based and a phraseological one. In addition, this chapter discusses previous studies on collocation patterns and current models of verb complementation.

Chapter 4 presents and discusses the data-bases of the study. With regard to the ToI corpus, the exact mode of compilation and the motivation for this approach are discussed in detail. This chapter also defines the concepts of collocational and complementational profiles on which the subsequent analyses are based and it concludes with an overview of the distribution of the analysed verbs as observed in the corpora.

Chapters 5-7 present the analyses of the ditransitive verbs *give, send*, and *offer*. For each, the verb-complementational and collocational patterns are identified and statistically evaluated. Whereas the analysis of *give* is solely based on ICE data, the chapters of *send* and *offer* also tap the BNC newspaper data and an equally large sample of the ToI corpus. The data indicate that both varieties exhibit variety-specific collocational preferences which in turn influence the complementation patterns. Some of these lexicogrammatical constructions also seem to have distinct functions in the two varieties (146).

Chapter 8 reflects on the methodological approach of this study against the background of the results of chapters 5-7 and other studies (e.g. Mukherjee and Gries 2009). In particular, this chapter reassesses the advantages and disadvantages of the adopted methodology and presents an elaborate model which accounts for the lexicogrammatical nativization of the extralinguistic CAUSE-RECEIVE processes encoded in ditransitive verbs.

Chapter 9 concludes the book with a brief summary and an outlook for further research.

A major accomplishment of this study is its ability to demonstrate that collocational and complementational patterns of Indian English are subject to structural nativization, in addition to more conspicuous phonological and morphosyntatctic features (168-172). Based on earlier analyses[1] and on construction grammar,[2] this study provides a functional model of structural nativization at the lexis-grammar interface which is able to account for dynamic nativization processes, and which is applicable not only to Indian English but to varieties of English in general (172).

Another merit of this study is the thorough discussion of the corpus and the web-derived data in terms of representativeness, comparability, intra-varietal variation and the repercussions these issues have on the results (167-168).

Moreover, the compilation of the 110-million ToI corpus is an additional achievement of this study as it does not only enable it to draw on an extensive database, but also demonstrates a way to tackle the problem of data-scarcity evident in many empirical cross-varietal studies (44-48).

However, the book also exhibits some less convincing aspects, particularly with regard to its data analysis: In view of the effort of compiling a 110-million word corpus, it is surprising that this data source is only tapped for SEND and OFFER but not for GIVE the analysis of which rests solely on the ICE data. Although the ICE data seems to offer enough data to allow for a thorough analysis, the non-consideration of the specifically compiled ToI-data is unexpected.

Moreover, the motivation for preferring a log-likelihood model to a Fisher exact test is not fully conclusive (22-23). Although it is unchallenged that the latter requires a higher computational effort, it is considered to be much more accurate than the model applied here.[3] Fisher exact tests would also have had the advantage of not

---

1 Cf. Mukherjee, Joybrato and Sebastian Hoffmann. "Describing Verb-Complementational Profiles of New Englishes: A Pilot Study of Indian English." *English World Wide* 27 (2006): 147-173.
2 Goldberg, Adele. E. *Constructions: A Construction Grammar Approach to Argument Structure*. Chicago: The University Press of Chicago, 1995.
3 E. g. Gries, Stefan Th. and Anatol Stefanowitsch. "Extending Collostructional Analysis: A Corpus-Based Perspective on 'Alternations'." *International Journal of Corpus Linguistics* 9.1 (2004): 97-129. 101.

requiring a token frequency of five instances for any bigram to be considered (cf. 55-56). Furthermore, the use of Chi-Square tests with up to 15 degrees of freedom cannot be considered unproblematic (cf. 65); configural frequency analyses to assess the differences in the complementation patterns would have been a preferable alternative.

In general chapters 5-7 would have been easier to comprehend if the entire discussion and motivation of the applied approach (chapters 3, 4 and 8) had preceded the analyses. The same is true for the model of lexicogrammatical structural nativization introduced as late as page 163.

In sum, this study constitutes a stimulating contribution to the field of variationist corpus linguistics. Particularly its way of overcoming data-scarcity by compiling a web-derived mega-corpus and its consequent attempt to integrate both quantitative and theoretical approaches to complementation and collocation into a unified functional framework make it a very inspiring study. Hence, for anybody interested in corpus linguistics, quantitative variationist linguistics, and/or the diffusion and nativization of World Englishes, this book will be of great interest.

Hamburg   GEORG MAIER

Björn Rothstein. *Wissenschaftliches Arbeiten für Linguisten.* **Tübingen: Narr, 2011. 218 pp.**

It seems fair to inform the reader that the reviewer is himself both a linguist and co-author of a monograph about scientific publishing and related issues[1] and is thus perhaps not quite as unbiased as he ought to be. Having said that, I will try hard to do justice to the book.

Among the plethora of books on the art of scientific writing, Björn Rothstein's (henceforth BR) guide stands out by specifically addressing students of linguistics and by devoting a more substantial share of the overall text (in fact chapters 1-5, pp. 19-98) to specialised matters such as gathering linguistic data, transcribing texts or obtaining statistically significant results.

Content. BR first addresses the problem of finding and properly delimiting a given topic and suggests that reading some introductory literature, devising a mind-map, gathering a series of key questions and converting them into a hierarchically structured table of contents may be useful. To illustrate his general tips, he adduces some concrete examples, most of which are taken from the realm of studies on German. While this approach works fine in a number of cases, in others the example chosen is too complex or lengthy to be of any real help. In section 1.3, dealing with methodology, for instance, BR tries to illustrate how a student might go about empirically verifying a linguistic model by referring to Marga Reis' criticism of an earlier article by Ross who argued that auxiliaries could be analysed as main verbs (27). This example is unfortunate on two counts: (a) It does not show how Ross' or Reich's model might be verified empirically and (b) the reported conclusion drawn by Reis quoted on p.27 is highly unsatisfactory because she appears to be at a loss how to decide which – if any – of the approaches sketched by her should be the "correct" one. The passage

---

1   See Standop, Ewald and Matthias L. G. Meyer. *Die Form der wissenschaftlichen Arbeit: Grundlagen, Technik und Praxis für Schule, Studium und Beruf.* Wiesbaden: Quelle & Meyer, 2008.

quoted could thus rather be used to illustrate an indeterminacy of analysis. Despite this, section 1.3 remains basically useful for its survey of the various angles from which a topic might be approached (27-31).

Chapter 2 on information gathering gives two valuable pieces of advice: (a) the necessity of including the canonical literature for a given field (as determined by figuring out which earlier studies are quoted in all or a majority of later studies) and (b) of making profitable use of the Ponzi scheme (G 'Schneeballsystem') by retrieving the latest article in a given field whose bibliography points to earlier articles – a step which can then be reapplied with those earlier articles. Here as elsewhere the strong bias towards German studies persists but students of other subjects can still profit from the references to the forum 'The linguist list' and to more general bibliographies such as the *Bibliography of Linguistic Literature.*

Chapter 3 exemplifies the use of the 'SQ3R' reading strategy which stands for five propagated stages '*Survey* (gaining a first survey of a text) – *Question* (asking *wh*-questions such as *Who/what/why X?*) – *Read* – *Recite* (recall essentials by summarising) – *Review* (check overall understanding)' by applying it to Marga Reis's study of subjects in German mentioned earlier. An entire 12 pages (45-56) are devoted to this, but the exemplification is at best partly felicitous. The excerpt from the bibliography included in Reis (1986) does not even reveal that her study focuses on subjects in German and when it is suggested that the reader jump from Reis's introduction to her conclusion to gain a preliminary survey, one finds that Reis ends up doubting the usefulness of the term 'subject' and that she suggests that, if it was to be retained, she would rather equate it with 'NP in the nominative' (47). The problem here is that while BR explicitly believes in the soundness of Reis's subject theory and presents it at length as an example supposed to resist closer scrutiny (at least to the extent to which it is quoted; 53-54), Reis's conclusion throws up puzzling questions such as 'How are traditional referential subjects distinguished (a) from predicative nominals such as *Lehrer* in *Hans beabsichtigt, Lehrer zu werden* and (b) from grammatical subjects as in *Es tanzen die Mäuse* when subjects are nothing but nominative NPs?' Or: Can Reis's model account for the substitutability of the clausal subject in *Dass er kommt, freut mich* by a nominative NP such as *sein Eintreffen?* Reis's full article might well provide answers here but BR's exposition of it does not. A shorter and less intricate argument that can be quoted in full would have been preferable.

Chapter 4 looks at linguistic argumentation and more specifically at making judgements about the validity of a thesis based on empirical evidence. Here BR's choice of examples seems more fortunate, though I would doubt that a student writing about a comparative study of the present perfect in English and German would profit from adducing additional languages to test a given claim (63). Very little can be concluded about the distribution or meaning of a category such as the perfect in one language by looking at another language. Similarly, BR's implicit background assumption that a category such as tense can reasonably be defined universally (84-5) needs to be challenged, as such a definition usually resorts to vague semantic criteria such as the placement of events in time that conflict with the distribution of the relevant morphemes in individual languages.

Chapter 5 deals with the use of the German online corpus COSMAS II, questionnaires and the gathering and interpretation of statistical data. BR's brief definition of a number of statistical key terms such as 'statistical certainty,' 'reliability' (93), 'split half method' (94) cannot ultimately conceal the impossibility of teaching even the most fundamental statistical basics in a concise book about linguistic writing. BR does not even try, but rather directs the reader to sample size calculators (93) or the capabilities of Excel (93), where it would have been better to refer him back to section 0.4 (12) where suitable books on corpus linguistics are listed. This is because inexperienced authors would otherwise be in danger of applying to their data various formulae whose function or validity they do not fully understand.

Chapters 6 through 8 deal mainly with form and cover issues such as quoting, the use of footnotes, tables of contents or title pages; some questions of content are, however, also addressed, such as what should go into a good introduction or conclusion (111-116). Section 7.3 deals with bibliographical entries. BR is not a resolute advocate of a given formal system but says: "Die linguistische Entsprechung dieser [bibliografischen] Angabe würde nach Standardkonvention wohl wie folgt ausfallen" (119). BR eventually advocates the model of the "MLA handbook for academic writers" (121-122.; a title that I could not find – perhaps Rosen's *Academic Writer's Handbook* was meant); yet his own bibliographical references are not fully uniform. First names of authors are sometimes spelled out and sometimes not (e.g. on p. 120) and '&' is recommended between two authors on p. 123 but a slash is also used elsewhere. Abbreviations of first names save little space while full names are appreciated by librarians. Only the most common types of bibliographical entries (excluding internet documents) are illustrated by BR, many of them being fictional. 11 pages are devoted to the proper use of direct and indirect quotes. For the sake of clarity BR's own indications of the sources for his examples should be placed outside the frame surrounding the latter because it took me some time to figure out that e.g. the example box on p. 130 is actually BR's literal quote from Öhl and not a fictional example illustrating how one might quote from him. (BR's directly addressing the reader inside an example box on p. 20 is equally confusing.) Contradictory to BR's claim, the shortening of the quote from Dürscheid (133) does not distort its meaning. The use of the German subjunctive is not illustrated though this is an area where many authors, possibly including Vogel quoted on p. 132, need help: "[Helbig & Buscha] präzisieren […], dass das Adverbiale hier notwendig ist [*read as* 'sei']."

Chapter 8 provides useful formal help with the most common elements of termpapers such as the title page, the declaration of academic integrity, the table of contents, the use and numbering of headlines (see section "Remarks on form" below on this). Helpful advice is also given on preparing sets of minutes, handouts, posters or (multimedia) presentations. The exclusive reference to PowerPoint should be avoided here. Section 8.7 on abstracts contains an example by Ralf Vogel (166) which should not have been used because of its bad English.

The final section of the book entitled "Service" (chapters 9-11) provides tips on word processing, drawing tree diagrams and transcriptions of oral texts. For the latter, the standard established by Ehlich and Rehbein in 1976 is recommended and illustrated in some detail (chapter 10). In chapter 11 the art of preparing glosses (verbatim translations of foreign language discourse) following the Leipzig Glossing Rules (also available online) is discussed. The latter kind of information is not easily found in other general guides on form and therefore particularly welcome.

Style. The exposition is largely clear but some sentences should be rewritten for stylistic or other reasons as in "Ein Korpus *ist im linguistischen Sinne* eine angemessen große Sammlung ..." → 'Ein Korpus *im linguistischen Sinne ist* ...' (67). "Die *Leipzig Glossing Rules* geben *mit anderen Worten* die Bedeutung [...] aller Morpheme [...] wieder" → '*Anders gesagt* geben die *Leipzig Glossing Rules* ...' (p. 185; see also p. 68 for a similar case). "[Fragebögen sollten auch eine neutrale Antwort anbieten], damit die Befragten sich nicht *von vornherein* festlegen müssen" (71) → 'sich *nicht in jedem Fall auf eine positive oder negative Antwort* festlegen müssen.' "Der Begriff Folie hat sich durch das *Schreib*programm PowerPoint *eingebürgert*" → '[...] hat durch das *Präsentations*programm PowerPoint *eine Bedeutungserweiterung erfahren*' (102). "[Zu Qualifikationsschriften] zählen *häufig* Doktorarbeiten ..." → '...zählen *insbesondere* ...' (103) (italics in all these examples are mine MM). These examples do not meet the author's own recommendation to opt for precision and to avoid ambiguities (145).

Remarks on form. In line with common practice, BR recommends decimal numbering for headlines (149) but the top level should be numbered '1, 2, 3 ...' instead of '1., 2., 3. ...' to make it consistent with lower levels numbered '1.1, 1.1.1' The logic here is to use a dot only as a separator of decimal hierarchies. The use of a major numbered heading for the book's own afterword, the section "Hilfreiche Literatur" and the bibliography goes against common conventions. Some tables lack proper right-justification of figures and/or vertical centering of the text.

Conclusion. My overall impression of the book is not as negative as my individual points of criticism might suggest and I have learnt quite a few things from it. It definitely fills a niche for authors of linguistic texts and the basic idea of teaching good writing by using pieces of texts written by professionals is basically sound.

Kiel   MATTHIAS L. G. MEYER

Isabel Karremann and Anja Müller, eds. *Mediating Identities in Eighteenth-Century England. Public Negotiations, Literary Discourses, Topography.* Farnham: Ashgate, 2011. 242 pp.

This collection of twelve essays explores how identities are mediated in the long 18th century. At the crossroads of identity politics and media research the essays thus probe the validity of concepts such as inner self or public persona for investigations of culture and society in 18th-century England. It is in particular the "opposition between coercive interpellation and volitional or intentional agency" (4-5) that the editors of, and most of the contributors to, this volume wish to transcend. "[R]egard[ing] the question of discursive structure and individual agency not as an either/or choice but rather as the two extremes of a continuum" (5), the essays in this collection focus on "historically specific social and aesthetic practices of media use" (5) to investigate processes of identification. The introduction by Isabel Karremann suggests that the essays can be divided roughly into two groups: the first four essays investigate the influence of narrative while the remaining eight essays all probe spatial constraints.

The scope of this collection is indeed impressive: Anja Müller investigates children's literature as a "site where competing notions of childhood were negotiated" (18). Clinging to features of orality and didacticism, Müller explains, authors of children's literature shunned literary aspirations so that their narratives of children being both innocent and needing improvement could be perceived as prescriptive. The didactic purpose of writing and reading is also explored by Isabel Karremann's reading of Defoe's *Journal of the Plague Year*. She contends, however, that the text – in its representation of individuals – remains inconsequential in propagating middle-class godly manliness and, instead "mediates most effectively the disorienting, meaningless experience of the plague" (43). Franz Meier compares the narrative situation in *Pamela* and *Fanny Hill* and argues that sentimental and pornographic texts with their primarily female narrators and focalizers will have resulted in "a potentially confusing gender performance" (54) that invite "a wide range of possible mediations of gender identities" (55). Focusing on paratexts, Katharina Rennhak looks at "how some female novelists use the metaphor of separate spheres in their construction of gendered identities" (64). She observes that female authors do not challenge the separation of spheres but remain apologetic about crossing the threshold and entering male territory. Construing themselves as addressing the public from the position of a detached private sphere, female authors asserted their claim to moral authority. Felicity Nussbaum presents the case of Kitty Clive, one of the first actresses, according to Nussbaum, who, "in fostering a sense of individuality and intimacy" (73), perfected a public 'interiority effect:' "a fluid, multilayered, situational and virtual" persona "bolstered by the circulation of celebrity gossip" (72). Onstage and offstage, Clive represented a new type of actress. These actresses, "savvy, moneyed, high-spirited with hearts of gold" (86), shaped identities with respect to class, gender, and, in Clive's case, English and Irish nationalities. Theatre as "meta-medium" is examined by Anette Pankratz who contends that 18th-century comedy established a dual vision of the public. Audiences were invited to conceive of themselves as part of an informed public vis-à-vis an "uniformed and gullible" public "taking the characters self-fashioning at face value" (94). Hence, comedy fundamentally fostered techniques of identity formation based on self-observation and the observation of others. Uwe Böker explores how far the attempt to control discursive behaviour in the court room can be understood as a reaction to notions of 'patchwork identities,' i.e. notions that "the ego, the self or identity, seemed to be discontinuous" (103). According to Böker, defiant behaviour of Quakers in court, documented in 18th-century reprints of 17th-century trial accounts, served "radicals [...] to articulate their subversive ideas" (106) outside the courts while Societies for the Reformation of Manners attempted to police citizens and to enforce their compliance in the courts. Anna-Christina Giovanopoulos examines the impeachments during the Exclusion Crisis as socio-political actions that bring to the fore that "identity attributions were based on exclusion rather than inclusion" (116). She claims that impeachments and their reflection in printed material were fundamental in shaping Whig and Tory identities. Christian Huck is "interested in finding out what kind of public (sphere) is created by advertising, especially by fashion advertisements" (127). He proposes to investigate a popular sphere "open to everyone who can be expected to have access to mass media" (130). Isabelle Baudino identifies a topographical turn in 18th-century paintings, sketches, and engravings by artists such as Hogarth, Thornhill or Wilson, who not only "conjured up a certain British reality" (155) but also sought to "contain aesthetics within national boundaries" (145). Landscapes and cityscapes, Baudino explains, thus "served as powerful tools in the forging of the British nation" (155) and helped propagate the identity of the British artist. Michael Meyer juxtaposes panoramas of London with oriental sceneries and claims that the orderly view of London and the depiction of a "land [that] could be easily appropriated and profitably used under colonial management" (159) complement each other. The panoramic gaze with its promise of control thus visualized and constructed a British imperial identity. Christoph Houswitschka identifies rambling and walking as political activities that played a crucial part in identity formation. Taking Thewall's *The Peripatetic* as his point of departure, Houswitschka investigates how the body itself can function as a medium. Exploring the "dialectic tension" (183) between ramblers in the countryside and urban flaneurs, he asserts that "the citizen as walker constructed democratic spaces" (190) at the time when "rambling the countryside becomes a symbolic act of practicing the disenfranchisement of urban spaces" (183).

The fact that two thirds of the contributors focus on space testifies to the legacy of Habermas' concept of the public sphere in this field of research. What emerges from the several approaches to mediated identities is the notion that 18th-century identities were in flux, both on the individual level of selves as well as on the social level of personae. It is thus hardly surprising that the critical responses included in this volume largely address the premises on which this notion is based. Rainer Emig's critical response is directed at the first four essays. He cautions us against using fictional prose for the investigation of historical debates and points out that conventions of realism, "genre boundaries, [...], and narratorial rules" (195) were instable throughout the 18th century. Hence, our speculations of who may have read what and for which purpose may construe identities that do not account for the "contradictions and *aporias*" (195) of mediated identities in the period. Christoph Heyl suggests in his critical response that the panoramas discussed by Meyer may be "not so much about control but about loss of control" (208), because they also expose the "spectacular downfall of capitalist enterprise" (208) and the hubris of imperial ambitions. Heyl reminds us that texts and images in their various mediated forms were fundamental for ongoing debates about identity and that historical investigations may only ever trace these debates while the identities shaped by them must remain largely obscure. Hans-Peter Wagner's response resonates with Brian Cowan's seminal paper "What Was Masculine About the Public Sphere? Gender and the Coffeehouse Milieu in Post-Restoration England." Wagner argues that the public sphere in 18th-century England may not have been as gendered and bourgeois as assumed by Habermas and most of his critics, and he suggests that we should distinguish between a normative sphere and a practical public sphere. Fairs and puppet theatres, for example, "were truly classless, attended and appreciated as they were by people from all walks of life and all social strata" (203). Is it possible that subjects in 18th-century England were all together and all distinct, as suggested by Hannah Greig in a recent article on London's Pleasure Gardens? If that is the case we may have to rethink the relationship of media use and identities in a much more radical fashion than *Mediating Identities* suggests. This volume has brought to the fore, perhaps inadvertently, that we still know very little about the media landscape once we shift our focus from the artefacts that have survived to the plethora of possible media uses. This is true for London but even more so for rural England. Proposing mass media *avant la lettre* may seem appealing but this idea will come at the prize of generalizing mediated discourse across a nation that was extremely heterogenic. The task for historically informed scholarship in the field, then, is to steer clear of generalizations without harboring idiosyncratic examples. The contributors to this volume have shown that this is a fine line to tread, and they should all be credited for the laudable achievement of having chartered a field with many obstacles.

Hamburg   FELIX SPRANG

LIST OF CONTRIBUTORS

BECK, Andrea, Dr., Ernst Moritz Arndt Universität Greifswald, Institut für Fremdsprachliche Philologien, Abteilung Anglistik/Amerikanistik, Steinbeckstraße 15, 17487 Greifswald, amb-beck@t-online.de.

BROSCH, Renate, Prof. Dr., Universität Stuttgart, Institut für Literaturwissenschaft: Anglistik/Amerikanistik, Keplerstr. 7, 70174 Stuttgart, ilwbrosr@ilw.uni-stuttgart.de.

BROWN, Ian, Prof. Dr., University of Kingston, Department of Drama and Dance, Penrhyn Road, Kingston upon Thames, KT1 2AL, England, United Kingdom, i.brown@kingston.ac.uk.

BUCKTON, Oliver S., Prof. Dr., Florida Atlantic University, Department of English, 777 Glades Road, Boca Raton, FL 33431, USA, obuckton@fau.edu.

DYMOCK, Emma, Dr., University of Edinburgh, Celtic and Scottish Studies, 27 George Square, Edinburgh, Scotland, United Kingdom, edymock1@staffmail.ed.ac.uk.

ENQVIST, Leena, University of Helsinki, Department of Modern Languages, PO Box 3, 00014 University of Helsinki, Finland, leena.enqvist@helsinki.fi.

FLÜGGE, Anna, Dr., Ludwig-Maximilians-Universität München, Fakultät für Sprach- und Literaturwissenschaften, Department für Anglistik und Amerikanistik, Schellingstraße 3, 80799 München, anna.fluegge@lrz.uni-muenchen.de.

GILBERT, Suzanne, Dr., University of Stirling, Literature & Languages, School of Arts & Humanities, Stirling, FK9 4LA Scotland, United Kingdom, suzanne.gilbert@stir.ac.uk.

GLAAP, Albert-Reiner OBE, Prof. Dr., Lerchenweg 16, 40878 Ratingen, glaap@philfak.uni-duesseldorf.de.

GNUTZMANN, Claus, Prof. Dr., Technische Universität Braunschweig, Englisches Seminar, Bienroder Weg 80, 38106 Braunschweig, c.gnutzmann@tu-bs.de.

GRIEM, Julika, Prof. Dr., Goethe Universität Frankfurt am Main, Institut für England- und Amerikastudien, Grüneburgplatz 1, 60323 Frankfurt am Main, griem@em.uni-frankfurt.de.

HAMES, Scott, Dr., University of Stirling, Literature & Languages, School of Arts & Humanities, Stirling, FK9 4LA Scotland, United Kingdom, scott.hames@stir.ac.uk.

HEDDLE, Donna, Dr., University of the Highlands and Islands, Centre for Nordic Studies, Kiln Corner, Kirkwall, Orkney, KW15 1QX, Scotland, United Kingdom, Donna.Heddle@orkney.uhi.ac.uk.

HEINEN, Sandra, Prof. Dr., Bergische Universität Wuppertal, Anglistik/Amerikanistik, Gaußstraße 20, 42119 Wuppertal, saheinen@uni-wuppertal.de.

HEINZ, Sarah, Prof. Dr., Universität Mannheim, Anglistisches Seminar, Schloß EW 280, 68131 Mannheim, sarah.heinz@uni-mannheim.de.

HÖPKER, Karin, Dr., Friedrich-Alexander-Universität Erlangen-Nürnberg, Department Anglistik und Amerikanistik, Bismarckstraße 1, 91054 Erlangen, karin.hoepker@gmx.de.

IORDĂCHIOAIA, Gianina, Dr., Universität Stuttgart, Institut für Linguistik: Anglistik, Keplerstraße 17, 70174 Stuttgart, gianina@ifl.uni-stuttgart.de.

KRÖLLER, Eva-Marie, Prof. Dr., University of British Columbia, Department of English, 397-1873 East Mall (Buchanan Tower), Vancouver, BC V6T 1Z1, Canada, emk@mail.arts.ubc.de.

LINDNER, Oliver, Prof. Dr., Christian-Albrechts-Universität zu Kiel, Englisches Seminar, Olshausenstraße 40, 24098 Kiel, linder@anglistik@uni-kiel.de.

LÖSCHNIGG, Martin, Prof. Dr., Karl-Franzens-Universität Graz, Institut für Anglistik, Heinrichstraße 36, 8010 Graz, Österreich, martin.loeschnigg@uni-graz.at.

MACKAY, Pauline, Dr., University of Glasgow, Scottish Literature, School of Critical Studies, 7 University Gardens, Glasgow, G12 8QH, Scotland, United Kingdom, pauline.mackay@glasgow.ac.uk.

MCCRACKEN-FLESHER, Caroline, Prof. Dr., University of Wyoming, Department of English Box 3353, 1000 East University Avenue, Laramie W 82071, USA, cmf@uwyo.edu.

MAIER, Georg, Universität Hamburg, Institut für Anglistik und Amerikanistik, Von-Melle-Park 6, 20146 Hamburg, georg.maier@uni-hamburg.de.

MEYER, Matthias, Prof. Dr., Christian-Albrechts-Universität zu Kiel, Englisches Seminar, Olshausenstraße 40, 24098 Kiel, m.meyer@anglistik.uni-kiel.de.

MEYER, Michael, Prof. Dr., Universität Koblenz-Landau, Institut für Anglistik – Institut für Kulturwissenschaft, Universitätsstraße 1, 56070 Koblenz, mimeyer@uni-koblenz.de.

MIESZKOWSKI, Sylvia, Dr., Humboldt-Universität zu Berlin, Institut für Anglistik und Amerikanistik, Unter den Linden 6, 10099 Berlin, mieszkos@cms.hu-berlin.de.

MOORE, Dafydd, Prof. Dr., Plymouth University, School of Humanities and Performing Arts, Portland Villas, Plymouth, PL4 8AA, England, United Kingdom, d.r.moore@plymouth.ac.uk.

NEUMANN, Birgit, Prof. Dr., Universität Passau, Professur für Anglistik/Cultural and Media Studies, Innstraße 25, 94032 Passau, birgit.neumann@uni-passau.de.

NITTEL, Jana, Dr., Universität Bremen, Fachbereich Sprach- und Literaturwissenschaften: English-Speaking Cultures/Literary and Media Studies, Bibliotheksstraße 1, 28359 Bremen, jnittel@uni-bremen.de.

NORQUAY, Glenda, Prof. Dr., Liverpool John Moores University, Dean Walters Building, St James Rd, Liverpool L1 7BR, England, United Kingdom, g.norquay@ljmu.ac.uk.

NYFFENEGGER-STAUB, Nicole, Dr., Universität Bern, Institut für Englische Sprachen und Literaturen, Längassstraße 49, 3000 Bern 9, Schweiz, nicole.nyffenegger@ens.unibe.ch.

RIACH, Alan, Prof. Dr., University of Glasgow, Scottish Literature, School of Critical Studies, 7 University Gardens, University of Glasgow, Glasgow G12 8QH, Scotland, United Kingdom, alan.riach@glasgow.ac.uk.

RUPP, Jan, Dr., Universität Heidelberg, Anglistisches Seminar, Kettengasse 12, 69117 Heidelberg, jan.rupp@as.uni-heidelberg.de.

SANDTEN, Cecile, Prof. Dr., Technische Universität Chemnitz, Institut für Anglistik/Amerikanistik, Reichenhainer Straße 39, 09107 Chemnitz, cecile.sandten@phil.tu-chemnitz.de.

SASSI, Carla, Prof. Dr., Università di Verona, Dipartimento di Lingue e Letterature Straniere, Lungadige Porta Vittoria 41, 37129 Verona, Italia, carla.sassi@univr.it.

SCHÄFER, Stefanie, Dr., Friedrich-Schiller-Universität Jena, Institut für Anglistik und Amerikanistik, Ernst-Abbe-Platz 8, 07743 Jena, schaefer.stefanie@uni-jena.de.

SCHULENBERG, Ulf, Prof. Dr., Katholische Universität Eichstätt-Ingolstadt, Sprach- und Literaturwissenschaftliche Fakultät, Universitätsallee 1, 85071 Eichstätt, ulf.schulenberg@ku.de.

SCHULZ, Dirk, Dr., Universität zu Köln, Englisches Seminar, Albertus-Magnus-Platz, 50923 Köln, dirk.schulz@uni-koeln.de.

SPRANG, Felix, Dr., Universität Hamburg, Institut für Anglistik und Amerikanistik, Von-Melle-Park 6, 20146 Hamburg, felix.sprang@uni-hamburg.de.

STRÄSSLER, Jürg, Dr., Universität Zürich, Englisches Seminar, Plattenstraße 47, 8032 Zürich, Schweiz, strassler@bluewin.ch.

TESKE, Doris, Dr., Pädagogische Hochschule Karlsruhe, Institut für Fremdsprachen und Sprachlernforschung, Bismarckstraße 10, 76133 Karlsruhe, teske@ph.karlsruhe.de.

TOKAR, Alexander, Dr., Heinrich Heine Universität Düsseldorf, Institut für Anglistik und Amerikanistik, Universitätsstraße 1, 40225 Düsseldorf, tokar@phil-fak.uni-duesseldorf.de.

WISCHER, Ilse, Dr., Universität Potsdam, Institut für Anglistik und Amerikanistik, Am Neuen Palais 10, 14469 Potsdam, wischer@uni-potsdam.de.

ZIEGLER, Heide, Prof. Dr., Universität Stuttgart, Institut für Literaturwissenschaft: Anglistik/Amerikanistik, Azenbergstraße 12, 70174 Stuttgart, heide.ziegler@ilw.uni-stuttgart.de.

STYLE SHEET

1. Only contributions written in English will be published. Please stick to either British or American English. Non-native speakers are requested to have their manuscripts proof-read by native speakers before submitting them.
2. The font size should be Times New Roman 10 (TNR 8 for footnotes).
3. Text and footnotes should be single-spaced. Please use footnotes instead of endnotes, numbered consecutively throughout the whole manuscript. For **book reviews**, please keep footnotes to an absolute minimum.
4. Italics are used for foreign words in the English text, for titles of books, plays, etc. Articles in periodicals or books are enclosed in double quotation marks (no italics), titles of periodicals etc. are given in italics.
5. Please use "quotation marks" instead of (typographic) "inverted commas" for all quotations not separated from the context. Quotations of more than three lines should be separated from the context and indented on the left margin (1 cm) without quotation marks. Omissions should be marked with square brackets [...].
6. Bibliographical references are included in the text and/or footnotes in shortened form and in round brackets, indicating author, publication date and page numbers. If a title has more than one author, please order their names alphabetically, separated by semicolons, e.g. (Frye 1957, 85; Rosier 1962, 4). Please provide full references in the Works Cited section at the end of your article (see examples).
7. Please observe AE conventions for punctuation (i.e. place commas and periods/full stops before the closing quotation marks): "Henry," she said, "please take them out."
8. Please send the manuscript by e-mail (Word- or rtf-version) to the following address: redaktion-anglistik@uni-koeln.de

Bibliographical references

Beowulf: A Student Edition. Ed. George Jack. Oxford: Clarendon, 1994.
Frye, Northrop. *Anatomy of Criticism: Four Essays*. Princeton: Princeton University Press, 1957.
—. *The Educated Imagination*. Bloomington: Indiana University Press, 1964.
Horwitz, Elaine K. "Preliminary Evidence for the Reliability and Validity of a Foreign Language Anxiety Scale." *TESOL Quarterly* 20 (1986): 559-562.
—, Michael B. Horwitz, and Joann Cope. "Foreign Language Classroom Anxiety." *The Modern Language Journal* 70 (1986): 125-132.
Lowi, Theodore, Benjamin Ginsberg, and Steve Jackson. *Analyzing American Government: American Government, Freedom and Power*. New York: Norton, 1994.
New, William H. "Panel." *Taking Stock: The Calgary Conference on the Canadian Novel*. Ed. Charles R. Steele. Downsview, ON: ECW Press, 1982. 34-37.
Schoeck, Eric. "An Interview with Ian McEwan." 1 January 1998. *Capitola Book Café*. 31 May 2010 <http://www.capitolabookcafe.com/andrea/mcewan.html>.

Other bibliographical references should observe the conventions set out in the *MLA Handbook for Writers of Research Papers* (7th Edition).

**Anglistik/Amerikanistik
Geschichte
Soziologie**

Universitätsverlag
WINTER
Heidelberg

GABRIELE LINKE (Ed.)

**Teaching
Cultural Studies**

Methods – Matters – Models
2011. 334 Seiten, 6 Abbildungen.
(anglistik & englischunterricht,
Volume 76)
Kart. € 23,–
ISBN 978-3-8253-5893-8

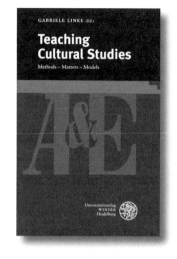

This volume presents reflections and systematizations of experiences, course design and teaching and learning techniques by recording instructors' experiences and insights to give successful models of instruction. It aims not only to broaden the scope of cultural studies instruction but also to facilitate the design of cultural studies courses. Therefore it contains case studies and examples of courses which demonstrate the effective integration into cultural studies of theories and models taken from well-established disciplines such as history, and sociology. Moreover, the brief overviews of a range of academic disciplines, methods and topics offered in the articles provide excellent introductory readings in classes on, for example, place, gender, identity, visual culture, reggae, or the Angry Young Men.
In addition, there are articles that focus on teaching (with) Web 2.0, on the nature and functions of stereotypes and on learning and teaching techniques for cultural studies classes.

D-69051 Heidelberg · Postfach 10 61 40 · Tel. (49) 62 21/77 02 60 · Fax (49) 62 21/77 02 69
Internet http://www.winter-verlag-hd.de · E-mail: info@winter-verlag-hd.de

CALL FOR DONATIONS

The German Association for English Studies has opened a special account for donations:

Sparkasse Paderborn (BLZ 47250101)
Account no.: 91140

In a period characterized by a growing number of foundations and by a communal and individual spirit of support for worthy causes, we ask each member of the German Association for English Studies to increase the Association's ability to further the cause of the study of English in all its variations.

On behalf of the Association
Christoph Ehland, Treasurer

CORRIGENDUM

Prof. Dr. Bärbel Diehr is based at the University of Wuppertal, not at the University of Munich, as erroneously stated in *Anglistik* 23.1. We apologize for the inconvenience this may have caused.